W9-BCZ-928

ST. JOSEPH'S UNIVERSITY

3 9353 00225 2102

THE GEORGETOWN SYMPOSIUM ON ETHICS

Essays in Honor of
Henry Babcock Veatch

Edited by

Rocco Porreco

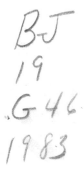

BJ
19
.G46
1983

UNIVERSITY
PRESS OF
AMERICA

LANHAM • NEW YORK • LONDON

241957

Copyright © 1984 by

University Press of America,™ Inc.

4720 Boston Way
Lanham, MD 20706

3 Henrietta Street
London WC2E 8LU England

All rights reserved

Printed in the United States of America

ISBN (Perfect): 0-8191-3777-4
ISBN (Cloth): 0-8191-3776-6

All University Press of America books are produced on acid-free
paper which exceeds the minimum standards set by the National
Historical Publications and Records Commission.

CONTENTS

v

PART III ETHICS AND LAW

PART IV ETHICS AND RELIGION

PART V ETHICS AND EDUCATION

PREFACE

On April 14 and 15, 1983, Georgetown University sponsored a two-day symposium on ethics to honor Henry B. Veatch on the occasion of his retirement from active teaching. A letter was sent to Henry's numerous friends and acquaintances, both within the profession and outside it, inviting them to attend the conference. The letter explained that those actually contributing papers would be from among Henry's distinguished colleagues and former students, many of them now following in Henry's footsteps. Response to the letter was amazing: more than one hundred and fifty professors, students and friends came from all over the United States to attend the symposium and more than eighty letters of regret, all of them praiseworthy and somewhat nostalgic, were received.

Almost without exception, everyone who was asked to give a paper, to introduce a panel discussion or to contribute in some way cheerfully agreed to do so. They most generously contributed their talents and their time, in Henry's words, "presumably for no other reason than that it gave them an opportunity to praise Henry, perhaps roast him, or perhaps just pass over him in discreet silence." But there was no doubt whatsoever about the high esteem and even great affection which everyone had for Henry. It was certainly not a matter of the conference participants' agreeing with Henry's philosophical position which, as he himself always pointed out, is a minority one. Many of them disagreed with his interpretation of Aristotle, his defense of natural law ethics, or his philosophy of education. And Henry was there listening to everything that was said, taking notes, but, uncharacteristically, keeping his silence throughout.

This silence was broken only when Henry delivered his "Remarks," as they were described on the program at the closing testimonial dinner. These "Remarks" appear in this volume as the first paper with the title, "Can Philosophy Ever Be a Thing for Hoosiers?" One has only to read this paper to be able to appreciate the encomia which were delivered on this occasion, both in letters received and at the dinner. Indeed, if Professor Ver Eecke, who was presiding, had not been firm in curtailing these encomia, the dinner would have continued past midnight.

As editor of this volume, I would like to present Henry B. Veatch to the reader through a mosaic of abridged comments made in connection with the symposium. Some of them will remain unattributed, their selection being based on the criterion that they say extremely well what many others have said and wrote on this occasion.

Howard Trivers, a retired Foreign Service officer and adjunct professor at Ball State University, described himself as "Henry's oldest friend" and told of how they "met in Heidelberg in June 1933, both German-American exchange students and both holders of Harvard philosophy scholarships in the amount of $1,000, a prodigious sum in those days." Trivers said that they were introduced by Jim Breasted, Jr., the son of the famous Egyptologist, and landed at the same *pension*. Of course, Henry, who already had his Harvard M.A. at the age of 21, was recognized as a precocious child prodigy. And he has well fulfilled the promise of those early days. . . ."

The tribute of the Dean of Georgetown College, Royden Davis, S.J., eloquently told about Henry's contribution to the university in the relatively short time that he was there.

> Professor Henry Veatch came to Georgetown in 1973—some ten years ago. Has it been so short a time for him to have done so much for his colleagues here, for his many students and for this university? He was already a scholar—I suspect he was always a teacher. He came to Georgetown as chairman of the Department of Philosophy—that means, as every good chairman knows, to mend tears and stitch patches, to build bridges and create castles, to prod and stimulate and lead with the staff one has been given until one makes many colors into a rainbow. They say there have been few, if any, Philosopher Kings who would be completely pleasing to Plato. There probably have been even fewer philosopher residents in Washington, D.C. There have been many—some say too many—chairmen of philosophy departments, but select is the number who are philosopher chairmen—wise and witty men and women who clearly do the necessary work of being a chairman but do so much more than the necessary. Henry Veatch was one of those chairmen at Georgetown. He was admired for his scholarship, enjoyed for his wit and humor, loved by his students— clear evidence of that student love was given when he received the Bunn Award for Faculty Excellence by vote of the College Senior Class.

There were many witty comments made on his retirement, several friends expressing the view that Henry would find it impossible to retire, and how impoverished the academic world would be if he really dropped out of sight. As one person put it, "The retirement is more symbolic than real, I suspect. . ." Others— professors of history, law and philosophy—wrote in a similar vein giving evidence of the high esteem in which Henry is held in the academic community.

> The notion that Henry Veatch could ever be retiring is simply incredible. In fact, I am inclined to believe that a retiring Henry Veatch is about as sensible as a square circle. Except for those exalted spirits that are able to believe in logical contradiction, no one will accept this description of him.

If they had written to say that Henry Veatch was fighting, thinking, provoking or provocative, even intelligent, I would be ready to believe that without difficulty. But I cannot imagine a Henry who would be a shrinking violet. Now, perhaps some other sense of "retiring" was intended. But examining all the meanings that occurred to me, none seemed applicable. Only one suggests itself as possible, and that is "retiring" in the sense of acquiring a new set of tires. In that case, I am ready to believe that Henry is starting one more bright, productive, and active phase of his life with a new set of tires and maybe even a new chassis to go with them. That is surely in character. . . .

Meanwhile, accept my warmest good wishes for a "retiring" which is more work, more productivity, old ideas moved in new directions, and above all a Henry Veatch who continues to be himself. He is a rarity in our field and in our world. Intelligence, wit, good humor, high integrity and a real sense of what matters are not qualities that often come together in one person—least of all one academic person. He has them all and because they make him who and what he is, he has the loyalty and devotion of so many good friends. I hope that I may have the privilege of counting myself among them.

****

On receiving the elegant printed invitation to the Symposium honoring him on "retirement from active teaching," I could not help wondering what sort of teaching he plans to engage in now if not *active* teaching—then passive teaching?. . .

****

As a brand new assistant professor at Northwestern I learned from you not only what a "professional Hoosier" was, but also what a professional philosopher was. Who could have asked for more? Congratulations on an illustrious career!

The search committee that brought Henry Veatch to Georgetown was amazed and pleased to discover that professors of diverse philosophical views had such great respect for him, even though his own position was always proposed with great vigor and staunchly defended. This widespread respect for Henry was also evidence in may of the letters received.

. . .You have. . .given some comfort to those of us who have disagreed with you from time to time. Though your good humor is barbed, you seem to enjoy our company and even to take us seriously. I have often suspected you as having the ingratiating manner of a dedicated philosophical social worker, but you disarm such suspicion with wit, warmth, and camaraderie. You may even have a case of the disease of the jaded social worker—secret identification with the client. Despite your scholarly assurance and obviously inexhaustible supply of cogent arguments, you don't seem completely immune to the reductive charms of PM (with its bare particulars) and the seductive charms of the transcendental (with its exotic *lebenswelten*). . . . You have remained, with all your forays into the underworld, a steadfast man of substance.

In the city of philosophy, where, all too often, the philosophical Cabots speak only to the philosophical Lowells, you have never been suspected of speaking only to God. Indeed, polemics aside, but, perhaps, even including them, you have done as much as anyone in my time to make the ideal of philosophical community an actuality. I say, "Long life! and keep the activity going!"

. . . But admidst all those lauds, Henry, please bring yourself to admit that there are only four predicables in Aristotle. You like the angels may be the only one of the kind, but that's not cause to make species a predicable!

Henry Veatch was always acclaimed as an excellent teacher. His awards from Georgetown and Indiana were two of many formally recognizing this excellence that he received during his long career. Furthermore, he was successful at all levels. A law professor who heard him lecture only for a period of ten days wrote:

Experiencing your work. . .was, for one who reveres excellent teaching, and himself aspires to that level of accomplishment, an inspiration. You held forth with intellectual strength and resiliency, and a touching degree of personal humility in the face of one of the toughest audiences anyone would ever have to face: a group of strong-minded-willed law professors. . . . I envy those who will be present in person at Georgetown on April 14 and 15th, but please know that an ever larger number of those to whom you have imparted knowledge, and with whom you have shared wisdom, will find the halls and rooms of the Symposium in spirit. . . . We are lucky to have shared in the excitement of your own intellectual voyage and to have benefitted from you genuine interest in ours. . . .

Several former students who are now professors wrote in the following vein:

Henry Veatch gave me one of the two "Bs" that I received in graduate school. And it is clear to me that his teaching worked by far the greatest effect on my subsequent development. For it taught me not to imitate others but to be my own philosopher.

. . . Though I must admit you didn't always get the very best from me, you're probably the best teacher I ever studied with. Even the few courses that I took with you made a big difference to me. In fact, if you hadn't been at Northwestern when I was there I probably would not be a philosopher today. So now you've got that on our conscience, old fellow!

Many former colleagues and students spoke of Henry's work in logic which might very well be the subject of another symposium. They regretted Henry's concentration on ethics during the latter part of his career because his work in logic had been so promising. Others reminisced about Henry's role as a proponent of faculty and student rights and also as someone who was unsparing of himself in giving advice and assistance to colleagues and students.

A former colleague wrote that two "memory clusters" of Henry stood out in his mind:

First is the warm wit of his conversations, even on the most subtle of philosophical issues. I treasure the copy he gave me of *The Two Logics* for its highly personal style, which so effectively evokes his face-to-face persona, disguising sharp and profound arguments under humorously exaggerated self-deprecation. (While I haven't got quite the right words, those who know and love him will recognize the image I'm trying to capture.)

The second is Henry Veatch as a steadfast, uncompromising leader of the fight for academic freedom, defending assistant professors against personally or politically biased tenure decisions. . ..

Another, in an "appreciation in the spirit of Henry", said:

The pleasantly intimidating, the humorous, the ironic, the argumentative, the comic Henry B. Veatch is leaving the classroom. This is a disaster for American philosophic education. Can one of the rest of us fill his shoes? Can ten of us? It is very unlikely. What will the poor undergraduate do? To whom will the graduate turn? The poor creatures will just have to do with the second best. Henry is a superlative teacher in every respect.

Now let the sophomore philosophy student sleep on in ignorant slumber, the graduate student in his dogmatic slumber. There is one less peal of the trumpet calling all to reason and to reality. Who will struggle in the name of Thomas against Russell and Husserl? Who will support Aristotle against Hume and Mill? Henry was a formidable philosophic antagonist.

Henry has left some students and some books. The graduate students will serve the next generation, and his books will outlive us. It was a grand day when we each met Henry Babcock Veatch. We remember our days together with fondness.

But this volume is not just a festschrift of laudatory essays to be put on the shelf in grateful memory of Henry B. Veatch. It is called *The Georgetown Symposium on Ethics* to signal the University's specialization in ethics at the graduate level and its emphasis on moral values in all its curricula. This volume is intended as a contribution to contemporary debate among ethical theorists, to the teaching of ethics and to moral education. The contributors were not asked to design their articles in terms of what Henry Veatch has said or written; rather, they were asked to contribute their best work in the various fields, related to ethics, in which they are working. The major papers are by Alan Gewirth, Alan Donagan, Manfred Vogel and Joseph Owens, all leading scholars well known for their teaching and scholarship in areas in which Henry Veatch has worked. Like the Symposium, this book is divided into shorter papers on the Foundations of Ethics, Ethics and Religion, Ethics and Law, and Ethics and Education. The reader will discover that these are not rigid divisions and that overlapping occurs. A kind of unity does appear in the volume from the fact that all of the issues raised in the various papers were investigated by Professor Veatch during his career. In this connection it was deemed useful to present a bibliography of his work because one has never been compiled, especially not by Henry. As a result, the book is presented not only as a tribute to Henry Veatch and a lasting memorial to him, but also a useful text for undergraduate and graduate courses that deal with ethical theory and moral education.

There are many persons at Georgetown who have made the Symposium and this volume possible. Georgetown sponsors of the Symposium included the School for Summer and Continuing Education, the Graduate School, the Kennedy Institute of Ethics and the Woodstock Theological Center. Michael Collins, Dean of Georgetown's Summer and Continuing Education school (SSCE), Rev. Royden Davis, S.J., Dean of the College, and Professor Wilfried Ver Eecke, Chairman of the Philosophy Department, gave the moral encouragement and financial support necessary to move it forward. There is also a debt to the Millie and Jerry Reed Fund which I gratefully acknowledge. I will not attempt to name and thank here the many administrators, professors and students at Georgetown who unselfishly gave assistance when it was needed. A few of them are Gerald Sullivan, Mary Greene and Nina Dryer of SSCE and Mary Dyer who has generously helped me with the editing of this volume.

Rocco Porreco
Georgetown University

PART I

VEATCH, VOGEL, OWENS, GEWIRTH AND DONAGAN

CAN PHILOSOPHY EVER BE A THING FOR HOOSIERS?

Henry Babcock Veatch
Georgetown University

Let me begin by confessing to an impertinence and a presumption. These are that I have actually given a title to these foreseeably somewhat empty and rambling remarks of mine this evening: I have called them, "Can Philosophy Ever be a Thing for Hoosiers?" And immediately, I can hear our chairman, Wilfried Ver Eecke, muttering to himself, "But who or what, in God's name, is a Hoosier?" For being, shall we say, the inveterate and almost irredeemable Fleming that he is, the last thing that Wilfried would ever allow himself to clutter his mind with is information to the effect that a Hoosier is someone from the State of Indiana. Yes, Wilfried, and I am afraid that the business may be a still more complicated one than that: for, after all, there are Hoosiers and Hoosiers, just as there are Belgians and Belgians; and so it is that a true Hoosier, as opposed to a mere Hoosier, is someone who is not just from Indiana, but from Southern Indiana!

With that, though, the question immediately becomes, "But why, and how come, this odd notion implied in my title that philosophy might possibly be a thing for Hoosiers?" For does not the very suggestion sound like a downright inanity, if not an actual contradiction: Surely, philosophy can only be a thing for intellectuals; and the one thing a Hoosier—at least a Southern Indiana Hoosier—neither is, nor should ever pretend to be, is an intellectual! No, for a Hoosier is, almost by definition, one who is sadly benighted, and often proud of it!

Before, though, I undertake to do the impossible by way of showing, not just that the poor Hoosiers need philosophy, but even that philosophy itself, oddly enough, needs the likes of Hoosiers—before getting caught up in demonstrations to this strange effect, let me first stop to pay just a few of the many thank-you's that I certainly owe on a happy occasion such as this—for it is an occasion that is a peculiarly happy one for me, even if for no one else. Not only the dinner this evening, but the entire Symposium of the last two days, have been billed as being "in my honor." Why? Well, some of you have doubtless got the impression that the business has begun to take on the appearance of "much ado about nothing." Perhaps so. But, then, I being the nothing on this occasion, is it any wonder that I should be most grateful!

Of course, it has occurred to me that given the circumstances, I probably could do no better by way of showing my gratitude tonight than to follow the example of General Grant at a testimonial dinner that was given in his honor

[1]

some 120 years ago in St. Louis. In the words of Grant's most recent biographer (*Grant: a Biography*, by William S. McFeely, New York, 1982, p. 154):

> After the toast to the general, the band burst into "Hail to the Chief." Grant rose, there were cheers, and he spoke—combining his distaste for speaking in public with a magnificent sense of how appealing unexpected brevity could be, "Gentlemen, in response, it will be impossible to do more than thank you."

And he sat down!

Note, though, that I am not sitting down! Alas no! Nor is it because, I assure you, I am any less sensitive than was General Grant to how "appealing an unexpected brevity" can be. Rather it is that in my case such a brevity would be so unexpected, so utterly out of character, so totally incongruous, as to be almost too great a shock for any and all of you. And so rather than shock you thus unexpectedly, I prefer to carry right on, boring you quite expectedly.

Accordingly, let me say, first off, how particularly grateful I am to Georgetown University as a whole, and to the Philosophy Department in particular, and, most particularly of all, to my beloved friend, Rocco Porreco—and grateful not just for this Symposium of the last two days, but even more for the fact that they all—Georgetown, the Philosophy Department, and my friends in the Department—have provided me, quite literally, with a haven of refuge for all of these last 10 years. Yes, 10 years ago I was indeed the proverbial stranger, and Georgetown took me in!

At the time, as it happens, Georgetown was looking for a new chairman. True, in fairness to Georgetown, let me hasten to add, they were in no wise looking for me! Quite the contrary. Rocco Porreco, whom I then did not know too well, had called me about another matter. And what did I do but quite confound poor Rocco right over the long distance telephone, when I had the temerity to suggest that maybe Georgetown might consider me for the chairmanship! And what was the response? Well, I will only say that at that point the phone went dead! Or if not the phone, then it was Rocco—or at least Rocco's voice—that went dead! Happily, though, communication was soon reestablished; and one thing then leading to another, I eventually did come to Georgetown—but not without the general feeling in the air, particularly among the Jesuits, that maybe the Philosophy Department, if it had not been "had," at the very least had bought a pig in a poke! In fact, I still remember the gruff, bluff Father Henle, who was then President of Georgetown, remarking at the interview that I had with him for the job. "Why, yes, I guess maybe you'll do. After all, I once used a book you wrote in one of my classes." Now even to this day I don't believe I quite know how to interpret this remark of Father Henle's: was it a reason, or a non-reason, that he was giving for hiring me?

Still, of all the Jesuits then at Georgetown, the one who really had to worry with that pig, once it had come out of the poke, was none other than poor, long-suffering Father Davis, the Dean of the College. Verily, I proved to be a heavy cross for him to have to bear—and for all I know, to have to bear vicariously for the entire Jesuit Community! Nor was Father Davis' cross-bearing in any wise alleviated, until one fine day he chanced to meet my good wife at some campus function or other. As usual, Father Davis wore his look of long-suffering on my account—at which Janie said to him cheerily: "Oh, Father Davis, you mustn't let such things worry you. For just consider that I am the only roommate whom Henry has ever had, who has not suffered a nervous break-down in consequence!" Well, that seems to have done it! From then on Father Davis found his lot to be not such an unhappy one after all. True, he could not be said to have been made any less miserable as a result of my wife's remark; and yet he did find that misery, when it has company, is somehow easier to bear!

But to return to the subject of my own gratitude. For on this particular occasion my gratitude is not just my long-standing one toward Georgetown, it is also the immediate one of my being grateful to all of those, my friends and former students and sometime associates, who have been good enough to give so generously of their time and effort as lecturers and participants in the symposium of the last two days. True, for them it may have been more of an occasion to roast me than to toast me. But then that's just fine! In fact, nothing could be better, if that be what it takes to get the likes of Father Owens and Alan Donagan and Alan Gewirth and all of the rest of you to come to Georgetown merely for such a much-ado-about-nothing. Thanks, and thanks again!

And now having paid my tributes and my thanks to both Georgetown and to the symposium participants, what is it that I can possibly say on the score of that egregious topic of mine having to do with Hoosiers and philosophy? Already I have remarked—and I am sure that none of you will hesitate to acknowledge it to be a fact—that philosophy, as it tends to be practiced now-a-days, is scarcely meet for Hoosiers—neither "meet" nor "meat." And with that, I can hear you rejoining, "But why should philosophy be either "meet" or "meat" for Hoosiers? Why not recognize that by its very nature philosophy is a subject solely for intellectuals, and indeed, even for the elite among the intellectuals?"

But no, I am afraid I just could not accept the notion of philosophy as being only for intellectuals. And that, not just because I am a Hoosier, but also because I have never been able to make the grade of being an intellectual! Indeed, will it surprise you if right here and now I make frank confession of the fact that throughout my whole professional career as a teacher of philosophy, I have had no end of trouble with philosophy and philosophers, particularly with the really sophisticated ones among them, especially the great philosophers—with Descartes, with Spinoza, with Leibniz; yes, especially with the likes of Hegel or Nietzsche, and even in our own day with Wittgenstein and Heidegger and all the rest. And what has my trouble with them been? Well, simply that I couldn't understand them!

Yes, even in my student days in the 1930s, when I was taking courses in philosophy, both undergraduate and graduate, it so happened that I was fortunate enough to be able to study under some of the most eminent among the then philosophers—Alfred North Whitehead at Harvard, Karl Jaspers in Germany, the remarkable pioneering logician, Henry M. Sheffer, C.I. Lewis, R.B. Perry, A.O. Lovejoy, *et al.* The only trouble was that, though lucky enough to be able thus to sit at the feet of some of the great—and there is no doubt about their all having been truly sophisticated philosophers and intellectuals—I, alas, found myself singularly unable ever to figure out quite what they were talking about! And even if on rare occasions I did manage to make some vague sense out of what Whitehead, for example, might be driving at with his talk of "actual occasions prehending the entire past actual world," or Jaspers with his notion of *Existenz*, or Sheffer with his "logic of forms and structures," I am afraid that the only sense I could make out of these esoteric doctrines was but a very feeble, remote, and even abstract sense, and not any firm, concrete sense that could in any way be related to my own fund and background of downright Hoosier experience.

Nor was it until after I had gotten my doctor's degree, and before I could find a regular job, that I came under the influence of my long-time, and I am afraid my sometime, friend at Harvard, the late John Wild. He it was who started me reading Aristotle, really for the first time. And with that, believe it or not, it was as if the scales began to fall from my eyes! At last, it seemed that a bit of philosophical light—not much, to be sure, but just a bit—began to penetrate my thick, dull, dense Hoosier skull. "Why," I said to myself, "Aristotle is a philosopher who really talks like a Hoosier."

Or maybe it is not quite accurate to say that Aristotle talked like a Hoosier, since he probably only spoke Greek; and even what he wrote was, or course, a very forbidding "Greek to me." Not only that, but the standard translations of Aristotle in those days had been done into the English of the eminent Aristotelian scholar and Oxford don, W.D. Ross. Alas, though, it must be said that the English of Oxford has never been quite the English of southern Indiana, no, not by a long shot! Still for all of that, whatever the language of Aristotle may have been, what he wrote certainly made good Hoosier sense—at least to me.

Likewise, somewhat later, I found myself able to say somewhat the same thing of St. Thomas Aquinas. For recall how St. Thomas in the Prologue to his mammoth theological *Summa* cites, as being his guiding principle in the work, the declaration made by St. Paul in *First Corinthians*: "For my part, my brothers, I could not speak to you as I should speak to people who have the Spirit. [No,] I had to deal with you on the merely natural plane, as infants in Christ. That is why I give you milk to drink, instead of meat (or solid food). For you are not yet ready for that." Very well, I ask you—or rather I put it to the formidable array of Thomistic scholars who are scattered through the audience this evening: when St. Thomas thought of himself as addressing people "on the merely natural plane," was he thinking of addressing people on any other plane than that of his master, Aristotle, and indeed in much the same vein as Aristotle? And what was this plane if not that of the natural man or, if you will, of the ordinary man, and not the plane of any mere sophisticated few among philosophers and intellectuals? Accordingly, why could one not say that very milk, as opposed to meat and solid food, which St. Thomas proposed to offer in his *Summa*, was, and is, nothing if not just such philosophical nourishment as even Hoosiers might be ready for?

Perhaps, also, the record as I am here reporting it would not be quite just or complete if I were not to tell you of the somewhat caustic comment that still another of my Harvard professors once made many years ago about Aristotle. "Why," he said, "Aristotle is really the only great philosopher who was able to enunciate the perfectly obvious, and still get away with it." True, the remark was not made so much in either irritation or disparagement, as rather in sheer amazement that a philosopher of Aristotle's presumed stature could ever have supposed that philosophy needed to be structured out of little more than commonplace truths, capable of being understood and appreciated by the common sense and common intelligence of all men everywhere—yes, doubtless even of Hoosiers. And need I add that the professor who made this remark was, after all, a Harvard professor, and as such was one who certainly fancied himself to be very much the philosophical sophisticate, if not actually a member of those select groups of professors and intellectuals, that seem to recur in almost every age, and that invariably think of themselves as constituting a philosophical elite. Hence for him the philosopher of all people was hardly one to traffic in the mere commonplace, but rather one to deal in the new, the original, the recondite, the abstruse—as, shall we say, only a Harvard professor can! Yes, for all I know, this particular professor may very well have gone along with the ever-fashionable view of the philosopher, as being nothing if not the creative thinker, the original genius, the one who spurns anything like common sense, and who is determined to shake the world with his brilliant insights and startling new ideas. To all of which I believe the pertinent retort is one made by the late great French Catholic thinker, Etienne Gilson, many years ago, when he said, "Just consider, is not one commonplace truth worth more than a hundred original errors?"

But enough by way of an account of my own Hoosier's difficulties with the elite among the great philosophers, as well as with the high-powered intellectuals among my own professors. And now let me come right out and say what it is that my thesis about Hoosiers and philosophy really amounts to. It amounts simply to the contention that philosophy is not really, and therefore ought not to be allowed to become, the mere resort or preserve of gifted intellectuals. Rather philosophy is for all men everywhere, and its teachings should speak directly to the common sense or common intelligence of all mankind. Oh, immediately, I can hear all of you muttering to yourselves that I am saying this only because, given my own self-confessed lack of even normal intelligence, much less of anything like a minimal competence for a subject like philosophy, I want to peddle a view of philosophy that will be largely by way of a self-justification, or maybe just a kind of protective coloration for my own philosophical limitations.

And yet I do not think that that is entirely it. For is it not simply a fact, whatever my own self-interest in the matter may be, that philosophy just is the one subject in the curriculum that is and ought to be for anyone and everyone? Thus so far as any college or university curriculum is concerned, philosophy is surely not the sort of thing that is for specialists only, or solely for those of superior talents and intellectual abilities, or even for those who have a kind of taste or liking for the sort of discipline that now-a-days goes by the name of philosophy. Rather philosophy is a subject that is decisively and peculiarly for human beings, and indeed for all human beings, simply in virtue of their being human.

After all, if man is a rational animal, then just what may that be taken to mean, if not that a human being, unlike any and all other beings in nature—trees, rocks, orangutangs, or squirrels—is just such a being as is not only able to know what he is about, but actually is under obligation—yes, a moral obligation—to find out what he truly is about and ought to be about, just as a human being. For surely, no human individual can qualify as a fully and properly rational animal, if life for him consists in no more than merely being aware that he has various desires, impulses and tendencies, and then being able to muster the necessary wit and ingenuity to figure out how he can best gratify these inclinations and tendencies. No, to be a truly rational animal, one needs to see to it that one's very desires and inclinations are the right ones for a human person to have, and therefore that one's very ends and purposes in life are rationally determined. In other words, for any human being—Hoosiers included—the business of living needs to be an affair of coming to desire and seek after those things which one ought to desire and aim for, and not merely a matter of figuring out how to get what you want, and then getting it.

Just where, though, is a human being—yes, any and every human being, insofar as he needs to be a rational and responsible agent—where is he ever to come by such knowledge of how to be and become human, if not from philosophy? For is not any and all human moral knowledge—i.e. any knowledge of what is required of a man, of what his very business in life is as a human person simply by virtue of his being human—must not any really basically human knowledge be thus a moral knowledge? And does not a moral knowledge in this sense call for a still further and all-embracing knowledge, or what one might call a knowledge of the whole—a knowledge of nature, man, and God, no less? For surely, how could a person ever hope to know, in the sense of rationally to understand, what he really ought to do and be as a human person—what it is that it is truly incumbent upon him to be, as over against merely responding to what his interests and inclinations impel him to be, or what his family or his community or his society try to condition him to be, or what he himself somehow fancies that his own conscience or supposed moral intuitions prompt him to imagine that he should be?—how could one ever hope to arrive at any such genuine and right knowledge of the moral and the ethical, if this moral knowledge be not set in the context of a knowledge of the entire order of being, and thereby of man's place in that order? And where else is such knowledge to be had, and what else is the nature of such knowledge, if not simply the knowledge that has traditionally been called philosophy?

Besides, is there not another point that needs to be made as regards this reputed philosophical knowledge which turns out to be, as we have been suggesting, both a moral knowledge, and a knowledge such as we have loosely termed a knowledge of the whole, in the sense of being a knowledge of the very order of being itself—of nature, man, and God? For in addition to its being a knowledge such as all men need to have, is it not also a knowledge, which all men, even if they don't have it, nevertheless can have, at least in the sense that they can all appreciate the truth of such things, once the truths be pointed out to them. To be sure, this proposition that there need be nothing especially abstruse or esoteric about philosophical kowledge,—it being a knowledge that is both indispensable to everyone, as well as available and intelligible to everyone—this may strike many of you as being somewhat far-fetched, if not downright wrong-headed, at least at first hearing and at first glance. And yet I wonder if such be not the conception of philosophy that is fundamental to Aristotle and Aquinas alike. For would they not both say that philosophy is somehow a properly and distinctively human knowledge, in that the very test of truth of philosophical knowledge is that such knowledge must somehow be ascertainable and certifiable by the common sense and common understanding and common testimony of all mankind. It is in just this sense that philosophy should be the concern of all men, and not the mere preserve of any intellectual elite. Or at least, they would say, philosophy could be and should be the concern of all men, unless by chance their economic or cultural circumstances might somehow prevent it.

Thus suppose, for example, we consider very cursorily some of the salient truths that are set forth in any Aristotelian type of physics, metaphysics or ethics. For would not both Aristotle and Aquinas hold that of course we human beings find ourselves simply to be and to exist in a world of people and things, that such things or substances, as Aristotle called them, have all sorts of characteristics or accidents attaching to them: they are of various sizes and shapes, are located in various places, are subject to change and motion, sometimes being acted upon by other substances, and sometimes being themselves the agents of changes in other substances. Of course, too, when substances thus undergo change, it is possible to determine roughly the sorts of causes that operate to produce these changes. For one thing, nothing could possibly undergo any change, be it of place or of quantity, or of quality, or even of substance, without its being able to be other and different, or without its having a capacity or potentiality to be in a different place, or to become larger or smaller, or to take on a different quality, say. Likewise, there could be no such changes in thing without some force or agent or active power to effect the change.

Similarly, what we have designated as being the potentialities of things to be or become other and different from what they presently are—these potentialities can also be recognized as being what a substance might be or could be—what, in other words, it has a capacity to become. Thus a young plant has a potentiality to attain to its full growth, and thus to enjoy a naturally flourishing condition. Or again, a human infant or young child has a potentiality to become a truly rational and responsible adult. Accordingly, we may say that the potentialities of any substance represent what that substance might be or could be, and thus what it ought to be or should be—though not necessarily an "ought" here in any moral sense. On the other hand, if we are talking about a human being's capacity or potentiality eventually to become and to act as a truly rational and responsible human person—this does represent what that individual ought to be, this time in an unmistakably moral sense, and what he therefore is under an inescapable natural and moral obligation to try to be and become simply as a human individual. In other words, the moral responsibilities of human beings are built right into their natural condition, or better these moral responsibilities are determined in the light of no less than the entire natural order of things as this pertains to men. Likewise, this same natural and moral order of the universe can surely be seen to be an order that would be scarcely intelligible, or even able to exist, without God, or the operation of a divine causality.

Oh, I realize that no doubt at this point I ought to go down on my hands and knees to all of you, and beg your forgiveness and indulgence for my thus rehearsing to you all of these several commonplace truisms drawn from Aristotelian philosophy. And yet does not the very point that I wished to make lie just here? Are not all of these truths of Aristotelian philosophy— almost all of them—little more than truisms, when you come right down to it? Moreover, if one should ask, "But how do we really know that as human beings we do exist in a real world of persons and things, that these things are, many of them, in process of change, and that when such changes pertain to human beings we have a responsibility for what we are to be and become— for what we make of ourselves?" Once this sort of question is put to us, do we not find ourselves constrained to answer such a challenge as to how we know such things, by responding, "Why these are things that are simply evident to us from our experience as human beings. Indeed, that is why they strike us as being little more than truisms and commonplaces, for what are they if not things that are palpable and evident just to the common sense and common intelligence of all men everywhere?"

But surely by this point, if not long before, there are many of you who will want to draw me up short and to say: "Is not, though, this whole business of philosophy as supposedly being a properly human knowledge in the sense of being a knowledge that is of and for all men—does this not run into one very obvious difficulty? For what about science and scientific knowledge, as these are purveyed by the modern natural sciences? For supposing that this reputed philosophic knowledge that we have been talking about is a knowl- edge that pretends to locate the moral and the ethical right within the very order of being itself—within the order of nature, man, and God, as we have termed it—how in the modern age can one possibly claim to a knowledge of man and of nature without one's relying heavily, if not exclusively, on the natural sciences?"

Surely not, though! And indeed, must not the answer to such a query be: "No, scientific knowledge, as we understand it today, is in no position to be in any way a substitute for philosophical knowledge. For scientific knowledge, instead of being what we have called a knowledge of the whole—a knowledge of the very order of being itself—is, of all things, a highly specialized knowledge. Rather than a knowledge that could ever purport to be in any way an all-encompassing knowledge of nature, man, and God, science necessarily restricts itself, and should restrict itself, to its own sphere. Accordingly, even to the extent to which science may rightly and properly be said to occupy itself with what might be called the order of nature, it does not and cannot envisage that order in such a way as to include the moral and the ethical. Instead, scientific knowledge in the modern sense is a knowledge that is radically value-blind and virtue-blind. And so the last thing that one could ever hope to learn from modern science is what it is that we human beings, simply by virtue of our human nature, ought to do and be, or of what our natural, human moral responsibilities in life are. No, for to take but a trivial example, it is of course possible to learn from physics that water seeks its own level. But the one thing that one cannot possibly learn' from any modern scientific study of physics is whether it is either right or wrong, or good or bad, that water should seek its own level—or for that matter that anything else in the scientific universe should either be the way it is, or do the things that it does.

Moreover, as a consequence of all of this, is it not now clear how scientific knowledge is to be contrasted with philosophic knowledge as being a specialized knowledge, rather than a knowledge for all? After all, in modern physics or chemistry or biology, the test of truth could never be based on the fact that scientific findings and principles are simply confirmable by the common sense and common experience of all mankind. Imagine submitting such things as the principle of complementarity in atomic physics, or Einstein's formula $e = mc^2$, or the business of recombinant principles of DNA in molecular biology—imagine submitting these to the test of their being directly evident to human experience everywhere—yes, even to the experience of Hoosiers! Why, the very idea of such a thing is ridiculous in the context of science. But in philosophy—at least in Aristotelian or Thomistic philosophy—it is surely quite different. There the test of truth just is its evidence to the common experience and common intelligence of all men everywhere.

No sooner, though, have we thus distinguished scientific truth and scientific knowledge, than immediately another objection suggests itself from another and very different quarter—this time an objection coming not from the scientists, but from the theologians, and maybe, for all I know, particularly from the Jesuit theologians! For why may we not imagine the theologians as contesting directly our fundamental contention in these remarks that it is philosophy, and philosophy alone, that is able to provide men with such knowledge as they need regarding the entire order of nature and being—a knowledge of nature, man, and God in short—a knowledge which men simply have to have if they are ever properly to know themselves, as Socrates would say, and thus be able to know what they ought to do and be simply as human beings? But no, we can imagine such theologians saying: any instruction for human beings that pretends to be an instruction in what we have called a universal and all-embracing knowledge, and that includes a moral or ethical knowledge as well—any such instruction can only be an instruction that must be based solely on faith, and be communicated only in the Faith.

Nor is it to be denied that such a theologian's objection is a difficult one to handle, particularly for me. For just as I confessed to you earlier my ignorance and lack of sophistication in the usual subtleties of intellectuals and of philosophers, so also must I now confess that I do just happen to be a Christian. Or perhaps if these words would seem to imply that one ever could be a Christian by mere happenstance, then let me just say that I happen to be a Christian, thank God, by the grace of God! Moreover, as a Christian I would certainly have to admit that there is just no way a human being can very well live as a human being ought to live, unless it be in the Faith. That, I think, is true. On the other hand, I would hardly take this to mean that the Faith which all men need to guide them is a faith that should ever be construed to the absolute exclusion of philosophy, to say nothing of being necessarily in opposition to the teachings of any and all philosophy. Quite the contrary, I would certainly want to affirm that the Faith needs philosophy—maybe not as much or as acutely as philosophy needs the Faith; but still in its own way, I should be inclined to say that I find it hard to see how the Faith could ever really dispense with philosophy at all!

And at this I don't doubt that the theologians will immediately come back at me, raining down upon my head all of those Pauline imprecations and condemnations in *First Corinthians*, where, quoting Isaiah, St. Paul says, "I will destroy the wisdom of the wise, and bring to naught the cleverness of the clever." For whom else and what else did St. Paul have in mind here, one will say, if not precisely philosophy and the wisdom of the philosophers?

Nevertheless, in my Scriptural ignorance and temerity both, I would venture to suggest that St. Paul is not here condemning philosophy as such, but rather a mere pseudo-philosophy, or philosophy as practiced by those whom we might call "the intellectuals," those who tend to be wise only in their own conceits, and whose philosophy turns out to be little more than a cleverness of the clever. For if we but undertake to supplement what St. Paul says in *First Corinthians* with what he affirms in the *Epistle to the Romans*, we there find that, although St. Paul complains and complains bitterly, that "in their wickedness men are stifling the truth," he promptly goes on to affirm in the very same passage, and in no uncertain terms, that "all that may be known of God lies plain before [men's] eyes. . . . [Indeed] His invisible attributes, that is to say His everlasting power and deity, have been visible, ever since the world began, to the eye of reason, in the things that He has made." And so St. Paul concludes,—if we may here render St. Paul's words in the rumble of the old King James version: "Thus men are without excuse!"

But now I ask you—and without my claiming to make even any minimal claims for myself in matters of Biblical exegesis—Is it not patent and obvious that St. Paul is here affirming that there is indeed such a thing as a true philosophic wisdom and knowledge of just the sort we have been advocating and even pleading for up to now? It is a knowledge and wisdom of the sort that we have termed a universal and all-embracing knowledge, in that it is a knowledge of the entire order of nature and being, as these have been "visible to the eye of reason ever since the world began." Besides, such a knowledge and wisdom of things as things visible to the eye of human reason—why is this not just that sort of philosophic knowledge which we have been claiming is both indispensable and accessible to all men every-where, and accessible to them simply because, in their capacity as rational animals, all men—even Hoosiers—possess that eye of reason; and access-ible to them, precisely as truths that are confirmable and verifiable in the common experience and common understanding of all mankind?

Not only that, but following St. Paul's lead still further, suppose we ask why it is that such philosophic truth as is thus available to all mankind would seem no longer to be recognized and appreciated by all men everywhere? Is not St. Paul's answer that this natural truth, this universal truth, available to all mankind, has none-the-less been "stifled by men in their wickedness"? And who and what is it that is thus primarily responsible for this stifling of the truth? Why, is it not just that "wisdom of the wise" and "cleverness of the clever" of which St. Paul speaks? In other words, is it not just those whom we have all along been calling the intellectuals among the philosophers— those who would scorn the idea that philosophy is after all something for human beings, yes all human beings, and who would insist instead that philosophy is very much a thing only of intellectuals, by intellectuals, and for intellectuals?

Yes, in this very connection why might we not venture to spot what I would suggest is, doubtless, the tell-tale mark of the so-called "intellec-tual"—not just the intellectual in philosophy, but the intellectual generally, as being a somewhat distinctive phenomenon of modern culture? For why not say that the intellectual is just such a one as ever seeks to replace our ordinary, everyday human and common sense criterion of truth with a criterion that is peculiarly the intellectual's own, or at least that of his own circle? Thus the common sense criterion of truth might be thought to be simply one which holds that those things are most basically and fundamen-tally true in human life that are evident to the common experience and common intelligence of mankind. In contrast, the intellectual would replace this everyday human standard of truth and meaning with some more or less private or esoteric standard that has been tailor-made, shall we say, in some one or other of those sophisticated circles in which intellectuals tend to move—for example, the cafes of the Left Bank in Paris, or maybe some literal "Vienna Circle," or perhaps the gatherings of the Bloomsburies in London, or maybe that one-time group of American neo-Marxists clustering around the *Partisan Review*? Or, still more prosaically perhaps, the intellectual's circle might be any one of those ever emergent cliques of professors and graduate students that are forever springing up in any of the various great multiversities of the modern world, Oxford, Berlin, Harvard, Berkeley, Chicago, Princeton, or wherever.

Why, though, rest only with these mere generalities? Why not consider at least one or two concrete cases of how in the course of modern philosophy, intellectuals have ever been prone to set up their own sets of truth-conditions or meaning-criteria by way of replacing the more traditional standards of truth as being evident to the common sense and common experience of mankind? And first off, why not consider the case of the great French philosopher, Descartes, the very founder of modern philosophy. For Descartes was nothing if not thoroughly convinced and imbued—if not even obsessed—with the idea that all of the knowledge and learning of his day, as well as all of the knowledge and learning inherited from the past, as the sort of common knowledge of Western culture—that all of this supposed knowledge was something so inadequate, so messy and confused, so haphazard and ill-ordered, that it really could not claim to be a proper knowledge at all? And so what did Descartes do? Well, he simply undertook to tear down the whole fabric of the then common fund of human knowledge, and to reconstruct it all from the ground up, simply according to his own, Descartes', method and specifications. For, as he said, the idea "that occurred to me was that frequently there is less perfection in a work produced by several persons than in one produced by a single hand. And so we notice that buildings conceived and completed by a single architect are usually more beautiful and better planned than those remodeled by several persons using ancient walls that had originally been built for other purposes." *(Discourse on Method,* Pt. II).

Really now, is not the import of such a Cartesian declaration almost breathtaking in its sheer assurance—yes, one might almost say in its very *hubris!* No longer was philosophic knowledge and wisdom to be the common heritage of mankind; instead, it was now to be a new creation set up by a single intellectual—viz., that exceedingly smart Frenchman, René Descartes! Nor is that all, for one might almost say that what Descartes thus did was to provide the very charter and title-deeds for what I might well call no less than "philosophy in a new key"—i.e., philosophy for and by intellectuals.

For in effect, what did Descartes do, if not simply erect as his own standard of truth—which was to say really nothing but the standard of clear and distinct ideas, as this might be said to operate in mathematics? Accordingly, for Descartes nothing was to be taken as true regarding the natural world, unless it could measure up to Descartes' own mathematical standard of truth. In contrast, Aristotle specified those things as being truths that are simply evident to the common sense of mankind, viz. such truths as that, as human beings, we live in a world of substances and their accidents, that these substances undergo change, that such changes always have their proper causes—there is always a something that undergoes the change, an agent of the change, and a proper terminus or end of the change etc., etc. But not so Descartes! He would have none of this. Instead, he insisted that none of these common-sense truths of Aristotle could possibly meet his (Descartes') mathematician's standard of clear and distinct ideas. And so Descartes simply read onto the face of nature a purely mathematized conception of matter as being no more than geometrical extension, the matter being simply disposed in countless different geometrical configurations, which are forever succeeding one another from instant to instant. And as for the causes of these successions of geometrical configurations one after the other, there of course could be no natural causes here of any sort at all. Instead it had to be no less than God Himself who needed to be invoked by way of quite literally recreating the entire physical world from instant to instant, each time with a slightly different material configuration from the one immediately preceding it.

Now, of course, such a Cartesian world is no longer a world in which any ordinary man can ever experience himself as actually living in, or being in, at all. Instead, it all turns out to be no less than a "brave new world" designed by Descartes, and aimed at providing the new physics with a framework within which the newly emerging modern natural science might be able to operate, and has indeed continued to operate pretty much right down to the present day.

Alas, though,—or maybe happily—there is no time for me to adduce other examples than that of Descartes, by way of showing how our modern philosopher-intellectuals have ever been given to setting up their own, often most ingeniously devised standards of truth, in order thereby to undermine completely the testimony of our common everyday human experience and human intelligence. For no less than Descartes, I could have used countless other examples—Bertrand Russell, Jean-Paul Sartre, F. H. Bradley, W. V. Quine, Karl Marx, Wilfrid Sellars, John Dewey, you name them—each and every one of them, each with his own standard or criterion of truth; and yet all of them to the same effect, viz. that of transforming the everyday world, in which we all of us as human beings live, into a world that is largely unrecognizable by the common sense and common experience of mankind.

And if now you should want to ask, but what's wrong with all of this? Why shouldn't different philosophers each set up their own private and personal and esoteric truth conditions? To this the answer surely is that if it be but a case of *suum cuique*—"to each his own"—in the matter of the philosophers' criteria of truth, then the upshot of this is to turn philosophy into no more than a matter of fashion, rather than truth. Nor is such mere fashion and arbitrariness necessarily the worst fate to befall philosophy when it thus forsakes the truth of common experience for truth as determined by the latest fashions of the intellectuals.

No, even more sinister would appear to be the new wrinkle that present-day philosophy has come increasingly to take on ever since Kant, and largely as a result of that transcendental turn which contemporary philosophers, nearly all of them, now tend to make largely as a result of Kant's influence. For one might indeed say that the decisive issue that our latter-day Kantian intellectuals have injected into philosophy is just the issue of whether there can really be any criteria of truth about the real world at all, be these criteria those simply of common human experience, or be they those of this, that, or the other passel of intellectuals, No, for perhaps no criteria of the truth of human experience will ever do, simply because, as Kant saw it, human experience, however conceived and however hedged about with criteria of truth and error, is somehow radically and in principle incapable of ever telling us anything about the way things really are, or the way the world is in fact and in itself.

Instead, what the Kantians insist upon is that the very framework or structure of the real world—the very order of being and of nature, if you will—is not anything that is even in principle ever discoverable in and through human experience. Why not? Why, it is simply because what we fancy that we experience as being out there, and in the facts, and in reality, is but a function of that order, or structure, or categorical framework, that the human mind itself brings to experience rather than finds in experience. Or if it be not the human mind that should thus be said to fashion the entire world, together with our experience of the world, then perhaps we might say that it is our human logical thought-forms or language forms by which we think about the world or talk about the world, that are responsible for the world appearing to be the way that it is. Indeed, as Kant himself suggested, rather than for human scientists and philosophers and human knowers generally having to worry about bringing their theories and ideas into conformity with objects, it is far better, to say nothing of being far easier and more fruitful, for scientists and philosophers simply to make objects conform to our own scientists' or philosphers' ideas of the way they would have objects in the world to be and to appear.

Clearly, with this Kantian development in modern philosophy, the triumph, then, of the so-called intellectual in philosophy—and indeed in science and in human knowledge generally—would appear to have become total and complete. No more need the intellectual worry about having to defer to the judgments of men's common human experience. Instead, it is now the intellectual who calls the tune, setting up his own standards and criteria of truth; and even determining what the very character of the world and the very order of nature shall be, according to the particular set of categories or hypotheses or theories with which he, the philosopher-intellectual, now approaches reality, and so makes it conform to his own conceptual patterns and frameworks.

With this, though, is it not now unmistakable what the consequence must be for philosophy of this determination and domination of all truth simply by the intellectuals? No longer will the truth men live by be in any way God's truth. Rather it will be only man's truth. Nor will it even be man's truth or a human truth, so much as it must now be but a truth cut to the cloth and to the measurements of the intellectuals' own standards and criteria. That is to say, it becomes largely a private truth, tailor-made and fashioned at the hands of whoever or whatever may be the regnant group of scientist-intellectuals or philosopher-intellectuals, whose particular world view happens to be the fashionable one at a particular time or place. For remember, if our human ideas are no longer to be brought into conformity with objects, but rather objects into conformity with our ideas, then there is just no way in which there can any longer be any objective standards of truth at all. Instead, truth will no longer be truth about the world or reality, or the truth of things as they are in themselves, but rather only such truth as but reflects the way things chance to appear to be when seen from the perspective of, and as filtered through, the particular hypotheses and theories and conceptual frameworks from which the currently fashionable philosophers and intellectuals may have chosen to view the world.

And so in conclusion I would but wonder, and at the same time, rather shudder to think, at what must be the eventual outcome of this whole notion of philosophic truth as something that is only cut to the particular specifications of philosophy's intellectuals. For as different intellectuals come to put forward their own very different and diverse standards of truth and evidence, and advocate their own radically different ordering schemes and conceptual frameworks for the picturing and structuring of reality and the world, just which standard, or which world-view, will it be that comes to prevail? For after all, if our present-day philosophical intellectuals are right, there is no longer anything like what we might call the fund of our ordinary human experience, or the common sense and intelligence of mankind as a whole, that now may be appealed to by way of deciding which world-view is the true one, or which set of intellectuals we should cast in our lot with.

Instead, all truth must become utterly arbitrary on this basis; nor will our own decision as to which truth we will go along with ourselves be anything more than a thing merely up for grabs. Yes, if there be no objective standards of any kind by which we can judge as between the innumerable rival truth-schemes and world-views of the intellectuals, then the only consideration that presumably can carry the day in favor of the one intellectual's scheme as over against another's will have to be none other than a consideration of mere persuasive force and power. And so what else does philosophy come down to in this present dispensation of our philosopher-intellectuals, such as we find ourselves to be in in today's world, if not simply the pursuit of what Nietzsche called "the will to power."

Is it any wonder, then, that in philosophical circles now-a-days, real dialogue as between different philosophical schools and positions, has tended to go pretty much by the board? And why should this sort of thing not have gone by the board? For so far from it being supposed that philosophic discussion should ever lead to greater knowledge and understanding, its only function is, as Richard Rorty would say, "to keep the conversation going" as between rival philosophical groups. And yet I ask you: why bother to keep the conversation going as between rival philosophies, if your own fashion in philosophy happens to be in the ascendancy—and in the ascendancy just in the sense that you and your own group control all the jobs, the promotions, the publication outlets, and just about anything and everything else in the profession—or indeed in the culture as a whole?

No, rather than keep the conversation going with your rivals, why would not the sensible thing be simply to concentrate on keeping your own in-group and its partisans in power, and your rivals out? After all, if the entire philosophic enterprise, as practiced by our present-day intellectuals, amounts to no more than a pursuit of the will to power, then why not do just that, and forget about anything so old-fashioned as the pursuit of truth? Yes, remembering Matthew Arnold's well-known concern with what he called "culture and anarchy," why not say that now-a-days our philosophical culture in the West bids fair to giving way to anarchy, indeed, and the anarchy to tyranny!

For myself, though, I am afraid that rather than merely acquiescing in this state of affairs, and even though I now be much too superannuated to do much of anything about it—I am still determined to go right on insisting that, notwithstanding all current philosophical fashions being to the contrary, I do believe philosophy to be a thing for Hoosiers after all. Nor is it merely a case of Hoosiers, and of ordinary men generally, needing philosophy; it is no less a case of philosophy needing Hoosiers, and indeed of its needing once more to respect the judgment of the common sense and the common experience of mankind, instead of being forever mesmerized by all the different sorts of ingeniously invented and imposed standards that today's philosopher-intellectuals would try to gull us into accepting.

Of course, I realize that in insisting that the criterion of truth in philosophy should be the common judgments of all men everywhere, I can hardly maintain that always and in each individual case the judgments of human beings will invariably reflect the ability of ordinary men to see the truth clearly and to see it whole. Far from it. And yet just recall how it was Abraham Lincoln who said that while you can fool all of the people some of the time, and some of the people all of the time, what you cannot do is fool all of the people all of the time! And surely Lincoln was right! Indeed, in enunciating as his standard of truth that no one can fool all of the people all of the time, was not Lincoln really only articulating a conviction that was common alike to Aristotle and to St. Thomas?

No, I would not go so far as to claim that Honest Abe ever read Aristotle; and I am almost as sure as I am standing here, that he doubtless never even heard of St. Thomas Aquinas. And yet, need I remind you once again of what I have already remarked on before, and that is that Aristotle was most unmistakably a Hoosier in spirit, if not in geography. And where was it, I ask you, that Lincoln grew up as a boy? Why, of course, you have already guessed it! He grew up in Southern Indiana, not far from the little town of Gentryville. Why, then, should it be so surprising that Aristotle and Lincoln should both have thought so much alike as regards the nature of philosophic truth, and whether such truth be not a thing for Hoosiers and for all men alike, and so is not just a thing merely for sophisticates and intellectuals? After all, anyone who has been to Gentryville, Indiana, can readily understand how that mere wide place in the road could have been a proper enough training ground for Honest Abe. But what it never was, and presumably never could be, would be any sort of rendezvous for intellectuals. No, not Gentryville, Indiana!

KIERKEGAARD'S TELEOLOGICAL SUSPENSION OF THE ETHICAL—SOME REFLECTIONS FROM A JEWISH PERSPECTIVE.

Manfred Vogel
Northwestern University

In some manifestations of the religious phenomenon the religious dimension is such that by its very essence it necessarily implicates the inner and inextricable intertwining of the ethical dimension with itself (we would designate these various manifestations of the religious phenomenon as belonging to type I). In other manifestations, however, the religious dimension in no way implicates the ethical dimension—the ethical dimension is constituted here as an independent and separate entity though the religious dimension can be brought from the outside to impinge upon it (and these manifestations we would designate as belonging to type II). Lastly, in still other manifestations even this possibility of having the religious dimension impinge from the outside upon the ethical dimension is excluded, thus leaving the two dimensions closed within themselves in a monadic-like fashion with no linkage or bridging between them (clearly these manifestations also belong to type II). Thus, we would submit that the first instance can be encountered, for example, in prophetic biblical faith and in non-mystical halachic Judaism; that the second instance can be encountered in some strands of Christianity (e.g., in Catholicism or Calvinism); and that the third instance may be encountered in some other strands of Christianity (e.g., in German Lutheranism particularly when associated with the pietistic expression) and in many of the nonbiblical religions (e.g., in Shamanistic primary religions, in Greco-Roman paganism and even in the religions of the Ancient Near East).

In as much as we are mainly concerned in this paper with the religious dimension as it expresses itself in mainstream Judaism (which is to say, in a structure of faith that is constituted by prophetic biblical faith and nonmystical halachic Judaism), we are evidently concerned with a religion that belongs to the first type of religions delineated above, i.e., to that type in which the religious dimension is by its very essence inextricably intertwined with the ethical dimension (where the very content of the religious act of witnessing is the ethical act and the ultimate signification of the ethical act is its being the fundamental act of religious witnessing). Now it should be quite clear that in such a type of religion the concern with the domain of ethics and religion, i.e., with the domain involved in delineating the relation between ethics and religion, must be central and of great significance. After all, this domain impinges upon the most fundamental and the most sensitive aspect of the structure of faith, to wit, it impinges upon the basic nature of the primary act of religious witnessing.[1] Likewise, it should be equally clear that in the context of this domain, i.e., that in the context of discussing the relation between religion and ethics, the real significant issue, the real problematic, which ultimately one must inevitably encounter is the issue of ultimacy and supremacy. Namely, sooner or later one must cope with the question of where ultimacy is being placed—is it to be placed in the ethical or in the religious domain—and commensurate to this ascertain which dimension—the ethical or the religious—is given supremacy over the other.[2]

I

Now, it is precisely with respect to this issue (an issue that is essential and inescapable for religions of type I as, for example, Judaism) that Kierkegaard's formulation of the teleological suspension of the ethical in *Fear and Trembling* receives its essential signification. For the formulation clearly states that the ethical is to be suspended for the sake of some higher end. As such the formulation clearly implies that ultimacy and supremacy are not vested in the ethical domain but rather in that other domain to which the higher end, the end for whose sake the ethical is to be suspended, belongs; and in as much as it is clear from the context that the higher end is none other than the divine will, the formulation clearly places ultimacy and supremacy in the religious domain. Thus, the essential signification of Kierkegaard's formulation cannot be mistaken—it places ultimacy and therefore supremacy in the religious and not in the ethical domain.

But Kierkegaard's formulation has not only the distinct merit of stating its position with respect to the issue before us with great clarity; it has the added important advantage that it expresses itself with unusual force and poignancy. This is derived from the fact that Kierkegaard's formulation of the teleological suspension of the ethical is articulated, as is well known, in intimate conjunction with the biblical story of the binding of Isaac (Genesis, 22:1–19). For as such it clearly precipitates the issue before us, i.e., the issue of supremacy between the religious and the ethical domain, in the most radical circumstances. It precipitates the issue in the context where, so to speak, the cards are stacked against the religious domain as far as it is conceivably possible to do—is the religious domain, i.e., is the divine command, to have supremacy and prevail even when it demands the murder of one's son? Here lies the force and poignancy of this formulation. It lies in the fact that it removes any and every subterfuge behind which one could hide and conveniently avoid facing the implications of the issue in all their force. It lies in the fact that the formulation here (i.e., the circumstances in whose context the formulation is articulated) does not allow one to be glib or superficial or less than crystal clear about what implications are contained in one's direction. For clearly it is not so difficult to affirm the supremacy of the religious when such an affirmation does not implicate the negation of the ethical; it is even feasible to affirm the supremacy of the religious without too much constraint when such an affirmation does implicate the negation of the ethical but only in some minor, peripheral and not too significant matters. It is, however, a totally different matter when the affirmation of the supremacy of the religious implicates the negation of the ethical in matters that are fundamental, in matters where the negation of the ethical would prove to be most offensive. Is one still prepared to grant the supremacy of the religious when the religious may demand the murdering of one's child? Yet, if such an affirmation is to be at all serious one must be prepared to accept its implications in all their dire possibilities as, for example, one must be prepared to accept sacrificing one's own son as a possible implication of such an affirmation. It is precisely in the making clear of this point that Kierkegaad's formulation of the teleological suspension of the ethical (taken, of course, in the context of the biblical story of the binding of Isaac) receives its special significance and impact. For clearly, any serious concern with the interrelation between ethics and religion is no longer able now to skirt, i.e., to circumvent or fudge over, the real, fundamental problematic which such an undertaking precipitates.

It is true, however, that Kierkegaard does not intend for his formulation of the teleological suspension of the ethical to be taken as an expression of a problematic; rather he clearly intends for it to be taken as an expression of a definitive answer. Namely, in the face of the most radical circumstances when the religious runs head on into the very grain of the ethical and contradicts it (i.e., when the religious implicates the murdering of one's son), Kierkegaard does not perceive the precipitation of a fundamental problematic but rather the presentation of the optimal situation in which to formulate one's position in full awareness of all its implications, even the most radical and difficult implications. Clearly the teleological suspension of the ethical articulates for him a definitive position rather than a prob-lematic—supremacy and ultimacy are accorded to the religious dimension over the ethical dimension in all conceivable instances even when the ethical is countermanded in its most fundamental signification.

That Kierkegaard can take this position, that he can claim through his formulation of the teleological suspension of the ethical the definitive position that the religious supersedes the ethical in all conceivable instances, is in a way not all that difficult to understand if we keep in mind the religious tradition from which Kierkegaard is coming and which he represents. For in coming from the Lutheran tradition Kierkegaard is clearly representing an understanding of religion in terms of the context of type II delineated above, which is to say, that for him the constitution of the religious does not necessarily implicate the ethical—the religious and the ethical are not internally bound and intertwined. Rather, the religious and the ethical are constituted here essentially as independent and separate dimensions, the former being delineated exclusively by the vertical relating while the latter is delineated exclusively by the horizontal relating. But clearly, in such a context where the religious does not necessarily implicate the ethical dimension in its very constitution, claiming supremacy and precedence for the religious dimension over the ethical dimension would not precipitate the problematic of internal self-contradiction (the religious does not have to be by its very constitution ethical!). Operating in such a context, therefore, Kierkegaard can clearly assert with no "ifs" or "buts" the supremacy of the religious while at the same time countenancing the possibility that it may well contradict and abrogate the ethical in its most fundamental values.

Indeed, the inner-logic operating here, i.e., the inner-logic operating in the context of those religions belonging to type II of our delineation above, would not only allow but would actually lead one to make such a claim. For in as much as salvation is placed, almost by definition, in the religious dimension, i.e., in the relating that is vertical, this means that the religious is invested with a worth and a validity that is supreme and ultimate. But this, on the other hand, also means that in as much as the ethical dimension, i.e., the relating that is horizontal, is constituted here as a separate dimension independent of the religious dimension, that inescapably there will be here a devaluation in the worth and validity of the relating that is horizontal, i.e., of the ethical dimension. Certainly, one would not be able to have here supreme and ultimate worth and validity vested in the ethical dimension, seeing that this has already been preempted by the religious dimension and that there is not internal intertwining, internal coalescence, between the religious and the ethical so that the status accorded to the religious is *ipso facto* shared also by the ethical. As such, it should not be surprising that a contradiction or abrogation of the ethical need not be viewed too seriously in this context. After all, such contradiction or abrogation does not touch the ultimate and supreme value. This is clearly arrogated to the religious dimension. Thus, in this context it is indeed the religious alone which takes precedence to the exclusion of all else (even ethics) and consequently one can acquiesce in what may be offensive to other dimensions (even to the ethical and, indeed, even when it is most offensive to the ethical as, for example, when it demands the murder of one's child) as long as the religious dimension is satisfied. This is the point to which the inner-logic operating here must lead and consequently this is the basic posture which one would ultimately encounter in religions belonging to type II. True, generally one would be more comfortable were the implications not pushed that far or expressed in such blatant and unambiguous terms. One could then extol the supremacy of the religious while conveniently fudging over its implications with regard to a possible contradiction of the ethical. Thus, the significance of Kierkegaard's formulation in this context, i.e., in the context of the religions belonging to type II, is precisely to counteract such fudging over by clearly and uncompromisingly spelling out the implications involved and then in full cognizance of these unpleasant implications proceeding to "bite the bullet."[3]

So, the analysis thus far has established the following: 1) that the teleological suspension of the ethical as formulated by Kierkegaard constitutes a statement which undertakes either to represent a certain state of affairs or to put forth a claim to bring about a certain state of affairs; 2) that Kierkegaard can formulate the teleological suspension of the ethical in this way as a statement is due to the fact that he comes from the Lutheran tradition, namely from a religious expression that belongs to type II; 3) that the formulation of the teleological suspension of the ethical as a statement is indeed feasible only in the context of religious expressions belonging to type II, seeing that the feasibility of such a formulation is contingent on the precondition that the vertical, i.e., the religious, dimension be separated in its very constitution from the horizontal, i.e., the ethical, dimension (for only in such a context of separation can the requirements of one dimension, as for example, the religious dimension, consistently go hand in hand with—or, even more poignantly, actually demand—the abrogation of the other dimension) and that, in turn, such separation is the distinctive mark exclusively of the religious expressions belonging to type II.

But in addition to these observations the analysis here clearly portends one further observation and, indeed, a further observation that is all-important. Namely, it portends the further observation that in the center of religious expressions where the religious dimension is not separated from the ethical dimension but rather is internally and inextricably intertwined with it, in other words, that in the context of religious expressions which belong to type I, the formulation of the teleological suspension of the ethical, far from articulating a demand that can be met, articulates in truth a demand that in principle cannot be fulfilled and thus rather than signify a possible state of affairs it signifies a problem. It portends that in the context of religious expressions belonging to type I the teleological suspension of the ethical is no longer a definitive exclamation-mark but a big question-mark. For by the same token that the analysis above of the factor of separation has shown that only in the context where separation is present, i.e., that only in the context where the religious dimension is separate from the ethical dimension, does the formulation of the teleological suspension of the ethical signify a demand that can be met, it will clearly also show that in a context where separation is not present the formulation of the teleological suspension of the ethical cannot possibly be a *bona fide* demand, i.e., a demand that can be met. Indeed, it will clearly show the diametrical opposite, i.e., that in a context where the religious is by its very constitution intertwined with the ethical the religious cannot go against the ethical nor conversely the ethical go against the religious. As such, a formulation of the teleological suspension of the ethical, seeing that it signifies the counter-manding of the ethical for the sake of the religious, must clearly precipitate a serious problematic when it is proposed in the context of religious expressions belonging to type I. For how can one affirm a formulation which by its essence implies a discordance between the religious and the ethical in a context whose very essence signifies a fundamental accord and correspondence between the religious and the ethical?

Indeed, as we have seen, the formulation of the teleological suspension of the ethical arises originally in the context of the religious expressions belonging to type II (we evidently have in mind its formulation by Kierkegaard in the context of Lutheranism) and there its affirmation is quite feasible and understandable. As against this, in the context of the religious expressions belonging to type I the formulation of the teleological suspension of the ethical can only arise as a "transplant" (a transplant from the previous context of religious expressions belonging to type II) and here its affirmation, far from being feasible and understandable, is actually very problematical. Thus, the whole point of our analysis above has been to show that there is such a "transplantation" occurring when one is moving from the context of religious expressions belonging to type II to a context of religious expressions belonging to type I and that in this process of "transplantation" the status of the formulation of the teleological suspension of the ethical changes radically in being transformed from a statement or a command into a big question-mark. We would submit, however, that it is precisely as a question-mark that the formulation of the teleological suspension of the ethical becomes really interesting. Namely, it is precisely in the context of religious expressions belonging to type I, where the teleological suspension of the ethical no longer signifies the positing of a fundamental principle but rather the precipitation of a fundamental problematic, that the analysis should become most intriguing and potentially also most instructive. For the analysis here will have to deal with how the religious expression (more specifically, the religious expression belonging to type I) responds to this problematic and attempts to overcome it and in doing this one is pushed *per force* to probing the structure of faith operating here in terms of its most fundamental inner-logic, thus gaining, almost inevitably, a much deeper knowledge and appreciation of the phenomenon. Thus, interesting as the analysis of the teleological suspension of the ethical in the context of type II may well be, its analysis when it is formulated in the context of type I is by far much more interesting and, indeed, much more substantive and challenging.

Indeed, the exemplification of this latter analysis delineated above is precisely the task which this paper set out for itself. This is clearly indicated by the title of the paper when it proposes to reflect upon the teleological suspension of the ethical from a Jewish perspective. For there can be no denying that Judaism, more accurately mainstream Judaism, is an example *par excellence* of a religious expression that belongs to type I. Thus, to reflect on the teleological suspension of the ethical from a Jewish perspective means reflecting on it from a perspective of a religious expression that clearly belongs to type I and this, in turn, means reflecting on it principally in terms of the fundamental problematic which it precipitates in this context. Given this context, therefore, the analysis which faces us in the remainder of this paper will have in the main two objectives: a) to determine the way and grasp the rationale underlying it in which a religious expression belonging to type I (in our case, mainstream Judaism) responds to the formulation of the teleological suspension of the ethical and b) to see if and to what extent it can overcome the serious problematic which the formulation inevitably must precipitate for it. It is to this task that we must now turn.

II

In addressing ourselves initially to the first objective we must readily admit that we do not have the means by which to determine the attitude of mainstream Judaism to the formulation of a teleological suspension of the ethical in a way that would be acceptable to the social sciences. Namely, we do not have a sufficiently clear-cut criterion by which to determine who does and who does not speak for mainstream Judaism. And even if one could suppose that this difficulty has been overcome, we certainly do not have the data at our disposal to make any definitive statement—no questionnaires were passed among the members and no statistics gathered. Finally, even if one opted to turn away altogether from the preceding, rather "sociological," head-counting approach to an examination of the theological-philosophical literature of Judaism to see what reactions it contains towards the formulation of a teleological suspension of the ethical (viewing the individual spokesmen in this domain as the authentic and legitimate articulators of the stance taken by the tradition—an approach, by the way, that has much to recommend itself), the fact is that there is hardly any explicit, sustained treatment of our topic in the theological-philosophical literature of Judaism. The one notable exception is Buber. And although Buber in this instance does not claim to represent the reaction of Judaism but only his own reaction to Kierkegaard's formulation, we would want to claim that his reaction here does indeed represent an authentic and basic reaction of mainstream Judaism. Of course, this claim of ours, as we conceded above, is based only on personal experiences and impressions; and under these circumstances it would only behoove us to be more careful and modest in our claim—we should not (and indeed we do not!) claim that it represents *the* reaction but only that it represents *a* reaction of mainstream Judaism. Still, Buber does articulate a most intriguing position and, for whatever it is worth, we do feel strongly that it authentically reflects a basic inclination and orientation within mainstream Judaism. But be this as it may, for better or worse, our analysis is based to a considerable degree on Buber's position and it is, therefore, to it that we must now turn in order to launch our analysis.

Buber's position, i.e., his reaction and attempted response to Kierkegaard's formulation of the teleological suspension of the ethical, is succinctly but forcefully expressed in his essay "On the Suspension of the Ethical."[4]

Turning first to the question of Buber's reaction to Kierkegaard's formulation, it is true that it is not stated explicitly in this essay; but implicitly Buber conveys his reaction in a way that is quite clear and unmistakable. Indeed, it would seem to us that it could not be denied that throughout the essay Buber's approach to the formulation is thoroughly respectful and serious, that he is even appreciative and admiring of its honesty and incisiveness. Certainly, we do not encounter here any derision or out of hand dismissal of the formulation as if it was an aberration, an expression of abnormal fanaticism. If anything, one gets the feeling that Buber is actually attracted to the formulation. At the same time, however, it cannot be denied that in the last analysis Buber finds the formulation unacceptable and does reject it. Thus, we encounter in Buber a reaction that is twofold, that essentially constitutes itself as a dialectical double movement towards its object, i.e., towards the formulation; it is a reaction that is both a yes and a no, that wants to draw near and is attracted and yet feels constraint to push away and reject.

Of course, in view of our claim above we should not take this reaction merely as Buber's private reaction, as the peculiar response of a certain isolated individual. For, as we have argued above, in this reaction Buber is quite authentic to his Jewish heritage—he is expressing a reaction that would be quite characteristic to mainstream Judaism. Thus, this twofold reaction, this dialectical yes and no, this attraction and rejection is not only Buber's reaction but a reaction authentic to mainstream Judaism, so to speak, a "Jewish reaction." The reaction thus becomes the expression of a much larger constituency and its status is commensurately strengthened. But the most significant advantage is accrued when one moves from the description of the reaction to attempt and provide a rationale for it. For at bottom it is really only in terms of the structure of faith of mainstream Judaism that a rationale can be construed.

Thus, the positive attitude towards the formulation of the teleological suspension of the ethical, i.e., the attitude expressing itself in the respect, seriousness and appreciation shown towards the formulation, receives its rationale, we would submit, from the fact that the very essence and thrust of the formulation lies in its poignant and radical expression of the uncompromised supremacy of the religious and that it is precisely this aspect which constitutes the very heart of the structure of faith of mainstream Judaism (or, for that matter, of any other authentic expression of biblical faith). Namely, what is at stake here is nothing else than the affirmation of the unconditioned, uncompromised, transcendence of the divine over-against any and every other aspect and being—the divine transcends any identification with or limitation by any other aspect or being no matter how elevated or ennobled it may be. This, after all, is what the formulation of the teleological suspension of the ethical is in the last analysis really saying. But this is also precisely what the notion of monotheism essentially signifies. For in clearly affirming the oneness, the singleness, the uniqueness of the divine the notion of monotheism must of necessity also implicate radical transcendence with respect to the divine. To safeguard the uniqueness of the divine, the divine cannot be allowed to be compromised by anything else no matter how elevated or ennobled this thing may be. Thus, both the teleological formulation and the monotheistic notion assert, in the last analysis, the same claim, to wit, they both ultimately assert radical transcendence on behalf of the divine.

Now, there can be no denying that the consensus of opinion will over-whelmingly agree that the notion of monotheism constitutes a fundamental, essential tenet in the structure of faith of mainstream Judaism.[5] And if this be the case then we can now understand why one encounters within mainstream Judaism a reaction to the teleological formulation that is basically sympathe-tic, respectful and appreciative. For after all what the teleological formula-tion expresses, in the last analysis, is nothing else but the same principle which finds expression in a tenet that is essential and fundamental in the structure of faith of Judaism, i.e., the tenet of monotheism. Namely, what mainstream Judaism must encounter in the teleological formulation is the expression of its own most fundamental principle, i.e., the expression of the radical transcendence of the divine; and, indeed, it encounters this principle here when it is expressed in a most forceful and poignant way. In these circumstances how could the reaction of mainstream Judaism to the teleo-logical formulation not be respectful, sympathetic and appreciative? Thus, given the fact that the thrust of the teleological formulation is to express, precisely in the most extreme circumstances, the supremacy of the religious dimension (or, in other words, the radical transcendence of the divine) and to safeguard such supremacy against any compromise, i.e., against any reduction whatsoever (even when the threatened reduction or compromise is to such an appealing dimension as the ethical!), it is quite understandable that the teleological formulation should elicit respect and appreciation when viewed from the perspective of mainstream Judaism.

But valid and significant as the above explication may well be, it is not as yet the whole story. For there is an additional consideration involved here which has not as yet been explicated. And since it is precisely this considera-tion which establishes the really ultimate and distinctive signification of the structure of faith of mainstream Judaism, it follows that without the explica-tion of this consideration one may not have touched upon the really ultimate and fundamental motivation which directs the reaction of mainstream Judism to the teleological formulation. Indeed, this consideration arises also in close association with the tenet of monotheism. But while it agrees that the tenet of monotheism is the fundamental and essential tenet in the structure of faith of mainstream Judaism, (thus agreeing that in dealing with any aspect of this tenet one is inevitably touching the very heart of main-stream Judaism) it wants to claim that there is a more fundamental and essential signification borne by the tenet of monotheism than the assertion of radical transcendence with respect to the divine being. Namely, while not denying that the tenet of monotheism does indeed implicate radical tran-scendence on behalf of the divine being, the consideration here wants to claim that the really fundamental and essential signification of the tenet lies in yet a further implication which the tenet carries, to wit, in its implication that the divine being is by its very essence constituted as a personal being. The fundamental and essential signification of the tenet of monotheism when it is embedded in the context of the structure of faith of mainstream

Judaism is to implicate that the divine being is by its very essence constituted not as a being-of-Power, an It-being but as a being-of-Consciousness, a Thou-being. Now, we would submit that a very strong case can be made on behalf of this claim; that indeed, the most distinctive and the most fundamental aspect of mainstream Judaism does lie in its assertion that the divine being is by its very essence constituted as a personal being or, in other words, that ultimacy resides in a being-of-Consciousness, in a Thou-being and not in a being-of-Power, in an It-being; and that this is, indeed, the fundamental signification which the tenet of monotheism carries in the context of mainstream Judaism.[6]

But if this be the case, then it follows that when the claim for the supremacy of the religious dimension over the ethical dimension is made in this context, i.e., in the context of the monotheistic expression of mainstream Judaism, then the claim really means to signify, in the last analysis, that supremacy and thus ultimacy are placed in a Thou-being and not in an It-being (in other words, it is placed in a god constituted as a Thou-being and not in a god constituted as an It-being). For in making the claim in any context whatsoever for the supremacy of the religious dimension over the ethical dimension one is really making ultimately the claim for the supremacy of a divine being over any and all ethical maxims and laws. But now, when this claim is made specifically in the context of mainstream Judaism, it is clearly tantamount to claiming supremacy for a Thou-being over an It-being, seeing that the divine being is by its very essence constituted here as a Thou-being and that ethical maxims and laws, no matter how spiritually imposing or uplifting they may be, are clearly impersonal entities, i.e., It-beings. Thus, the really distinctive and fundamental aspect of mainstream Judaism, when one pushes things all the way, lies in its claim that supremacy and ultimacy reside in a Thou-being and not in an It-being, not even when the It-being is represented by the most edifying and inspiring ethical maxims and laws. In other words, the really distinctive and fundamental characteristic of mainstream Judaism lies in the fact that in its context ultimately one encounters a person (i.e., spontaneity, intentionality, contingency) and not a set of maxims and laws (i.e., necessity, detachment, universality) no matter how profound and worthy they may be.

This point may well need stressing because in the way Judaism is usually perceived the distinctive and fundamental characteristic of the tradition is located in its contribution to ethics, in the highly developed and profoundly sensitive sense of social justice which it introduces into the world. Indeed, very often the very essence of the tradition is equated with (in other words, reduced to) the social ethics it constitutes. And, as we shall see below, there is much truth in this. For there is no denying that the very essence of mainstream Judaism is intimately connected with the expression of social ethics. But, and this is the crux of the point we are trying to make here, such an expression of social ethics with which the tradition is so intimately connected is not perceived within the tradition as grounded in itself, namely, as grounded in its own foundational principles which, in turn, are taken either as axioms or as grounded in some universal reason; rather, it is understood within the tradition as ultimately grounded in the personal being of the divine, i.e., in the spontaneous will of the divine, so that ultimately one encounters here neither inherent ethical maxims nor impersonal universal reason but a particular spontaneous will, a specific personal being.[7]

Again, it is to Buber that we are indebted for having perceived and appreciated the significance of this point. For in his essay "Religion and Ethics"[8] where, as the title indicates, he is concerned with the relation between ethics and religion, Buber first suggests that the central issue in this context is the need of the ethical to ground itself in the religious. The way he puts it is that there is a fundamental need "to bind the radical distinction between good and evil to the Absolute."[9] Secondly, Buber further suggests that in the spiritual history of man there were essentially two attempts to do this. The one attempt which appeared rather universally in Oriental and Greek antiquity (and which we would typologize as "pagan") tried to achieve this absolutization of ethical values by making them the expressions of cosmic law, "the moral order is identical with the cosmic."[10] The second attempt, on the other hand, which appeared in a rather isolated manner in Ancient Israel (and which we would typologize as "biblical faith") tried to establish the absolutization of ethical values not by incorporating them into the continuous, constant and all-encompassing cosmic or heavenly order (as the first attempt did) but rather by referring them to a specific being, to wit, by referring them to the "God of Israel" who, on the one hand, is seen as the Absolute while, on the other hand, He is encountered as "a giver and protector of law."[11] Thus, in as much as the precepts of the law are promulgated by the divine who is the Absolute, the precepts of the law, i.e., that which constitutes the ethical, are themselves also endowed with Absoluteness. To paraphrase Buber, now it is no longer the cosmic order that is decisive but rather He who is its sovereign, the Lord of heaven and earth.[12]

We need not follow Buber any further in his pursuit of this theme for the point which is of interest to us here has already been clearly implicated in what he has said thus far. For the exposition above clearly shows that in Buber's judgment on the linkage between the religious and the ethical as such is by no means unique to Judaism. In many other traditions is the religious intimately linked to the ethical, seeing that it is the religious which introduces and sustains the universal principle underlying the pattern of right behaviour, be it called Tao in China, Rita in India, Urta in Iran or Dike in Greece.[13] Thus, the linkage between the religious and the ethical, indeed the implication of the ethical by the religious, can by no means be as such the distinctive characteristic of Judaism. But this is not to say that for Buber Judaism does not, indeed, have a distinctive characteristic which sets it apart from all other religious formulations. Indeed it does, except that Buber locates this distinctive characteristic not in the mere implication of the ethical by the religious (this is rather widespread) but rather in the nature and status of the ethical thus introduced. Namely, in Judaism the law, being the expression of the ethical points beyond itself to another being who promulgates it; it does not as in the other religious formulations come to rest within itself as but a particular reflection of its all-encompassing, universal self. Thus, the implication is clear that for Buber the distinctive characterization of Judaism lies not in its introduction of the law *per se* but rather in its introduction of a law-giver. Even more fundamentally, it follows by clear implication from the foregoing, that the distinctive characterization to be attributed to Judaism here lies in the fact that it encounters the ultimate, i.e., the Absolute, not in some immutable universal law (be it the heavenly order or the cosmic order or the world of pure forms) but in a particular law-giver—in Judaism one encounters ultimately not a law but a law-giver. Finally, there is one further implication that can be clearly derived from the foregoing and with it we do indeed come to the very heart of the matter. Namely, it clearly follows from the above that the ultimate which one encounters in Judaism is a personal being, a being-of-Consciousness, a Thou; as against this, the ultimate which one encounters in the other religious formulations is an impersonal entity, a being-of-Power, an It. For clearly, a being that is itself not a law but the giver and protector of law is of necessity a personal being, a Thou.[14] Conversely, there can be no question that when speaking of a cosmic order or a heavenly law or the world of Forms one is inescapably dealing with impersonal entities, with an It, no matter how elevated or edifying they may well be.

Thus, Buber's incisive insight that in Judaism, in contrast to the other religious formulations, one ultimately encounters not a law but a law-giver, carries with it the further all-important and pregnant implication that in Judaism the ultimate being, the Absolute, is constituted as a personal being, as a Thou, while in the other religious formulations it is constituted as an impersonal being, as an It. As such, although Buber is using a different vocabulary, i.e., the vocabulary of law versus law-giver, and although his immediately explicit concern is not with the question of how the ultimate is constituted but rather with the question of how can ethics be best ab-solutized, Buber nevertheless succeeds, as we have tried to show above, to clearly implicate the most fundamental observation that can be made with respect to Judaism, namely, that in the last analysis, the real decisive, distinctive mark of Judaism lies in the fact that in contrast to the other religious formulations where it is blind Power that is encountered as the ultimate (be it in the benevolent or malevolent manifestation of its brute force or in the necessity and regularity and consequently in the predictability and lawfulness of its expression), in Judaism the ultimate is encountered beyond blind Power in a being that is personal (i.e., in spontaneity, in freedom and in awareness).

But if this be the case, then we can see a second and, indeed, a more profound rationale for why the teleological formulation should be congenial to Judaism. For now it is not only the affirmation of the supremacy of the religious over everything else (even over the ethical) that makes the formula-tion congenial; it is also the clear implication that the God involved in the formulation, namely the God who supersedes everything else, who can, indeed, suspend the ethical, is a personal being, a Thou. For clearly the fundamental contingency and spontaneity of the act (and in terms of the formulation the suspension is certainly not continuous or necessary), the notion of suspension and most evidently the very notion of a *telos*, of a higher goal, can make sense only with respect to a personal being, to a Thou—with respect to an impersonal being, to an It, they would simply not make sense. Thus, it is understandable that Judaism in clearly sensing that the God implicated in this teleological formulation is a personal being should respond to the formulation with an underlying basic feeling of respect and appreciation.

But if the rationale (actually, the twofold rationale) for the positive reaction of mainstream Judaism towards the teleological formulation has been thus far adduced, one hopes, in a manner that is fairly straightforward and convincing, the rationale for the negative reaction of mainstream Judaism towards the formulation, namely, the rationale for the fact that, in the last analysis, mainstream Judaism must reject the teleological formulation, can now be adduced, we would submit in a manner that is by far more forthright and convincing. For the negative reaction of mainstream Judaism to the teleological formulation follows directly and without ambiguity from the fact that mainstream Judaism belongs to, indeed, is an example *par excellence* of, type I of the religious formulation delineated above, namely, that it belongs to that type of religious formulation in which the religious and the ethical dimensions are inextricably intertwined, to that type of religious formulation in which the religious act (i.e., the vertically-directed act) inescapably expresses itself through the ethical act (i.e., the horizontally-directed act) and, conversely, the ethical act inevitably points beyond itself to the religious act, so much so that at one and the same time the religious act is the ethical act and vice versa the ethical act is the religious act. For as such it should be quite evident that in this context, i.e., in the context of the religious formulation belonging to type I, a suspension of the ethical is in principle not feasible—the very option of a suspension of the ethical is not available. For there is no higher end, a further *telos*, that would justify it, seeing that the religious aspect, which really is the only aspect that could have served as the higher end, the further *telos*, for whose sake the ethical could have been suspended, is not available here. And it is not available because in the context of the religious formulation belonging to type I, where the ethical is inextricably part and parcel of the religious and conversely the religious is inextricably part and parcel of the ethical, the suspension of the ethical is *ipso facto* and inescapably at one and the same time also the suspension of the religious and as such nothing is left for whose sake the suspension could have been undertaken and, indeed, justified. Suspension is feasible only if that which is to be suspended does not constitute the ultimate; only if beyond it there still exists yet another being which as such constitutes the ultimate and, moreover, which demands its suspension. Suspension is feasible only with respect to a penultimate but never with respect to an ultimate being and then only if the ultimate dictates it. But clearly these two conditions do not obtain with respect to the ethical in the context of the religious formulation belonging to type I. For while, strictly speaking, the ultimate here is indeed constituted by the religious (this being so almost by definition), the ethical, being constituted here as the inextricable expression of the religious, is as such, so to speak, built into the ultimate, certainly to the extent that its suspension cannot be justified, leave alone required, by the ultimate. Thus, any and every religious formulation that belongs to type I—mainstream Judaism being a foremost instance of such a religious formulation—will, in the last analysis, have to reject any claim for the suspension of the ethical.

Indeed, it follows from our analysis above that in the context of the religious formulation belonging to type I, the teleological formulation no longer presents the articulation of the highest truth regarding such a religious formulation (as, indeed, is the case with respect to the religious formulation belonging to type II) but rather it presents the posing of a most fundamental problematic. For while with respect to the religious formulation belonging to type II the teleological formulation in its claim for the suspension of the ethical signifies the radical, uncompromised supremacy of the religious dimension over any and every other dimension (including the ethical), and this certainly constitutes the articulation of the highest truth connected with such a religious formulation, with respect to the religious formulation belonging to type I the teleological formulation in claiming the suspension of the ethical is claiming something which is not feasible. For as we have seen above, in the context of the religious formulation belonging to type I the suspension of the ethical is not feasible; and this unfeasibility constitutes a fundamental characteristic of the religious formulation belonging to type I. Indeed, in view of this, one would be inclined to conclude that while the teleological formulation may well apply to the religious formulation belonging to type II, it certainly should not apply to the religious formulation belonging to type I. For it certainly does not make sense to apply demands which by the very nature of things cannot be delivered.

But it is not so easy, precisely in the context of the religious formulation belonging to type I, to give up the challenge of the teleological formulation, i.e., the challenge of the suspension of the ethical. For this challenge arises from another, yet equally fundamental, aspect which characterizes the religious formulation belonging to type I, namely, it arises from the aspect that the ultimate encountered in the religious formulation belonging to type I is constituted as a personal being. For as a personal being its very essence lies in its freedom and, being ultimate, this means moreover that its freedom must be absolute which, in turn, would require that it be granted the possibility of suspending any and every thing it chooses including even the ethical. To reject, therefore, the claim of the teleological formulation, i.e., the claim of the suspension of the ethical, is tantamount to rejecting that the ultimate is constituted as a personal being; one may be left with a personal being but not with both, i.e., with an ultimate that is a personal being. Yet, it is precisely this demand, i.e., the demand for an ultimate that is a personal being, which constitutes the essential, *sine-qua-non* requirement of the religious formulation belonging to type I. Thus, the signification of the challenge presented by the teleological formulation is not peripheral or incidental. It is not as if it arises arbitrarily or superficially, the product of fancy or passing whim carrying no special significance so that it can be removed without any serious consequences. Rather, it arises out of the most fundamental aspect of the religious formulation belonging to type I, i.e., the assertion that the ultimate is constituted as a personal being, and its removal, therefore, since it clearly undermines the validity of this assertion, must of necessity carry the most serious implications. As such, one cannot extricate oneself from the difficulty here by conveniently excluding the teleological formulation from impinging upon the religious formulation that belongs to type I. And if, indeed, there is no escaping the teleological formulation impinging upon the religious formulation that belongs to type I, then there is also no escaping the contradiction and ambivalence which are built into the way by which the religious formulation belonging to type I relates towards the formulation, namely, that while on the one hand, one cannot dismiss here the teleological formulation (for that would undercut the assertion essential to such a religious formulation, to wit, that the ultimate is con- stituted here as a personal being), on the other hand, one cannot at the same time really accept it either (for its demand for the suspension of the ethical is not feasible in terms of the religious formulation that belongs to type I).

But this ambivalence and contradiction regarding the status of the tele- ological formulation here is actually the direct result and, indeed, but the reflection of the signification which the teleological formulation carries when taken in the context of the religious formulation belonging to type I. For what the teleological formulation really signifies in the context, namely, what it really does here is to lay bare the head-on collision, the contradiction, which exists between the two fundamental and essential principles that are necessarily implicated in the religious formulation belonging to type I, to wit, the principle that the ultimate be constituted as a personal being and the principle that the ethical may not be suspended here. Both these principles must be present in the religious formulation belonging to type I and yet their respective implications, as we have tried to show above, are clearly and inescapably contradictory to each other. This inner contradiction and ambiv- alence which are built into the very structure of the religious formulation belonging to type I are, however, brought to the fore, i.e., are revealed, most poignantly by the teleological formulation precisely by their forcing the issue in pushing the principles all the way with respect to their implica- tions. Thus, in the context of the religious formulation belonging to type I, the teleological formulation, far from making a statement to be proclaimed, is really raising a problem to be overcome. The teleological formulation here does not signify an exclamation-mark but a question-mark. And as such, the most challenging and fundamental issue here connected with the teleologi- cal formulation is the issue of how the religious formulation belonging to type I manages to overcome the problematic posed by the formulation, i.e., manages to get around the clash, mitigate its detrimental effects or, indeed, prevent it from actually arising. In conclusion, therefore, let us briefly examine two possible approaches that have been proposed to see how well they succeed in coping with the problematic.

III

One of these approaches is very cogently presented by Buber in an article to which we had already occasion to refer, i.e., in his article "On the Suspension of the Ethical."[15] It is perhaps not too unfair to suggest that the thrust of Buber's strategy here is not to allow the problematic delineated above, i.e., the problematic precipitated by the clash between the absoluteness of the free will of the divine and the unfeasibility of suspending the ethical, to actually come before us. For clearly if the problematic is not before us then no decision and choice between the two contradictory aspects have to be made and consequently neither of the two aspects need be undermined or compromised and this, for all intents and purposes, is tantamount to canceling the problematic. Now, Buber accomplishes this goal by introducing and leaving unsolved yet another problematic, a problematic which logically precedes the problematic delineated above and whose solution (and thus removal) is indeed a necessary presupposition for the problematic delineated above to arise. Namely, Buber finds another problematic on whose solution the actualization of our problematic is made contingent, which means, in other words, that he finds another problematic which when left unsolved acts as a "repressor" of our problematic, and he then proceeds to argue that this problematic does indeed remain unsolved for us today and, therefore, we are saved from the necessity of choosing and deciding with respect to our initial problematic thus canceling, for all intents and purposes, its sting.

In translating this strategy into more concrete terms (which means here as it meant all along in connection with this issue a turning to the story of the binding of Isaac), we can put the case as follows: our problematic arises from the fact that God's command here (i.e., sacrifice your son) goes against the ethical judgment (i.e., do not murder). For in these circumstances any choice, any decision, that we may make (what Buber refers to as "the decision of faith") is bound to undermine one or the other essential aspect characterizing the religious formulation belonging to type I, i.e., the absoluteness of God's free will (even to the point of commanding the sacrifice of one's son) or the unfeasibility of suspending the ethical (in commanding an act which is deemed by ethical judgment to constitute an act of murder), and in either case a serious problematic is necessarily precipitated. That much in the situation seems to be irrefutable and one must resign oneself to accepting it.

But then, how is one to extricate oneself from the problematic which this situation necessarily precipitates? Well, Buber's strategy is to focus on the point that before one can really be confronted with this problematic one must be ready to grant and clearly uphold that the God who is addressing one here is indeed the true, authentic God (and this, of course, even though the address goes against the ethical). For clearly, if the God involved here is not the true, authentic God but only Moloch (for Moloch imitates the voice of God")[16], our problematic dissolves of itself. Thus, Buber is shifting, so to speak, the place where the battle is to take place. It is now to take place on the question of whether one can really uphold with surety that the God involved is the true God. Namely, if our problematic is to be overcome, it can be overcome not in its own terms but only by being blocked from materialization in the first place by raising the further problematic of whether the God involved is the true God. As Buber observed, "the problematics of the decision of faith is preceded by the problematics of the hearing itself. Who is it whose voice one hears?"[17] And again, "where, therefore, the suspension of the ethical is concerned, the question of questions which takes precedence over every other is: Are you really addressed by the Absolute or by one of his apes?"[18]

Now, on the new battlefield Buber can make his move to salvage the situation. In essence his move consists in the claim that in our time one can no longer uphold with surety that the God involved is the true God and not "one of his apes." It is important, however, to note the inclusion of the qualifier "in our time" in the claim. For while Buber readily concedes that it has always been risky to make such claims, that, indeed, the danger of being fooled by an imitator of the true voice is intrinsic to the very relationship that obtains here, he nonetheless suggests that in the past man did possess images of the Absolute which, although inadequate in many ways, could and did function as guides, as reference-points, safeguarding man from succumbing "to the deception of the voices."[19] Thus, it should be underlined that the claim here is not made with respect to any feature that is intrinsic and inescapable to the situation which, in turn, would mean that the claim here is not normative but only descriptive. But even further it should be noted that even as mere description the description is by no means universal in its applicability. Buber clearly excludes the past and gives strong intimations that he would also exclude the future—the future in the sense of being messianic, of being the point where "the new conscience of men has arisen."[20] The claim is strictly confined to the present, to the era in which, to use Nietzsche's words, "God is dead," or in other words to the modern era. For it is precisely the death of God, which in Buber's interpretation comes to signify the decline in the image-making power of the human heart, that is responsible for the inability to uphold with surety that the God involved is the true God, seeing that it is the presence of the images of the divine (the Absolute) which allows one to distinguish the voice of the true God from the voice of Moloch, thus allowing one to uphold with surety the voice of the true God, and that it is precisely the weakening and, indeed, disappearance of these images which the death of God phenomenon manifesting itself in the modern era signifies. Thus, it is specifically with respect to our era, to the present (and not with respect to the past or to the future), that Buber puts forth his claim that one cannot take for granted that the voice addressing one is the voice of the true God. Still, this allows Buber, at least as far as the present is concerned, as far as we are concerned, to overcome our initial problematic, what he called "the problematics of the decision of faith," by blocking its materialization through the introduction of "the problematics of the hearing itself." For if we cannot be sure that the God involved is the true God, then clearly "the problematics of the decision of faith" is of necessity suspended, so to speak "bracketed," till a time when we can be sure of this.

Now, how are we to react to this approach? Well, first of all it certainly would not have escaped noticing that the way in which the approach here is attempting to overcome the problematic is not at all on the theoretical level but exclusively on the practical level. Namely, the logical head-on collision between the implications of encountering the Absolute as a personal being (i.e., as a free and spontaneous being) and the implications of maintaining the unfeasibility of suspending the ethical is in no way overcome. The logical contradiction between the two basic and essential tenets of the structure of faith stays untouched as it was. Rather what this approach offers in the way of overcoming the problematic is the removal of the practical consequences that may follow the suspension of the ethical. What constitutes for it the overcoming of the problematic is the ability to block from coming to materialization, thus to neutralize, any of the practical consequences that may ensue from the suspension of the ethical (evidently what would constitute the problematic here is the constraint to execute a demand for the sacrifice of one's son). That this is so is really not surprising. For, it seems to us, that there is really no way of removing the logical contradiction. Thus, on the theoretical level there is no escaping the fact that an unerasable tension, dialectic, is built into the structure of faith of the religious formulation belonging to type I. But what is most important to realize is that precisely because we are dealing here with the religious formulation belonging to type I, i.e., with a formulation where the religious by its very essence expresses itself through the ethical domain, it is indeed the practical, concrete act rather than the purely abstract theoretical inconsistency that counts. What offends is the concrete act of murdering one's son (or even of breaking a promise) rather than the logical inconsistency of maintaining both the supremacy of a personal being possessing absolute freedom and the unfeasibility of suspending the ethical. Thus, the approach here is offering after all an authentic overcoming of the problematic when it proposes to block the unsavory practical consequences of the suspension of the ethical rather than remove logical inconsistencies. Indeed, it would seem to us, this predilection towards the practical rather than the theoretical would characterize all viable approaches to the problematic here for it is determined by the very nature of the context in which the problematic arises. As said, the problematic really arises here when one has to act contrary to the ethical and therefore, correspondingly, it is overcome when the possibility for such acts is removed. Thus, far from being a weakness, the predilection towards the practical, the concrete act, is a distinct advantage for this approach.

Secondly, as we have seen, this approach attempts to overcome our initial problematic, i.e., "the problematic of the decision of faith," through the agency of "the problematic of hearing" which it introduces into the picture. Now, there can be no denying that when manipulated by a clever and skillful dialectician (and Buber is certainly that!) this strategy appears very attractive and promising. For it is, indeed, the case that the overcoming of "the problematic of the decision of faith" is contingent upon the inability to overcome "the problematic of hearing" and on that basis it is only too clear that the overcoming of "the problematic of the decision of faith" will indeed depend on what results the handling of "the problematic of hearing" may produce. But to produce the right results, the handling of "the problematic of hearing" must be just right—an order that is not so easy to fulfill. Buber, however, is handling the task with great insight and consequently succeeds in using the agency of "the problematic of hearing" to its greatest effect. Let us briefly point to one or two aspects of this remarkable handling as we understand it.

Thus, for example, Buber very wisely does not hold that "the problematic of hearing" remains unresolved universally, namely, that at no time and under no circumstances was it, is it or will it be possible for man to distinguish between the voice of the true God and the voice of Moloch. He does not hold this position even though holding this position would have clearly insured that "the problematic of the decision of faith" would have been completely neutralized, i.e., overcome, for all times and all circumstances—certainly a most desirable state of affairs.

And let it be known that Buber's basic religio-philosophic stance could have readily provided a convincing rationale for the claim that the irresolution of "the problematic of hearing" is universal, i.e., for the claim that at no time could one uphold with surety that the voice is the voice of the true God and not the voice of one of his apes. For there is no denying that in the context of Buber's religio-philosophic formulation any claim on behalf of the divine is always and inescapably a risk and a gamble that it may be false. After all, there can be no demonstration and no proof with respect to these claims. There can be, therefore, no escape from the possibility that one could be fooled. In the last analysis, uncertainty is built into the very structure of things here and as such it can obviously express itself in the past and in the future just as well as in the present. Now, on this basis, Buber could have easily claimed a universal irresolution of "the problematic of hearing." And it is not that he is unaware of this implication flowing directly from his position. On the contrary, he dwells on it at great length, waxing very dramatic—all relations with the divine are embedded in holy insecurity.

Yet, Buber does not use this basic, ineradicable underlying uncertainty as a spur and a rationale for claiming a universal irresolution of "the problem of hearing." Rather he seems to take this uncertainty as constituting the "normal" substratum underlying the whole of the human-divine realm, the ether, so to speak, engulfing its totality and thus bathing each of its items in this basic modicum of uncertainty and in return demanding the taking of risk, the placing of trust, as the fundamental acts of affirmation. But it would seem that precisely because this uncertainty is perceived as all-pervasive and inescapable that Buber is not inclined to take it as an acceptable spur and rationale for positing the irresolution of "the problematic of hearing." For this an additional factor which can increase the uncertainty would seem to be required. And indeed, Buber does introduce precisely such a factor—the image of the divine which the human soul may cultivate and develop. For no matter how inadequate the image may be, its presence decreases while its absence increases the uncertainty as to whose voice is being heard—the voice of the true God or the voice of one of his apes. (This possible increase or decrease is, however, in terms of that uncertainty that is already beyond the uniform, all-pervasive uncertainty.) Now, it is precisely in terms of this increased uncertainty due to the absence or the weakening of the image rather than in terms of the constitutive all-pervasive uncertainty that Buber opts to posit the irresolution of "the problematic of hearing." But this means of course that he is transforming the kind of cause which is responsible for the irresolution—it is no longer an innate, constitutive cause but an external cultural or historical cause. For clearly, the genesis, the strengthening or the weakening of the image of the divine within us is essentially culturally and historically conditioned. And this, in turn, would further mean that while in terms of the innate, constitutive causation the irresolution of "the problematic of hearing" which is brought about is inescapably necessary and universal, the irresolution which is brought about in terms of cultural and historical causation is inescapably contingent and in all likelihood partial.

In view of the fact that, as we have just seen, a necessary and universal irresolution of "the problematic of hearing" would have provided by far the best means for overcoming "the problematic of the decision of faith" and that a contingent and partial irresolution must be commensurately far less effective, it is interesting to note that Buber's thought follows nonetheless the latter and not the former alternative. Now, in all probability Buber was not concerned with the particular considerations which we have introduced and his thought was motivated and directed by some other considerations. But whether or not he was aware of our considerations, it seems to us that his opting for an irresolution of "the problematic of hearing" which is contingent and partial rather than necessary and universal is, in the last analysis, the right move precisely for the sake of our considerations. For to have opted for an irresolution of "the problematic of hearing" which is necessary and universal would have certainly meant the exclusion of any and every possibility of upholding with surety that a divine communication has occurred, that one could hear and distinguish the voice of the true God. And such a total exclusion would have certainly meant, in turn, the cancellation, i.e., the disintegration, of the religious pole, seeing that the religious phenomenon is by its very essence built on there being a relation, a communication, between the divine and man. Thus, to have taken up this position would have been tantamount to throwing out the baby with the dirty water and this would not do. One certainly wants to overcome "the problematic of the decision of faith" but such overcoming would be pointless if in the process the very feasibility of the religious phenomenon is taken away. Buber's restraint, therefore, in not applying the irresolution of "the problematic of hearing" also to the past and to the future is not only not a shortcoming but is a distinct advantage for his approach.

Yet another insightful aspect which emerges from Buber's handling of "the problematic of hearing" lies in the fact that it is precisely to the present and not to some other span of time, as for example the past or the future, that the irresolution of "the problematic of hearing" is confined. For as such, indeed, one is provided with a span of time which in our context proves to be the only suitable span of time, i.e., the only span of time where the real encounter and the real overcoming of "the problematic of the decision of faith" can take place. For after all, since "the problematic of the decision of faith" really precipitates itself, as we have seen, in the concrete choice, even more precisely, in the concrete external act and furthermore since, commensurate to this, the real overcoming of the problematic is likewise with respect to the concrete external act (namely, the rub of the problematic lies in the actual carrying out of an act that is contra-ethical and correspondingly the problematic is neutralized and overcome when likewise the act is not actually carried out), it should be clear that the real arena for both the encounter and the overcoming of the problematic here is the present rather than the past or the future. It is only in the present (not in the past or the future) that concrete choice is presented, that concrete decision can be made and that concrete action can be executed. With respect to the past all is finished and known; with respect to the future all is "iffy" and speculative. It is only in the present that one encounters concreteness and open-endedness which as such call for one's decision, choice and action but also open up the possibility for being thrown into the throes of agony and perplexity if and when confronted by a command coming from the divine yet going against the ethical. Thus, to the extent that one can exclude the possibility of being confronted by "the problematic of the decision of faith" in the present (though leaving intact the possibility of being so confronted with respect to the past and to the future) one has succeeded in safeguarding oneself against the sting of this problematic. Indeed, it would seem that this approach by succeeding in confining the irresolution of "the problematic of hearing" to the present only (but not to the past or the future) succeeds in achieving the enviable feat of eating the cake and having it too. For it can with respect to the past continue to affirm the absolute supremacy of the divine will even when it countermands the ethical and yet at the same time remove the offensive implications of such an affirmation regarding the ethical by excluding with respect to the present the possibility of the divine clashing with the ethical. Thus, with reference to the past (which is the temporal dimension that would be congenial to such expressions) it establishes in abstraction and in theory the supremacy of the divine free will while with reference to the present (which is the temporal dimension where alone such actions count) it safeguards in practice and actuality that the ethical not be suspended.[21]

We should be clear, however, that in Buber's approach (and in clear contradistinction to the immediate foregoing analysis) the terms "past," "present" and "future" are not to be used in their general denotation referring to the abstract categories of time, to the permanent dimensions of temporality, dimensions that inhere in the very nature of things. Rather, they are to be used in a very limited, specific denotation referring to particular, contingent segments of history. Indeed, Buber does not much use in this connection the terms "present," "past" and "future." Instead, he refers to our time or even more precisely to a time whose *geist* is characterized by the "death of God" or the "eclipse of God" syndrome (this span of time so characterized clearly constituting with reference to us the present), to the "biblical period," the "period of the patriarchs and the prophets" (clearly constituting with reference to us the past) or to "a time when the new conscience of men has arisen" (constituting with reference to us the future).

We should be wrong, however, to dismiss this as an insignificant pecularity on Buber's behalf. Rather, it is a reflection of the precision and consistency of his approach. For this usage, it would seem to us, expresses the tendency to get away from universality in the positing of the irresolution of "the problematic of hearing" as far as possible, thus even to the point of trying to get away from the universality implicated in the use of the abstract categories of temporality (i.e., the universality implied in the claim to cover *every* present, *every* past or *every* future). The approach tries to establish as far as it can the contingency and particularity of the irresolution of "the problematic of hearing" which it must claim; it tries to confine and specify as much as it can this necessary irresolution. For as such it can sustain as much as is possible the viability of the religious pole—it can keep open as widely as is possible the potentiality of the divine communication to man. Clearly here, in protecting the viability of the religious pole in such a committed and consistent way, lies the special strength of this approach.

But at this very same point where its maximal advantage is manifested, lies also its gravest shortcoming. For although there can be no denying that it succeeds in safeguarding against the suspension of the ethical by introducing the irresolution of "the problematic of hearing" into our present, this is done so minimally, so stringently and narrowly, that one is not at all sure that the feasibility of safeguarding against the suspension of the ethical is adequately provided. Thus, as we have seen, the irresolution of "the problematic of hearing" and consequently the safeguarding against the suspension of the ethical could be established with respect to our present only because our present is characterized by the "death of God" (or the "eclipse of God") syndrome. Namely, strictly speaking, the irresolution can be established only because of the "death of God" syndrome—the coupling is between the "death of God" syndrome and the irresolution. And from this it follows that only with respect to spans of time that are characterized by the "death of

God" syndrome, but then to one and every such span of time, can the irresolution of "the problematic of hearing" be established. But this is evidently much too contingent and limited to adequately protect the interests of the ethical pole, i.e., to adequately safeguard against the suspension of the ethical. For our era, our present, for example, could easily have not been characterized by the "death of God" syndrome and then the irresolution of "the problematic of hearing" could have not been established which, in turn, would have culminated in our being confronted by "the problematic of the decision of faith." Likewise, there is no compelling reason and certainly no guarantee, that the "death of God" syndrome would continue in the future, thus providing spans of time, i.e., "presents," which would be characterized by the "death of God" syndrome. And certainly many of the previous "presents" constituting now the past were not characterized by the "death of God" syndrome.

Thus, although a solution with respect to our present situation can be attained on the basis of Buber's approach, namely, although we can establish on the basis of this approach that we can be saved the agony of "the problematic of the decision of faith" and the dread of the suspension of the ethical, the application of the approach is so contingent that it does not really remove sufficiently the possibility of being confronted with "the problematic of the decision of faith" so that one can be comfortable with the approach. Although it is true that in terms of this approach we are spared a direct encounter with the problematic, other spans of time in which the problematic may well have to be confronted are pressing hard on us from all directions. The dreadful either/or which the problematic precipitates for us, although strictly speaking is still but a theoretical question, is too close and too real a possibility not to impress itself on us as a concrete problematic. We may even feel that the way in which this approach extricates us from this dilemma is rather superficial and unsatisfactory. As such, one cannot really relate here to "the problematic of the decision of faith" on a purely theoretical level as if it were exclusively hypothetical. This certainly cannot be a reassuring position for the ethical role which is concerned to remove as much as possible the precipitation of a decision. Indeed, given the drift of this approach, the likelihood is that if a decision were to be precipitated it would go for the religious and against the ethical pole.[22]

Thus, there is no question that this approach formulated by Buber acquits itself well with the religious pole. It is a different matter, however, when one views it from the vantage-point of the ethical pole. Here it becomes clear that it fails to convincingly provide sufficient protection against the suspension of the ethical. Obviously as such, the religious formulation belonging to type I in any of its manifestations—as, for example, mainstream Judaism—cannot be fully content with the approach formulated by Buber.[23] For it the solution must come from a different approach. Such an approach is, indeed, available and has been embraced, for example, by the fundamental orientation of mainstream Judaism both in the biblical and the post-biblical periods. Let us in conclusion outline in a most schematic way the main thrust of its strategy as it manifests itself in mainstream Judaism.

IV

The essential thrust of the strategy which this second formulation, to which we may refer as the classical prophetic approach, presents may be summarized in the following two statements: 1) the personal being of the divine, thus its spontaneous free will, constitutes here the ultimate and therefore, in the last analysis, the divine free will must prevail in all circumstances; 2) it is taken, however, as an axiomatic act of trust that this divine being by his own free will never suspend the ethical.

Clearly, this formulation should satisfy completely both the religious and the ethical pole. It satisfies the religious pole by asserting with no qualifications whatsoever the absolute supremacy of the divine being in its spontaneous free will in all conceivable circumstances. It satisfies the ethical pole by excluding the possibility that in *practice* in reality, God would suspend the ethical. And as we have seen, while for the religious pole it is the theoretical affirmation of divine supremacy which is important, for the ethical pole it is rather the practical absence of the counterethical act which is important (rather than any theoretical speculations as to its supremacy).[24] Furthermore, the exclusion of the possibility of the suspension of the ethical is made in this approach completely universal. There is no limitation, no contingency applied here. And obviously, since the exclusion of the suspension of the ethical is attained here by quite different means than was the case in the previous approach formulated by Buber, such universalization carries here no threat whatsoever to the viability of the religious pole (as was the case with the former approach). As such, the approach can satisfy completely again both the ethical pole (by universalizing the exclusion of the suspension of the ethical) and the religious pole (by in no way limiting the possibility of the divine communicating with man).

Evidently, the way this approach is formulated it is tailor-made to the requirements of the religious formulation belonging to type I. It encompasses the tension and contradictory pulls which are built into this formulation and as such, it can fully overcome "the problematic of the decision of faith," seeing that the problematic here constitutes itself as nothing else but the laying bare of such tension and contradiction. True, the approach here can attain all this because, in the last analysis, it constitutes itself on an act of trust—it is an act of trust of the believer that God will not act in such a way. Of course, within an act of trust, within an axiom, one can arrange matters to one's satisfaction. Now, an act of trust may not be legitimate or acceptable in the philosophic domain but it is completely legitimate and acceptable in the religious domain. For it is the distinctive characterization of the religious perspective that it recognizes the limitation of all human powers, particularly rationality, and thus opens itself to the going beyond them through the act of trust. In the religious domain, therefore, sooner or later one must come to the act of trust. And in as much as we are dealing here with a religious domain, it is perfectly legitimate and acceptable to establish one's strategy by which to overcome "the problematic of the decision of faith" on an act of trust.

Lastly, it becomes clear that the real problem in this context is precipitated if and when our experience contradicts the act of trust which says that God does not suspend the ethical. Namely, in having overcome so nicely and neatly "the problematic of the decision of faith," the problematic of holding on to both the supremacy of the personal being of the divine and the unfeasibility of suspending the ethical, we prepared the ground for a new problematic to arise—the problematic of theodicy. The act of trust allows us to overcome "the problematic of the decision of faith" but it also makes it possible to raise the problematic of theodicy.

Indeed, in mainstream Judaism the question of theodicy is the fundamental religious act. Far from being an expression of atheism, a rejection of the divine, it is a question that arises from within the very bosom of religion. True, it is a challenge to the divine (how come that this is the case?") and therefore implies a critique. Yet, and much more profoundly, the challenge and critique can be raised only because one first accepts the axiomatic act of trust that God is bound to the ethical and would not act against it. Thus in each challenge one reaffirms the underlying act of trust which makes possible the raising of the challenge. Thus, the challenge of theodicy is at bottom the primary act of religious witnessing, the primary act witnessing to the inextricable bond between the divine and the ethical. It is an act which through the challenge affirms the essential characteristic of the religious formulation belonging to type I, namely the insoluble bond between the divine and the ethical. It is not surprising therefore that throughout its history from Abraham to the post-holocaust era mainstream Judaism raises and wrestles with the question of theodicy. It may not have the answer but it must raise the question. It is in the raising of the question that the authentic religious orientation expresses itself. Just as the religious formulation belonging to type II (the type in which the religious is *de jure* severed from the ethical) is captured in its very essence by the resignation "Let your will be done!" so the religious formulation belonging to type I is captured in its very essence by the challenge "Is the Judge of all the earth not to do justice?"

NOTES

[1]Something which clearly is not the case with respect to the other types of religion where the religious is essentially separated from the ethical and where, indeed, in consequence the concern with the domain of ethics and religion is much more peripheral and of far less moment.

[2]It may be helpful at this juncture to briefly indicate what the notion of the religious dimension and that of the ethical dimension essentially signify in the context of this discussion. Indeed, we would suggest that "religious" essentially signifies here the reality of the personal being of the divine and its free will while "ethical" signifies the acceptance of a set of maxims or laws as guidelines or criteria by which the desired human action is determined. Thus, in asking

whether the religious or the ethical dimension is ultimate and supreme one is really asking whether it is God in his free will or a set of maxims and values which is taken to provide the ultimate and supreme authority and justification for the course of action which man ought to pursue. This, in the last analysis, is the real issue which is at stake in the discussion here.

[3]In all probability, however, there would be some uneasiness and queasiness as to the validity of associating so closely Kierkegaard's teleological suspension of the ethical with expressions of the religions which belong to type II. This uneasiness, in turn, is most probably due to a difference which we have not had occasion to refer to above but which nonetheless does validly obtain between the implications of the inner-logic operating in the context of religious expressions belonging to type II and the situation depicted by Kierkegaard's teleological suspension of the ethical when it is formulated in close conjunction with the story of the binding of Isaac. This difference lies in the fact that in the context of the story of the binding of Isaac the ethical is undermined (the suspension of the ethical is achieved) by an overt act—the religious dimension requires the performance of an evil act, e.g., the murdering of one's son. As against this, in the context of religious expressions belonging to type II, the inner-logic operating there can only take one as far as sanctioning acquiescence in the presence of evil but certainly not to the point of prompting the active perpetration of evil. The ethical is countermanded here not by the actual doing of evil but by the absence of active resistance to evil. Thus, we do indeed have here a difference—the difference between activity and passivity, between actively perpetrating evil and passively not resisting its on-going existence.

Of course, in the context of the religious expressions belonging to type II one can argue that underlying these acts of passive acquiescence and, indeed, providing the very possibility for their expression, lies the further act which on the premise of having cut asunder the vertical from the horizontal (excluding the possibility of the former impinging upon the latter or of the latter being at the service of the former) proceeds to renounce and abdicate the horizontal dimension, i.e., the this-worldly dimension. And this act is clearly active and not passive—it does not signify the suffering of a certain state of affairs but the actual bringing about of it. Furthermore, and most importantly, this act is not just one among a great many other run-of-the-mill acts (which in contrast to the others happened to be active rather than passive). No, in the context of the religious expressions belonging to type II this act is the most fundamental act; in this context it is the essential and distinctive act. For in as much as it signifies the renunciation and abdication of the horizontal dimension the act in the context of the religious expressions belonging to type II clearly underlies all other possible acts and in this sense constitutes a most fundamental act; and in as much as the act not only underlies all the other acts but actually makes their expression possible the act is clearly essential; finally, in as much as the act in signifying renunciation and abdication of the horizontal dimension clearly captures the central feature by which the religious expressions belonging to type II are distinguished from all other religious expressions the act is clearly distinctive of this type. Thus, one could argue that in spite of all the passive acts of acquiescence encountered here one can also encounter here an active act and, indeed, encounter it in the very fundamental, essential and distinctive act which underlies all the other acts in this context (all of which, to be sure, being acts that are passive). But this means that, in the last analysis, one would have to concede that the countermanding of the ethical in the context of the religious expressions belonging to type II is achieved ultimately also here by an active rather than a passive act (for after all it is the fundamental act of abdicating the world before the divine which, in the last analysis, is the primary act in the countermanding of the ethical and this act is clearly active) thus equating the situation here with that encountered in the story of the binding of Isaac. Surely, Kierkegaard must have made such an equation in his mind. For he clearly perceives his renunciation of Regina Olson in terms of the sacrifice of Isaac. The renunciation of Regina Olson is also an act of sacrifice. And though there are no doubt any number of similarities between the two instances to justify the equation (as, for example, that in both instances the act is constituted as a rejection of the horizontal dimension for the sake of the vertical dimension, that in both instances the act, i.e., the sacrifice, is brought about because of a demand emanating from the vertical, i.e., from the divine, or that in both instances the act clearly implicates a countermanding of the ethical), the equation would not have held if the two acts were not also perceived as ultimately being constituted as the same kind of act, i.e., as active rather than merely passive acts. Thus, even in the context of the religious expressions belonging to type II, as encountered, for example, in the thought of Kierkegaard who clearly represents the impact of the Lutheran tradition, the countermanding of the ethical does not express itself exclusively in passive acts of acquiescence but ultimately and fundamentally one encounters behind these many and various passive acts of acquiescence an active act of renunciation where the countermanding of the ethical is really effected. Still this argument may not be all that convincing after all. For there is no denying that the overwhelming preponderance of acts in which the ethical is countermanded in the context of the religious expressions belonging to type II are passive acts of acquiescence. The argument above could point to only one act (albeit a fundamental and essential act but nonetheless numerically speaking only one act) that is an active act of renunciation. As such, one cannot close one's eyes to the fact that in this context the countermanding of the ethical is overwhelmingly associated with passive acts of acquiescence. And with respect to such a context the question may well be raised as to how valid is the application of the teleological suspension of the ethical seeing that it is formulated in close association with the story of the binding of Isaac and that consequently it establishes only too clearly without any doubt or ambiguity that the countermanding of the ethical is associated specifically with an act that is active. Can it really be meaningfully applied to our context where with one exception (though granted this one exception is constituted by an act that is fundamental, essential and distinctive) the acts involved are passive acts of acquiescence?

Evidently, one must come up with a rationale that would go beyond the rationale offered above, namely, one must come up with a rationale that would go beyond attempting to formulate its justification in terms of the single act of renunciation underlying the multiplicity of the passive acts of acquiescence and would formulate its justification in terms of the very passive acts of acquiescence themselves. Not, it would seem to us, that such a rationale is indeed available. For if one were to examine the matter more carefully one would realize, we would submit, that the difference between the active and passive act really receives its significance only when it is assessed from the standpoint of the ethical. Namely, from the standpoint of the question of responsibility or guilt, i.e., the degree of responsibility or guilt implicated, there is indeed a significant difference between the act countermanding the ethical being active and its being passive. Thus, for example, there is clearly a significant difference with respect to the guilt or responsibility incurred between actually murdering someone and failing to take action when seeing someone else murdering someone. In this context the difference between the active and passive act, the difference between the active and passive countermanding of the ethical, is real and significant and must be taken into consideration. As such, indeed, it would be highly problematical, from the perspective of the ethical standpoint, to compare (leave alone equate or transfer) a state of affairs where the countermanding of the ethical is active with a state of affairs where it is passive (it would be like comparing apples and pears). In other words, from the perspective of the ethical standpoint, it is indeed highly problematical to associate the teleological suspension of the ethical in conjunction with the story of the binding of Isaac (where the countermanding of the ethical is active) with the religious expressions belonging to type II (where the countermanding of the ethical is passive.) But the ethical standpoint, i.e., the question of the degree of responsibility or guilt, is not the issue at stake here—it is not the issue that the teleological suspension of the ethical precipitates. The issue at stake here, the issue which the teleological suspension of the ethical precipitates, is the issue of the relation between the religious and the ethical, or more specifically, the issue of the supremacy and ultimacy of the religious over the ethical. And with respect to this issue the difference between the active and the passive act evaporates. For the way the ethical is countermanded, the question of the "how," is really immaterial here. What is significant is the claim that the ethical is counter-manded and that it is countermanded because of considerations or dictates brought forth by the religious. For this, and this only, establishes the supremacy of the religious over the ethical. The question of whether the countermanding of the ethical expresses itself in an active or a passive act is beside the point here as it does not affect the question of articulating the supremacy and ultimacy of the religious over the ethical—a passive act of acquiescing in the on-goingness of evil is just as much a countermanding of the ethical as is an active act of perpetrating evil (and as such it is just as much an act establishing the supremacy of the religious over the ethical as is the active act of actually perpetrating evil). Thus, if the issue at stake is indeed the issue of the supremacy of the religious over the ethical then the discrepancy between the active countermanding of the ethical as finding expression in the teleological suspension of the ethical when formulated in conjunction with the story of the binding of Isaac and the passive countermanding of the ethical as finding expression in the preponderance of the religious expressions belonging to type II is not really of any significance. And as such, indeed, the two expressions can be consistently and meaningfully linked even though in the one expression (i.e., the former expression) the ethical is countermanded by an active act while in the other expression (i.e., the latter expression) it is countermanded by a passive act.

⁴This essay appears in a volume of collected essays by Buber entitled *Eclipse of God* (Harper Brothers, New York, 1952), pp. 115–120.

⁵Indeed, commensurate to this it is now also understandable that in terms of the structure of faith of mainstream Judaism the cardinal sin, i.e., the main and fundamental transgression, be the sin of idolatry. For what, in the last analysis, idolatry really signifies is precisely such a compromise of the radical transcendence of the divine. This can be seen fairly easily. Thus, the usually accepted understanding of idolatry is as follows: idolatry is constituted by an act in which one relates to a non-absolute being (no matter how important, ennobled, powerful or enduring it be) as if it were absolute—the taking of a contingent being as the ultimate being. But clearly, this understanding implies that the act of idolatry is, in the last analysis, but an act compromising the radical transcendence of the divine, i.e., the absolute, being. For in relating to a non-absolute being as if it were an absolute being idolatry constitutes its divine, i.e., absolute, being in terms of a non-absolute being—in truth, its divine being is a non-absolute being. Thus, idolatry identifies its divine being with a non-absolute being and as such it clearly compromises the radical transcendence of its divine being. It turns out, therefore, that both idolatry and monotheism impinge on the same aspect, i.e., the radical transcendence of the divine, except that monotheism impinges positively, i.e., affirming and safeguarding the radical transcendence, while idolatry impinges negatively, i.e., compromising and negating the radical transcendence. Idolatry is but the other side of the coin from monotheism. As such, a reverse correspondence between monotheism and idolatry should indeed obtain—the centrality of monotheism should indeed implicate idolatry as the cardinal sin and, vice versa, taking idolatry as the cardinal sin should clearly point to monotheism as the central tenet.

This consideration, however, beside being interesting for its own sake is also relevant to the point we are trying to make here, namely, that the notion of the radical transcendence of the divine is fundamental in the structure of faith of mainstream Judaism. For it follows from the above that this claim can be established not only by the direct observation of the fundamental and central status that the notion of monotheism commands here, but also by the further indirect observation that idolatry is taken here as a cardinal sin. Consequently, the fact that in mainstream Judaism idolatry is indeed taken as a cardinal sin is a further buttressing observation in support of our claim.

⁶For further elaboration on this point see my article "Monotheism" in *Encyclopedia Judaica* and my essay entitled "Some Reflecions on the Jewish Idea of God," *Concilium*, No. 123, March 1977, pp. 57–65.

⁷It is important to note in this connection that the *Halacha*, i.e., the legal formulation, fully reflects this understanding. For in terms of the *Halacha* the authority of the precepts is in the last analysis grounded exclusively in the fact that they are commanded by God. Thus, it is the divine will, i.e., the personal being of the divine, and not the apprehension of any ethical maxim, which constitutes here the ultimate point of reference. Venerable and old as the tradition of trying to find a rationale for the various precepts may well be, the obligation to observe the precepts in no way depends on the availability of such a rationale but exclusively on the fact that

they are expressions of the divine will. And to the extent that the *Halacha* expresses the very essence of mainstream Rabbinic Judaism this stance taken by the *Halacha* should, therefore, be most instructive.

[8]This essay appears also in *Eclipse of God* (Harper Brothers, New York, 1952), pp. 95–111.

[9]*Ibid*, p. 99. Since "the radical distinction between good and evil" clearly signifies the inextricable foundational act on which ethics is constituted and since "the Absolute" is provided only in the domain of religion, the above statement is tantamount to saying that there is the need of grounding (i.e., of binding) the ethical in the religious.

[10]*Ibid.*, p. 99. And after this absolutization is undermined by sophistry (*ibid.*, p. 101) it reasserts itself in Plato by making ethical values the expression of immutable ideal forms (*ibid.*, pp. 101–102).

[11]*Ibid.*, p. 103.

[12]*Ibid.*, p. 104.

[13]*Ibid.*, p. 99.

[14]Indeed, the way in which this being is further depicted by Buber in this essay—as, for example, its depiction as the particular, specific "God of Israel," or as the "Covenantal God," or as the God who teaches man by the example of his own choosing between good and evil—clearly and indubitably establish this being as a personal being, a Thou.

[15]See *op. cit.*, in particular pp. 117–119.

[16]*Ibid.*, p. 118.

[17]*Ibid.*, pp. 117–118.

[18]*Ibid.*, pp. 118–119.

[19]*Ibid.*, p. 119.

[20]*Ibid.*, p. 120.

[21]By the way, this strategy in Buber's approach whereby the intervention of the divine is relegated to the past and future but excluded from the present, namely, where it is determined that the address of the voice of the true God can be upheld with surety with respect to the past or the future but not with respect to the present, readily reminds me of the strategy adopted by the rabbis with respect to revelation. For as is well known, while the rabbis of the Talmud quite clearly accepted the revelation of God in the past, e.g., Sinai, and in the future, e.g., the messianic era, they at the same time just as clearly suspended God's intervention by revelation during the interim period, i.e., during the present. The parallel is quite striking with the difference, of course, that in the case of Buber's approach one is concerned with the question of the conduct of man and the aim is to safeguard the applicability of an independent ethical judgment while in the case of the Talmudic rabbis one is concerned with the question of legislation (or hermeneutics) and the aim is to secure the applicability of independent rationality. The underlying structure, however, is the same. Thus, in both cases the expression of the religious pole, i.e., the expression of the direct impingement of God on man, is relegated to the past and the future while the expression of the human pole, i.e., the expression of the activity of man, is defended in terms of the present. In view of our analysis above, we should be in a position to better appreciate the tendency towards such an arrangement and the advantages that accrue from it.

[22]Thus, for example, one gets the strong impression from Buber's handling of this issue that when a head-on collision between religion and ethics occurs (as it may well have occurred in the past), the religious pole wins—one is to obey the divine even at the cost of suspending the ethical.

[23]Indeed, in this respect, when the chips were really down, Buber showed himself to be more the existentialist thinker than the representative of mainstream Judaism.

[24]By the way, this should help us to better appreciate the significance of the fact that in such stories as that of the binding of Isaac or of Job the narrative in which one would seem to encounter the suspension of the ethical by the divine is introduced and qualified by the notion of trial—God is merely placing Abraham or Job through a trial. For this means that the suspension of the ethical is presented here merely for the sake of the trial but that in reality it has no standing. Thus, since God does not suspend the ethical here in actuality, in practice, once and for all, the sting of the problematic is removed or at least greatly mitigated.

HOW FLEXIBLE IS THE ARISTOTELIAN "RIGHT REASON"?

Joseph Owens, C.Ss.R.
Pontifical Institute of Mediaeval Studies
Toronto, Canada

I

In traveling through the *Nicomachean Ethics* of Aristotle today's attentive observer may soon become aware of a disconcerting phenomenon. Two apparently contradictory strands of thought keep clashing with each other. On the one hand the entire fabric of Aristotelian moral philosophy is woven from premises that hold only "roughly" and "for the most part," with conclusions that have correspondingly flexible nature (1.3.1094b20–22). On the other hand what today would be called moral absolutes are resolutely upheld. Adultery, theft, murder and the like are always (ἀεί—2.6.1107a15) and absolutely (ἁπγῶζ—a17) wrong. In fact, the whole moral structure is based upon a stable virtuous habituation acquired in a framework of authoritatively enforced laws (10.9.1179b29–1181b15). The two thrusts seem contrary. Yet they are continually operative throughout the Aristotelian moral thinking.

In spite of these prima facie opposed aspects, however, the three Aristotelian *Ethics* feature a single philosophical criterion for moral goodness. The criterion is introduced as "right reason" (ὁ ὀρθὸς λόγοζ). Presumably right reason is meant to account for—perhaps even to generate—both of the allegedly opposed aspects in the Aristotelian morality. One may of course readily grant that the term "reason" in the phrase allows considerable room for internal flexibility. But the notion "right" quite obviously implies conformity to some standard. How can the standard, or the conformity to the standard, be flexible enough to give rise to principles and conclusions that without exception of any kind hold only roughly and for the most part? Moreover, if that same standard, or the conformity to it, is so thoroughly flexible, how can it ever require that some types of conduct be always right and other types always wrong?

Can there be any doubt that the flexibility is meant to be all-pervasive? Hardly. In general, the subject matter of moral philosophy is regarded by Aristotle as having "no fixity."[1] In every individual case and according to the ever-varying circumstances of the moment, the practically wise man (the

The significations of both Greek words, *orthos* and *logos*, have therefore to be kept in mind when probing the historical origin and meaning of the phrase for Aristotle. The phrase occurs in earlier Greek literature in non-technical senses of the right word or the correct account.[7] In the authentic works of Plato it is found used on sixteen occasions, but still without any definite technical stereotyping. An examination of the passages by a German scholar has shown that for Plato the phrase had widely varying meanings in accordance with the different senses of *logos*. Nowhere with certainty, however, did it have the "objective" sense of a moral law, this study has shown, and only in three places (*Plt.*, 310C4, *Lg.* 2.659D1–4; 3.696C8–10) had it with some certainty the "subjective" meaning of correct moral thinking.[8]

No further background for the phrase in a technical moral context has been traced. Nevertheless Aristotle, without any apparent hesitation or explanation, introduced it in the *Nicomachean Ethics* as the commonly accepted norm for moral conduct: "Now to *act* according to right reason is commonly accepted, and let it be assumed here; later there will be a discussion concerning right reason, both as to what it is and how it is related to the other virtues" (2.2.1103b31–34; Apostle trans.). The deeply Platonic background of the *Nicomachean Ethics* is commonly acknowledged, and has been pointed out in detail by Burnet in his commentary on its first book.[9] This indicates at least that the hearers to which it was directed enjoyed a thorough Academic training and were steeped in the Platonic mentality. That would hold true in a special way in regard to the notion of *logos*.[10] Apparently the hearers were considered to accept without question the formulation *orthos logos* as the commonly known phrase for the norm of moral conduct, even though in introducing the formula the *Nicomachean Ethics* asserts that it will require further discussion both as regards what "right reason" is and what its relations are with the "other virtues."[11] Aristotle seems to be telling his audience that though by common consent people have now accepted "right reason" as the norm for moral conduct, they still have only a hazy notion of what it means. No clearly defined ethical conception of it, in fact, can be gathered from what we know of its historical background before Aristotle. What he himself understands by it, then, has to be sought from his own writings. True, he claims no originality for the expression in its moral context. Yet the way is unmistakably left open for an understanding of it that may be profoundly innovative and distinctive of his own ethical thought. The sources for the investigation, however, have been the Aristotelian treatises themselves.

III

The notion of "right reason" as ethical norm is found in all three series of Aristotelian ethical treatises. There is as yet no agreement on the chronology of the three works, or on which of the two major works should be considered the more mature and authoritative.[12] The *Nicomachean Ethics*, however, is the series in which "right reason" occurs most frequently and is given its most significant explanations. This collection, in consequence, is indicated as the basic text for a thoroughgoing study of the notion.

The two elements of the phrase are used in the opening book of the *Nicomachean Ethics*. In summarizing the knowledge of the soul required for the approach to the study of moral philosophy, the last chapter of that book keeps up a running contrast between reason and the irrational part of the soul (1102a23–1103a3). Of the irrational side, one part is vegetative and does not share in reason. The other part, the emotive, does share in reason by obeying reason in the case of a self-controlled person or of a person who is temperate or courageous. Yet this emotive side can also resist and struggle against reason (τῷ λόγῳ—1102b18). In such struggles reason is regarded as praiseworthy, because it urges the moral agent in the right way (ὀρθῶς—b15), that is, towards what is best.

There can be no doubt about the meaning of "reason" (*logos*) in the ethical context of this first book of the *Nicomachean Ethics*. Used with and without the Greek definite article in this passage, it signifies the part of the soul that is not shared by plants and brute animals, and which in man gives the right guidance to the emotions and passions.[13] As a term it covers in this section the faculty by which the soul reasons and guides conduct, as well as the acts by which it exhorts and guides, and the content of that guidance as shared by the emotive part.

The notion "right," however, is mentioned just once in this passage. The only explanation given of it, with the Greek *kai*, is that reason directs the emotions and passions towards the best: "since it urges them aright and towards the best objects" (1102b15–16; Oxford trans.). This reads as though directing "towards the best" were a proper characteristic of reason. Reason would seem of its very nature to be "right." "Right" would be merely explicative of "reason," as the ground by which reason is praiseworthy. It would be adding nothing new, but merely bringing out an acknowledged characteristic. If that is the case, one may expect to find "reason" and "right reason" used interchangeably in the Aristotelian ethical treatises. For the moment the passage in the first book of the *Nicomachean Ethics* introduces the term "reason" in the moral context with sufficient clarity as the part of the soul not shared by brute animals, while "right" is given no further determination than that of something characteristic of reason in directing human conduct towards the best of things. Yet that seems enough to suggest that the two notions taken together will focus upon the high point of excellence in human conduct.

The combination of the two notions, in the phrase "right reason," first makes its appearance in somewhat abrupt fashion early in the second book of the *Nicomachean Ethics*. After having shown in its opening chapter that good moral habituation is acquired by actions, the book proceeds at once to specify the kind of actions. They are actions performed "in accord with right reason" (2.2.1103b32;33). The first remark made about this norm is that it cannot be expected to have a rigid character. Rather, it comes under a type of *logos* that has to take into account the changing circumstances of the moment, just as in the arts of medicine and navigation the correct action depends upon the actual condition of the body or the weather at the time (1104a1–10). In conduct it will consist in striking the mean between excess and deficiency, as is readily illustrated in the domains of temperance and courage. Correct (*orthê*) education will be the habituation in relishing what one should in that regard, and in being grieved by what may be opposed (1104b12–13). The object attained by conduct of this kind is regularly described as "what one *should* do" or as the *kalon*, the right thing to do when all the circumstances of the moment have been taken into consideration.[14]

The result is that the moral mean is "determined by reason and in the way the wise man would determine it" (*E N*, 2.6.1107a1–2). The wise man will take all the relevant circumstances of the moment into consideration, including his own condition. What is right, what is morally good, what ought to be done, is in this way determined by reason. Here the notion "reason" fits in neatly enough with the way the term was used in the opening book of the *Nicomachean Ethics*. The notion "right" now appears as something that is determined by reason, and accordingly as rational in origin. Although a mean in relation to wrong extremes, it is always what is best, and in that way is essentially the high point or extreme of moral goodness in the actual conduct (a6–8). Yet with this understanding of moral goodness so carefully set out, Aristotle can go on without hesitation to say that "in all things the mean is an object of praise, while the extremes are neither right (*ortha*) nor praiseworthy" (2.7.1108a15–16). It would seem that for him every moral act can be construed in a way that would make it lie between two extremes, even though from another viewpoint the act may be named solely from the extreme of goodness, for instance in the case of temperance or courage. Further, he notes (2.9.1109b20–21) how difficult it is to determine by reason (τῷ λόγῳ) the degree and extent of the blame, again (cf. 1107a1) assigning to "reason" just alone the task of determining the moral mean, without the explicit addition of "right."

What can be gathered from the first occurrence of "right reason" in the *Nicomachean Ethics*? It keeps the notion "reason" aligned sharply enough with the rational side as distinguished from the non-rational nature of the soul in the opening book of the series. But whether it is understanding "reason" as the faculty or as the activity or as the content of the reasoning is not brought out clearly. The notion "right" undoubtedly implies the grasping of the golden mean between excess and deficiency, thereby attaining the extreme of moral goodness. Yet the ground on which the determination of the goodness is to be made is still left vague. The ground seems somehow to be intrinsic to reason itself, so much so that Aristotle can routinely speak of moral goodness as determined by reason without feeling impelled to add the qualification "right," even though "right reason" is used again in the summary at 3.5.1114b29.

In the third book of the *Nicomachean Ethics* (11.1119a20) the temperate man is said to enjoy pleasures in the way "right reason" prescribes. But the term "reason" alone, without the "right," continues to suffice for the notion (12.1119b11; 14–15; 16; 17–18). Quite as in the opening book, sense appetite is contrasted with reasoning (*logismon*—b10). In the fourth book (5.1125b35) "reason" by itself is used in regard to the correct regulation of anger, while in the fifth (11.1138a10—on the reading see Gauthier-Jolif, II, 424–425; infra, n. 15) "right reason" occurs in the context of justice. But "right" is also used alone, without mention of any standard (e.g., 4.2.1122b29;5.10.1137b14–21).

The promised (*E N*, 2.2.1103b31–34) discussion about the nature of "right reason" and the way it is related to the other virtues is then given in the sixth book of the *Nicomachean* treatises. This book commences with an explicit backward reference to the tenet that the virtuous mean is what "right reason" (ὁ λόγος ὁ ὀρθός—1138b20) prescribes. It likewise refers back expressly (1139a3–15; cf. ὁ τὸν λόγον ἔχων at 1138b22–23) to the division of the soul into rational and non-rational parts in the last chapter of the opening book of the series (1.13.1102a27–1103 a 3). It uses the phrase "right reason" three times (1138 to 25; 29; 34) in noting that so far the meaning of the expression has remained vague and unspecified. Yet, it continues, actual conduct requires detailed guidance, just as in the care of one's health the overall norm of taking what medical science and its practitioners lay down has to be specified in detailed remedies.

The text then notes that truth for the practical intellect means correspondence with correct (*orthê*) appetency (2.1139a30–31), and that choice is the origin of conduct (a31). This sets the stage for the presentation of the intellectual virtue *phronêsis*. The term is none too easy to translate into English. The closest translation would be "wisdom," as the noun, and "wise" as the adjective, in the way these words are understood in ordinary conversation. A person who makes the right decisions in everyday conduct is customarily regarded as "wise" or as endowed with "wisdom." But in the Aristotelian context the term "wisdom" just by itself has been preempted to translate the Greek term *sophia* in the sense of theoretical wisdom, even though *sophia* originally denoted a skill in some activity. To use the word "wisdom" just alone as a translation of *phronesis* in some places (e.g., *E N*, 6.11.1143b15) would occasion considerable difficulty. Accordingly "practical wisdom" has been used successfully, though not without some awkwardness, as a regular translation of *phronesis* in ethical contexts. However, to translate *phronimos* as "a practically wise man" is hardly felicitous. The traditional Latin translation was *prudentia* (basically *providentia*), giving rise to "prudence" and "the prudent man" in English and to their equivalents in the modern languages derived from the Latin. But these translations are none too satisfactory and require explanation. Perhaps the best policy is to use "wise" and "wisdom" where there is no danger of confusion with theoretical wisdom, and to add the specification "practical" where there is. In any case the relation between the *phronimos* who determines the moral mean (2.6.1107a1–2), and the virtue *phronesis* discussed in the present book (6.5–13,1140a24), should appear at once in the translation.

After a protracted discussion of the virtue *phronesis*, the sixth book of the *Nicomachean Ethics* returns in its final chapter to the theme of "right reason." It notes again (cf. 2.2.1103b32) that at the time all those (presumably in the Academic circles[15]) who defined virtue added to its generic characteristics the notion of conformity with "right reason" (6.13.1144b23). Immediately "right" is explained as conformity with practical wisdom, a wisdom which in itself is "right reason" (b23–28). Without it one's choice cannot be "right" (*orthê*—1145a4), nor can it itself be "right" without the orientation given by moral virtue towards the goal of human conduct. The morally good action itself, then, has to conform with practical wisdom.

What does this mean? The text explicitly makes "right reason" identical with practical wisdom as the moral standard. To be morally good the actions must conform with practical wisdom, which in turn depends upon the habituation given by morally good actions, in what has been called a "virtuous" circle. This locates the moral standard in reason itself.

The identification of "right reason" with the virtue of practical wisdom may well be taken as Aristotle's "last word" on the topic.[16] Whether the sentence be translated as "right reason about such things is prudence" (Apostle) or "practical wisdom is a right rule about such matters" (Ross), the meaning, as Burnet (ad loc.) noted, is that the *orthos logos* may be regarded as identical with the *phronesis* of the man who has the *logos*. The picture rounds out neatly, from the notion of "reason" outlined in the opening book of the *Nicomachean Ethics*, into the guidance of conduct originating through choice in a properly habituated moral agent. Here truth means conformity of the action with correct moral habituation. The practically wise man plans and directs his conduct in accord with that orientation. The plan and the directing constitute "right reason" or "practical wisdom." The notion of "right," accordingly, means conformity with the moral habituation developed through actions performed under human reason that has been true to its deep urge "towards the best." That is the ultimate standard involved.

The role of "virtuous" circularity in this explanation will call for careful consideration. But these texts suffice to show what the elements "reason" and "right" meant for Aristotle in the phrase "right reason." In their light the problem whether the Greek *orthos logos* should be translated "right reason" or "right rule" fades away. Stewart (I, 173–174) had warned against the translation "according to right reason" because the Greek article used with it should indicate a more general sense than "faculty" for *logos* and because in back of Aristotle's thinking in regard to it there must have been the notion of standard or proportion or law, etc. Yet Stewart noted that here the faculty and the object "can be distinguished only logically; for the two are really one." Nevertheless Anglophone scholars have tended to use "principle" or "ratio" or "norm" or "standard" in the translation. This has not escaped notice on the continent.[17] But once right reason is seen to coincide with practical wisdom there is no place for a distinction of that kind between the faculty and the act and its content. The norm or standard for conduct in each particular case will have no original being outside the act of practical wisdom, and the act itself will have no content over and above the direction it gives. Human reason will in this way engender its own rectitude, instead of conforming to a standard external to itself such as a Platonic Idea or a natural or eternal law.

The other instances of "right reason" in the Aristotelian corpus do not add substantially to what can be gleaned from its use in the first six books of the *Nicomachean Ethics*. In the seventh book it stands for the correct judgment against which the acratic errs (1147b3), and for the virtuous mean (b31; 1151a12; 21; 22; cf. 29–b4). Similarly in the *Eudemian Ethics* (2.5.1222a8–10) it is the virtuous mean in relation to ourselves, with corresponding forward reference (b7–8) to the treatment about its nature and bearing. It is likewise what determines the way things should be done (3.4.1231b33), and may be found expressed simply in the one word "reason" (7.15.1249b3–5). In the same vein the *Magna Moralia* tends to use "reason" alone when covering these topics, though "right reason" is found at 1.35.1196b6–11 three times and further at 1198a14 and a18 in regard to the virtues, and six times at 2.6.1202a11–1204a10 in the treatment of acrasia. At 2.10.1208a5–20 it is explained as what keeps the passions from hindering the mind's performance of its own work, with the phrase "right reason" likewise used six times in this short passage.[18] All these texts serve to confirm the notion of right reason given in *Nicomachean Ethics* I-VI, though without any important doctrinal addition. The English translation "right reason" stands up satisfactorily throughout. It renders with sufficient force the pertinent senses of faculty, act and content as combined in the Greek phrase *orthos logos*.

IV

As its notion emerges from the texts, then, the Aristotelian "right reason" is identical with practical wisdom. It is "right," because in every particular and always different case it conforms to the habituation of a person properly brought up. Its rightness is based upon the internal moral virtue required for a person's practical reasoning, and not upon any externally set standards. That explains why Aristotle can so readily use the term "reason" just by itself to carry the notion expressed by the whole phrase, for there is a relevant sense in which all mind may claim to be right.[19] That is also why he can say that the practically wise man (the *phronimos*—*E N*, 2.6.1107a1–2) or the morally good man (the *spoudaios*—3.4.1113a32) functions as the norm and measure of truth in matters of conduct. The measure is intrinsic to the fully developed practical reason, reason habituated by wisdom. One can, of course, represent its judgments as objects for discussion, and thereby regard them as moral standards, moral principles, moral norms. But as exercised they are identical with the human thinking. They have no other "objective" existence in themselves.

With "right reason" so understood, what conclusions may be drawn about its flexibility? Is it flexible in regard to one's supreme goal? Even without explicit texts in Aristotle, one may grant that right reason plays some role in the choice of the highest goals.[20] The correctly brought up person chooses contemplation, and even in an acratic act he retains that choice (*E N*, 7.4.1148a4–17) though only in habitual fashion. The choice remains in accord with right reason, and involves right reason. It is true that practical reason has to presuppose orientation towards the correct ultimate end through the moral virtues. But just as surely that virtuous habituation depends reciprocally on right reason (3.5.1114b26–30; 6.13.1145b1–2). Moreover, the knowledge of the virtuous orientation is required for the choice, and that knowledge is not a function of the moral virtues but of the intellectual virtue of practical wisdom. Because in its very nature practical wisdom is based upon orientation to the correct ultimate end, it cannot choose any other without self-destruction. Right reason, like anything else, has to respect the first principle of demonstration. It could not remain itself while changing into its contradictory. So while a person may choose sensual indulgence or fame as his greatest good (1.5.1095b19–23), right reason cannot. That would not be flexibility but annihilation. In that regard right reason is not flexible, though a person is. Its nature, like that of any other virtue, is stable.[21] The decision when and how long to engage in acts of contemplation pertains, however, to right reason. In that respect it is flexible. Similarly happiness in a secondary phase (Δευτέρως—10.8.1178a9), the life of moral virtue, exhibits the same flexibility.

Aristotle himself (*E N*, 7.12.1144a–7–9; 20–22; 13.1145a4–6) preferred to stress the angle in which moral virtues envisage the end, practical wisdom the means. The context was deliberation. In any deliberation, the end is accepted, the means debated (3.3.1112b11–16). But concrete goal can in turn be debated.[22] The actions have their origin in choice, undetermined by antecedent cause. The moral agent is free to accept or reject, to say yes or no (3.5.1113b7–21).

The right choice demands awareness of the pertinent circumstances. But these vary with time and place. Right reason has to be flexible enough to take account of all that are relevant. As Plato had noted, "the differences of men and of actions, and the fact that nothing, I may say, in human life is ever at rest, forbid any science whatsoever to promulgate any simple rule for everything and for all time" (*Plt.*, 294B; trans. Fowler). No lawgiver can adequately meet this situation: "For how could anyone, Socrates, sit beside each person all his life and tell him exactly what is proper for him to do?" (295AB). Yet right reason has this task. It has to extend to every circumstance. As intellectual it is entirely undetermined as regards its objects (*De an.*, 3.4.429a18–22; 8.431b21), and in the case of conduct it is dealing with an object that has not been determined in the nature of things. From these angles its flexibility is unlimited. It is not bound by the strictures of any law or rule outside itself.

Yet in the deliberation that leads up to its decision, right reason has to take into consideration natures that are fixed and stable. There is the nature of the moral agent composed of soul and matter, a body that can stand only so much heat or cold, a body that requires food, air, rest and recreation, a spirit that needs activity, education, friends, public order and government. Other material things likewise have their own stable natures. What is poisonous does not serve as nourishment. What is asphyxiating does not sustain life. Right reason cannot wave a magic wand over these things and render them innocuous. It has to respect their natures, whenever it makes decisions in which they are involved. It is not flexible in that regard. Further, the habituation in the virtues acquired through correct moral life from earliest years has its own type of stability. It is a stability that functions in a variable way, just as in regard to temperance right reason has to determine in each case the mean required by varying bodily condition of the moral agent and the type of food or drink in question. But in each case the determination comes under the one abiding notion of temperance. This stable orientation remains in the moral agent, even when through weakness of will (acrasia) he fails to act according to it. Although the general run of people in a civilized community do not come strictly under Aristotle's classification of virtuous, but rather in between the self-controlled and uncontrolled—with greater tendency towards lack of control (*E N*, 7.7.1150a15–16; 10,1152a25–27)—the basic habituation towards the good remains stable no matter how frequently they act against it. From the side of the moral agent the ground for making genuinely universal judgments continues to be present under all the variations of practical life.

In this way the Aristotelian notion of the *kalon* or the morally good maintains its universality and its own characteristic obligatory force. Like any other universal aspect, it is seen first in its individual instances, then in ever-increasing universality in the virtues and finally in the principles of moral philosophy. But as the condition of both moral agent and external circumstances keeps changing incessantly, the judgment of right reason has to be made according to the relation that these two ever-varying sides have to each other at the given moment. It has no fixed model by which it can decide. Unlike the plan or design that directs art and craftmanship, the basic principle here is free choice (*Metaph.*, 6.1.1025b22–24). But in accord with the rational nature of the moral agent, the choice has to be rational. There is nothing haphazard or merely arbitrary about it.[23] It has to be made in accord with the required deliberation. The awe of bringing something entirely new into the course of the universe, of initiating an action not determined by what has gone before it, carries its sense of responsibility and obligation that Aristotle (*E N*, 3.5.1113b7–21) compares to the attitude a man has towards the children to whom he has given life. Even though the basic moral judgments are made on the response of a properly habituated person to a proposed course of action, quite as the judgment whether chords are musical or not is made by a person with an ear for music, there is nothing ante-cedently fixed that can serve as the norm for finalizing the decision. The fact that a definite way of acting was morally right on a previous occasion does not in itself guarantee that it will be right under present and different circumstances. Morally the act is not repetitive, like chords in music. It is radically new in each instance.

The flexibility of the Aristotelian right reason, then, is thoroughgoing in spite of the strong grounds in both agent and object that give it genuine stability. Murder is always wrong. Yet for a particular act of killing a human being to come under the notion murder the variable circumstances have to be taken into account, making the decision often difficult for a jury. It is for right reason to determine whether the physical act is or is not murder under these circumstances. To this extent there may be agreement with Locke's (*Essay*, 3.10.19) observation that here the nominal coincides with the real essence, and endorsement of Aquinas' (*In E N*, 1.1.1) stand that the moral order is *made* by reason in considering its own act while the order of natural things is not made but only considered by it. The rigid determination of the natural order does not freeze moral entities into any of its molds. The flexibility of right reason is as extensive as their basic origin, rational choice.

V

How, then, is the prima facie clash between flexible and stable to be assessed? Are they really opposed to each other in the Aristotelian setting? As just seen, the requirement of distinctive moral categories, of stable virtuous habituation, of laws, customs and strict discipline, is not something alien to right reason or imposed upon it from without. It is flexible enough to allow for and prescribe absolute types of moral goodness and evil, such as the virtues and the vices and the actions by which these are specified. That extension pertains to its flexibility, and is required by its flexibility. In a civil community the common culture will not remove all differences of temperament and habituation. Each person's reasoning may be expected to differ considerably in detail, giving rise to indefinitely varied judgments on the same case. "Be reasonable, do it my way" is an attitude that will continually crop up. Right reason, along with efforts at compromise, has to meet that attitude with fixed laws that all are bound to obey, with penalties to enforce those laws and equity to supply for their deficiencies. Right reason, after Aristotle's time, will even be found open to an eternal law, and to the requirements of the elevation of man to a supernatural order, and to the divinely revealed positive laws of the Judeo-Christian tradition. In itself the flexibility of the Aristotelian "right reason" is sufficiently thoroughgoing to extend to all those possibilities.

In fact, the theoretical circularity always present in and always permeating the Aristotelian "right reason," may strongly suggest the need of a supernaturally revealed morality even though it does not at all substantiate the fact. For Aristotle "right reason," as practical wisdom, depends upon the habituation given by the moral virtues. But the moral virtues depend just as much on right reason. The dependence is reciprocal. The habituation of the virtues is brought about by acts performed under the guidance of "right reason." But "right reason" cannot act unless the virtues are already formed in the moral agent. Good laws and customs are required for the upbringing and education of the citizens. But good laws can be made only by persons who have been properly habituated. The rightness or correctness in "right reason" is measured only by right reason itself. Everywhere there is circularity, if the problem is approached on the theoretical level.

But in his *Ethics* Aristotle is not approaching his subject matter on the theoretical plane. He is meeting it in the practical order. He is taking his first principles or starting points from the practical life of the Greek city-state. That practical life was there before his eyes. The first principles were the judgments being made in everyday life about what was morally right and morally wrong. The historical origin of culture was not an immediate concern for practical science. But even if the question had been introduced, it could hardly have caused Aristotle discomfort. Cosmic change was eternal, every change had one before it, and accordingly civilizations had kept rising and falling without any absolute beginning. Before each there was always one preceding, to bequeath to it the rudiments of moral habituation. But where the eternity of human history is not accepted, some other origin would seem required. Yet with Aristotle himself, for whom the succession was taking place from all eternity, the question of absolute origin does not arise. In other settings, however, it draws attention as obviously as a flashing hazard light.

Correspondingly, there is for him no question about whether the stable aspect or the flexible aspect of right reason comes first. Neither aspect can be viewed as basic, with the other as something superadded. Physicists could not see the classical conceptions of wave and particles in light as reducible one to the other. They are obliged to seek a photon whose nature will account for both facets. In Aquinas, (*In Peri herm.*, 1.14.Spiazzi no. 197) human choice, because both caused and free, required a source that transcended the orders of necessity and of contingency. Though in a way radically different from these two examples, Aristotelian right reason has to be of a nature that gives rise to both the flexible and the stable aspects with equal immediacy. The flexibility is not to be understood by way of exceptions to or dispensations from an already stable law. It is not an equitable supplying of deficiencies that the legislator would have attended to had he known. It is not a concession made to human weakness. It is a flexibility that antecedes all laws, and that is found in the root of the moral order. The root is rational choice, the first principle of conduct, involving the individual's own responsibility for his actions. Nor is the stability basically a restraint upon an already existent flexibility. Rather, it is an aspect that follows with equal immediacy upon the rational side of human choice. Instead of clashing, the two aspects blend. Right reason is equally the source of both facets. In it the flexible is not hindered or restricted by the stable, but is extended into the stable and enhanced by the expression given to the rational character of human choice.

Aristotle himself does not spell out these reflections. In fact, the phrase "right reason" is somewhat infrequent in his treatises, outside two or three clusters of instances. An overview of the situation makes it appear like an apt expression encountered by him in the vocabulary of the Academic circles in his time. He recognized its usefulness for driving home a basic moral tenet. The tenet fitted neatly into his own moral philosophy in the framework of the virtues, under the caption of practical wisdom. His explanation of the already current phrase "right reason" was accordingly given in terms of identification with the intellectual virtue, both in regard to its nature and to its relations with the other virtues. In this way it played its cooperative role in a moral philosophy built upon virtuous habituation.

Far more frequent, however, than recourse to either right reason or to practical wisdom for pinpointing the morally good in Aristotle, is the mere mention of the *kalon* and the "ought." They occur everywhere. The moral facts of right and wrong are regarded as straightway recognized by the person who has been properly brought up. Those facts are the starting points of the Aristotelian moral science. Explanation through right reason and practical wisdom can but offer a philosophical understanding of them. Aristotle's own philosophical explanation is given in terms of a morally self-sufficient human reason. This has made the Aristotelian ethic appear as "grace's worst enemy." Yet the Aristotelian "right reason" was flexible enough to extend beyond its initial self-sufficiency while remaining true to the exigencies of its own deepest nature in tending towards the best. It became a tenet with which Thomas Aquinas could feel perfectly at home. Equally amenable as Aquinas to right reason, I would suggest, is the sturdy and vigorous proponent of the Aristotelian conception of practical science whom we are honoring in the present symposium, the distinguished contemporary scholar Professor Henry Veatch.[24]

Notes

[1]*E N*, 2.2.1104a4; Oxford trans. John Alexander Stewart, *Notes on the Nicomachean Ethics of Aristotle* (Oxford: Clarendon Press, 1892), I, 174, suggested "nothing *absolutely* fixed," on the ground that the wording "is too strong, and is apt to mislead." But even with this qualification, the presence of moral absolutes would still have to be explained. As it stands in the text, the assertion is unqualified and calls for consideration on its own merits before the qualification is inserted.

[2]On the etymology, see Hjalmar Frisk, *Griechisches etymologisches Wörterbuch* (Heidelberg: Carl Winter, 1970), s.v. λέγω. G. B. Kerferd in Paul Edwards' *Encyclopedia of Philosophy*, s.v. *logos*, notes how "attempts to trace a logical progression of meanings in the history of the word are now generally acknowledged to lack any secure foundation." For literature, see bibliography to Kerferd's article. The early use of the term is studied in Heribert Boeder's article "Der frühgriechische Wortgebrauch von Logos and Aletheia," *Archiv fr Begriffsgeschichte*, 4 (1959), 82–112. In the opening book of the *Nichomachean Ethics, logos*

is set in contrast with the non-rational part or nature (*physis*—13.1102b13) of the soul, as though it itself were another part or nature.

3See Frisk, s.v. Examples of *orthotês* are given by Aristotle at *E N*, 6.9.1142b8–33. On the contrast of "right" choice with choice "of any kind at all," see 7.9.1151a29–35. On *orthotês* in Plato as applied to laws, see *Lg.*, 1.627D, and to moral goodness, *Men.*, 97BC and *Cri.*, 46B.

4On the history of *recta ratio*, see Karl Bärthlein, "Zur Lehre von der 'recta ratio' in der Geschichte der Ethik von der Stoa bis Christian Wolff," *Kantstudien*, 56 (1965), 125–155. Bärthlein (p. 154) quotes Wolff's assertion (*Philosophia Practica Universalis*, 456) "Additur quidem vulgo, quod sit dictamen rectae rationis; sed per modum pleonismi: ratio enim non est, quae recta non est." Bärthlein (ibid.) attributes it to Wolff's reduction of the practical order to the theoretical, making the *recta* "überflüssig: denn von Vernunft könne eben nicht mehr die Rede sein, wenn sie nicht richtig wäre." On the other hand, Robert Hoopes, *Right Reason in the English Renaissance* (Cambridge Mass.: Harvard University Press, 1962), going over much of the same history, had undertaken to offer another account of "the two principal and controlling elements investing 'right reason' with its unique meaning, a meaning no longer possessed by the single term 'reason'" (p. 4).

5For a listing of modern versions, see William K. Frankena, "The Ethics of Right Reason," *The Monist*, 66 (1983), pp. 22–23.

6Cf.: "Third, 'reason' becomes relevant when we move to the agent-related dimensions of moral value. Here the moral value of an action will depend on: . . . (c) whether he acted "for the right reason,' . . ." S. F. Sapontzis, "Moral Value and Reason," *The Monist*, 66 (1983), p. 157.

7See instances from Herodotus ("rightly so called"—2.17; "in very deed"—6.68; trans. A. D. Godley) given in Liddell and Scott, *Greek-English Lexicon*, s.v. ὀρθός, III, 2. Similarly Antiphon, *Fr.* 44 (Diels-Kranz, II, 349.10–11. Archytas' *logismos (tf(DK Fr.* 3; Freeman trans. "Right Reckoning"), though functioning as a standard, can hardly serve as a Pythagorean antecedent for the phrasing "right reason."

8Karl Bärthlein, "Der ὀρθὸς λόγος und das ethische Grundprinzip in den platonischen Schriften," *Archiv für Geschichte der Philosophie*, 46 (1964), 129–173. Bärthlein (pp. 136–173), however, sees rich Platonic background for the "objective" sense of the *orthos logos*. On pp. 130–136 he collects and anlyzes the Platonic instances of the phrase. Ingemar Düring, "Aristotle on ultimate principles from 'nature and reality': *Protrepticus* fr. 13," in *Aristotle and Plato in the Mid-Fourth Century*, ed. Ingemar Düring and G. E. L. Owen (Göteborg: Studia Graeca et Latina Gothoburgensia, 11,1960), had regarded Plato as the first philosopher of "right reason": "As far as our evidence goes, it was Plato who first developed a philosophy of ὀρθὸς λόγος" (p. 36), a philosophy that Aristotle "seems to have adopted . . . with a significant difference" (p. 37). On the instances in the *Magna Moralia*, see Bärthlein, "Der 'ΟΡΘΟΣ ΛΟΓΟΣ' in der *Grossen Ethik* des *Corpus Aristotelicum*,"*AGP*, 45 (1963), 213–258.

9John Burnet, *The Ethics of Aristotle* (London: Methuen, 1900), pp. 6–61. The Platonic terminology need not imply any acceptance of a non-Aristotelian Platonism at the time. It is a question rather of exploiting the language familiar to the audience.

10See Bärthlein (1964), pp. 164–171. There can hardly be any doubt that *logos* carries over from Plato the requirement that human action should conform to some intelligible standard, as in the passage "Tell me what is the nature of this idea, and then I shall have a standard to which I may look and by which I may measure actions, whether yours or those of any one else, and then I shall be able to say that such and such an action is pious, such another impious." (*Euthyphro*, 6E).

[11]The ἄλλαζ (1103b34) in this text need not be merely pleonastic. It is open to interpretation in the sense that right reason is one virtue among the others. See infra, n. 16. Cf. Franz Dirlmeier, *Aristoteles: Nikomachische Ethik* (Berlin: Akademie-Verlag, 1967), p. 298.

[12]On this topic see Franz Dirlmeier, *Aristoteles: Magna Moralia* (Berlin: Akademie-Verlag, 1958), pp. 93–110; 185. Anthony Kenny, *The Aristotelian Ethics* (Oxford: Clarendon Press, 1978), pp. 1–5; 213–239.

[13]*E N*, 1.13.1102b25–28. The use of the Greek article with *logos*, accordingly, does not restrict the term to an "objective" sense.

[14]A discussion of this theme may be found in my paper "the KAΛON in the Aristotelian *Ethics*," in *Studies in Aristotle*, ed. Dominic J. O'Meara (Washington, D.C.: The Catholic University of America Press, 1981), pp. 261–277. The Aristotelian *kalon* carries its own sense of moral obligation (pp. 263–264; 273–275).

[15]"Tout le monde est d'accord aujourd'hui pour reconnaître dans ces 'modernes' les Académiciens disciples de Platon." René Antoine Gauthier and Jean Yves Jolif, *L'éthique à Nicomaque*, 2nd ed. (Paris: Béatrice-Nauwelaerts, 1970), II, 556. Similarly, "'all' probably refers to all of those who are, or have been, associated with the Academy, or at least to the *soi-disant* successors of Socrates." J.M. Rist, "An Early Dispute about *Right* Reason," *The Monist*, 66 (1983), 39.

[16]"Voilà sur le problème son dernier mot: la droite règle, c'est la sagesse; on dirait mieux ancore: c'est le sage." Gauthier-Jolif, II, 557. The opposite view is that the *orthos logos* is neither a virtue nor identical with *phronesis*—Burnet, p. 286. Burnet regards the identification "in this bald form" (p. 80) as post-Aristotelian.

[17]Bärthlein (1963), p. 213; Dirlmeier (1967), p. 298. Apostle, however, uses "right reason" regularly in his translation, and in the Oxford translation of the *Eudemian Ethics* it is used by J. Solomon at 1222a9; b7; 1227b17; 1231b33. In the 1963 article Bärthlein finds the "subjective" meaning of *orthos logos* in *M M*, 2.6., and the "objective" meaning in *M M*, 2.10.

[18]See Bärthlein (1963), pp. 230–258, for an analysis of these texts.

[19]In contrast with appetency and imagination, mind is always right—*De an.*, 3.10.433a26. In what it immediately knows, mind is always right, and also in the validly reasoned knowledge and practical wisdom based upon this immediate cognition. But in mediate cognition, insofar as conclusions may be drawn invalidly from premises in reasoning, thinking can be wrong—*De an.*, 3.3.427b8–14.

[20]Cf.: "Sans doute, c'est la vertu morale qui, en le maintenant tourné dans la bonne direction, permet à sa sagesse de voir le vraie fin, mais il reste que c'est elle qui la voit, et c'est elle aussi qui découvre les moyens de la réalizer." Gauthier-Jolif, II, 557; cf. 784. Pierre Aubenque, "La prudence aristotélicienne porte-t-elle sur la fin ou sur les moyens?" *Revue des études grecques*, 78 (1965), 40–51, argues against this stand in defending *prudence* as the appropriate translation of *phronesis*. "Prudence" accords with the viewpoint from which moral virtue gives the end, practical wisdom selects the means.

[21]E.g., the *physis* of equity, *E N*, 5.10.1137b26. In accord with the different senses of *physis*, its use to designate what a virtue is does not at all imply any derivation of moral entities from the world of matter and form.

[22]For a discussion, see Rist, pp. 41–44. Choice, which applies to concrete ends and to means, has two different but related senses in Aristotelian moral philosophy. It can mean the basic choice of a way of life, which in habitual fashion remains intact even while the acratic is

deliberately acting against it (*E N*, 7.9.1152a17). It can also mean the acceptance of one particular action in preference to others (3.2.1112a17; cf. 3.3.1112b31–1113a7 and *E E*, 2.10.1226b6–8). On the historical background of this distinction, see Pierre Aubenque, *La prudence chez Aristote* (Paris: Presses Universitaires de France, 1963), pp. 119–132.

[23]At *Metaph.*, 12.10.1075a19–23, the nature (*physis*) of the free man, in contrast to the slave and the lower animal, makes him subject to set order. The blending of freedom and stability in a single source is accordingly no more mysterious or odd than the living human person. One must always keep in mind that for Aristotle (*E N*, 3.3.1112b31–32) the person is the origin of all the actions, and (*De an.*, 1.4.408b1–15; 3.8.432a1–2) the soul with all its faculties exercises but an instrumental role. In this way the free moral agent is the measure of both the stable and the flexible in good conduct.

[24]My thesis is that normative or practical science, to use the more traditional and in many ways more felicitous term, is perfectly legitimate as science." H. Veatch, "Concerning the Distinction between Descriptive and Normative Sciences," *Philosophy and Phenomenological Research*, 6 (1945), 284. In that tradition, as Frankena, p. 3, notes, "the use of the concept of right reason in the formulation of an ethical theory is explicit and central." For Aristotle practical philosophy has its principles in the habituation of the moral agent (*E N*, 1.3.1095a2–8) and its conclusions in the person's actions (7.3.1147a28), a conception of science that intimately involves the Aristotelian notion of right reason. On the theme "that moral or practical reasoning is of a different type from practical reasoning and not merely an application of it," see D. Stephen Theron, "Morality as Right Reason," *The Monist*, 66 (1983), 26–38.

NATURAL LAW, HUMAN ACTION, AND MORALITY

Alan Gewirth
University of Chicago

I am very pleased to participate in this symposium in honor of Professor Henry Veatch. I have known Henry for many years, and have always admired his philosophical acumen, his broad and deep learning, and his real warmth and generosity of spirit.

My present paper is offered as a contribution to a discussion that Henry and I have carried on for a long time. The discussion has revolved around the question of the adequacy of a certain conception of natural law as a theory of morality. I wish to explore here some of the main issues on this question.

My paper is divided into two very unequal arts. In the bulk of the paper, I make critical examination of some central theses of the Aristotelian-Thomist theory of natural law, and I indicate certain difficulties that beset the theory. In a brief concluding section, I give an outline of my own moral theory, based on the concept of human action, and I try to show how it avoids the difficulties of the natural-law theory. But I also suggest how, with certain qualifications, my own theory may also be construed as a theory of natural law.

1. The Aristotelian-Thomist Theory of Natural Law

The Aristotelian-Thomist theory of natural law may be viewed, for present purposes, as having three central features. First, it holds that natural law is *universal* in its validity, in that it sets justified prescriptive requirements or precepts for the conduct of all human beings. By this normative universality, natural law is differentiated from all particular institutional conventions, including those of etiquette, of variable municipal laws of different states, and of the diverse ceremonial precepts of the various religions. Unlike these, natural law does not derive from any particular institutions, arrangements, or preferences of human beings. For any such source would remove the normative *universality* of natural law.

An important consequence of this universal validity is that natural law is held to have *normative primacy and necessity*, in that no human action, policy, or institution, including positive law, can be justified, valid, or legitimate if it violates the requirements of natural law. Thus, natural law stands as the most basic criterion of moral rightness, whether in the sphere of individual, social, political, legal, economic, or any other kinds of action or policy. It is this enormously important feature of natural law, its normative primacy and necessity, that provides the connecting link from Thomas Aquinas to Richard Hooker and John Locke, and that hence underlies the modern constitutionalist doctrine of limited government.

Thus far, the universal validity of natural law has been explicated only in negative terms: I have indicated from what sources natural law does *not* derive. There is, then, a second definitive feature of the Aristotelian-Thomist doctrine of natural law, which I shall call *ontological groundedness* or, more simply, *ontological*. Natural law is held to have universal validity and normative primacy because it requires the protection and promotion of goods or interests that are based on the very nature of human beings. Its requirements are not imposed on humans from sources outside their own essential natures; on the contrary, those requirements simply reflect and promote goods or interests that are inherent in fundamental tendencies and strivings of human nature as such.

By this ontological feature, natural law is differentiated not only from moral principles or criteria that are transcendent in ways that go counter to human nature; it is also differentiated from all ethical relativisms that try to base moral precepts on variable desires, emotions, commands, or social institutions. Not only do such sources fail to satisfy the first feature of natural law, universal validity, but they also fail to satisfy the second, ontological feature. For, although they derive from human beings, they do not derive from human *nature* in the sense of essential characteristics that pertain to all humans by virtue of their own inherent potentialities.

A third central feature which this doctrine attributes to natural law is that it is based on *reason*. This feature serves to bring even closer together the first two features. For it is reason that sets the universally valid moral requirements of the first feature of natural law, and reason sets these requirements by virtue of what it ascertains about the ontologically based goods of human beings that constitute the second feature of natural law. Thus reason is both prescriptive and descriptive: it issues the moral precepts of natural law, and it bases these precepts on the ontological characteristics it discovers about the nature of man, of humanity.

Of these three features of natural law—normative universality, ontological groundedness, and rationality—it is the second, the ontological feature, that especially differentiates the Aristotelian-Thomist version of natural law theory from alternative versions, including those of the Stoics and John Locke. Although aspects of the ontological feature can indeed be found in these alternative versions, in none is this feature made as central to the *justificatory basis* of natural law as in the Aristotelian-Thomist tradition. Hence, my discussion will focus especially on this ontological feature.

I now wish to examine the philosophical adequacy of this conception of natural law as thus briefly sketched. For this examination, we must consider two main interrelated questions. The first bears on the *descriptive* use of reason as ascertaining the ontological characteristics of human nature. The question is: What are the *contents* of the precepts of natural law that derive from these ontological characteristics? This question of contents breaks up into two sub-questions, which I shall call the *substantive question* and the *distributive question*. The substantive question is: *What* are the onto-logically-based goods or interests of human beings that natural law requires us to protect or promote? The distributive question is: Of *which* humans are we required to protect or promote these goods or interests?

In addition to these questions of the contents of natural law's precepts, there is also a second main question. It bears on the *prescriptive* use of reason as issuing precepts or commands based on the descriptive use. The question is: How do the ontological characteristics of human nature set *obligatory* or *prescriptive requirements* for human conduct? What is there about those characteristics that makes it mandatory to secure or promote the goods that derive from them? I call this the *authoritative* question because it asks for the basis of the authority that is claimed for the precepts of natural law.

I shall also refer to the first general question, with its substantive and distributive parts, as the question of the *contents* of natural law, and I shall also refer to the second, authoritative question as the question of the *obligatoriness* of natural law. Put more succinctly, then, the two main questions are: First, what is it that natural law tells us to do, and second, why ought we to do it? I shall deal with the first question in some detail and with the second question much more briefly.

2. *The Contents of Natural Law*

The answer to the first main question, that of contents, especially in its substantive part, is initially given by a pair of insights that are so plausible that we might well call them intuitions—not, indeed, in the technical Aristotelian sense of *nous* as providing incorrigible cognitions of first principles, but rather in the more colloquial sense of very plausible assump-tions. The first intuition is that the content of the precepts of natural law, what they require us to do, is to act for the good of human beings, or at least to act in accordance with that good. The second intuition is that the good of human beings is based on, or is determined by, their nature, by what at bottom, or ontologically, humans essentially are. In particular, it is by considering the essential needs and strivings of human beings that we can ascertain what is good for them, and hence what constitutes the good of human beings. And it is, of course, by reason that such ascertainment is to be made.

I shall refer to these two insights, respectively, as the *human-good intuition* and the *naturalistic intuition*. It is these two intuitions that underlie the answer that the Aristotelian-Thomist theory of natural law gives to our first main question, the question of the *contents* of natural law.

The human-good intuition has been criticized both on the axiological ground that there are entities besides humans which have value, and on the deontological ground that the moral 'ought' is *sui generis* and hence cannot be logically derived from any considerations about goods. The first ground, however, does not remove the great importance of human goods, and the second ground may give the moral 'ought' a kind of arbitrariness which is antithetical to the rational basis of morality. Hence I shall not spend any more time at present defending the human-good intuition.

Let us now turn to the second intuition about the content of natural law, which I have called the naturalistic intuition. This intuition has two parts. The first part says that the good of human beings is based on or is determined by their nature. The second part says that this basis is ascertained by reason. I shall refer to these parts, respectively, as *the naturalistic determination thesis* and the *rationalistic thesis.*

Each of these theses raises some very profound, and to some extent very familiar, questions. The naturalistic determination thesis, in particular, incurs all the meta-ethical problems that, especially in this century, have been held to beset ethical naturalism, including problems about the meaning of "good," the definability of "good," the relation of fact and value, the 'is-ought' problem, and so forth. Also, when we say that *the good* of a man is determined by his nature, there is the question of the relation between such a *substantive* use of the word "good" and its *attributive* use, as in the expression "a good man." This distinction is sometimes put as the difference between non-moral and moral uses of "good." If some man attains or achieves *his good* or *the good of* man, is this the *same* as his being *a good man*? Can't he achieve even *the* highest good—*eudaimonia*, happiness, well-being, or flourishing—and yet not *be* good?

For the most part I shall here deal with these questions only indirectly. The usual interpretations of the questions rest on meta-ethical and meta-physical assumptions that are drastically different from those upheld in the Aristotelian-Thomist theory of natural law. It will be only certain specific bearings of the questions for that theory that I shall consider here.

3.   *The Naturalistic Determination Thesis*

The primary question about the naturalistic determination thesis with which I want to deal is this: In just what ways does the nature of human beings determine their good, what is good for them?

Obviously, the meaning of the word "determine" is important for dealing with this question. In Aristotelian terms, the word can be understood either in the sense of *formal cause* or in the sense of *efficient cause*. In the sense of formal cause, the question means: how does the nature of human beings serve to *define* or at least to provide the *criterion* for the good of human beings? In the sense of efficient cause, the question means: how does the nature of human beings serve to *generate* or *effectuate* the good of human beings? While these two meanings of the question are closely related, I shall deal primarily, though not exclusively, with the formal-cause interpretation.

Our question, then, is this: How does the nature of human beings serve to *define* or at least to provide the *criterion* for the good of human beings? At least two sets of distinctions are relevant to this question. First, when the naturalistic determination thesis says that the good of human beings is based on or determined by their nature, this basis or determination can be taken in the sense either of *necessary condition* or of *sufficient condition*. In the sense of necessary condition, the statement would mean that human nature sets the outer limits on what can count as the good of man, but it does not exhaustively define or constitute that good. In the sense of sufficient condition, the statement would mean that derivation from man's nature is itself sufficient to define or provide the content of man's good.

Now it does seem plausible that man's nature sets the outer limits of, and hence the necessary condition for, what can count as the good of man. Indeed, the Kantian dictum that 'ought' implies 'can' may be regarded as one variant of this position, since it entails that the capacities of human nature set the outer bounds of human obligations and attainable values.

But it is a quite different matter, and far less plausible, to say that man's nature is a *sufficient* condition of man's good, in the sense that man's good is itself derivable from man's nature and hence can be read off from that nature. Yet this is what seems to be said in Thomas Aquinas' theory of natural law. For example, he writes: "all those things to which man has a natural inclination, reason naturally apprehends as good, and consequently as having to be pursued by deed."[1] Here, human nature, as found in man's natural inclinations, seems to be set forth as the *sufficient condition* of human goods, in that the content of those goods can be derived simply by a consideration of man's nature or natural inclinations.

To understand the difficulties I am suggesting in the sufficient-condition interpretation, we must consider a second distinction, or rather pair of distinctions. These concern the meaning of the concept of nature, including human nature. This is, of course, a crucial question in understanding the naturalistic determination thesis. Now, to begin with, we must distinguish between *holistic* and *specific* meanings of "nature," between nature in the large or as an undifferentiated physicalistic whole, and nature in the sense of specific *natures*. It is the latter, pluralistic meaning that figures centrally in Aristotle's philosophy, and also to a large extent in Thomas Aquinas's. In this sense, we talk of the nature of specific kinds of things; thus, the nature of a caterpillar is different from that of a rock, and both of these are different from the nature of a human being.

In this specific sense, Aristotle, followed by Aquinas, defines nature as "the principle or cause of motion and rest in that to which it belongs primarily and essentially."[2] In other words, the nature of a kind of thing is the internal source or cause of the distinctive modes of operation of that kind of thing, and these distinctive modes of operation derive from the primary essence, the essence which is peculiar to that kind of thing. Thus the nature of a caterpillar is its internal structure and constitution that enable it to operate in the distinctive ways that it does, including, for example, its slithering movements on the ground. And similarly with the nature of humans: this too consists in the internal structure and constitution that enable humans to operate in the ways that are distinctively human.

But here we come to some crucial questions. What *is* the distinctive mode of operation of human beings? What is the internal principle or cause of motion and rest that is *distinctively* essential to man? What is it that man does by his own nature, or naturally? And is there a *single* distinctive natural mode of operation common to all humans?

To deal with these questions, we must recognize another distinction as to the meaning of "nature." It can refer either to the material cause or to the formal and final cause. Taken in the first way, as material cause, the nature of a thing consists in its primitive, inherent but undeveloped constitution that comprises only the potentialities for its distinctive mode of functioning. Taken in the second way, as formal and final cause, the nature of a thing consists in its ideal fulfillment, in the perfection of its essential characteristics. Thus the nature of an animal, taken in the material sense, consists in its flesh and bones or other physical constituents and in the operations that derive simply from these. But the nature of the same animal, taken in the formal and final sense, consists in its distinctive structure that directly enables it to operate in the ways peculiar to itself as that kind of animal—for example, as a caterpillar, a dog, or a man. What this means, among other things, is that not everything that is natural in either the holistic or the material-cause senses is natural in the sense of the formal and final cause. Thus Aristotle holds, for example, that deformities in animals are not natural. For, although they derive from the workings of nature viewed globally, and they are attributes of the underlying matter or material causes of the animals that have them, still, deformities do not pertain to the *fulfillment* of the animals' distinctive modes of functioning; rather, they *impede* that functioning because they are *imperfections* in the animal's development.[3]

Now in asking what is the distinctive mode of operation of human beings, we are obviously asking about the nature of humans in the second sense, that of formal and final cause. Hence, when the naturalistic determination thesis says that the good of man is based on or is determined by man's nature, this thesis now means that the good of man follows from, or is defined in terms of, the full development of man's distinctive mode of functioning.

4.   *The Problem of Determinacy*

Having analyzed to this extent the meaning of the naturalistic determination thesis, I now wish to raise what I regard as a crucial question about it: How *determinate* is the basis for man's good that is provided by man's nature, when we interpret this nature as formal and final cause? By a basis or principle's being "determinate," I mean that it has or entails definite contents, such that the *opposite* contents are ruled out or prohibited. So the question of determinacy may also be put in this way: Do we get a single, consistent set of characteristics for the content of man's good if we try to derive it from man's nature in the sense just indicated? Can we read man's good off from man's nature in this sense?

Now it may well be the case that the nature of man, in the sense of his distinctive mode of functioning, is a sufficient condition for determining certain components of the good of man—for example, his physical health and even parts of his mental health. Since man's distinctive mode of functioning requires certain bodily and mental attributes, we can say that the good of man, constituted by such functioning, also requires those bodily and mental attributes.

But there still remains the question of the more general good of man, including his further psychological and ethical qualities. This extension is especially important if we ask either about man's good as a whole or about his highest good. In dealing with the problem of how determinate a basis man's nature provides for ascertaining man's good understood in such a comprehensive sense, it is also very important to avoid begging the question by directly construing man's nature in a certain way. If we define man's nature by using such *value* terms as *"optimal"* functioning or *"ideal* fulfillment or development," then, of course, since the optimal and the ideal are at least *good*, the question of whether man's nature determines his good would be answered automatically. For the question would now mean: Does man's *optimal* or *ideal* condition serve to define his *good* condition? Even on this tautological construal, however, there would still be the problem of indeterminacy insofar as there are plausible divergent criteria of what is "optimal" or "ideal." Hence, to avoid begging the question, the problem of determinacy should be stated as follows: Does man's nature, understood as his *distinctive* mode of functioning, provide a determinate definition or criterion for man's good?

When the question is put in this more neutral non-question-begging way, the answer seems to me to be negative. Thus, I am here suggesting two basic criticisms of the theory of natural law that I am examining. If man's good is identified with or derived from his nature in the sense of his distinctive mode of functioning, then, first, we get very different and indeed incompatible contents for man's good, and, second, we get morally unacceptable contents for man's good. The Aristotelian-Thomistic theory of natural law seems to me to incur these two failings because the concept of human nature as distinctive mode of functioning, on which it tries to ground its precepts, is too diffuse and varied to provide a determinate set of contents for natural law. On the other hand, insofar as the concept of human nature used in the theory of natural law is not too diffuse and varied for this purpose, the theory incurs the fault of begging the question. For it then proceeds by incorporating into its concept of human nature just those valuable attributes that it wants to use in order to derive the contents of natural law.

To grasp the basis of these suggested criticisms, let us ask the following question: What are we to look for as man's nature in the sense of formal and final cause, taken as specifying what is distinctively human in man's operations? The answer that is traditionally given, of course, is *reason*. But this answer at once raises a further question: Is reason the *only* operation that is *distinctively* human and hence specifically natural to man?

Consider the following: using an opposable thumb; being capable of lying, cheating, and stealing; following out the will to power; and, if we believe Freud, laboring under an Oedipus or Electra complex. Each of those modes of operation pertains *only* to human beings; and on at least some plausible theories of human nature, they pertain to *all* human beings. This is, of course, a very old point. Let me remind you of what Plato had Glaucon say in the second book of the *Republic*: that "*by nature* all [human] beings pursue as good their own self-aggrandizement [*pleonexian*]" so that for all men "*by nature*, to commit injustice is good."[4]

Hence, if man's good is identified with his nature in the sense of his distinctive mode of functioning, then we shall have to say that man's good consists in his own self-aggrandizement or his pursuit of the will to power or his acting out the Oedipus or Electra complexes, and so forth. But these versions of man's good, and the accompanying precepts, are, of course, very different from those upheld by Aristotle and Thomas Aquinas. We therefore get results that are both indeterminate and morally unacceptable.

Now it may be objected that the non-Aristotelian and non-Thomist views I have just cited take man's nature not in the sense of formal and final cause but only in the sense of material cause; not in the sense of distinctive fulfillment but only in the sense of primitive preconditions; not in the sense of man's supreme ability but only in the sense of his subordinate abilities. But is this really so? After all, Glaucon was referring to what men naturally pursue as their *good*, and hence as the optimal *development* and *fulfillment* of their distinctively human operations and strivings. Similarly, Nietzsche regarded the will to power as the ideal manifestation of man's best and supreme mode of functioning. If we are going to look at man's nature objectively, in terms of what men actually pursue by virtue of their inherent strivings or tendencies, then how can we exclude such modes of operation?

It may also be objected that even on these views of man's nature and resulting goods, *reason* still has a certain primacy, since the protagonists of Glaucon, Nietzsche, and the rest must all use reason to attain their objectives. The most that this would prove, however, is that for such views reason is the slave of the passions or of the will, so that its role among man's distinctive modes of functioning would still be ancillary, not primary. Moreover, this objection would admit that reason can be used for evil as well as for good purposes, so that the appeal to reason as the distinctive power or function of man would still lead to indeterminate and morally unacceptable results.

The criticism I am suggesting, then, is that if we take man's nature even in the sense of formal and final cause, this does not give us a determinate set of characteristics which can serve as sufficient conditions for deriving man's good, because the distinctive operations and functionings of human beings are too diffuse and varied to yield such determinacy. Hence, we must reject the naturalistic determination thesis which holds that man's nature is a sufficient condition for determining man's good.

5. *Aristotle's Rejection of the Naturalistic Determination Thesis*

There are important respects in which this rejection of the naturalistic determination thesis was also the view of Aristotle. In the *Posterior Analytics*, the *Topics*, and especially the first book of the *Parts of Animals*, Aristotle pointed out the very great difficulties that confront philosophers or scientists who try to ascertain the characteristics that comprise the *essential nature* of each species. He showed that there is no simple way of equating this essential nature either with the ultimate matter, or with the sensible form, or with the generic functioning, or even with the specific functioning of each species.[5] These difficulties bear directly, of course, on the problem of determinacy that arises when we try to derive man's good from his essential nature.

Here, however, I want to focus on a more specific criticism that Aristotle brings against the naturalistic determination thesis. This criticism is that the thesis results from confusing the theoretical sciences with the practical sciences, and thereby also confusing man's biological and psychological *nature* with his moral or ethical *states of character*; it confuses *physis* with *hexis*.

It will be worth looking at this Aristotelian point in a little more detail for two reasons. On the one hand, Aristotle's elucidation of the point seems to me to explain in a rather profound way why the naturalistic determination thesis is untenable. But on the other hand, the explanation derives from a philosophy, that of Aristotle, which, unlike modern metaphysical doctrines, is basically congenial to, and indeed serves as the basis of, Thomas Aquinas's doctrine of natural law.

To begin with, we must note that in an important respect there is no gap between fact and value in Aristotle's concept of nature. As we have seen, Aristotle views each species or natural kind of thing as having its own specific nature, i.e. its own distinctive mode of operation or function. This nature consists in the formal cause, which is the specific mode of organization or structuring of underlying materials. By virtue of this formal cause, each species is able to operate in a way peculiar to itself, and this distinctive mode of operation is its final cause, which constitutes the *good* of each species.

According to Aristotle, however, there is a very important contrast as to the way in which this good is related to the distinctive mode of functioning in the biological and psychological spheres, on the one hand, and in the ethical sphere, on the other. This contrast derives from the sharp distinction Aristotle draws between the theoretical and the practical sciences. The most familiar way of interpreting this distinction, of course, is in terms of their *final causes*: the theoretical sciences, which include mathematics and the physical and biological sciences, are pursued for the sake of *knowing the truth*; while the practical sciences, which include ethics and politics, are pursued for the sake of *action*. But this way of interpreting the distinction is grounded by Aristotle in a more fundamental way, namely, in terms of the respective *material causes* or *subject-matters* of the theoretical and the practical sciences.

According to Aristotle, the subject-matter of the theoretical sciences consists in essences or natures that exist and have their basic characteristics quite independent of human control or contrivance. The subject-matter of the practical sciences, on the other hand, consists in human actions, characters, and institutions that depend upon and vary with the choices, deliberations, and actions of human beings. Thus in the case of the theoretical natural sciences, their objects operate from principles inherent in their own natures or essences, which is why those objects, as such, cannot be affected or varied by human action. But in the case of the practical sciences, the objects with which they deal exist and have their distinctive modes of operation from the choices or wills of agents, and this is why those objects are variable in ways that the theoretic sciences' objects are not.[6]

This difference in the subject-matter of the theoretic and the practical sciences has a direct bearing on the naturalistic determination thesis that the good of man is exhaustively determined by his nature. To see this more clearly, we must connect the points just made with some even deeper metaphysical concepts of Aristotle. He holds that the theoretic natural sciences trace a sequence of movement or development from potentiality to actuality. Each natural species of thing has certain distinctive potentialities or powers of movement or development deriving from its essence or nature, and, unless there are impediments, these potentialities are actualized in correspondingly distinctive ways, which, for biological entities, constitute their respective goods. Thus plants and animals tend to develop in their own distinctive ways, and humans also actualize their unique intellectual powers along lines inherent in their intellectual natures. These developments are their final causes or goods.

In the case of the practical sciences, on the other hand, the movement or development of their subject-matter cannot be accounted for by this simple scheme of the actualization of inherent potentialities. Rather, an *intermediate* concept must be invoked: that of *habit* or *habituation*. This is intermediate between potentiality and actuality, in the following sense. As we have seen, the subject-matter of the practical sciences consists in actions, characters, and institutions that are alterable by man. This subject-matter is indeed *based on* inherent natural powers or potentialities of humans, as its material cause or *necessary condition*. But—and this is the crucial point— these potentialities can be turned in many different directions so far as concerns the various virtues, vices, and other ethical conditions that may be developed on the basis of them. This is the *diffuseness* to which I referred before. For example, humans, like the other animals, have natural potentialities to feel various emotions or passions. But these potentialities in humans can be developed in different ways, so that some men become cowards, others reckless daredevils, still others heroes, saints, or martyrs, and others still courageous in an intermediate way. Thus Aristotle emphasizes that the development of the various states of character cannot be accounted for by *nature (physis)*, where nature is the efficient and formal cause that derives natural entities along the path from potentiality to actualization. As he puts it, if man's moral virtues were generated by nature, then, since "nothing that exists by nature can form a habit *contrary* to its nature,"[7] it would follow that there are no moral *vices*. But of course there are. Hence, moral virtues must have a different source than nature, including human nature, and this source consists in the way in which our passions or emotions are *conditioned* in one direction rather than others. Thus it is by *habituation (hexis or ethos)* that the various states of character are developed, in that there must be a certain kind of training of the emotions, which proceeds not only or mainly by intellectual instruction but rather by discipline, force of example, legislation, and other ways. Hence, the human goods, including the moral virtues, cannot be derived from or accounted for by man's nature alone, as the naturalistic determination thesis holds; this nature is not the *sufficient condition* of man's good. For since man's nature is so diffuse as to the states of character that may be developed on the basis of that nature, a formal and efficient cause other than man's nature must be invoked to elucidate which, from among those diverse possible states of character, constitutes man's *good* states of character, his *virtues*, and hence *the good* of man.

There is also another important context that supports the view that Aristotle rejected the unqualified interpretation of the naturalistic determination thesis. In the famous Book I, Chapter 7 of the *Nicomachean Ethics* where he undertakes to ascertain the highest good of man, Aristotle does not simply *identify* man's good with his distinctive function. Rather, he says that man's good "is thought to reside *in* the function" (*en tō ergō*).[8] In other words, the function of man is where we must look to locate man's good; it is the *necessary* condition of man's good; but the good is not simply *identical* with the function; the function is not the *sufficient* condition of man's good. Thus Aristotle does not say that man's good *is (esti)* his function (*to ergon*), rather he says that man's good is to be found in the *area of* his function (*en tō ergō*). It is rather with the *good* functioning of man, not with his functioning *per se*, that Aristotle identifies man's good. Thus, after repeating that "the function of man . . . is an activity or action of the soul in accordance with reason," Aristotle then adds: "the function of a *good* man is the *good and noble* performances of these activities. . ."[9] In other words, the human good is not simply the same as certain functions; rather, the human good is the *good* performance of those functions. This means that Aristotle is not a *pure* naturalist in the practical sphere; he defines the human good not simply in terms of certain facts of human operations or activities, but rather in terms of the *good* performance of those activities. He goes on to say that such good performance means that the activities are carried on "in accordance with *virtue*" i.e. with *excellence*.

In these ways, then, Aristotle himself provides the basis for rejecting the naturalistic determination thesis that is a central part of the theory of natural law I have been examining. The good of man is not simply determined by man's nature as its sufficient condition; other considerations besides man's nature must be adduced to define that good or to provide its definitive criterion. According to Aristotle, of course, these other considerations, so far as concerns efficient causes, consist in certain kinds of habituation; and so far as concerns formal causes, they consist in certain rational moderations or intermediate conditions that are imposed on the natural materials of the passions so as to constitute good or virtuous states of character. Both points, especially the latter, bear on what I have called the rationalistic thesis, so I shall now turn to consider it.

6. *The Rationalistic Thesis*

It will be recalled that the rationalistic thesis says that it is *reason* that ascertains what is man's good and how it is grounded in or determined by his nature. This thesis is upheld, although in very different ways, by both Aristotle and Thomas Aquinas.

Now it may be contended, to begin with, that this rationalistic thesis supplies the answer to the criticisms I have just brought against the naturalistic determination thesis. For, despite my earlier qualms, suppose we accept that man's nature and hence his distinctive mode of functioning consists solely or mainly in reason or rational activity. And suppose we accept also the rationalistic thesis that it is by reason that man's good is ascertained. On the basis of these two assumptions, it will have been shown, at least indirectly, that it is man's nature that determines his good. For man's nature is to use his reason, and by the use of his reason man ascertains his good. Hence, after all, the good of man is determined, at least in the sense of ascertained, by man's nature, i.e. by reason.

Now, even if we accept this argument, we must note the strong limitations it imposes on the naturalistic determination thesis. It entails that, so far as concerns efficient causes, man's good does not exist by nature in the way in which his bodily functions and his passions exist by nature. For we have had to invoke the *normative* criterion of rational ascertainment. Hence, the existence of man's good does not follow the semi-automatic sequence from potentiality to actuality; rational ascertainment must intervene in order to find out, from among the many possible upshots of the original diffuse potentialities of man's passions and actions, which of these upshots are for man's good.

We must also recognize another important limitation on the way in which we can say that, because reason is natural to man, what is ascertained or produced by reason is also natural to man. If the rationalistic thesis is interpreted in an unqualified way, it would entail that all human *artifacts* are also natural. For they are all ascertained and produced by reason, which is natural to man. We must hence confine the rationalistic thesis to areas where the materials on which reason works are themselves also directly parts of or inherent in man's nature, at least in the sense of material causes—i.e. man's passions and actions. It is when man's reason works on *these* (passions and actions) that the human goods consisting in the moral virtues are ascertained and generated. In this way, while taking account of the distinctions emphasized above between the subject-matters of the theoretic and the practical sciences, we could still make a qualified affirmation of the naturalistic determination thesis, the qualification consisting in the distinction just noted between existence by nature and the normative criterion of rational ascertainment. With such qualifications, we could still say that the goods or final causes of the practical subject-matter, which are determined by choice and deliberation, are thereby determined by man's nature, since choosing and deliberating are operations of man's practical *reason*, which is his nature.

In order to come to closer grips with this rationalistic thesis, we must note a further connection between it and the naturalistic determination thesis. Thomas Aquinas raised against himself precisely the same objection about indeterminacy that I have raised against the naturalistic determination thesis, and he answered the objection in a way that is at least very close to what I have called the rationalistic thesis. St. Thomas raises the objection in the context of the article in which he asks "Whether the law of nature is *one* among all men." He states the objection as follows: "To the law of nature pertains that to which man is inclined in accordance with his nature, as was said above. *But different men* are naturally inclined to *different things*, some men to lust for pleasures, other men to the desire for honors, and other men to other things. Therefore, there is not *one* natural law among all men."

Aquinas answers this objection of indeterminacy or plurality as follows: "just as, in man, reason rules and commands the other powers, so all the natural inclinations that belong to the other powers must be ordered according to reason. Hence it is uniformly right for all men that all their inclinations should be directed according to reason."[10]

This reply assumes what I have called the rationalistic thesis, that reason ascertains man's good as grounded in his nature. It is also pertinent to note here what Aquinas says in the body of the same article. He asserts that the derivative propositions of natural law are not known by all men, because "some men have a reason that is corrupted by passion, or by bad customs, or by a bad habituation of nature." Here again it is assumed that the good of man can be ascertained by the uncorrupted use of man's reason.

The crucial questions raised by this rationalistic thesis are these: What is meant here by "reason"; how does reason operate to ascertain the good of man; how conclusive is this use of reason; and how morally acceptable are its results?

I shall now briefly indicate how these questions are to be answered for Aristotle's and Thomas Aquinas's uses of reason.

7.   The Use of Reason in Aristotle

Let us begin with Aristotle. In his ethical doctrine, reason functions in several ways. One central way is dialectical, through analogical comparisons. He accepts as a common assumption that one must act according to right reason; and he specifies what is right reason in action by comparing men's good psychic qualities to their good bodily qualities and to good works of art. Just as in the bodily and artistic spheres the good is destroyed by *excess* and *defect*, and is produced, preserved, and augmented by a *mean* or *moderate* condition, so it is with men's good psychic qualities or virtues.[11]

In this familiar doctrine of Aristotle, it is difficult or impossible to separate the respect in which reason deals with ends from the respect in which it deals with means. The means is that which produces, preserves, and augments the good end, and the good end is characterized as the psychic condition which is analogous to recognized goods in the bodily and artistic spheres. Reason, then, is here both intuitive, grasping what is the common element in these various goods, and also calculative, grasping the means of producing, augmenting, and preserving these goods. It is on these grounds that Aristotle says, in his definition of moral virtue, that it is a mean or moderate state of character "determined by reason" (hōrismenē logō).[12]

How conclusive are the results of this use of reason? And to what extent are the results morally acceptable? Aristotle has, of course, warned us not to expect more precision in the practical sciences than their practical subject matter admits of. But he has also said that just as the physician must know the facts about the body, so the ethicist, using his reason, must know the facts about the soul.[13] This analogy, however, incurs a well-known difficulty. In the case of the body, there are trans-culturally recognized norms of physical health that specify the ends toward which the physician must work. It is these norms that constitute man's bodily good; and reason can operate to ascertain the means to this end. But there are not similar trans-culturally recognized norms or ends in the case of the moral virtues. What constituted a good man in Nazi Germany, for example, was different in important respects from the criteria upheld in the Soviet Union, and both of these were different from the criteria upheld in the western democracies, in various parts of Asia and Africa, and so forth. Now, as we have seen, Aristotle does not accept the naturalistic determination thesis in the sphere of the moral virtues. Instead, he accepted the views of his own class, time, and place about what constitutes good psychic qualities. Hence, his ethical results about the good of man, based on his use of reason, are far from conclusive. The intuitive and calculative uses of reason which Aristotle employs to arrive at the contents of the moral virtues are limited by the sociopolitical context from which he explicitly acknowledges those contents are partly derived.

While this inconclusiveness can be found in many segments of Aristotle's discussions of the moral virtues, including courage, highmindedness, and others, I wish to consider here only his discussion of the morally crucial virtue of justice. It is in this context, indeed, that he comes closest to the subsequent tradition of natural law. In the *Rhetoric* he refers to a "common law" which is "in accordance with nature,"[14] but in that work he is not so closely stating his own views. In the *Nicomachean Ethics*, however,

Aristotle introduces the concept of "natural justice"; he says that natural justice "has the same validity everywhere and does not depend on men's thinking one way or another"[15]—i.e. it does not depend on men's variable opinions (tō dokein ē mē). This negative point seems designed to exclude from natural justice the indeterminacy that would be antithetical to its having "the same validity everywhere." Aristotle goes on, however, to acknowledge that even natural justice partakes of the variability that characterizes all practical subject-matters, just as "by nature the right hand is stronger, yet it is possible that all men should come to be ambidextrous." But he concludes with the significant statement that while political constitutions, and hence arrangements about justice, vary from one place to another, "there is *only [monon]* one constitution which is everywhere *in accordance with nature* the best."[16]

Previously in the *Nicomachean Ethics* Aristotle has noted that distributive justice requires that awards of honors and other goods be made "in accordance with merit" (*kat' axian*), but he points out that different political groups have different criteria of merit: freedom according to the democrats, wealth according to the oligarchs, and virtue according to the aristocrats.[17]

Now Aristotle makes his own normative selection from these varying criteria of justice—or, as we might say, of natural law or of political morality. The criterion he upholds for what he calls the best constitution is virtue. But the content he provides for virtue has the relativity to his time, place, and class that I noted before. Thus, Aristotle interprets the role of virtue in the best constitution in such a way that not only is slavery natural for men who lack intellectual virtue in sufficient degree, but even farmers and mechanics should be slaves.[18] For the absolutely best constitution is one where the state is dedicated to the maximal development of reason, i.e. of the moral and intellectual virtues, so that only those humans should be genuine parts of the state who can participate in and contribute to such development. All other humans should be mere means to this end—i.e., slaves. And Aristotle claims that all of these discriminations are based on his use of reason in the double sense of the jointly dialectical-intuitive grasp of the end and the calculation of the most effective means to the end.

Now it is clear that other philosophers, also claiming to use reason, have come up with quite different results from those of Aristotle. Hence, so far, considerable indeterminacy is allowed by the rationalistic thesis which says that reason determines the good of man, including his political good. And it is also obvious that Aristotle's results are morally unacceptable so far as they allow slavery and the severely stratified society he endorses as the absolutely best state. Hence, Aristotle's application of the rationalistic thesis does not serve to remove the difficulties we have found in the naturalistic determination thesis.

8. *The Use of Reason in Thomas Aquinas*

Let us now turn to Thomas Aquinas. Unlike Aristotle, his use of the rationalistic thesis is inextricably linked to his acceptance of the naturalistic determination thesis. In a passage from which I have already quoted, Aquinas says that "all those things to which man has a natural inclination, reason naturally apprehends as good, and consequently as having to be pursued in deed, and their contraries as evil and having to be avoided."[19] Here we have the naturalistic determination thesis, that the things that constitute man's good are the things to which man has a natural inclination. And to this the rationalistic thesis makes no independent contribution, for it says simply that reason apprehends, as the criterion of the things that constitute man's good, that man has a natural inclination to them. Hence, the rationalistic thesis in Aquinas suffers from the same indeterminacy and other difficulties that we have seen to mark the naturalistic determination thesis.

These difficulties are not removed by the fact that Aquinas has a quite technical meaning for "natural inclination." If we were to take "natural inclination" in an ordinary sense and were to apply it to his statement that "all those things to which man has a natural inclination, reason naturally apprehends as good," this statement would entail, for example, that reason naturally apprehends as good the self-aggrandizement (*pleonexia*) which Glaucon said all men naturally desire and pursue. But in Aquinas's technical meaning for "natural inclination," the natural is that which derives from man's essential nature in the sense of his formal cause, and "inclination" signifies the impulsions or tendencies which men have in consequence of their essential nature. Indeed, "inclination" is a universal ontological concept for Aquinas; thus he says that "all things participate in some way in the eternal law, namely, insofar as from the impression of that law they have inclinations to their proper acts and ends."[20] Since the eternal law is God's plan for the universe as a whole, the concept of natural inclination has here a definite theological connotation. But since Aquinas also insists on the purely rational character of natural law, his use of the concept of natural inclination can be abstracted from the broader theological context, and it is subject to the difficulties of indeterminacy that I have raised about the interpretation of man's "proper acts and ends."

Let us now briefly consider how determinate and morally acceptable is Aquinas's use of reason to derive the precepts of natural law from man's natural inclinations. He lists three different sets of precepts of natural law, in accordance with three different parts or phases of man's nature.[21] The use of reason in the derivation of these precepts can be interpreted either as means-end calculation or as conceptual analysis. Interpreted in the former way, reason presents the precepts as indicating the means to the ends or goods determined by man's natural inclinations. Interpreted as conceptual analysis, reason analyzes the ends or goods determined by man's natural inclinations and sets forth their components. In either case, reason is viewed not only as knowing or apprehending the naturally-based goods but also as prescribing or commanding their effectuation.

The three parts or phases of man's nature that Aquinas distinguishes are, first, the nature which man has in common with all other substances; second, the nature which man has in common with all other animals; and third, the nature which is properly human, namely, reason. Thus reason figures in the precepts of natural law not only as that which ascertains and prescribes the components of man's naturally-based good, but also as itself a crucial component of that good.

Let us briefly examine how Aquinas deals with the precepts concerned with the second and third parts of man's nature. The second part, the nature which man has in common with other animals, had been the basis of some of the most cynical doctrines of natural law, including those of Callicles and other expositors of the naturalness of the pursuit of power and self-aggrandizement. How can their doctrines be avoided by a philosopher who adverts to the biological basis of man's nature? Aquinas writes as follows: "Secondly, there is in man an inclination to some more special [goods] according to the nature which he has in common with the other animals: and according to this, those things are said to pertain to natural law which nature has taught all animals, such as the commingling of male and female, and the raising of children, and the like."

The question which arises here is the following. On what ground can Aquinas *exclude* from this biologically-based segment of natural law the violence which "nature has taught all animals," including Spinoza's observation that in the sea the big fish eat the little fish,[22] and so forth? If it be said that such violence is not part of the natural inclination which men have according to that part of their natures which they share with the lower animals, it is difficult to see how this can be supported. The right answer here, of course, is that it is by the moderating influence of reason, which is peculiar to man, that such violence is to be avoided. But Aquinas, in this segment of natural law, moves directly from man's animal inclinations to the rational apprehension of the goodness of their objects, and from this to the precepts whereby those objects are to be secured. The latter step seems to proceed by means-end reasoning, with no *independent* place for a rational *moderation* of the inclinations which constitute its base.

Another reply that may be given to my objection about the violence of animals is that such violence is not good. But this reply would, of course, beg the question. For Aquinas has undertaken to establish what is good on the basis of men's natural inclinations, including their inclinations in accordance with their biological natures. Hence, he cannot reject certain natural inclinations or their objects on the ground that they are not good.

A comparable difficulty can be found in Aquinas's third part of natural law, based on man's "inclination to good in accordance with the nature of reason, which is proper to him." Aquinas gives, as examples of such inclinations, knowing the truth about God and living in society, and he says that the precepts of natural law designed to fulfill these inclinations include "that man avoid ignorance, that he not offend against those with whom he must associate, and other such . . ."

Now these are valuable precepts. But, as in the case of Aristotle, they allow for considerable indeterminacy. Even if we agree that men have a natural inclination to live in society, this inclination can be satisfied in very diverse ways; and indeed Aquinas, like Aristotle, recognizes many different kinds of political society as legitimate. At two points he briefly says that the "best" form of government is the "mixed" regime which combines features of monarchy, aristocracy, and democracy.[23] But he also says that kingship is the best of the pure forms of government,[24] and he bases most of his political discussions upon it. Aquinas does not, like Marsilius of Padua,[25] declare that the only legitimate state is one where the whole people have the final legislative and electoral authority. Moreover, Aquinas provides for the persecution and killing of heretics.[26] and like Aristotle, he upholds natural slavery.[27] He briefly qualifies the natural basis of slavery by saying that it derives not from the *jus naturale* but from the *jus gentium*; but since the latter proceeds "through human reason for the utility of human life,"[28] this is only a slight modification of the natural-law basis of slavery.

9.   The Distributive Question

It will have been noted that the issues I have just been discussing bear not only on the substantive question of what are the goods of man, but also on the distributive question of who should have those goods, and in which proportion they should be distributed among men. Both questions are parts of what I previously called the question of the contents of natural law and of the precepts that are either required or permitted by that law. And we have seen that both Aristotle and Aquinas uphold a drastically unequal distribution of the emoluments which they have specified as the goods of man.

One point must be stressed concerning the distributive question. To say that natural law has the feature of universal validity, which we noted at the outset, does not entail that natural law, as such, must embody egalitarian universalism, i.e. the idea that all humans have equal rights, at least to certain basic goods. Thus, both Aristotle and Aquinas, while upholding the universal validity of natural law and natural justice, can accommodate within it such doctrines as natural slavery and other great inequalities of freedom and well-being in political, legal, social, and economic rights.

It may also be held, however, that we must distinguish between what is *essential* to the ontological version of natural law theory in general and the particular inegalitarian *aberrations* upheld by some exponents of the theory. It may well be the case that an ontological natural law theory can be developed without such aberrations so that they are accidental to it.

While this caution must be taken most seriously, the very fact that the Aristotelian-Thomist natural law theory can include morally unacceptable doctrines like the ones I have mentioned shows at least that the theory allows a dangerous degree of indeterminacy. Moreover, it is not entirely clear that the inegalitarian doctrines are so accidental to the general theory. For, as we have seen, the theory holds that the moral good is determined by the specific nature of man, and it interprets the latter in terms of formal and final causes that constitute the maximal development of reason. It is because most humans cannot achieve this maximal development, or can achieve it only in varying degrees, that the theory readily lends itself to the inegalitarian extremes found in Aristotle's and Aquinas's versions of the theory. In the egalitarian natural law theory of John Locke, on the other hand, reason is given a much more minimal interpretation, and his theory is not an ontological one such as we have been examining here.

I conclude, then, that as Aristotle and Thomas Aquinas use the rationalistic thesis that reason ascertains man's good as grounded in his nature, their use of it does not remove the indeterminacy we found in the naturalistic determination thesis, and it involves morally unacceptable results.

10. The Authoritative Question

In the remainder of this paper, I want to deal very briefly with two points. One is the *authoritative* question, the question of the obligatoriness of natural law: How do the ontological characteristics of human nature set obligatory or prescriptive requirements for human conduct? Why ought we to act in accordance with the precepts of natural law?

The most direct answer to this question is that the precepts of natural law are for the good of human beings; indeed they are intended to contribute to human flourishing and perfection. I think this is a very cogent answer, so far as it goes. But it suffers from all the difficulties we have noted in the answers to the substantive and the distributive questions. For the precepts of natural law are not for the good of all persons equally; hence, why should the precepts be accepted by those persons who are treated disadvantageously? Moreover, the precepts interpret the human good in ways that some humans may not regard as *their* good; so again, why should these persons accept the precepts?

It may be replied that this objection confuses *justification* with *motivation*. Even if some persons are not *motivated* to accept the precepts of natural law, still these precepts have a rational *justification* in the ways sketched above, and this is a sufficient ground for accepting them.

While I accept the distinction between justification and motivation in general, it has the following difficulty when it is applied in the present context. The use of reason in the theories we have examined is tied so closely to the substantive and distributive doctrines that it cannot be severed from them. The precepts of natural law have not been shown to be *inherently* rational, such that to reject them is to incur self-contradiction. Rather, they are rational as subserving the very substantive and distributive doctrines whose lack of general cogency was seen to cast doubt on the obligatoriness of the precepts. Thus, it is difficult to see how these precepts have the universal *validity* which we listed as the first purported feature of natural law.

11. An Alternative: Human Action and the Principle of Generic Consistency

The second and final point I want to take up here, also very briefly, is my own alternative to the natural law theories I have been examining. Since I have developed this alternative in considerable detail in my book *Reason and Morality*,[29] I shall simply try to show how its position is related to the Aristotelian-Thomist theory of natural law.

One of the central differences is this: Instead of the *ontological* ground-edness of natural law, my doctrine is based on *human action*. Now while human action is indeed a pervasive feature of the general human condition, human action reflects not human nature *per se* but rather a certain development of it, since it consists in man's purposive or intentional control of his natural tendencies. Thus human nature is the *necessary* condition of human action, but not its *sufficient* condition. At the same time the concept of human action is morally neutral and hence not question-begging in the present context, because a concern with how persons are to *act* is common to all moralities, regardless of their highly divergent contents. The justification for basing moral theory on human action is, indeed, that all moral precepts deal, directly or indirectly, with how persons ought to act, especially toward one another.

My moral theory is grounded, then, in the generic features of human action and the prudential and moral judgments that logically derive from those features. The theory establishes that every agent, on pain of self-contradiction, must accept that he and all other prospective agents have equal rights to the necessary conditions of action, freedom and well-being. Thus the theory achieves and upholds the egalitarian universalism that we saw to be lacking in the Aristotelian-Thomist natural law theory.

Let me briefly sketch the main line of argument that leads to this conclusion. As I have said, the argument is based on the generic features of human action. To begin with, every agent acts for purposes he regards as good. Hence, he must regard as *necessary goods* the freedom and well-being that are the generic features and necessary conditions of his action and successful action in general. From this, it follows that every agent logically must hold or accept that he has *rights* to these conditions. For if he were to deny that he has these rights, then he would have to admit that it is permissible for other persons to remove from him the very conditions of freedom and well-being that, as an agent, he *must* have. But it is contradictory for him to hold both that he *must* have these conditions and also that he *may not* have them. Hence, on pain of self-contradiction, every agent must accept that he has rights to freedom and well-being. Moreover, every agent must further admit that all other agents also have those rights, since all other actual or prospective agents have the same general characteristics of agency on which he must ground his own right-claims.

What I am saying, then, is that every agent, simply by virtue of being an agent, must regard his freedom and well-being as necessary goods and must hold that he and all other actual or prospective agents have rights to these necessary goods. Hence, every agent, on pain of self-contradiction, must accept the following principle: Act in accord with the generic rights of your recipients as well as of yourself. The generic rights are rights to the generic features of action, freedom and well-being. I call this the Principle of Generic Consistency (*PGC*), because it combines the formal consideration of consistency with the material considerations of the generic features and rights of action.

In this way, then, the use of reason in the deductive sense of logical necessity, including conceptual analysis, when it is applied to the generic features of action, serves to establish an egalitarian-universalist moral principle, the Principle of Generic Consistency.

The *PGC* and the argument leading to it have the three characteristics of natural law theories that I listed at the beginning of this paper. The *PGC* has *ontological groundedness*, but only in the modified form I have indicated, since the generic features of action do not derive from man's nature *per se* but from a certain purposive development of it. The *PGC* also has *universal validity* because it is derived from the *generic* features of human action— features that characterize *all* actual or prospective agents. And the *PGC* is based on *reason* in the most stringent sense, because it can be denied or violated only on pain of self-contradiction; hence, it is inherently rational.

Let me now briefly indicate how the *PGC* avoids the difficulties we have found in the Aristotelian-Thomist natural law theory. First, on the *substantive* question of what are the goods or interests of human beings that moral precepts require us to secure and promote, the *PGC*'s answer is much more specific than is the one given by the ontological natural law theory. For the *PGC*'s argument is based on the necessary goods of *action*. Now human *action* is a much more specific and restrictive basis for goods than is human *nature*; moreover, there is far less of a gap between goods and *action* than there is between goods and human *nature*. For every action, because of its purposiveness, aims directly at what seems to the agent to be good. There is, of course, considerable indeterminacy in the contents of these *particular apparent* goods. But this indeterminacy is halted as soon as we come to the necessary conditions of all actions and successful action in general, namely, freedom and well-being. For these conditions have quite determinate contents precisely because of their necessary role in all action. And it is on these necessary conditions of action that the *PGC* is directly grounded, because the principle proceeds through the rationally-grounded conceptual necessities of action.

Secondly, on the *distributive* question of *whose* goods should be promoted by moral precepts, the *PGC* also gives an answer that is at once more determinate and more egalitarian than the one given by the Aristotelian-Thomist natural law theory. Unlike that theory's preferred criterion of virtue, with its aristocratic implications, the *PGC* requires that all actual or prospective agents have equal rights to freedom and well-being, because all agents have equal needs for these necessary conditions of action. Since every human is an actual, prospective, or potential agent, the *PGC* is a principle of equal human rights.

In this regard, the ontological natural-law theory suffers from not having a *formal* distributive criterion of *consistency*. It does, indeed, adduce a criterion of distributive justice, but this proceeds not by formal considerations of consistency and universalizability but by material considerations of virtues or excellences. As a result, the natural-law theory allows either for considerable indeterminacy or for a morally dangerous degree of inequality in the distribution of goods and rights.

Thirdly, on the *authoritative* question of why persons ought to obey the precepts of the moral law, why these precepts are *obligatory* for the conduct of all persons, the ontological natural-law theory's use of reason and of the rationalistic thesis, as we have seen, is not sufficiently rigorous to provide a conclusive answer. In the case of Aristotle, there are debatable analogies and contingent means-end inferences. In the case of St. Thomas, his use of reason in natural law is tied so closely to the naturalistic determination thesis that it suffers from that thesis's limitations. Thus, in neither case does the use of reason suffice to give the resulting moral precepts a *categorical* obligatoriness.

The moral precepts of the *PGC*, on the other hand, do have categorical obligatoriness, for two interrelated reasons. First, their substantive base is in the generic features and necessary goods of *action*; hence, no *agent* can fail to be obligated by the requirements set by these necessary goods. Secondly, the argument's use of reason is far more rigorous than that of Aristotle and Aquinas, for it proceeds by logical necessities. This means that, on pain of self-contradiction, no agent can deny or reject either the steps leading to the *PGC* or the principle itself and its derivative precepts. This logical necessity gives the *PGC* and its precepts a normative inescapableness and hence a categorical obligatoriness, since no agent can *rationally* reject them, in the most stringent sense of "rational."

I should like to conclude this paper as I began it by saying that I offer the above reflections to Professor Veatch as a continuation of the discussions he and I have carried on for many years. I wish to emphasize that I by no means think that the criticisms of natural law theory that I have presented here necessarily apply to any of Professor Veatch's own views. His published writings on this subject, especially in his fine books *Rational Man* and *Toward an Ontology of Morals*, although they have been characteristically thought-provoking and indeed brilliant, have been tantalizingly brief on the specific subject of natural law. One of my hopes for my present paper is that it will lead Professor Veatch to develop his own views on natural law more fully, or at least to do so for publication. I know that many other members of the philosophical community, as well as I, would strongly welcome and profit from such a development.

Notes

[1]Thomas Aquinas, *Summa Theologica*, II. I. qu. 94, a.2, Resp.

[2]Aristotle, *Physics*, II. 1. 192b22.

[3]See Aristotle, *Generation of Animals*, 1. 18. 724b32. See A. L. Peck's introduction to his translation of his work (London: Loeb Classical Library, 1943), p. xiv.

[4]Plato, *Republic*, II, 358E, 359C.

[5]See Aristotle, *Posterior Analytics*, II. 13; *Topics*, VI-VII; *Parts of Animals*, I. 1–4.

[6]See Aristotle, *Metaphysics*, E. 1. 1025B 19ff.; *Nicomachean Ethics*, VI. 3–7.

[7]Aristotle, *Nicomachean Ethics*, II. 1. 1103a20.

[8]*Nicomachean Ethics*, I. 7. 1097b27.

[9]*N.E.*, I. 7. 1098a14.

[10]*Summa Theologica*, II. I. qu. 94. a.4, obj. 3 and ad 3.

[11]Aristotle, *Nicomachean Ethics*, II, 2.

[12]*N.E.*, II. 6. 1106b36.

[13]*N.E.*, I. 13. 1102a 16ff.

[14]*Rhetoric*, I.13. 1373b 4ff.

[15]*Nicomachean Ethics*, V. 7. 1134b 28ff.

[16]*N.E.*, V. 7. 1135a4.

[17]*N.E.*, V. 3. 1131a 25ff.

[18]Aristotle, *Politics*, I.2. 1252a30; I.5. 1254b 15ff; VII. 9. 1329a26; VII. 10. 1330a 26ff.

[19]Thomas Aquinas, *Summa Theologica*, II. I. qu. 94, a.2, Resp.

[20]*S.T.*, II. I., qu. 91, a.2, Resp.

[21]*S.T.*, II. I., qu. 94, a.2.

[22]B. de Spinoza, *Tractatus Theologico-Politicus*, ch. 16, para. 2.

[23]Thomas Aquinas, *Summa Theologica*, II. I. qu. 95, a.4, Resp.; qu. 105, a. 1, Resp.

[24]*S.T.*, II. II. qu. 50, a.1, ad 2; *De Regimine Principum*, I.2.

[25]Marsilius of Padua, *Defensor Pacis*, I. xii-xiii, xv.

[26]*S.T.*, II. II. qu. 10, a.8, ad 3; qu. 11, a.3, Resp.

[27]Thomas Aquinas, *Summa contra Gentiles*, III. 81.

[28]*Summa Theologica*, II. I. qu. 94, a.5, ad 3.

[29]Alan Gewirth, *Reason and Morality* (Chicago: University of Chicago Press, 1978).

TELEOLOGY AND CONSISTENCY IN THEORIES
OF MORALITY AS NATURAL LAW

Alan Donagan
University of Chicago

This paper resembles a carnival monster: a great papier-maché head, in which controversial conclusions about the teleological foundation of the conception of morality as natural law are drawn from confessedly indirect evidence, supported by a ridiculously unimpressive body and legs in which those conclusions are tested by investigating how any theory of natural law can meet the fashionable contemporary charge that it cannot be consistent. Still, however grotesque my monster, its topic is timely.

Its first part, in which I present my unorthodox view of St. Thomas Aquinas's theory of natural law, is the one most directly and deeply indebted to the philosopher we are met to honour—Henry Veatch. As I look back on the quarter of a century in which I have known him, it is impossible to disregard the numerous topics on which he has had no choice but to try to set me right, or to escape acknowledging that on most of them, including some non-philosophical ones in comparison with which nothing philosophical matters much except the fundamentals of all thought whatever, after stubborn resistance I have tamely succumbed. It would be agreeable to my self-esteem to call to mind some matter of philosophical importance in which Henry has capitulated to a view of mine; but in confessing that I cannot, I must also confess that, on the matters on which we persist in differing, I wish I were more confident that my future will be less ignominious than my past.

I

In several recent articles Henry Veatch has powerfully upheld the position taken in *For an Ontology of Morals* (Evanston: Northwestern University Press, 1971) that any true moral theory must, like Aristotle's, be eudaimonistic, and primarily concerned with virtue rather than with law.[1] In doing so he has sided, although in his inimitably original way, with the main body of Thomist philosophers. Of course neither he or any other Thomist has ever denied that the Jewish and Stoic conception of moral law is an integral element in Christian ethics, nor has he ever pretended that Aristotle anticipated that conception—here some other Thomists have been less accurate. And finally, he has never failed to recognize that, unlike Aristotle's, St. Thomas's ethics is in part a revealed moral theology, in which neither the greatest virtues nor the highest states human beings can attain are discoverable philosophically. Moral philosophy is therefore at best only a part of ethics. And certain notions that have recently been agitated in the philosophical journals, for example that of a sanctity that is purely moral, are therefore strictly unintelligible.[2]

It has been said that the best is the enemy of the good; and I believe that in a Christianized Aristotelian eudaimonism, in which eudaimonia is identified with the intellectual good, the beatific vision gets in the way of our grasping certain essential truths about the everyday moral good, even though it is perfectly compatible with them. Aristotle has told us why.[3] The being whom to see is the supernatural end of all rational creatures, the only thing that will satisfy the longing they have by virtue of being rational, is nevertheless not a natural object of the human intellect. Our philosophical habitation is in the physical world of animate and inanimate creatures, so far as we can arrive at intelligent beliefs about it by reflecting on what is offered to us in sensation. The Christian faith, and the Jewish faith too, tell us that in the end there is no eudaimonia for human beings unless they are of good will. But, since no merely philosophical theory of eudaimonia can be true, no moral theory of good will that rests on a purely philosophical theory of eudaimonia can be well-founded; and philosophical experience supports Kant's contention that building on such a foundation is always disastrous.

Perhaps there is a hint of this in Aristotle's famous statement of what eudaimonia, the human good, is: namely, 'activity of soul in accordance with virtue, and if there are more than one virtue, in accordance with the best and most complete . . . in a complete life' (*Eth. Nic.* 1, 1098a 16–18). The familiar Kantian objection to this begins from Aristotle's ready concession that 'external goods' such as friends, riches, political power, good birth, good children and even beauty are necessary to eudaimonia, because 'it is impossible, or not easy, to do noble acts without the proper equipment' (*Eth. Nic.* ,1 1099a 31–1099b7), and from his acknowledgement that virtues (which are dispositions to actions of certain kinds) are acquired by practice (*Eth. Nic.* 11,1103b 14–25). Henry Veatch rightly reminds us that Aristotle does not contend that 'a life of virtue' is 'an absolute guarantee of happiness' but only that 'a good man, while he may not be completely happy under circumstances of adversity, is at least happier under such circumstances than the non-virtuous man would be.'[4] Kant primarily objected, however, not to this (although he might fairly have complained that it dodges the problem of adverse circumstances brought about by refusing to act viciously), but rather to Aristotle's implicit doctrine that the radically unfortunate (for example, gifted persons born to slavery in the Hellenic world of the fourth century B.C.) cannot live a humanly decent life at all because they lack the external goods necessary for the good actions that must be done if the virtues are to be acquired.

Yet is there a serious philosophical alternative to Aristotelian eudaimonism? The usual Thomist answer is that there is not; and Henry Veatch has put the reason for it in a nutshell: namely, that if we reject eudaimonism we abandon teleology for deontology, and 'the deontologist invariably tries to . . . maintain that our moral obligations may be seen ultimately to be rationally justifiable just in themselves, and without any appeal to any prior notion of the good or of an end.'[5] Although Kant's remark that it is necessary to purge moral theory of 'whatever is . . . is derived from the special predisposition of humanity, from certain feelings and propensities, and even, if this were possible, from some special bent peculiar to human reason'[6] may seem to lend force to this objection, I think it can be conclusively shown to be false. Kant explicitly grounded his deontology upon a teleology, although a teleology of a distinctive kind. The soundness of that teleology is indeed controversial, but not its existence or its fundamental character. But that is not all. After briefly setting out the nature of Kantian teleology and its function in his moral theory, I shall proceed to argue that, if we scrutinize the structure of St. Thomas's theory of natural law, we shall find that the teleology underlying it is not a Christianized version of eudaimonism, but an anticipation of the very same teleology Kant was to arrive at a little more than five hundred years later.

Let us begin with Kant. His objection to taking eudaimonia as the end by reference to which the moral law can be determined differs from, but is equivalent to, the objection I have already made to identifying it with the human good. In the actual circumstances of human life, Kant repeatedly points out, it may not be possible for a human being to attain natural this-worldly happiness, yet it must be possible for every human being to observe the moral law. And the same point can be made about every other material or psychological state of affairs the production of which can be proposed as an end: circumstances can make its production impossible, but as long as free human action (i.e., the condition of either moral or immoral action) is possible, then the observance of the moral law is possible. Hence, Kant reasoned, 'in the idea of a will that is absolutely good . . . there must be a complete abstraction from every end that has to be produced.'[7] What has concealed Kant's teleology from most recent philosophers (from Henry Sidgwick and Sir David Ross, for example) is that it is not a teleology of producible ends, and they can conceive no others.[8] However, in view of *Summa Theologiae* 1–11, 2, 8, where the question, 'Is man's happiness realized in any created good?', is answered by a quotation from St. Augustine, 'As soul is life for flesh, so God is the blessed life for man' (*De Civ. Dei,* xix, 26), it is surprising that the concept of a non-producible good should be unfamiliar to any Thomist. The end on which the moral law depends, according to Kant, 'must . . . be conceived, not as an end to be produced, but as *sebstandiger Zweck'*—[9] as an independently existing end with which we are confronted. And the primary demand that such an end makes on us, as rational beings who recognize it as an end, is that we not act against it, and hence that 'in all our willing we never rate [it] merely as a means, but always at the same time as an end.[10]

One reason why Thomists have failed to perceive the concept of a non-producible end in their own moral tradition has been their mis-understanding of the place in that tradition of what St. Thomas called 'the first principle in practical reason' that 'good is to be done and pursued, and evil avoided,' a principle which in turn depends on the identification of good as 'what all things seek': *bonum est quod omnia appetunt.* [11] On the face of it, this suggests that human action is a matter of producing—of doing things that can be done, and of pursuing things that can be obtained on one hand, and of bringing about states of affairs in which things that can be avoided are avoided. But appearances deceive. As Germain Grisez has pointed out in his brilliant paper, 'The First Principle of Practical Reason,' [12] that principle, as St. Thomas conceives it, is the principle of all rational action as such, moral or immoral; and what it says, in effect, is that rational action is by its very nature *sub ratione boni.* '[I]f "good" denoted only moral goods,' Grisez wrote, 'either wrong practical judgments could in no way issue from practical reason or the formula we are examining would not in reality express the first principle of practical reason.' [13] Since most rational action is directed to the production either of producible goods or of states of affairs in which evils are avoided, the terms in which St. Thomas expressed his principle harmlessly suggest production, but they do not imply it. As it stands, St. Thomas's principle tells us that if we believe (as Kant did) that reducing a self-existent end to a mere means is something that is rational to avoid—an evil—that will be a *rationale* for avoiding it. Whether or not it is in fact rational to avoid such conduct is something that awaits investigation.

Where, if anywhere, does St. Thomas carry out such an investigation? Not in the treatise *de Lege* in *Summa Theologiae,* although he lays the foundation for it in the article *Quae sint praecepta legis naturalis?* (1–11, 94, 2) in which he introduced the first principle of practical reason. And not in the elaborate investigations of the theological and cardinal virtues of the second part of Part II of *Summa Theologiae,* although in that part a great deal is said about the more specific precepts of morality. Rather, the cardinal exposition of natural law is where a Christian biblical scholar might have been expected to put it: in the treatise on Mosaic law (*de lege veteri*) where he takes up the Pauline theme of what fragment of the Mosaic law coincides with natural law. But that portion of *Summa Theologiae* has not hitherto attracted much attention from moral philosophers.

Let us, however, look at the foundation laid in 1–11, 94, 2. St. Thomas begins by inquiring what are the goods to which human nature as such inclines, because human reason 'naturally apprehends as good all those things to which [man] has a natural inclination.' Three kinds of thing fall into this class: first, the good which a man has in common with any substance whatever—his own existence; secondly, the goods which he has in common with all other animals—heterosexual intercourse, the rearing of offspring, and the like; and thirdly, the goods proper to him as rational—which include a due relation to God, and such relations with his fellows are as necessary for living with them in a civil society.

Taken in conjunction with the first principle of practical reason, this list of human goods (and a corresponding list of evils) provides us with a series of moral precepts which are not only self-evident (*per se nota*) but are recognized in practice by all civilized human beings. '[W]ith regard to common principles of reason, whether speculative or practical, truth and rectitude are the same for all, and are equally known.' However, St. Thomas recognized that, even with regard to common principles, a given person's knowledge may be depraved 'by passion, or by bad custom or native proclivity (*ex mala habitudine naturae*)'. His example of the third of these was the Germans of Julius Caesar's time, who saw nothing wrong in robbery.[14]

The fundamental common principles (*principia communissima*) of the natural law cannot, according to St. Thomas, be eradicted from the human heart.[15] Unless there is some depraving force they will assert themselves. But it is quite otherwise with the secondary, more specific precepts that are derived from them. They are not written in every heart. About them, honest errors are made, and in consequence honest differences of opinion are found.

Well, what are the *principia communissima* of natural law? While this is not explicitly answered in 1–11, 94, it is in *de lege veteri*, the authority appealed to being that of Jesus commenting on Moses, not that of Aristotle. The *prima et communia praecepta* of the Mosaic law, *all* the precepts of which are declared in some sense to belong to natural law,[16] are identified as *Thou shalt love the Lord thy God* and *Thou shalt love thy neighbour;* and it is further laid down that all the precepts of the Mosaic decalogue are related to these as conclusions to *principia communia.'*[17]

What is loving one's neighbour in the sense in which the second of these two precepts commands it? I was long persuaded by what amounted to a scholarly consensus that it would have been anachronistic to interpret it in a sense anticipating Kant. However, the only non-Kantian interpretation proposed is that loving your neighbour is promoting in him the goods necessary to human flourishing, and never acting against them.[18] And there are two reasons against it. First, it is difficult to find a sound argument for it on the basis of St. Thomas's first principle of practical reason. While it follows from that principle that action in pursuit of any good necessary to human flourishing is rational in the sense of being *sub specie boni,* it in no way follows that acting against those goods is always wrong (for example, when full human flourishing is impossible, and one is confronted with a choice of evils). And secondly, it implausibly entails that the scriptural analogy between loving God and loving your neighbour is remote. Loving God presumably means treating him as the independently existing end of all your actions. You can, indeed, try to make the world better for God's sake; but you simply make a fool of yourself if you imagine that if you succeed you will make God's situation better. And that the analogy between loving God and loving your neighbour is not remote follows from the intimate relation between them authoritatively (for Christians, at least) laid down in St. John's first epistle (4:20): 'he that loveth not his brother whom he hath seen, how can he love God whom he hath not seen?' His neighbour is the image of the unseen God, and the love he reasonably elicits is an image of the love God reasonably elicits. If the love God reasonably elicits is the will to treat him as the ultimate independently existing end of any action whatever, it is hard not to infer that the love your neighbour reasonably elicits is the will to treat him as an independently existing end in any action that concerns him.

That St. Thomas's theory of natural law in certain respects anticipates Kant's metaphysics of morals is confirmed by comparing what both found to say about motivation. Both recognized the existence of a state of a rational being in which it cannot will evil: Kant called that state holiness, and described a holy will as one that necessarily wills according to reason.[19] The only actual holy will he mentions is divine: the will of 'the Holy One of the gospel.'[20] St. Thomas indeed went further. The divine will is holy in Kant's sense, but, by divine grace, every human being can also attain a holy will through the beatific vision, which will ultimately be granted to all who avail themselves of the means of grace.

St. Thomas and Kant were agreed that it is possible for human beings to will either according to what they perceive to be requirements of reason or according to the promptings of other inclinations (desires, passions, even hatred of the human condition itself). The objects of such requirements and inclinations *all* confront us *sub ratione boni*. To gratify a natural desire, to avoid or reduce the power of what we perceive as harmful, and to rise above the limitations of our present condition are all in themselves rational things to attempt, but not when they have such further characteristics as preventing others from gratifying desires for elementary necessities, or avoiding or harming what will otherwise prevent us from doing wrong.

If I am not mistaken, St. Thomas also agreed with Kant that reason unconditionally requires that we treat God and the rational creatures that are his images as what Kant called independently existing ends (*selbständige Zwecke*). Kant's remark that 'morality and humanity, inasmuch as it is capable of morality, alone have dignity'—where dignity is identified with intrinsic worth—seems to make essentially the same point as St. Thomas's 'because to subsist in rational nature is of great dignity, every individual of rational nature is called a "person." '[21] To reject this is to deny the ground on which the natural desires of rational creatures are held to have a different and more fundamental significance for practical reason than those of irrational animals. The story is told that Voltaire, when a thief who had picked his pocket justified himself by saying 'A man must live,' replied, 'I don't see the necessity.' St. Thomas and Kant were at one that Voltaire was wrong: confronted with a person whose life can be preserved only by consuming some superfluous property of yours, his dignity as a person—an individual of rational nature—imposes a categorical obligation on you to relieve him. But only as an independently existing end. It would not be a categorical obligation to provide for his needs if you could unless he were such an end.

Finally, Kant's observation that *Achtung,* the consciousness of an immediate determination of the will by an imperative of reason, 'is properly the representation of a worth that abashes my self-love (*meiner Selbstliebe Abbruch tut),*'[22] seems to me to be an enlightening (although of course unwitting) gloss upon a much discussed passage in St. Thomas.[23] There, in the course of showing that human beings first sin mortally when, beginning to have the use of reason, they discern a due (*debitum*) end according to their capacity but fail to direct their lives according to it, St. Thomas remarked, 'At that time the first bit of thinking it falls to a man to do is to deliberate about his own self.'[24] T. C. O'Brien here rightly warns that 'There is no need . . . to posit the disjunction; either God is somehow chosen as final end, or self is.'[25] The point appears rather to be that, deliberating on one's own self, one both discerns one's own dignity as an individual of rational nature, and at the same time recognizes that, if an individual of rational nature is a *finis debitus,* then there are rational constraints on what one may do to gratify one's desires and passions.

II

St. Thomas, I have argued, understood the second of his *prima et communia praecepta* of natural law, 'Thou shalt love thy neighbour,' as Kant did: namely, as equivalent to 'Thou shalt treat all rational beings (for every rational being you encounter is, in the relevant sense, your neighbour) always as independently existing ends.' The ground I have so far given has been that only so understood can that *praeceptum* generate the specific precepts of the Mosaic decalogue as a common principle generates a specific conclusion. If it is understood simply as 'Thou shalt promote the various goods necessary to thy neighbour's flourishing' it will not absolutely exclude (say) murder and bearing false witness, as the decalogue does; for there may be situations in which the consequence of a murder may be that more lives will be saved than lost, and of an act of perjury that more truth will become known than otherwise would have. The connection of the *prima praecepta* with the specific precepts of the decalogue in turn shows that in that part of St. Thomas's first principle of practical reason which prescribes that good is to be done and pursued, 'good' cannot be confined to what is necessary for human flourishing (*utile*), but must also include what practical reason demands of us out of respect for the dignity of rational beings (*honestum*). And I have also found passages in St. Thomas's treatment of practical reason in relation to morality that appear to bear out this interpretation.

This argument is indirect, but unavoidably so; for St. Thomas has not provided us with the only evidence that would enable us directly to confirm or disconfirm it: namely, an explicit derivation of the *prima et communia praecepta* of the Mosaic law in accordance with the first principle of practical reason.

St. Thomas's omission to provide such an explicit derivation has tempted some interpreters to the fatal course of reconstructing what his conception of natural law was from his general discussion of it alone, without considering what he wrote about the Mosaic law at all. The gist of what is written about the secondary precepts of natural law in the general discussion is simply that from the principle that it is true and right that we act according to reason (which I take to be equivalent to the first principle of practical reason itself) it follows as a proper conclusion that goods held in trust are to be restored; but 'the principle is insufficient (*deficere invenitur*) the more one descends to particulars', as is shown by the fact that the conclusion drawn from it, although generally true, admits of exceptions—as when what is held in trust would, if restored, be used against one's country.[26] On this, James F. Ross has commented that to St. Thomas 'The common principles of natural law are not, therefore, universally general truths applied by universal in-stantiation to individual cases but are *policies* which must be realized where possible (wherever reason permits) and must *not* be encrusted with qual-ifications.[27]

When we turn to the treatise *de lege veteri,* however, we find that the precept that goods held in trust are to be restored is presented as a conclusion from the precept of the decalogue, 'Thou shalt not steal';[28] that every precept of the decalogue is described as 'knowable straight off from the first common principles with a little thought';[29] and that the precepts of the decalogue are *omnino indispensabilia* as embodying the divine intention, from which it follows that they allow of no exceptions.[30] The precepts of the decalogue are therefore, contrary to Ross, 'universally general truths'. However, they are insufficient for deciding many particular cases, because the more we descend to particulars, the more questions arise as to whether those particulars do or do not fall under the general precept. To determine whether they do or do not, additional premises are needed, which are not implicit in the general precepts themselves. In the case in question, whether the goods of enemies of one's country that have been left in trust are to be restored, some premise is required which defines what an enemy's property rights are. The precept, 'Thou shalt not steal' is rightly said to 'fail' (*deficere*) to settle this, but such failure is in no sense a defect.

The precepts of the decalogue, therefore, are applied to particular cases, not by 'universal instantiation', but by the mediation of additional premises which lay down whether or not certain more specific cases fall under their terms. What St. Thomas calls 'secondary precepts' of the natural law are not written in every heart because these mediating premises are not. And that is why the secondary precepts we use are often only approximate, and admit of exceptions. However, it does not follow that moral theorists should not try to discover mediating premises by means of which exception-free secondary precepts can be deduced. Indeed, when St. Thomas spoke of precepts not expressly included in the decalogue 'which are found by the diligent inquiry of wise men to be in accordance with reason', and which are 'contained in [the precepts of the decalogue] as conclusions from principles',[31] was it not presupposed that the more diligent the inquiry, the fewer would be the exceptions to those secondary principles?

This outline of the structure of natural law as St. Thomas conceived it may well seem to you to be out of date in scholarship and moral style alike. In refusing to abandon part at least of its moral style, namely that according to which any adequate theory of right reason must certify as 'imperatives' such 'derivative obligations' as 'not to murder, not to steal, not to commit adultery, not to bear false witness etc.' I am content with the support of Henry Veatch.[32] And, despite the readiness of respected scholars to abandon natural law as inessential to St. Thomas's moral theory, their own scholarly integrity must in the end forbid it.

The following remarks, by Vernon J. Bourke, a scholar and philosopher to whom all students of St. Thomas are indebted, are representative of this readiness.

> While the notion of natural law does play a part in Aquinas's teaching on morality, it does not seem to me to be a central role. Indeed there are many reasons why it might be better, today, to stop talking about natural moral law, both in the context of Thomistic philosophy and in the broader context of contemporary ethics. What I now advocate is the position that right reason (*recta ratio*) is the key theme in the ethics of Aquinas.[33]

Whether the role of the notion of natural law in St. Thomas's ethics is 'central' or not is a vague and unprofitable question. If one wants to determine whether or not St. Thomas was 'a natural law ethicist' it seems to me that there are two questions that matter: (1) Did he think that certain kinds of action are permissible or impermissible by their very nature? and (2) If so, did he think that their permissibility or impermissibility is to be ascertained by procedures implicit in his discussion of natural law? To these questions there are straightforward answers. That he did think that certain kinds of action are permissible or impermissible by their very nature is obvious: the *Secunda Secundae* is full of questions of the form '*Utrum X sit peccatum?*' '*Utrum Y sit licita?*' where only the natures of X and Y are in question. And in answering these questions, when he is invoking neither revealed divine commandments nor human positive law, the procedures he follows are those implicit in his discussion of natural law. That is why students have always gone to the treatment of such questions in the *Secunda Secundae* for examples of arguments on points of natural law. It does not matter that in these treatments the phrase 'natural law' is seldom used. As Senator Ervin observed in the Watergate hearings: If you draw a good picture of a horse, you needn't write 'horse' underneath it.

None of this contradicts Bourke's assertion that 'right reason (*recta ratio*) is the key theme in the ethics of Aquinas.' But the question is whether an ethics of right reason involves a morality of natural law—a strict deontology. St. Thomas, I contend, unmistakably held that it does.[34]

III

Besides being corroborated or weakened by the indirect evidence of how its secondary precepts are derived from its primary common principles, and of how those principles are established in accordance with the first principle of practical reason, theses about the nature of the teleological foundation of St. Thomas's theory of natural law may also be tested by comparing what they imply about why its secondary precepts cannot be inconsistent with one another with what St. Thomas found to say about implicit objections that they are.

In carrying out this test, the only objections examined will be implicit, because St. Thomas had a far clearer grasp of what a consistent set of secondary precepts of natural law would be than any of his contemporaries known to me. According to any natural law theory of morality, moral precepts are commands of practical reason. And St. Thomas clearly perceived that no set of precepts can be a set of commands of practical reason unless (1) any conjunction of what is commanded by members of the set is also commanded by practical reason, and (2) whatever is commanded by practical reason can be carried out. It follow that precepts of natural law cannot come into conflict *simpliciter*; for they could do so only if situations were possible in which obeying some of them would make it impossible to obey others, that is, only if there were a conjunction of what is commanded by precepts of natural law that cannot be carried out, even though, by (1) and (2), all such conjunctions are commanded, and whatever is commanded can be carried out.[35]

St. Thomas, however, saw clearly what some moral theologians did not, that not all moral conflict is moral conflict *simpliciter*. It is perfectly possible for human beings to find themselves in situations in which they cannot obey some precepts of the natural law without disobeying others, not because the natural law is inconsistent or inapplicable to the actual human situation, but because they have already violated it.

St. Thomas described a person in such a situation as '*perplexus secundum quid*': he is, in the idiom of today, in a moral conflict, not simply speaking, but by reason of a special circumstance for which he is to blame. Logically, as St. Thomas saw, to conclude that a set of precepts is inconsistent because it can give rise to moral conflict *secondum quid* would be as absurd as to conclude that a set of axioms is inconsistent because it generates a contradictory when combined with the contradictory of a theorem that follows from it. A set of precepts is consistent if anybody to whom it applies can obey it in all situations to which it applies; but there is no assurance that disobeying one of its members will not entangle him in situations in which he cannot avoid disobeying others. 'It is not *inconveniens*,' St. Thomas drily observed, 'that a person in mortal sin be perplexed.'[36]

Although distinguishing moral conflict *simpliciter* from moral conflict *secundum quid* disposes of unsophisticated accusations of inconsistency brought against the natural law as traditionally understood by numerous theologians in the Dark Ages [37] and numerous academic philosophers today, it cannot dispose of objections that the natural law gives rise to moral conflict *simpliciter*. Such charges are made, and they are acknowledged to be serious.

Among contemporary Thomists, the objection of this sort that is most discussed is that natural law, as traditionally conceived, is inconsistent in forbidding murder, but permitting killing in self-defense, killing enemy combatants in a just war, and capital punishment. The alleged contradiction is not direct (murder is defined as killing the materially innocent, and an assailant threatening life or limb is not materially innocent), but arises from the usual non-Kantian interpretation of the ground on which murder is held to be contrary to natural law, namely, that life itself is a good intrinsic to persons—rational individuals—and so has a dignity in virtue of which it should be respected and protected. On the same ground one's own life is to be defended against murderous attack. But a moral conflict *simpliciter* appears to follow if one can only save one's life by defensive measures that will cause the assailant's death. For, on one hand, one is forbidden to kill one's murderous assailant; and on the other hand, one is forbidden not to defend oneself—and the only effective defense is to kill one's assailant.[38]

St. Thomas's solution of the casuistical problem, 'Whether it is licit to kill another in defending oneself?' is as controversial as it is celebrated.

> Nothing forbids there being two effects of one act, of which only one is in intention, and the other is beyond intention. However, moral acts receive [their] species according to what is intended, and not, be it added, from what is beyond intention, which is *per accidens* as appears from things said above. Therefore, from the act of somebody defending himself two effects follow: one indeed is the preservation of his own life, but the other is the killing of the attacker. It is because of this, that the preservation of his own life is intended, that an act of this kind does not have the character of an illicit one, since it is natural to anybody that he preserve himself in being as far as he can. Yet any act proceeding from a good intention can be rendered illicit if it is not proportioned to its end. And so if anybody to defend his own life uses more violence than is needed, it will be a wrong. If indeed it repels violence with moderation, a defense will be licit; for according to the laws [the *Decretals of Gregory IX*] *it is licit to repel force by force with the moderation of a blameless guardianship* . . .

> But because it is not licit to kill a man except by public authority for the common good, as is clear from things said above [11–11, 64,3] it is illicit that man intend to kill man in order to defend himself, with the exception of one who has public authority, who intending to kill a man in self-defense refers it to the public good, as appears in a soldier fighting against enemies, and in an officer of the court fighting against robbers.[39]

That this passage should commonly be received as showing that St. Thomas took it to be always wrong directly to attack human life is extraordinary, and only a little less so that it should be interpreted as 'an enunciation of the principle of the double effect as we understand it today, and as an application of that principle to the lawfulness of killing in self-defense.'[40]

What it does show, plainly and unmistakably, is that St. Thomas held that human life may licitly be *intentionally* taken by those with public authority acting for the common good. Since homicide in the line of duty by soldiers and officers of the court is perfectly licit when intentional, St. Thomas would have held it to be an error to seek to justify it only when *praeter intentionem*. The long and honourable line of philosophers who, like Grisez, have taken St. Thomas to maintain 'the inviolable dignity of human life as a natural law principle,' and have proceeded to treat his theory of justifiable killing by private persons in self-defense as fundamental to whatever is sound in his entire theory of justifiable homicide, have stood his theory on its head.[41] The foundation of St. Thomas's theory of justifiable homicide is his theory that public authority is justified in killing for the common good; his theory of justifiable killing in self-defense, far from being its foundation, has to do with a special exception to the prohibition of private persons from usurping a function of public authority. His reason for holding that private persons may not intentionally kill even in self-defense is set out in 11–11, 64, 3:

> to kill a wrongdoer is licit inasmuch as it is ordered to the safety (*salutem*) of the whole community, and so it pertains to him alone to whom is committed the charge of keeping the community safe . . . But charge over the common good has been committed to rulers holding public authority, and so to them alone is it licit to kill wrongdoers, but not to private persons.

In 11–11, 64, 7 St. Thomas did no more than point out that, in saving his own life, which he is 'more bound (*plus tenetur*)' to do than to save another's a private person may *praeter intentionem* do what an officer of the court would do intentionally in the course of duty, without usurping a function reserved to public authority. Not only is it not true that those having public authority are permitted to kill grave wrongdoers *praeter intentionem* because private persons are, it is on the contrary true that private persons would not be permitted to do it *praeter intentionem* if those having public authority did not have the duty to do it *in intentionem*.

At a symposium in honour of Henry Veatch it is unnecessary to dwell on the point that the common good, as St. Thomas conceived it, is not the good of the many as opposed to that of the few, but, since human beings are social, a good willed in every act of will for a particular good.[41] That they live in a peaceable and law-abiding society is a good robbers and murderers will, and of which they do, take advantage. 'Hence,' St. Thomas reasoned, 'if any man is dangerous to the community, and corruptive of it because of some sin, he is killed *laudabiliter et salubriter,* so that the common good may be preserved.'[42]

Grisez has found this unsatisfactory for three reasons: that, except for the muddle that only wrongdoers endanger the common good, it would justify killing the innocent; that killing wrongdoers is not necessary to preserve the common good; and that it depends on the false Aristotelian doctrine that the good of individuals is less 'godlike' than the good of the social whole of which they are parts.[43] Now, while I concede that St. Thomas's use of the Aristotelian notion that individuals are related to their communities as parts to wholes prevented him from expressing his point exactly, it seems to me that his recognition that the good of the community to which an individual belongs matters morally only to the extent that it is genuinely common to its members invalidates in advance morally objectionable conclusions drawn by preferring social goods that are not common to the good of individuals. And I contend that the point St. Thomas was trying to express is that an individual who wills gravely to wrong his fellows, by attacking the human dignity that is the independently existing end of all rational human activity, attacks a fundamental good common to himself and them, and so makes a good life for himself as well as for them impossible.

But is it not evil in itself *(malum secundum se)* to kill any human being whatever, even one who acts in this way? Not at all, St. Thomas answered:

> By sinning a man turns his back on the order of reason; and so falls away from human dignity, inasmuch as he is indeed naturally free and existing for himself, and in a certain way falls into the servile condition of the beasts, so that from himself he is rather ordered to what is for the good of others . . . And so although to kill a man remaining in his natural dignity is evil in itself, yet to kill a sinner can be good. Just as to kill a beast. For an evil man is worse than a beast, and does more harm, as Aristotle says.[44]

Although this is inexactly expressed—Grisez rightly points out that self-degradation beginning 'even if it is conceived as a kind of existential suicide, cannot alter one's human nature or detract from one's inherent dignity as a human person'—[45] it can reasonably be interpreted as anticipating something like the following:

> By sinning a man turns his back on the order of reason, which requires him to respect himself and all other rational beings as ends in themselves. In so doing he degrades himself to a condition like that of the beasts, who act in natural instinct, without conceiving either ends in themselves or means. If in this degraded state he hinders other rational beings from following the order of reason, they may forcibly hinder his doing so, without infringing his dignity as a rational being. And, since the order of reason ordains that civil societies be estab-

lished, so that laws enabling all to follow the order of reason may be
made and upheld, the public authorities in such societies may suppress
actions violating the law by lethal force if necessary, and may impose
punishments for lawbreaking proportionate to the offence, without
infringing the dignity of lawbreakers as rational beings. To put a
murderer to death by due process of law does not infringe his dignity
as a rational being, provided his death is 'kept entirely free of any
maltreatment that would make an abomination of the humanity residing in the person suffering it.'[46]

That this is the substance of what underlies St. Thomas's treatment of
homicide in *Summa Theologiae* 11–11,64 seems to be an inescapable
conclusion when articles 2, 3, and 7 are read in order. It follows that the first
principle of natural law, *Thou shalt love thy neighbour,* cannot be construed
as implying *Thou shalt treat the goods essential to thy neighbour's well-
being, for example life, as inviolable.* St. Thomas, like Kant, held that what
follows from the principle about the inviolability of the goods necessary to
your neighbour's well-being is that they are inviolable if he 'remains in his
dignity,' that is, if he does what his dignity requires, but not otherwise.

The preceding investigation whether my thesis that the teleology underlying St. Thomas's theory of natural law is substantially identical with the
Kantian one can be tested by examining how St. Thomas treated charges that
its precepts are inconsistent, while complex in detail, has been simple in
design. It began with his own clarification of what it would be for the
precepts of a system of natural law to be inconsistent: briefly, they would be
so if and only if situations to which they would apply should be possible in
which they would be in conflict *simpliciter*—conflict *secundum quid* would
not count. It then turned to his treatment of homicide, because it contains the
article (11–11, 64, 7) that is widely believed to show both that he held a
certain good necessary to human well-being, namely life, to be an inviolable
end, and also that he resolved the apparent conflict between the duty not to
take life and the permissibility of defending one's own life at the cost of
taking another's by anticipating the modern theory of the double effect.
According to that theory, while it is illicit intentionally to take a human life,
it is licit to take one *praeter intentionem* if the loss of that life is an
unintended effect of any course of action by which you can preserve your
own life. There is no conflict *simpliciter*, because acts are assigned to
species according to their intentions; hence the species of the acts performed
in such cases is *preserving one's own life*, and not not *taking the life of
another*.

In developing a consistent natural law theory of homicide along these
lines, Grisez has persuasively argued that public authority acting for the
common good cannot licitly take human life except on a ground analogous to
that on which private persons can: namely, community self-defense. And
even then it may not intentionally do so.

As in self-defense, a soldier on a battlefield can shoot straight at an enemy soldier, intending to lessen the enemy force by one gun, while not intending to kill. Similarly a military camp or a factory producing military goods can be bombed. But an enemy hospital or non-military area cannot be justly attacked. The enemy soldier may not be killed if he can be inactivated otherwise, or if he has surrendered.[47]

Despite my difficulties with the theory of the double effect,[48] I find this theory of natural law intellectually attractive, especially in its conclusions about the conditions under which it is licit to engage in war at all, and about the means by which it is licit to wage it.

The question before us, however, is not what is the best theory of natural law, but what was St. Thomas's. Grisez takes the theory of the double effect developed from 11–11, 64, 7 both to render consistent the interpretation of the natural law principle *Thou shalt love thy neighbour* as laying it down that the various goods necessary to human well-being are to be promoted wherever possible and never acted against, and also to be indirect evidence that at some deep level of his thought St. Thomas himself endorsed that interpretation. Hence he leaves himself no choice but to dismiss St. Thomas's explicit recognition of the permissibility of intentional killing by public authority for the common good as an irrational accommodation to contemporary prejudice.[49]

On the other hand, if instead of assuming that St. Thomas's natural-law framework took human life as such to be an inviolable good, we infer what his framework was from how he defended the consistency of the precepts to which it gives rise, we shall not take it to be an aberration that, like Kant five hundred years later, he not only expressly affirmed that public authority has the duty intentionally to take human life when only so can internal law and order and external peace and justice be protected, but also defended the consistency of doing so on the ground that human life as such is not inviolable. True, his reason for declaring that to kill a sinner can be good is defective because of its uncritical reliance on the Aristotelian conception of civil society as a whole of which human beings are parts. However, if this defect is corrected on Kantian lines, his treatment of homicide can be accepted as a philosophically coherent whole, superior in a number of specific details to Kant's.[50] By contrast the entire structure of 11–11, 64 is in conflict with the 'framework' on which Grisez maintains that it is erected.[51]

Notes

[1]Especially "Telos and Teleology in Aristotelian Ethics," in Dominic J. O'Meara, ed., *Studies in Aristotle* (Washington, D.C.: Catholic University of America Press, 1981); and "Variations, Good and Bad, on the Theme of Right Reason in Ethics," *The Monist* 66 *(1983): 51–70.*

[2]Cf. Susan Wolf, "Moral Saints," *Journal of Philosophy* 79 (1982): 419–39.

[3]Aristotle, *Physics* 1, 184a10–21.

[4]Henry B. Veatch, *Rational Man: A Modern Interpretation of Aristotelian Ethics* (Bloomington: Indiana University Press, 1962), p. 179, commenting on Aristotle, *Eth. Nic.* 1, 1100b23–1101a8.

[5]*Monist* 66 (1983): 68.

[6]Immanuel Kant, *Grundlegung zur Metaphysik der Sitten* (2nd edn., Riga, 1786), pp. 59:60 (Ak. edn. p. 437). Here and hereafter I have drawn upon the translations of L. W. Beck, James Ellington, and H. J. Paton.

[7]*Ibid*, p. 82 (Ak. edn. p. 437).

[8]For classical examples, see Henry Sidgwick, *The Methods of Ethics* (7th edn., London: Macmillan, 1907), p. 390; Sir David Ross, *Kant's Ethical Theory: a Commentary on the Grundlegung zur Metaphysik der Sitten* (Oxford: Clarendon Press, 1954), p. 51. Henry Veatch has described as 'sharp and decisive' a remark in R. P. Wolff *The Autonomy of Reason: A Commentary on Kant's Groundwork of the Metaphysics of Morals* (New York: Harper 1973), p. 131:'[A] categorical imperative cannot "directly command a certain conduct without making its condition some purpose to be reached by it," for that is the same thing as saying that it commands an agent to engage in purposive action with no purpose' (quoted by Henry Veatch in *Monist* 66 (1983): 55). It is perfectly understandable that Kant's critics should take the word of professedly sympathetic commentators *after* Paton and Beck that Kant drew no distinction between engaging in purposive action and engaging in action to produce some end believed to be producible, but it is inexcusable that such commentators should give their word that he drew none. For the necessary corrections for Wolff see Marcus G. Singer, 'Reconstructing the *Groundwork*,' *Ethics* 93 (1982–3); 566–78. Singer appropriately concludes: 'To be sure, the *Groundwork* needs interpretation. But it is not in need of this sort of *transformation*, in which it is divorced from the whole of Kant's developing and developed philosophy' (p. 578).

[9]Kant, *Grundlegung*, p. 82 (Ak. edn., p. 437).

[10]*Ibid.*

[11]'*Bonum est faciendum et prosequendum, et malum vitandum*' *(Summa Theologiae, I-II, 94,2. (I have used the Latin-English edition published in 61 volumes by Blackfriars, London, between 1964 and 1981.)*

[12]First published in *Natural Law Forum* 10 (1965): 168–96. Its substance is readily accessible in Anthony Kenny (ed.) *Aquinas: a Collection of Critical Essays* (Notre Dame: University of Notre Dame Press, 1976), pp. 340–82.

[13]Grisez, in Kenny (ed.) *Aquinas,* p. 368.

[14]*Summa Theologiae* I-II, 94, 4. Two articles later, this is inconsistently referred to as a *praeceptum secundarium*.

[15]*Ibid.,* I-II, 94.6.

[16]*Ibid.,* I-II, 100, 1.

[17]*Ibid.,* I-II, 100, 3 *ad* 1.

[18]Germain Grisez, "Toward a Consistent Natural Law Ethics of Killing," in *American Journal of Jurisprudence* 15 (1970): 65–66, 90–96 splendidly exemplifies this approach, with respect to the good of human life itself. Henry Veatch appears to take a similar line in *Monist* 66 (1983): 67–68.

[19]Kant, *Grundlegung*, pp. 39, 86 (Ak. edn., pp. 414, 439).

[20]Kant, *Grundlegung*, p. 29 (Ak., edn., p. 408).

[21]Compare Kant, *Grundlegung*, p.77 (Ak. edn. p. 435) with St. Thomas, *Summa Theologiae*, 1, 29, 3 ad 2. (The latter should be taken together with *'persona significat id quod est perfectissimum in tota natura'* (I-II, 29, 3 c.).

[22]Kant, *Grundlegung*, p. 16n (Ak. edn. p. 401 *n.* 2).

[23]St. Thomas, *Summa Theologiae* I-II, 89, 6c. In Appendix IV to Vol. 27 of the Blackfriars editions, its editor, T. C. O'Brien, comments on it at length (pp. 125–33).

[24]*'sed primum quod tunc homini cogitandum occurrit est deliberare de se ipso'* (*Summa Theologiae*, I–II, 89, 6 c).

[25]In the Appendix cited in note 23, p. 128.

[26]St. Thomas, *Summa Theologiae* I-II, 94, 4 c.

[27]James F. Ross, "Justice is Reasonableness: Aquinas on Human Law and Morality." *Monist* 58 (1974): 90.

[28]St. Thomas, *Summa Theologiae*, I-II, 100, 4 *ad* 2.

[29]*Ibid.,* I-II, 100, 3 c.

[30]*Ibid.,* I-II, 100, 8 c.

[31]*Ibid.,* I-II, 100, 4 c.

[32]Veatch, *Monist* 66 (1983): 65–66.

[33]Vernon J. Bourke, "Is Thomas Aquinas a Natural Law Ethicist?", *The Monist* 58 (1974): 52.

[34]In both Sections I and II I have made use of hitherto unpublished material presented in a paper "Morality and Natural Law in the Philosophy of St. Thomas Aquinas," read at a symposium devoted to St. Thomas's ethical theory on October 11, 1974, at Aquinas College, Grand Rapids, Michigan as part of a celebration of St. Thomas's 700th anniversary.

[35]My formulation of the presuppositions (1) and (2), by reference to which natural law theorists hold any putative set of moral precepts that generates moral conflict *simpliciter* to be inconsistent, derives from an analysis by Bernard Williams, in a paper "Ethical Consistencey" in *Problems of the Self* (Cambridge: Cambridge University Press, 1973), pp. 166–86, esp. 179–80.

[36]St. Thomas distinguishes perplexity *simpliciter* from perplexity *secundum quid* in several places: *Summa Theologiae* I-II, 19 6 *ad* 3; II-II, 62, 2 *obj.* 2; III, 64, 6 *ad* 3; and *Quaest. Disp. de Veritate*, 17, 4 *ad* 8. G. H. von Wright, in *An Essay on Deontic Logic* (Amsterdam: North Holland Publishing Co., 1968), p. 81*n.* 1, has pointed out (with acknowledgements to P. T. Geach) the importance of St. Thomas's distinction, but he appears not to have been heeded.

[37]E.g. St. Gregory the Great, *Moralium Libri sive Expositio in Librum B. Iob*, xxxii, 20 (in Migne, *Patrologia Latina*, vol. 76, pp. 657–58). St. Gregory, holding a command theory of morality, and so not accepting the presuppositions of a natural law theory, simply argued that the moral law gives rise to moral conflicts. But his argument can be used against the theory that morality is natural law, and St. Thomas's reply suggests that it was.

[38]While I have constructed a possible theoretical position, and do not attribute it to anybody, I have kept in mind Germain Grisez's subtle and powerful argument in "Toward a Consistent Natural-Law Ethics of Killing," *American Journal of Jurisprudence* 15 (1970): 64–96, esp. 65–66, 73–4, 87–91.

[39]St. Thomas, *Summa Theologiae*, II-II, 64, 7c. My translation is as close to the original as I could make it. The passage is thoroughly discussed, and more elegantly translated, by Grisez, *American Journal of Jurisprudence* 15 (1970): 73–75, 87–91. The concept *'praeter intentionem,'* as St. Thomas uses it, is clarified and illustrated by Joseph M. Boyle, Jr., *The Thomist* 42 (1978): 649–65.

[40]Joseph T. Mangan, S.J., "An Historical Analysis of the Principle of Double Effect," *Theological Studies* 10 (1949): 49. This important paper, while it establishes that *Summa Theologiae* II-II, 64, 7 'is the historical beginning of the principle of the double effect as a principle' (*ibid.*, p. 61), is less successful, in my opinion, in showing that it ought to have been.

[41]St. Thomas, *Summa Theologiae*, I-II, 19, 10 c.

[42]Ibid. II-II, 64, 2 c.

[43]*American Journal of Jurisprudence* 15 (1970): 67–69.

[44]St. Thomas, *Summa Theologiae*, II-II, 64, 2 *ad* 3.

[45]*American Journal of Jurisprudence* 15 (1970): 69.

[46]The final sentence is from Immanuel Kant, *Metaphysik der Sitten* (2nd edn., Königsberg, 1798), vol. i, *Rechtslehre*, p. 229 (Ak. edn., p. 333). I have used John Ladd's translation.

[47]Grisez, *American Journal of Jurisprudence* 15 (1970): 91–91.

[48]See my *Theory of Morality* (Chicago: Chicago University Press, 1977).

[49]E.g., "[Working in a framework that assumes that human life is inherently a good to be protected and respected, Aquinas is precluded from defending capital punishment and killing in warfare. Yet as a theologian, Aquinas was confronted with a tradition which justified capital punishment and took warfare for granted" (*American Journal of Jurisprudence* 15 (1970): 72n).

[50]While remembering that Kant's treatment of homicide in *Metaphysik der Sitten* has a number of details best explained as lapses into dotage, it is hard to imagine St. Thomas even in his dotage deviating into such cant as 'If legal justice perishes, then it is no longer worth while for men to remain alive on this earth' (*Metaphysik der Sitten*, vol. i, p. 227, Ak. edn. p. 332)—as though in human history legal justice has not many times perished and been restored.

[51]In Part III, I owe a great deal to Professor Joseph M. Boyle, Jr., of St. Thomas University, Houston, for allowing me to read unpublished work of his, and for criticism in correspondence. While there was no time to send him the present paper before submitting it for publication, I trust to his professionalism to correct my errors in Thomistic scholarship.

PART II

THE FOUNDATIONS OF ETHICS

FOUNDATIONS, OBJECTIVE AND OBJECTIONS: ADLER AND FINNIS ON OBJECTIVE GOODS AND REPLIES TO FOUR OBJECTIONS

Thomas Russman, O.F.M. Cap.
University of St. Thomas

Those who would defend the objectivity of morals and ethics by claiming it has a basis in human nature have generally been thought to face the serious problem of going from *is* to *ought*. This has been variously described as the problem of going from fact to value, from descriptive to prescriptive language, or from hypothetical to categorical imperatives. The problem is weighty because it is a problem of sheer logic. An argument is invalid if there are modalities in the conclusion that are not present in any of the premises. It is invalid to infer an ought-statement conclusion from nothing but is-statement premises—similarly for inferring value-statement conclusions from fact-statement premises, prescriptive statement conclusions from descriptive premises, and categorical conclusions from hypothetical premises. What we are dealing with here is a genuine logical fallacy, and any natural law theory of morality that depends upon it is indefensible. But the fallacy is not as common as is often thought—the large majority of natural law ethicians avoid committing it. Even so, the specter of the fallacy serves a useful purpose. It focuses our attention upon those parts of natural law ethical theories in virtue of which they are *not* guilty of the fallacy; for arguments that avoid it may be nevertheless otiose.

In this paper I shall examine the views of Mortimer Adler and John Finnis at this foundation point of their natural law theories. I shall then reply briefly to four common objections to the theory of objective goods. I choose these two authors because their recently published positions can get us to the issues quickly and effectively and also because Henry Veatch's definitive position on the issue has not yet been forthcoming.

In his *Six Great Ideas* (New York, 1981), Mortimer Adler addresses the problem in the following way. He grants that ethics begins with is-statements in descriptive language. These descriptive statements tell us what things are good for all humans, not just for some, and not just because they are chosen. Such goods are "objective" human goods and Adler distinguishes them from subjective human goods. The latter are goods, but only relative to the desires of individuals, and not goods as such for everyone. Adler does not deny that both objective and subjective goods are objects of desire, but he distinguishes between two different sources of such desire, which correspond to the two kinds of goods. The desire for objective goods springs from human "needs," the desire for subjective goods springs from human "wants." Needs are inherent in human nature just as are various physical characteristics, the shape of the human skeleton or the size of the human brain, for example. Objective goods include such things as life, health, friendship, freedom, knowledge, skill, and aesthetic satisfaction. Subjective goods include things like an ice cream cone, a house at the shore, a red sports car, or shaking hands with the president—when these happen to be desired by some individual. I assume Adler would agree that attraction to a specific good thing may spring from both kinds of desire. My desire to eat fettucini with white clam sauce can express both my desire (need) for health and life (objective goods) and also my personal preference (want) for this dish given the alternatives on the menu (subjective goods).

Notice Adler's way of categorizing these various statements and expressions. He says that statements classifying things as objective human goods are descriptive rather than prescriptive. Yet they are also evaluative. According to Adler, then, there are at least two kinds of evaluative statements, descriptive-evaluative and prescriptive-evaluative. For Adler the distinction between fact and value does not correspond to the distinction between description and prescription.

Because Adler claims that statements about objective human goods are descriptive, he must explain how we can go from description to prescription without committing the is/ought fallacy. He does this by supplying a self-evident prescriptive premise: "We ought to want and seek that which is objectively good for us." This premise, when combined with "descriptions" of objective goods (i.e. things which are good for everyone) gives us prescriptive conclusions enjoining the pursuit of each of these objective goods upon everyone.

Adler calls his prescriptive premise a self-evident truth because, he says, it is impossible to think the opposite. "Without knowing in advance which things are, in fact, really good or bad for us, we do know at once that 'ought to desire' is inseparable in its meaning from the meaning of 'really good,' just as we know at once that the parts of a physical whole are always less than the whole." The imperative is categorical, says Adler, because it does not depend upon anything other than itself. By this last point Adler apparently means that the imperative to do the objectively good does not depend upon choice the way hypothetical imperatives do. If you choose to join a club, then you must comply with the admission requirements. The *imperative* to comply operates only on the *hypothesis* that one chooses to join. No such hypothesis is needed, says Adler, for the imperative to seek what is really good. One is obliged to do it prior to any choice to do it. This priority of the imperative can be seen, says Adler, from the very meaning of the terms "ought to desire" and "really good." These meanings are inseparable and do not depend upon any hypothesis of choice to join them.

We know at once that these two meanings are inseparable, says Adler, even "without knowing in advance which things are really good or bad for us . . . ." Now this claim seems to be true in one sense, but not in another. We can readily imagine someone who sincerely and coherently says he wants to do the right thing, but is not sure, in a given case, what the right thing is. Such a person is expressing Adler's categorical imperative to pursue the really good, but without knowing what the really good is *in a particular case*. To this extent Adler is right about the separability of his categorical imperative and knowledge of what is good or bad. But there is another sense in which they are not separable. How could anyone understand the meaning of "really good" or "objectively good" without understanding some examples? Unless one knows that such things as life, health, etc., are objectively good, the expression "objectively good" will be a meaningless expression. But if its meaning is not understood, then the necessary connection between its meaning and the meaning of "ought to desire" will not be recognized. It follows that the knowledge that certain things such as life and health are objective goods must precede knowledge of Adler's categorical imperative which requires us to pursue the objective good.

But then we begin to suspect that, as a separate step in the argument, this categorical imperative is a redundancy. If it is true that the imperative is self-evidently linked with the meaning of "objective good," then one cannot know that something is an objective good without knowing that it ought to be pursued by everyone. But then it is not possible for someone to know life or health or whatever is objectively good only descriptively and not prescriptively. If health is an objective good, it is a good to be sought. It follows that Adler's analysis of the foundation of natural law morality is faulty. His attempt to isolate a merely descriptive use of "objective good" and then, as a separate step, to claim that such an objective good is self-evidently prescriptive, is incoherent. Either prescriptivity is present in the original ascriptions of objective good or it is not self-evidently linked to objective good at all.

How damaging is this criticism to the natural law position? John Finnis (*Natural Law and Natural Rights,* Oxford, 1980), for one, believes it is not the least bit damaging. He proposes from the outset that things like life and health are goods to be sought by everyone. He therefore does not believe there is some is/ought gap yet to be traversed once we recognize these things to be objective goods. Objective goods are already on the side of the ought.

Finnis does not, like Adler, arrive at this ought by invoking a single categorical imperative. He claims that one arrives at it by reflection upon human activities. When one has had some experience of life and observed the difference between health and illness, for example, one is able to recognize that health is good and illness bad. One does *not* infer this by strict logic from any number of non-evaluative descriptions, simple or complex. It is an insight that comes to any sufficiently experienced and reasonable human being. That health is an objective good to be pursued by everyone is simply evident. Finnis says it is "self-evident." By this he does not mean that it can be known without prior knowledge of many other things. To understand the meaning of "health" and "illness" requires enough experience of them to provide a rich and accurate sense of how it is to be healthy or ill.

Once one has achieved this sufficiently rich and accurate understanding of health and illness, it is self-evident that health is good for everyone. Such insight, says Finnis, is the foundation of morality and ethics. Adler avoided the is/ought fallacy by invoking a single self-evident categorical imperative—the really good ought to be desired by everyone. Finnis avoids it by claiming that, life, freedom, etc., are each self-evidently and objectively good and to be desired by everyone. Finnis improves on Adler by avoiding the incoherence of separating the categorical imperative from the recognition of objective goods.

Now let's consider four common objections to the theory of objective goods.

1. "Good" cannot be an objective property in the real world.

2. The objective goods often contradict one another; therefore they cannot be prescriptive. If they were prescriptive we would be obliged to do contradictory things, which is impossible.

3. The objective goods express only hypothetical imperatives, not categorical ones.

4. The objective goods, as presented by Finnis, lack metaphysical foundation.

I will examine these objections in turn:

1. "Good" cannot be an objective property. This objection is a commonplace among empiricists, among whom I would number J. L. Mackie (*Ethics: Inventing Right and Wrong,* New York, 1977) and Gilbert Harman (*The Nature of Morality: An Introduction to Ethics,* New York, 1977). The granddaddy of this kind of argument is Hume's attack upon the reality of factual relations. Hume denies the reality or objectivity of the cause/effect relation because it is impossible even "by the most accurate examination of (something's) sensible qualities to discover its causes or effects." (*Inquiry,* Bobbs-Merrill, p. 42.) Hume was saying that, since the causal tie cannot *itself* be observed, and since the causal tie cannot be deduced from properties which can be observed, it must be a relation that is entirely supplied by the mind. Hume's argument works just as well against spatial relations. No amount of scrutinizing the sensible properties of a blue color blob will show that it must be to the left of a green color blob. One cannot "see" the relation "to the left of" nor can one deduce it from the properties of either blob. This extension of Hume's argument would conclude that spatial relations are also supplied by the mind and are not real or objective.

But all Hume's argument shows is that factual relations are not colors and are not deducible from colors. He does not show that only colors and properties deduced from them are objective. He needs the second premise to conclude that relations are not objective. But it is just this premise which was the issue in the first place. I will not present the arguments in favor of the existence of real, objective relations here. I will only say that I regard the case against Hume by F. H. Bradley, Rom Harre, and others to be overwhelmingly successful on this point. Everyone agrees that relations are not colors, but the case in favor of real relations shows that properties other than colors are objective.

J. L. Mackie's argument against the objectivity of values is like Hume's against relations. Mackie claims that, if values were properties, they would be very "queer" properties. He concludes that properties so queer could not be objective. But in what sense would value properties be queer? It seems that for Mackie they would be queer simply because they are not colors, shapes, or relations. But why does this show they are not objective? I might as well say that relations are queer, and therefore not objective, because they are not shapes, colors, or values. Mackie wanted to show that values are not objective properties, but instead he showed only that they are not identical with any property he considers objective.

Harman takes Mackie's argument a further step. He admits the objectivity of some properties other than commonsense colors, shapes, and relations. He grants objectivity to the protons, electrons, etc., which are postulated by scientists to explain commonsense entities and properties. But then he makes the inevitable empiricist move. He observes that values are not only *not* properties like colors and shapes, they are also not properties like "spin" and "charm," properties that subatomic particles have—therefore, Harman concludes, they are not objective properties! The argument has the same form as Hume's and Mackie's and is just as successful. Harman has simply added the further observation that values are not identical with the properties of microentities. When someone learns from observation and experience what it is like to be healthy and what it is like to be ill, and he recognizes from this that it is a good thing to be healthy, shall we say that he has observed "good" as a property of "health"? Why not? Successive revisions of empiricism have recognized the objectivity of relations, though Hume did not, and the objectivity of scientific microentities, though whole generations of instrumentalists did not—perhaps we are now poised for the recognition of objective values. This, like the earlier medicines, will be hard for strict empiricists to swallow, but gagging on it will not show that it is not good for them.

2. The objective goods often contradict one another; therefore they cannot be prescriptive. If they were prescriptive we would be obliged to do contradictory things, which is impossible. Among the goods which can be recognized as such by a sufficiently experienced and reasonable person is the ability to adjudicate value conflicts and make decisions with regard to them. This ability has traditionally been called "prudence" (but "practical reasonableness" by John Finnis). The prudent person sees that it is impossible to pursue every objective value at all times and with all one's strength. It is obvious, therefore, that choices must be made. The pursuit of one value may force the neglect of another. To become a serious student, one may have to spend less time conversing with one's friends. To choose to do so is not to act immorally. Such choices are inevitable. But if such choices are not immoral, then neglecting one value (say, friendship) for the sake of another (say, learning) does not violate the prescription to pursue the friendship. But then how can the good of friendship or any other objective good have any

prescriptive force at all?

An objective good is to be pursued by everyone, but not at all times and in every circumstance. An objective good as such has general prescriptivity but not specific prescriptivity. Its demands upon us are subject to the refinement and reasonable application that we have called prudence. Such refinement produces moral principles and finally specific moral choices. It is the exercise of prudence that translates general prescriptivity into specific prescriptivity. Moral principles tell us under what circumstances an objective good *must* be protected or pursued. Prior to the exercise of prudence, objective good itself specifies no such thing. We can summarize the distinction in the following way:

a) General prescription: an objective good enjoins its own pursuit upon everyone, but not at all times or under all circumstances.

b) Specific prescription: the result of prudent reflection specifies *when, where,* and, *how* the objective goods are to be pursued.

Prudent reflection produces moral principles such as: "One may not directly take innocent human life"—complete with commentary telling us the relevant meaning of "directly" and "innocent." It specifies the obligation to keep one's contracts, to provide for one's children, to pay one's taxes, and so on. It also carries us to the level of individual choice. It is immoral for me to let someone next to me choke to death while I pursue the good of learning by reading a book. Such action is not a reasonable way to adjudicate the claims of learning and life in such circumstances. On the other hand, I may choose to be a teacher rather than a physician, even if this means some people may die who might have been saved through my practice of medicine.

A great deal more can be said about the connection between objective goods and prudence. John Finnis says much that is valuable in his chapter, "The Basic Requirements of Practical Reasonableness," but he does not make explicit the important distinction between general prescription and specific prescription. This distinction is needed to explain how objective goods can have prescriptive force even though they often pull in opposite directions. The key to the distinction is the objective good of prudence or practical reasonableness itself. The development of prudence enables one to adjudicate successfully the conflicting claims of various objective goods, respecting them all, but integrating them so as to protect and bring to a full measure of being the good that talent and circumstance make possible.

3) The objective goods express only hypothetical imperatives, not categorical ones. The arguments I have heard that try to show that objective goods are only hypothetical imperatives make the following mistake: they confuse natural obligation with natural necessity. They point out that objective goods only become effective *if* one chooses to pursue them. If one chooses not to pursue them, they are ineffective. But this shows only that the objective goods are not categorical *necessities*. It does not show that they are not categorical *imperatives*. A human being can go against his moral obligations, after all. When he does so, he shows that he was not necessi-

tated; he does not show that he was not obligated.

Some, after making this mistake, think the only way to bridge the gap between the hypothetical and categorical is by bringing God into it. This is done in one of two ways:

a) God is seen as commanding that we pursue the objective goods. This is supposed to make the hypothetical imperative categorical by showing its connection with the categorical moral will of God. This solution fails, however, because the categorical will of God is effective only *if* one *chooses* to *do* the categorical will of God. The effectiveness is just as hypothetical as in the case of objective goods. The only way out is to distinguish between necessity and obligation in the first place. God's will obliges, but does not necessitate. But objective goods also oblige without necessitating. Therefore, objective goods can carry the categorical imperative without explicit reference to God.

b) God is seen as making us in such a way that the pursuit of objective goods is necessary for our fulfillment. This is supposed to make the hypothetical imperative categorical by connecting it with the categorical creative will of God. This argument is no more successful than the more voluntarist (a). The creative will of God is morally effective only *if* one *chooses* to *act* in accordance with it. Effectiveness is just as hypothetical as in the case of objective goods. Once again, the only way out is to distinguish between necessity and obligation in the first place. But once we do this, the objective goods can carry the categorical imperative without explicit reference to God.

4) The objective goods, as presented by Finnis, lack metaphysical foundation. The issue here is whether ethics must be based upon metaphysics, whether the valid recognition of objective goods requires a prior understanding of the philosophical issues surrounding such terms as "soul," "freedom," "matter," "spirit," "substance," "existence," "mind," "universals," "God," etc. I agree with Finnis that such understanding is not required. One can begin philosophy by doing ethics; all that is required is sufficient experience of life, a capacity for reasonableness, and teachers by word and example. But this is not to deny that in a particular case—or even in many cases—a preliminary excursus into metaphysical issues may be helpful or even necessary in order to persuade someone. The fact that such metaphysical discussion can sometimes be helpful or necessary does not show that it is necessary *per se*.

Suppose Mabi is a native of the New Guinea Highlands and believes that the earth is flat. Suppose he is convinced of this because of the religious beliefs of his tribe. Because of his convictions he may be unwilling even to consider evidence that the earth is spherical. In such a case it may be helpful or even necessary for Mabi to begin to question the infallibility of some of his religious beliefs before he will be open to evidence about the shape of the earth. Does this mean that proof that the earth is spheroid requires *per se* a prior argument about Mabi's religious beliefs? Clearly not. No such argument is relevant when discussing the matter with an American six-year-old.

Similarly in the case of metaphysics. If someone's prior metaphysical convictions prevent his seriously entertaining the possibility of objective goods, then discussion of these larger metaphysical views may be helpful or even necessary for persuasion. *Which* metaphysical issues need to be discussed will vary from person to person, and *no* metaphysical discussion will be necessary *per se*. Indeed, even in such a case, the most promising course may nevertheless be to pursue the ethical issues first. It may be that a discussion of ethics may spark a re-thinking of metaphysics. Neither is founded on the other, but not every metaphysics is consistent with every ethics. A re-thinking of one can engender a re-thinking of the other, and a starting point for such re-thinking can be found in either metaphysics or ethics.

VEATCH AND MACINTYRE ON THE VIRTUES

Michael H. Robins
Bowling Green State University

This is a time in which philosophy seems to be enjoying a golden age. The elegance and scope of recent philosophical theories on a variety of subjects, the high technical competence with which issues are commonly discussed— a competence which was impossible to achieve just a short time ago—and, recently, the public recognition of philosophers as bona fide consultants and social critics all underscore a most auspicious epoch.

But in this chorus of accolades there are a few voices of discontent. One philosopher inveighs against the discipline as not being a natural kind, suggesting instead that it be absorbed into literary criticism. In other quarters, the complaint is that moral philosophy in particular should be the subject of an obituary column. And to the extent that moral philosophy is a reflection of the culture, the warning is that, instead of enjoying a golden age, we are on the brink of a new dark age, on the brink, that is, if we have not already made our descent into the abyss. The only way out—before it is too late—is to reclaim in both philosophy and morality a virtue-based ethics structured on the classical tradition.

Certainly one would think that the combination of the last diagnosis and cure is so singular that it can be the product only of one mind. But not so! There is not one, but two, distinguished moral philosophers who have said just that. Not only said that, but arrived at it independently. The first is Henry B. Veatch; the second is Alasdair MacIntyre.

In this paper I intend to confine my remarks to their positive thesis, leaving the negative thesis to others, there being no dearth of whom willing to take up the challenge. Before this even gets off the ground, however, both thinkers will protest that the only "positive thesis" they share is a terminological one which masks the radically different conceptions of the virtues to which they subscribe. I do not depreciate this point, in fact will do much to develop it, but I believe that Veatch and MacIntyre may have a lot more in common than they care to admit. For these admittedly disparate conceptions of the virtues seem open to roughly the same kind of criticism.

I. What is a Virtue Based Morality? — Veatch's Conception

A good starting point is MacIntyre's observation that "one of the features of the concept of a virtue . . . is that it always requires for its application the acceptance of some prior account of certain features of social and moral life in terms of which it has to be defined and explained."[1] This is a statement

[117]

with which Veatch would agree if you delete from it "social [life]." Veatch would also agree with MacIntyre's subsequent observation that this prior account is the good life for man conceived as the *telos* of human action.[2] But it is in the specification of this prior good that they would emphatically part company. I shall first discuss Veatch's specification of this prior good[3] and then MacIntyre's.

Veatch's account is best understood against the setting of Aristotle's metaphysical biology—an account which, we shall see, MacIntyre rejects. For Veatch, everything that undergoes change has its own nature, which is a concept that does double duty in both explaining its behavior, i.e., its reaction to and interaction with changes in its environment, and in providing a normative standard, indeed a rule or law, as to how it is supposed to react. The metaphysical biology is superimposed on this if we focus next on things that undergo growth and development. "Immediately," writes Veatch, "we are led to think of and speak of the thing's natural growth or development, i.e., a development that is determined by the thing's very nature, or by the law of its nature. And from here the next step can only be to acknowledge that the very notion of such a natural growth or development implies the further notion of some sort of end-point or point of completion of that natural growth of development. Call this the natural end of that thing's development."[4]

Such a natural end or *telos* is the actualization of the thing's nature, which it possesses only in a potential state when it enters the world. In living things, Veatch says, anyone can recognize the difference between a healthy specimen and one that is diseased or stunted; one cannot help seeing the former as a perfection or completion of the latter—completion both in the explanatory, descriptive sense and in the normative sense. For things in a potential state are ordered to reach their actual, flourishing state precisely by the law that governs their nature.

When it comes specifically to humans, however, we should not interpret these biological notions to imply that their *telos* consists of just physical health. Otherwise, Veatch reminds us, a perfect physical specimen like Jane Austen's Sir Walter Elliot would have achieved his perfection even though he is nothing if not a pompous ass.[5] No, when it comes to man, his *telos* or good life consists of living intelligently, i.e., bringing reason and moderation to bear on his whole life. Connected with this is that, unlike non-humans, man can achieve his natural end only by *knowing* what it is and devising the means to reach it. These "means" and methods carve out a space that is occupied precisely by the virtues. And in this sense, writes Veatch, one can compare living well to practicing an art, in the sense that you cannot be, say, a good sculptor or doctor without acquiring the necessary skills.[6]

Does this mean that moral virtue, i.e., the methods used for mastering the art of living, is simply a matter of skill as in the other arts? Not quite. What the art of living shares in common with the other arts is that of intellectual virtue, i.e., the know-how to achieve the objective. But the art of living is supposed to require more than just know-how; one must actually choose in accordance with that know-how, especially when one may be deflected from its proper path by fears, prejudices, self-deception, slothfulness, flagging commitment, and a host of other afflictions. Hence these "virtues of choice" are called the moral virtues. The upshot is that, presumably, the art of living consists of exercising both the moral and the intellectual virtues, while the other arts consist just of the intellectual virtues appropriate to them.

As an aside, I think this contrast between the art of living and other arts is overdrawn. I don't see why a good practitioner of the other arts doesn't also require moral virtue in Veatch's sense. It is hard to fathom how one could be, for example, a good philosopher or scientist by just possessing intellectual virtue. Doesn't one also have to have, in the psychologist's terminology, achievement motivation, which might consist in good study habits, self-discipline, especially to resist the inclination to laziness, and other sources of flagging commitment that beset one in the art of living? And what is this achievement motivation if not "virtue of choice"?

In *Rational Man*[7] Veatch draws out the difference between the art of living and other arts in terms of the implications for each of making an intentional mistake. (This is an odd juxtaposition unless one is talking about *akrasia*. What Veatch means in the case of arts is intentionally violating a rule of skill.) The difference is that such "intentional mistakes" do not reflect on the competence of the practitioner in the arts, but they do reflect on the competence of the practitioner in the art of living. In the latter case there is no *point* to making an intentional mistake.

However, I again see this as open to the same objection. According to Veatch, a scientist, like Cyril Burt, who intentionally falsifies or manufactures data to support his conclusions, or a Dr. Mengele, who perverts the practice of medicine to perform "experiments" on prisoners of concentration camps, is no less competent a scientist or doctor. But one need only recall Plato's argument in the *Republic* that a doctor who practices medicine to line his pockets rather than to heal the patient at that moment ceases to be a doctor in the best sense of the term. There is a sense, of course, in which Veatch is right if we consider the narrow sense of "competence," but Plato was also right to point out that "doctor" and "scientist" have an ethical dimension as well as an intellectual one; so it is not surprising that the real practice of the arts requires moral as well as intellectual virtue in Veatch's sense. Alternatively, if the narrow sense of "competence" is maintained, then it would be said that the *akrates'* competence or judgment is no more impugned for being *akratic*.

One final thing, in rounding out Veatch's account—and this will be especially important in contrasting it with MacIntyre's—is that on his conception, private acts are both normatively and conceptually prior to social acts. Were it not liable to misunderstanding, Veatch takes the virtues to designate duties that in the first instance are duties to oneself, not duties to society. And he thinks it a modern perversion to think of duties to oneself as mere prudence or even self-interest. Thus he writes: "To the extent that a human being is a rational animal and ordered to human perfection, he must [first] make something of *himself*. And this is interpreted to mean that the possession of the virtues is a do-it-yourself job or it is nothing."[8]

In the second part of his book, Veatch develops this notion into an intriguing theory of rights, striking what he takes to be a proper balance between the licentiousness of libertarianism (my terminology) and the paternalism of the welfare state. Time and space prevent me from going into this, but perhaps we can note that the do-it-yourself aspect of the virtues implies a negative right of the individual against societal, paternalistic interference. Any such paternalism, or conception of the state as one of making its citizens virtuous or looking out for their well-being would be missing the entire point of the virtues. What the virtues require of the state is only the opportunity that they be exercised, which appears to mark exactly the concept of a negative right.

Veatch thus provides us with a conception of the virtues that is both compelling and inspiring. The criticism that I shall make by no means detracts from its overall elegance. Accordingly, the most vulnerable part of this scheme is, presumably, the metaphysical biology. As I see it, the three pillars of that scheme, nature as an explanatory concept, development as a normative concept, and natural law as a normative concept, all stand together or fall together. In my opinion they fall together.

Take "nature" first. The idea that the nature of a thing explains its behavior, strikes me as either pleonastic or circular. When someone asks, "Why does water seek its own level?" and is answered by saying, "Because that is its nature," the answer sounds like a restatement of the question, which might have been elliptical for "Why is it the nature of water to seek its own level?" And if it is not pleonastic, then it seems either eliminable or circular. For if the answer, "It is the nature of water to seek its own level," is followed up with the question, *"Why?"* it either admits to reducing nature to atomic theory, in which case there is an explanation, but only at the cost of making nature eliminable, or it suggests the circular reply that water does (typically) seek its own level. As I see it, "nature" is playing an analogous role to "fittest" in the aphorism "The fittest survive." In this case the circle is that a species is said to be the fittest because it survives, but it also survives because it is the fittest.

Next, consider the normative concept of development, which Veatch takes to be something read off the faces of things rather than a human construct imposed on them. Given the rival conceptions of flourishing—a point well made by MacIntyre—it is hard to define development or actualization in any but the most circular terms. For example, in the case of humans, is a person developed when he has reached the stage we identify with maturity? But this might mean that while his intellectual powers and perhaps self control are in full flower, his physical powers might already be headed downhill. In one sense he is past his prime; in another he is enjoying it. If we count this naturally as development, is that because we are reading the flourishing of human nature off the face of the man—even if we concede that by that time he "has the face he deserves"—or are we smuggling in our value predilection for intellectual prowess over physical prowess? So the circle is that the attribution of "natural development"—viz., that the thing developed possesses perfection or actualization, health or well-being—was supposed to support the implicit value judgment; yet it looks as though that value judgment might have been smuggled in exactly to support the attribution of development. Incidentally, this kind of point is most in order concerning the question whether the chemical and biological changes occurring throughout the earth's history constitute "evolution"—a loaded term if there ever was one—or "involution," or perhaps just "change."

This point is absolutely critical for the doctrine of the virtues, for if the prior notion of the good that it implies is something that admits of rival interpretations, then, as MacIntyre notes so well, the upshot might be rival tables of the virtues.[9]

These criticisms come to a head in assessing the normative conception of natural law. For this seems to imply, implausibly, that it is wrong to change or supplant the natural end of something with our own artificial ends— especially if those artificial ends result in a perversion of the natural end. In agriculture, for example, certain kinds of domesticated livestock are weaker and not as "fit" to survive as their natural counterparts. If this is a perversion of their natural end, is it wrong? In agronomy, perhaps some of our own ends are better served by harvesting certain plants before they are ripe, or even by stunting their development. "Green wood" for example, sometimes makes a longer lasting fire in the fireplace than does ripe wood. Or perhaps corn that is not ripe might make better alcohol (say, for gasahol) than ripe corn. Perhaps the day might come when diseased corn might serve some useful purpose overriding any served by healthy corn, which would be such as to make it desirable to increase the production of such at the expense of healthy corn. (Compare the making of penicillin from mold.) And these examples are dwarfed by the dazzling possibilities presented by molecular biology. The day is not far off when, genetically speaking, we may be able to produce any kind of man we want.

II. MacIntyre's Conception of the Virtues

According to MacIntyre, "the use of 'man' as a functional concept is far older than Aristotle and it does not initially derive from Aristotle's metaphysical biology. It is rooted in forms of social life to which theorists of the classical tradition give expression. For, according to that tradition, to be a man is to fill a set of roles each of which has its own . . . purpose: member of a family, citizen, soldier, ..."[10] Man comes into the world already equipped with these social roles which he can opt out of only at the cost of "making himself disappear."[11] "It is only when man is thought of as an individual prior to and apart from all roles that 'man' ceases to be a functional concept."[12] As a preliminary matter, we can see that MacIntrye, having rejected the metaphysical biology, but (as we shall see) having maintained Aristotle's formal structure, starts at the opposite end from which Veatch begins. The exercising of virtues for MacIntyre is in the first instance a social act because it is so intimately attached to social roles. (Actually, given MacIntyre's conception of the common good[13] and of the bonds of friendship that keep it in place, the distinction between social acts and private acts is a distinction without a difference. But that is getting ahead of the story.)

MacIntyre's conception of the virtues is tied to three fundamental concepts: the notion of a practice, the idea of the narrative unity of a life, and the concept of a tradition. As it turns out, these are also listed in descending order of importance, and I shall omit discussing the last. Let us start with the concept of a practice. Before we can get a handle on this, we must, following Aristotle, first define two kinds of means-end relationships. Any traditional conception of the virtues implies a means-end relationship in some sense if we remember MacIntyre's observation that the concept of the virtues is supposed to ride piggyback on a prior conception of a good, in relation to which the virtues stand as means. This is also essential to preserve the teleological conception. (On this both MacIntyre and Veatch agree.) But, as MacIntyre astutely observes, there are two kinds of means-ends relationships: external and internal. In an external relationship, the means are one of several alternatives for reaching the end, and the end itself is conceptually independent of any description of the means. Writing or playing chess to achieve fame or fortune is exactly like this. The money and the recognition are external goods or ends in relation to the skill.

An internal means-end relationship in contrast is such that "the end cannot even be described apart from the skilled activity, and can be identified and recognized only by experienced participants of the practice."[14] The means are the virtues and the end (or the goods) is something the very specification of which involves reference to those virtues. We may refer to the kinds of goods or ends that result from doing a thing well as internal goods. Armed with this distinction, MacIntyre focuses on the definition a practice "as any coherent and complete form of *socially* established cooperative human activity through which the goods internal to that form of activity are realized in course of trying to achieve those standards of excellence which are appropriate to that activity, with the result that human powers to achieve excellence and human conceptions of the ends and goods involved are systematically extended." This is to say that the goods of practice are edifying and uplifting to the human spirit. Doing philosophy would undoubtedly be a practice but attending philosophy department meetings apparently would not.[15] Parasitic upon this, virtues are defined as "acquired qualities [habits] the possession or exercise of which tends to enable us to achieve those goods which are internal to practices and the lack of which effectively prevents us from achieving any such goods."[16] So conceived, virtues are both necessary conditions of, and in that sense (partially) constitutive, of internal goods, and they also tend to be sufficient, without really being so.

This, however, is where the problem comes in, for, as I see it, how is one to figure out exactly what the difference is between the virtues specific to a practice and the internal goods which they constitute. Granted that there is the constitutive relationship, such that the goods cannot be completely separate, the problem is how we can account for this internal, constitutive relation without making the goods and the virtues collapse into the same thing.

Obviously MacIntyre intends to keep them at least quasi-separate when he maintains that the virtues are inherently tied to a teleology. Thus he remarks, "when teleology is abandoned, there is always a tendency to substitute for it some version of Stoicism. The virtues are now not practiced for the sake of some good or other, or more than the practice of the virtues itself. Virtue is, indeed has to be, its own end, its own reward and its own motive."[17]

What is elusive about this internal teleology is that elsewhere he says:

It is the character of a virtue that in order that it be effective in producing the internal goods which are the rewards of the virtues it should be exercised without regard to the consequences. ["Consequences" has to mean internal goods here.] For it turns out to be the case that—and this is in part at least one more empirical factual claim—although the virtues are just those qualities which tend to lead to the achievement of a certain class of goods, nonetheless unless we practice them irrespective of whether in any particular set of contingent circumstances they will produce those goods or not, we cannot possess them at all.[18]

Perhaps we can reconcile these passages by saying that, motivationally, we are to be somewhat "Stoic," but not in giving a third person, philosophical account of the virtues, which is to be teleological. But if the goods really are internal in his sense and not external, why should we be Stoic even motivationally? In this light the last passage now makes sense only if he really means to be talking about external goods, but that certainly is at odds with what he actually says.

Perhaps we can get a better handle on this problem if we only had a few examples of what an internal good is. But on this score MacIntyre apparently leaves us empty handed. Nevertheless, I want to try out two plausible examples of internal goods, and then show how they miss the mark. The first one, in the context of the "practice" of chess, is that of winning. I mean by winning, of course, not winning a prize or winning recognition, but winning as defined by the rules of the game. Since winning in this "internal sense" implies playing the game as opposed to cheating, one might want to say that here is a good of which the virtues are both constitutive and necessary conditions—or let us suppose that they are—but not sufficient. (If the virtues are not even necessary, then this good has even more problems with it than the ones cited.) But if the virtues are not sufficient, what else is required? If one doesn't win at chess because of his virtues, but, say, by luck or by some element of luck, then to that extent winning begins to look like an external good. Alternatively if the internal notion of winning is exhausted by playing the game well, then it seems to be nothing *other than* exercising the virtues of chess playing—the "means" to it, and thus incidentally seems to collapse into the Stoic perversion.

MacIntyre's remarks specifically on chess playing only underscore our difficulty:

> We may hope there will come a time when the child [who in this example is learning to play chess and is first motivated by external goods—candy] will find *in* those goods specific to chess, *in* the achievement of a certain highly particular kind of analytic skill, strategic imagination and competitive intensity, a new set of reasons, *reason* now not just *for winning on a particular occasion,* but for trying to excel in whatever way the game of chess demands. (Emphasis added).[19]

MacIntyre conceives the internal goods as reasons for the sake of which one is to try to win and to excel, and so they must refer to something other than winning. But what *are* these reasons? If they are not external goods, they seem not to name reasons, goods, or ends at all other than the exercise of the very virtues which "tend" to produce them.

The other candidate for an internal good that comes to mind is a psychological good, something like pleasure or satisfaction, not in the external "utilitarian" sense, but in the supervenient Aristotelian sense, where the pleasure supervenes upon excelling in a practice "as the bloom of youth supervenes upon someone in the flower of his prime." The trouble is that on both Aristotle's and MacIntyre's account, pleasure—even in this benign sense—is strictly *verboten* as a *bona fide telos* for the sake of which the virtues are practiced. Happiness for Aristotle, of course, is, but this is meant, not in the psychological sense, but in the metaphysical sense of the well being of the entire person, which in turn means exercising the moral and intellectual virtues.

Structurally, then, there is a kind of circle in MacIntyre that I ascribed to Veatch's metaphysical biology. In MacIntyre, the virtues are practiced for the sake of internal goods, but the internal goods are so internal as to be inseparable from those very virtues. This gives rise to a circle that is best cast in the normative idiom: while the virtues are supposed to be practiced for the sake of internal goods, the internal goods are *valuable* because they are produced by the virtues.

One MacIntyre expert, Andrew Altman, thinks this criticism misfires because I have misidentified exactly the kinds of things virtues are in relation to social practices.[20] Virtues, according to him, are not the skills of a specific practice, but rather general character traits, which, as a matter of empirical fact, have a strong tendency to enable a person who possesses them to acquire as well those specific abilities that are useful to particular practices such as chess-playing. MacIntyre would, however, endorse my

claim that these specific abilities *are* the same thing as the internal goods of that practice. For example, in chess, the ability to anticipate reliably the moves of an opponent is both a "virtue" of (notice the scare quotes) and an internal good to, chess playing. But the definition of virtues cited above, namely as "acquired abilities [habits] the . . . exercise of which tends to enable us to achieve [internal goods of practices] . . ." is meant to apply to virtues as general character traits whose connections with internal goods in the real world is contingent. This is also buttressed by another passage quoted above, to wit: "For it turns out to be the case—and this is in part at least one more empirical factual claim—although the virtues are just those qualities which tend to lead to the achievement of a certain class of goods
. . . ."

On this interpretation something counts as a virtue only if it actually has that connection to internal goods. Specific abilities (such as those specific to chess) would not count as virtues because their connection to internal goods is not contingent. (An implication of this is that there is a possible world in which different character traits would count as virtues, i.e., that the term is not a rigid designator.

Having made this distinction, Altman can then claim to make sense out of MacIntyre's "motivational Stoicism." In the last passage just partially quoted, MacIntyre makes the point that although virtues empirically lead to the achievement of internal goods, "unless we practice them irrespective of whether in any particular set of contingent circumstances they will produce those goods or not, we cannot possess them at all" (see above). This again is an empirical observation on the psychology of the virtues, that we cannot exhibit them selectively, i.e., only on those occasions when we think that doing so will (probably) lead to the internal good we are after on that occasion.

Finally, Altman thinks that MacIntyre's justification of the virtues is not circular because internal goods are valuable, not because they are produced by the virtues (which would be circular), but because of their connection to social practices which make a person who he is and without which he would "disappear." That is what makes internal goods more valuable than external goods. Since virtues are empirical means to those internal goods, their value is derived from those goods.

Altman's interpretation has much to recommend it. Particularly plausible is the interpretation of the "psychology" of the virtues just mentioned. The habits of character that tend to lead to proficiency at chess have to be exemplified all the time if they are to be had as habits of character, and to fail to see this is to fail to secure not only the virtue but also the specific proficiency which is its internal good.

As plausible as this interpretation is, however, it leaves us with two gaping holes. The first is that if virtues are only contingently related to the internal goods of practices (contingently means to those ends), then what exactly was the *point* of MacIntyre's emphatic distinction between internal means-ends relations and external ones? Do the *virtues* so interpreted stand to those goods in an *internal* or an *external* means-end relation? Insofar as they are contingently connected, it would appear to be external. True, they would still be partially constitutive of the goods or skills of practices, but this would merely mean that they are causally necessary conditions for possessing those specific skills, not logically necessary conditions. Since any event has causally necessary conditions, there is nothing special being marked here. And if that is true, then the whole grandiose distinction between the internal and the external is a wheel that turns nothing. Moreover, in calling the goods of practices internal goods, did MacIntyre mean to imply that they were *identical* with the skills of those practices? If so, he certainly chose a circuitous way to express it! But I think the chief reason for questioning this interpretation is that it fails to accommodate the whole point of the distinction in question, which point was to clarify the special *teleology* involved, i.e., to clarify the relation between the *virtues and the goods or rewards* they lead to.

The other problem with this interpretation—and this I think is a stronger rejoinder—is that I don't see how this rescues MacIntyre's scheme from a vicious circle. Recall that the circle was supposed to be straightened out by deriving the value of the virtues from the internal goods of practices, and by making the value of internal goods derive from the social role of practices, and finally, by securing the social role of practices to making a person who he is. But if we ask *why* do these social roles play so essential a part in constituting our moral identity, the answer seems to be—and this seems congruent with his definition of practices *qua* practices—that they give us an opportunity to exercise the virtues. That is what distinguishes *practices* from other structured social activities or rule-governed games. So in this reading, the circle is back with us. Altman's alternative answer to the question is that the value of social roles is that they allow the self to be expressed essentially. That is to say that the value is grounded in a metaphysics of the self, which does not, of course, smuggle in the virtues. Not only is this undeveloped, but it would also have to be a kind of theory that avoids all the markings of "metaphysical biology." To be sure, no one can say what is or is not possible in philosophy, but, until this foundation is really laid, it is risky to put very much weight on it.

We come now to the next pillar of MacIntyre's theory: the narrative unity of a life. This is necessitated by the fact that if virtues are just tied to practices, some of them might have internal goods which are incompatible with those of other practices. Since practices *qua* practices are supposed to, as I said, extend the opportunities for exercising general virtuous character traits, these goods make conflicting demands on us, and this brings us face to face with the *tragic* conflict of some goods with others. The purpose, then, of relating practices and their derivative virtues to the unity of life is to give us a better perspective on tragedy.[21] Another, related purpose, concerning Aristotelian justice, is to enable us to ascertain the relative desert of people who contribute to different practices.[22] However, unlike the historical Aristotle who denies tragic conflict in life, the narrative unity of life does not remove or dissolve the tragic conflict, and therefore does not constitute, in the Aristotelian sense, the unity of the virtues. What, then, does it do? The answer is that it enables us to understand that while there is *no right* choice to make, the madality of our choice can be *better or worse,* "heroic or unheroic, generous or not generous, graceful or graceless, or prudent or imprudent."[23] Understanding the narrative unity of our life and how it intersects with those of other people helps us in the end to know and to choose the right modality.

This unity is derived from his analysis of action, which in order to be intelligible, has to be explained in terms of the longest range intention or goal, but this intention is intelligible in turn only within a larger narrative setting linking it in a story-like way to other intentions. "The unity of a life consists of living out that narrative," and "the good life consists of living out that specific unity in the best way possible."[24]

The trouble is that our knowledge of what the narrative unity is *while* we are living in face of tragic conflicts is partial at best. Schneewind, I think, overstated it when he said that "narrative" is a retrospective concept—something that can be written only after a life is finished—while the decisions—especially the tragic ones—have to be made prospective to the knowledge of that unity.[25]

I say he overstated it because there is a sense in which—if we are not too demanding—human agents can be likened to novelists, "writing" and giving narrative unity to their own lives as they go along. Novelists may do this often, not knowing how the story is going to end or even what exactly is going to come next.[26] But there is a critical difference, one that makes human agents much less "authors." In a novel, the ensuing events, characters, social practices and traditions, can be seen to flow from the narrative that was so far written or from the control of the novelist himself. The continuity is imposed from either source. Sometimes this happens in real life, of course, but sometimes, perhaps quite often, it does not. When it does not, the agent is much less in a position to know how his "story" is going to unfold, and this uncertainty may bar him from correspondingly bringing to his decisions the right modality.

It is worthy of note that MacIntyre half concedes this point when he construes the proper living of a life as a *quest* for narrative unity, and the purpose of the virtues as one of sustaining that quest in the face of temptations and other distractions. In this context his provisional definition of the good life for man is "the life spent in *seeking* the good life for man, and the virtues necessary for the seeking of those which will enable us to understand what more and what else the good life for man is."[27]

Again, however, we seem to run up against a circle or *petitio,* although this time it is a circle that circumscribes somewhat different elements. On the one hand, the strength of this stage of his theory is that, while the virtues are justified derivatively as leading to the good life or narrative unity, these latter notions do seem to be partially separate and prior to those virtues. But, on the other hand, we are saddled with the idea that living the good life (through living a narrative unity) consists of seeking it; and given the disparity between the prospective and retrospective points of view, this amounts to Schneewind's observation that we—at least often—can't say anything more about *what* we seek (the good life) except that we seek it.[28] Perhaps the reader will be pardoned if he sees this as something of an anti-climax to a theory that is supposed to rescue modernity from the dawn of a new dark age.

III. The Two Concepts of Virtue Summarily Compared

Although these two perspectives of classical virtues differ radically in the content of their teleology, foremost in the conception of the *telos* for the sake of which the virtues are valuable, there is in the end a kind of *petitio* that perhaps underpins them both. For Veatch, the critical concepts of nature and development are supposed to support the correct value judgment as to the good life for man, but these notions seem impotent in playing such a normative role unless one puts the cart before the horse by sneaking in a prior, question-begging value judgment about what the good for man is. In MacIntyre, the virtues are supposed to derive their value from being tied to the internal goods of a practice, yet the value of these goods seems to be entirely exhausted by those virtues. His notion of the narrative unity does look like a bona fide, conceptually prior good, until we inquire in what it consists, to which we are given the answer that it is the fulfillment of our question for that unity

Notes

[1]Alasdair MacIntyre, *After Virtue* (Notre Dame, Indiana: University of Notre Dame Press, 1981), p. 174. All subsequent references to MacIntyre are to this book.

[2]*Ibid.*

[3]Except where otherwise noted, all of the material on Veatch is taken from his most recent book manuscript, *Positive Law and Natural Law as Guarantors of Individual Liberty (unpublished).*

[4]*Ibid.*, p. 57.

[5]*Ibid.*, p. 69.

[6]*Ibid.*, p. 72.

[7]Henry Veatch, *Rational Man* (Bloomington: Indiana University Press, 1962).

[8]Natural Law Ms., p. 105.

[9]MacIntyre, *op. cit.*, p. 171.

[10]*Ibid.*, p. 56.

[11]*Ibid.*

[12]*Ibid.*

[13]*Ibid.*, pp. 141–143.

[14]*Ibid.*, p. 176.

[15]*Ibid.*, p. 175.

[16]*Ibid.*, p. 178.

[17]*Ibid.*, p. 217.

[18]*Ibid.*, p. 185.

[19]*Ibid.*, pp. 175–176.

[20]From private correspondence about this paper.

[21]MacIntyre, *op. cit.*, p. 187.

[22]*Ibid.*, p. 188.

[23]*Ibid.*, p. 208.

[24]*Ibid.*, p. 203.

[25]Schneewind, "Review of *After Virtue*", *Journal of Philosophy* 79 (Nov., 1982), 659.

[26]Again, I am indebted to Andrew Altman and to some of the participants in The Veatch Symposium for this point.

[27]MacIntyre, *op. cit.*, p. 204.

[28]Schneewind, *op. cit.*

ARISTOTLE ON PRACTICAL KNOWLEDGE AND MORAL WEAKNESS

Fred D. Miller, Jr.
Bowling Green State University

When Aristotle takes up the task of establishing the foundations of ethics in the *Nicomachean Ethics*, he understands this task quite differently from many modern philosophers. This is largely the result of his conception of ethics as a practical inquiry. He explicitly distinguishes ethics and politics from more precise disciplines such as mathematics, and emphasizes that their end is action (*praxis*) rather than knowledge (*gnosis*) (I, 3, 1095a5–6). Moreover Aristotle differs from many moderns in the importance which he places upon knowledge of what to do *in a concrete situation*. Practical knowledge for Aristotle has two indispensable, interrelated components: (1) apprehension of the ultimate end of human action, and (2) practical rationality in virtue of which one knows how to pursue this end in concrete situations. As a moral epistemologist Aristotle is exceptional in the emphasis he places upon practical rationality. As Henry Veatch remarks in his illuminating book on Aristotle, even if one correctly apprehends the ultimate end, knowing how to attain it in action is no trivial matter of perfunctorily applying general precepts. Veatch quotes Sartre's anecdote of the young man who sought his advice during World War II as to whether he should stay with his mother or join the Free French forces. Veatch contends that Aristotle would agree with Sartre that a general apprehension of the end will not provide us with *a priori* recipes for answering "concrete moral questions," such as the dilemma posed in Sartre's anecdote. And he would agree that the young man must work out the answer for himself in the immediate context of action. But Veatch also maintains contra Sartre that moral agents can and should work out answers through "practical moral knowledge."[1] Part I of this essay will defend this way of understanding Aristotle on practical knowledge against an opposing interpretation.

Another important contrast with moderns is that Aristotle believes that being a virtuous person depends upon having practical moral knowledge. A failure to have or exercise practical knowledge can undermine one's resolve to do right and lead to moral weakness. Part II of this paper will argue that Aristotle's approach to the problem is comprehensible only when it is viewed in the light of his theory of practical knowledge, so that his practical interest in moral weakness is different from the theoretical interest of recent analytic philosophers like Donald Davidson.

I. Practical Knowledge

The account of practical knowledge in Aristotle's ethical writings[2] involves a set of interlocking concepts, including *phronesis* (practical rationality), *bouleusis* (planning or deliberation), *nous* (practical insight), *syllogismos ton prakton* (practical syllogism), and *aisthesis* (perception). He uses these concepts, in connection with a variety of notions of desire, passion, choice, habituation, and moral virtue, to explain how we come to have good and bad goals, how we construct life plans which are more or less satisfactory in achieving these goals, and how we carry these plans out, or fail to carry them out, in action.

Practical rationality is an intellectual virtue or excellence, which enables a person to plan well about what is good or useful for living well or being happy (VI, 5, 1140a25–28). It is his function to plan well concerning goods attainable by humans (7, 1141b8–12). The function of every part of the intellect is to reach the truth (11, 1139a27–31), and practical rationality is a truthful state or capacity, involving thought, for acting with regard to human good and evil (5, 1140b4–7). There is strong *prima facie* evidence that practical rationality is confined to identifying the means to ends. For, in addition to the bald statement that we deliberate about means and not ends (III, 3, 1112b11–12; cp. *EE* II, 10, 1226b10, 1227a8), Aristotle states that practical rationality makes our means right, in contrast to excellence of character or moral virtue which makes the end right (VI, 12, 1144a7–9; cf. also VII, 8, 1151a18–19).[3] Aristotle in Book III compares the process of planning or deliberating to the process of scientific discovery, for example, the problem of geometrical construction (3, 1112b16–24). Just as problem-solving terminates in the recognition of something ultimate which forms the first step in the construction of a figure, planning terminates in the recognition of something ultimate which is the "first cause" in action. Practical rationality, the state of deliberating well, is a cognitive state which produces imperatives: "for what should (or must) be done or not be done is its end" (VI, 10, 1143a8–9). The truth for such a cognitive state will, evidently, depend on whether the imperatives to act are derivable from true indicative statements relating means to ends in a justified manner.

What, then, is the relationship between the employment of practical rationality, so understood, and the actions and observations of the agent at the time of action? Two interpretations have been suggested:

(I) The employment of practical rationality in the planning process can be completed only at the time of action; and it includes, as its terminus, a practical syllogism.
(The action-terminating interpretation)

(II) The process of planning or deliberation is completed when the agent decides upon a specific type of action, a decision which may be implemented at an appropriate subsequent time; and the activity of planning does not include or require in any way a practical syllogism. (The action-type-terminating interpretation)

The former interpretation is (as indicated in the introduction to this essay) favored by Henry Veatch. But recently John Cooper has defended the second interpretation, on the basis of two lines of argument: that there is a fundamental difference between the logic of deliberation and that of the practical syllogism which Aristotle would not have overlooked; and the action-terminating interpretation imputes to Aristotle a serious epistemological confusion for which there is no basis in the text: "On this interpretation Aristotle will be representing as part of the process of deliberative analysis what is in fact the work of perception by which one brings the conclusion of deliberations to bear on the actual conditions in which one finds oneself."[4] Cooper develops these arguments with a persuasive selection of supporting texts and examples, but they are not in the end convincing, and there is good reason to adopt instead the action-terminating interpretation.

Cooper's first line of argument turns upon the claim that there is a fundamental difference between the logic of deliberation and the practical syllogism. "Deliberation as Aristotle represents it does not take a form that remotely resembles an Aristotelian syllogism, and Aristotle never says or implies that it does." Means-to-end reasoning involves relational logic, whereas the practical syllogism involves subsuming a particular case under a more general "ought" statement. This line of argument is mistaken: Aristotle clearly indicates that he regards deliberation as yielding syllogisms, and it is anachronistic to think that he would have been clear on the distinction between syllogistic and relational logic which has come to be widely accepted by philosophers only during the past century.[5]

Cooper supports the action-type-terminating interpretation (II) with another, epistemological line of argument: The practical syllogism, narrowly constructed, makes an altogether different contribution to practical reasoning from that of the deliberative process, which Aristotle would not have failed to see. For the practical syllogism, as such, represents only the work of perception by which one brings the conclusion to deliberations to bear on the actual conditions in which one finds oneself. Cooper appeals to two examples: A doctor completes his deliberations by deciding to give his patient an emetic in midafternoon, tells him to come back then, and only later carries out the decision by looking among his medicines, selecting the emetic, and giving it to the patient to drink. Similarly, having deliberated, a person decides to flip the light switch; when he perceives a switch, he simply reaches out and flips it.[6] In both examples the deliberation is clearly completed before the time of action and perception is required only in order to implement its results. At this point I will only suggest that both these examples seem suspiciously cut and dried. In normal cases of planning, in business, warfare, or teaching, it is far from clear that the process of working out what to do is completed before action and that perception of the field of action makes no contribution to this process. Even if one has drawn up contingency plans for a battle, these will be necessarily incomplete, in that the final crucial stages of the plan can be identified only by coming *in medias res*. Even a deliberating doctor should take into account the observable peculiarities of a patient, as Aristotle emphasizes: "While, on the whole, rest and abstinence from food are good for someone with a fever, for a particular person they may not be" (*EN* X, 9, 1180b8–10). Moreover, a patient's condition changes in observable ways, which requires continuing revisions in one's plan of treatment. (One hopes that Cooper's doctor would take any such changes into account before administering the emetic.)

Cooper contends, however, that completion of Aristotelian deliberation does not presuppose observation of the individual circumstances of action. Cooper's interpretation is hard to reconcile with passages which characterize practical rationality as concerned with particulars (*kath' hekasta*) and ultimate things (*eschata*). The most natural way of taking these passages is that practical rationality, excellence in deliberation, is concerned with action involving individual things and concrete circumstances.[7] It terminates with the identification of such individuals, and hence can be completed only at the time of action. This is the action-termination interpretation (I). Further support for it is found in Aristotle's remark that practical rationality is concerned with the ultimate, that is, the object of *perception* (VI, 8, 1142a26–27). However, Aristotle connects perception with the working of insight (*nous*) in practical contexts (11, 1143b5). Therefore, it is necessary to consider whether Aristotle's treatment of insight and perception also agree with the action-terminating interpretation (I).

Insight or intelligence is an indispensable mental capacity in the sphere of purposeful action as well as of theoretical wisdom (VI, 2, 1139a33–35; 7, 1141a18–19). Nevertheless, the term "insight" performs a quite different role in Aristotle's account of practical knowledge from its role in his account of theoretical knowledge. For example, whereas theoretical insight secures the causal principles which form the major premises of scientific explanation, practical insight is supposed to supply the *minor* premises of practical syllogisms (VI, 11, 1142b35-1143b5). Corresponding to the two interpretations of practical rationality, there are two interpretations of practical insight in Aristotle:

(I*) Insight, in its practical application, brings deliberation to completion, through the identification of suitable means, within the observable field of action, for the realization of the agent's ends.
(The deliberation-completing interpretation)

(II*) Insight, in its practical application, merely connects completed deliberation to action, through the perception of a concrete instance of the specific type arrived at independently by deliberation.
(The deliberation-implementing interpretation)

In view of the fact that Aristotle states that practical insight and practical rationality are directed toward the same thing (VI, 11, 1143a25–29), one would expect a close correspondence between the interpretation of these two concepts. Thus, not surprisingly, Cooper defends (II*) the deliberation-implementing interpretation of practical insight: its job is "to apply one's calculations about how an end is to be achieved to the circumstances in which action actually begins."[8] Given (II) Cooper's action-type-terminating interpretation of practical rationality, practical insight could have no more than this job to do if its job were to provide the factual minor premise of a practical syllogism. Contrariwise, (I*) the deliberation-completing interpretation of practical insight complements the (I) action-terminating interpretation of rationality: rationality must include something like insight if it is to complete its work of selecting individual actions in concrete situations.

On either of these interpretations, (I*) or (II*), there is a marked contrast between the roles of practical insight and theoretical insight. The contrast between theoretical and practical insight is explicitly stated in the following passage:

> And insight is of ultimate things in both directions; for insight and not reasoning is of the primary bounding principles and of the ultimate things, and insight, *in demonstrations,* is of immutable bounding principles, whereas insight, *in matters of action,* is of the ultimate and of the contingent and of the minor premise . . . [1143a35–b3].

One might well ask why Aristotle uses the same word "*nous*" for these theoretical and practical excellences, if they differ so strikingly. The most likely reason is that insight, in either context, has a close connection with *perception* or *observation.* This is quite evident in the case of theoretical insight in the *Posterior Analytics.* Theoretical insight is a capacity to grasp universal principles as a result of repeated sense experiences. For insight is an epistemic capacity acquired through the process of induction (VI, 3, 1139b28–29) and 6, 1141a7–8; cf. *Apo* I, 18, 81b2; II, 19, 100b3–5, 12); and induction presupposes experience (*empeiria*), which consists of sense-perceptions retained in the form of memories (II, 19, 100a3–9). For example, one might observe visually that spherical bodies wax and wane in a specific manner. One sees the connection between the properties of being spherical and waxing and waning in a certain way, and has the insight that it must be so in all cases (cf. I, 31, 88a16–17). One grasps such a generalization through a process of induction on the basis of accumulated experience.

Aristotle's account of practical insight resembles this in important respects. For he speaks of insight as the perception of particulars (*aisthesis, haute d'esti nous,* VI, 11, 1143b5). But the precise relationship between practical insight and sense-perception is quite subtle. Insight involves an act of sense-perception, but it also presupposes the possession of accumulated experience. This can be inferred from two passages. In the first he is arguing that one cannot be *morally* virtuous without having insight. *Natural* virtue is a necessary, but not sufficient, condition for moral virtue in the full sense. For natural virtue without insight *(aneu nou)* can be harmful, "as a strong body which moves without sight may stumble badly because of its lack of sight" (1144b9–12). Aristotle notes that this deficiency is especially characteristic of *children,* which seems to recall the second passage where young people cannot have practical rationality because they lack *experience*(8, 1142a12–16). Evidently, the "lack of *nous*" of the young involves their inexperience and resulting inability to identify particular ways of attaining their goals.

Aristotle does not go into detail about the precise contribution of insight and experience in these passages, but he evidently has in view the necessity of perception in order to *find the mean.* For example, a youthful person may possess natural generosity, but due to inexperience, may blunder disastrously in trying to act generously. He may err in identifying the proper beneficiaries of his actions. He may be mistaken in the form his generosity should take, so that he ends up insulting or humiliating his beneficiary. He may be wrong about the magnitude of the gratuity, about the beneficiary's true interests, his timing may be off, and so forth. "In the case of such particular matters, the decision rests with perception" (IV, 5, 1126a31–b4; II, 9, 1109a24–30, b20–23). But, as the foregoing passages about youngsters suggest, the ability to perceive available opportunities in one's field of action presupposes *experience.* The role of experience in practical cognition is, in a way, analogous to its role in theoretical inquiry. For by experience one can "go on" to new and difficult cases and identify specific means for attaining one's ends.

The text, therefore, supports the action-terminating interpretation (I) of practical rationalty and (I*) the deliberation-completing interpretation of practical insight. Insight is spoken of as perception, and insight and practical rationality are directed to the same thing, the concrete object of perception. Insight is, in effect, the perception that an individual thing will serve one's needs. Since practical rationality is excellence at deliberation, the implication is that deliberation can be completed only at the time of action by the agent observing the field of action, and that insight brings deliberation to completion through the identification of suitable means in the field of action.

Moreover, this interpretation permits the most natural reading of Aristotle's description of insight as the perception of "what is ultimate *and* contingent *and* of the minor premise," which serve as the starting points for the goal (11, 1143b3). Insight is the perception that a perceptible means (the ultimate thing) is required to reach one's end, described in the minor premise.

On the other hand, to limit as severely as Cooper does the role of insight to merely implementing deliberation leads to absurd results. For it is hard then to make good sense of Aristotle's suggestion that youngsters blunder as a result of their lack of insight. The suggestion would have to be that although youthful persons may be able to complete the process of calculation and deliberation, for example, to conclude that they should eat chicken in order to make themselves healthy, they are unable to identify chicken! Surely, it is more plausible, in view of Aristotle's remarks elsewhere about perception and the mean, to suggest that they are unable to do so because of lack of experience. For example, the youth wants to act courageously but does not know how to identify opportunities as such as they present themselves in battle. Aristotle's theory of virtue as a mean requires this account of insight. The experienced soldier can pick out the appropriate sorts; as he is at the time of action identifying these opportunities, he is also supplying the materials for the practical syllogism.

This concludes the defense of the interpretation of Aristotle on rationality in action according to which practical rationality is exercised at the time of action, practical insight is indispensable to completing rationality, and the practical syllogism is a part of deliberation. This interpretation seems to be in fundamental accord with that of Veatch, who points out that the complexities and uncertainties of concrete action situations are not peculiar to moral dilemmas of the sort illustrated by Sartre—they are found in ordinary practical cases. For example, Veatch describes a fisherman who finds himself in a dilemma in which, if he reels a fish in too slowly or too quickly, he will lose it. There is no *a priori* rule on hand for handling the situation and no one else can tell him what to do. Veatch also argues that, from the fact that such difficult problems arise, it cannot plausibly be inferred that the fisherman, or the moral agent, is acting without practical knowledge.

Practical *moral* knowledge differs from productive knowledge of the sort exhibited by the angler, insofar as the means to the end grasped by practical rationality and insight is itself a *constituent* of the end sought (cf. VI, 5, 1140a24–28). Practical rationality and insight enable one to grasp in a concrete situation what the generous or courageous act is, an act which is valued for its own sake (cp. II, 4, 11105a26–69). Hence, it is by means of practical rationality and insight that the end of human conduct is to be fully articulated (cf. VI, 5, 1140b4–7).

II. Moral Weakness

Virtuous conduct on Aristotle's account requires not only a disposition to act virtuously but also practical knowledge at the time of action. A fully virtuous person is correctly guided by reason and has desires in agreement with reason. A morally strong or continent person is correctly guided by reason but has bad desires; however, such a person is not led by them. A morally weak person succumbs to base desires or emotions, but apparently recognizes that this is not the right thing to do. In his analysis of moral weakness Aristotle places great emphasis on the fact that a failure to have or to exercise practical knowledge at the time of action can undermine one's resolve to act virtuously. This is an insight which has been underappreciated by modern commentators. When Aristotle's analysis of moral weakness is viewed in light of the action-terminating interpretation of practical ration-

ality and the deliberation-completing account of practical insight, it will be
apparent that it does accommodate familiar instances of moral weakness.
Moreover, it will become apparent that his interest in moral weakness differs
fundamentally from that of recent analytic philosophers such as Donald
Davidson. The following discussion focuses on implications of the issues
taken up in Part I for Aristotle's understanding of moral weakness. It is not
intended to be a full treatment of either Aristotle's entire account or the
immense secondary literature on the subject.

Aristotle has been often taken to task for his characterization of the
morally weak person: "Now, since the final premise (*teleutaia protasis*) is a
belief about a perceptible thing and is decisive (*kuria*) for actions, this one
either does not have being in a passionate state, or has it, not in the sense in
which to have is to know but [in the sense in which it is] to speak, as a
drunkard speaks the verses of Empedocles" (VII, 3, 1147b9–12). Aristotle
is diagnosing moral weakness as involving a failure to use practical cognitive faculties fully and effectively in an occasion for action, and he
distinguishes himself from Socrates by locating the breakdown at the level
of the particular rather than the universal (b13–17). This approach to the
problem seems especially implausible if it is supposed that the work of
deliberation is complete before the time of action so all the agent needs to do
at the time of action is to perceive the particular instances of a specific course
of action decided on beforehand. Such an interpretation would require
Aristotle to say that moral weakness involves the following: one has fully
worked out what to do before the time of action but is unable to perceive a
present opportunity to act accordingly. This suggests preposterous examples
(e.g., one concludes beforehand that one should have chicken for lunch but
an urge for sweets prevents one from recognizing some chicken clearly in
view) and leaves Aristotle open to the charge that, for him, suffering moral
weakness is like suffering a lapse of memory.[8] But on the interpretation that
insight and perception at the time of action are required to complete one's
deliberations about what to do, Aristotle will be saying that the influences of
desire may interrupt or beguile the deliberative process in its final stages.

Aristotle believes that people act as they do because they desire certain
ends and they have beliefs based on the evidence of their senses as to how
these ends can be attained. It is a real problem for Aristotle when people who
have deliberated about how to attain their ends do not behave accordingly
but act against their better judgment. Consider, for example, a gambler who
spends her day at a racetrack instead of meeting her obligations to her
employer or family. Aristotle offers two possible explanations: Either her
deliberations about how to spend her time and money were interrupted or
they were somehow preempted. Aristotle accordingly recognizes two forms
of moral weakness: impetuousness and lack of fortitude (VII, 7,
1150b19–28). Of these, impetuousness (*propeteia*) poses no problem,
because the person does not *complete* the process of deliberation which
would have specifically forbidden the weak action. For example, the
gambler motivated by a desire for the excitement of the track might not

calculate the costs to her family should she lose a bet or determine what specific tasks she should be doing at work. (It seems no exaggeration to say that such calculations do not tax the minds of most bettors.) Aristotle probably has impetuousness in mind when he says that, due to passion, a person may simply not *have* (6, 1147b20*f.*) the final premise of the practical syllogism. And, as argued in Part I, the identification of the final premise is *part* of an act of insight which terminates the process of deliberation. The impetuous gambler will simply not employ her practical insight to locate the particular features of a complex situation which will enable her to further her other goals: e.g., pursuing her career or taking care of her family. Although impetuousness does not puzzle Aristotle (cf. 1147a8–10), he is and should be puzzled abut the other type of weakness of will, lack of fortitude *(astheneia)*, where the agent who has deliberated fails to carry out the results of deliberation. Aristotle's explanation is that deliberation may not issue in action because it is preempted or impeded by another piece of practical reasoning.[9]

> When, therefore, the universal premise in us holds us back, *(ko-luousa)* from tasting, but there is the premise, "Everything sweet is pleasant" and "This is sweet" (and this premise is exercised), and desire exists in us, the one [viz. the premise] tells us to avoid this, but the desire guides us; for it [viz. desire] can move the parts [of the body]; so it follows that being weak-willed is under reason in some manner and under a belief, not opposed as such but only incidentally to right reason, for the desire and not the belief is opposed <to it as such> [1147a31–b3].

In this example there are two opposing syllogisms. The first has a universal premise that would hold us back from tasting, e.g., "A second piece of pie is not to be tasted. This is my second piece of pie. So this is not to be tasted." The second is: "Since I desire pleasure and a sweet is pleasure, a sweet is to be tasted. This is sweet. So this is to be tasted."[10] The final premises of the second syllogism is exercised *(energei)* and the desire for pleasure leads us to act. Aristotle denies that our rational faculty accepts a principle opposed to right reason (e.g., that health is a good thing and whatever this implies). Rather desire is opposed (in a causal sense) to reason. Why does the first syllogism fail to impede the second? Aristotle indicates that the strength of the conclusion to be enacted is a result not only of a general desire, such as for health, but also of the strength of the *minor premise,* which identifies the particular aspects of the field of action tending to satisfy the desire. After the passage above, Aristotle alludes to an earlier comparison (1147b6–9):

> It is clear, therefore, that weak-willed persons should be described like the preceding cases [viz. sleepers, psychotics, and drunkards]. The fact that they state propositions derived from knowledge signifies nothing; for people influenced by such passions state demonstrations

and words of Empedocles, and those who are first learning can string propositions together, without at all knowing them; for it has to grow into them, and that takes time, so one should suppose that the weak-willed people make statements just like those who play a part on a stage [1147a17–24].

In spite of the comparison to sleepers, psychotics, and so forth, Aristotle is not here claiming that in every case of weakness of will the agent is rendered unconscious, blind, or insane as a result of his desires. The examples in this passage suggest a much broader view. The weak-willed person is able to make relevant statements but *either* he does not know what they mean *or* he does not believe them *or* he does not understand why they are true. In general, he "has" knowledge in the sense that he can make statements which express it, but these statements are not epistemically well grounded. There follows the notorious claim quoted earlier: "The final premise[11] is a belief involving what is perceptive and decisive for action, and this [the weak-willed person] *either* does not have being in a passionate state, *or* has it, not in the sense in which to have is to know but [in that sense in which it is merely] to state, as the drunkard says the words of Empedocles" (1147b9–12), he is covering both types of weakness: The impetuous person lacks the minor premise altogether, whereas the one lacking fortitude "has" it only in the weak sense. If a person's deliberations and practical syllogisms resemble the recitations of drunkards or demonstrations by undergraduates, they may be preempted.

As in other parts of ethics Aristotle is not content with offering a correct analysis of a concept such as *akrasia*. He is also concerned with how the morally weak person is to be "cured" (cf. VII, 2, 1146a33–34). He is accordingly interested in giving an etiology (in the Aristotelian sense of *aition* or "cause") of this disorder with a view to its cure. He concludes that of the forms of moral weakness, impetuosity is easier to cure than lack of fortitude and that weakness due to bad habits is easier to cure than the innate type (VII, 10, 1152a27–33).

Aristotle probably cannot be acquitted of the often heard charge of taking an overly "intellectualist" approach to moral weakness. And it is not surprising that he finds lack of fortitude more intractable than impetuosity. His analysis of impetuosity is straightforward and plausible: Impetuous persons present no problem because their deliberations are interrupted due to the passions. As much cannot be said for his analysis of those suffering from a lack of fortitude: Aristotle may well be right in many cases that the causal chain proceeding from noble ends to virtuous acts is preempted by other practical reasoning leading to reprehensible acts—but it cannot invariably be claimed that the preemption occurs *because* the moral agent's final premise is not epistemically entrenched enough. Aristotle wants to maintain that practical rationality *(phronesis)* is the strongest of all states and that, if it is fully exercised at the time of action it *must* lead to action (VII, 2, 1146a5–7). But he seems to go too far in confining the subversive role of such desires solely to weakening our knowledge of the minor premise. It has often been objected that one may recognize the minor premise which completes one's deliberations, and yet fail to act accordingly. Hence, Aristotle has at best a partial "cure"—in the sense of a cure for moving a person from moral weakness to moral strength or continence. Strengthening one's practical rationality is part, but not all, of the answer.

To appreciate more fully the point of the foregoing interpretation of Aristotle on moral weakness, it will be useful to contrast his interests with those of the contemporary analytic philosopher Donald Davidson in "How is Weakness of the Will Possible?". Davidson offers an interpretation of Aristotle which is

> As long as we keep the general outline of Aristotle's theory before us, I think we cannot fail to realize that he can offer no satisfactory analysis of incontinent action. No doubt he can explain why, in borderline cases, we are tempted both to say an agent acted intentionally and that he knew better. But if we postulate a strong desire from which he acted, then on the theory, we also attribute to the agent a strong judgment that the action is desirable; and if we emphasize that the agent's ability to reason to the wrongness of his action was weakened or distorted, to that extent we show that he did not fully appreciate that what he was doing was undesirable. [12]

Davidson here presumes that Aristotle's problem of weakness is the same as the problem which Davidson is attacking in his own paper. This seems to be wrong. The purpose of the present discussion is not to take Davidson to task for an interpretation of Aristotle which he offers in a modest and tentative way, but merely to point out *how* different Aristotle's technique and interest are from Davidson's.

There are, of course, similarities. Like Davidson, Aristotle thinks that agents act as they do *because* they have the ends and the beliefs which they do, and that they recognize morally weak agents as acting intentionally and for reasons. [13] And Aristotle is troubled by the occurrence of moral weakness because he takes for granted rationality in human action. But Davidson's approach differs fundamentally insofar as he sees weakness of will as a *conceptual* problem, consisting in an inconsistent triad of propositions:

P1.   If an agent wants to do x more than he wants to do y and he believes himself free to do either x or y, then he will intentionally do x if he does either x or y intentionally.

P2.   If an agent judges that it would be better to do x than to do y, then he wants to do x more than he wants to do y.

P3.   There are incontinent actions [i.e. for some action x, the agent does x intentionally, the agent believes that there is alternative action y open to him, and the agent judges that it would be better to do y than to do x]. [14]

Davidson's tactic for solving the problem is to distinguish between two senses in which one can "judge that *a* is better than *b*." Briefly, one can make an "unconditional judgment," or one can make a conditional judgment or relativized judgment that *a* is prima facie better than *b* relative to certain considerations. Davidson's solution is that "judge" has the unconditional sense in *P2* and the conditional sense in *P3*, so that there is no inconsistency.

A critical discussion of Davidson's solution is beyond the scope of this paper. But it is necessary to challenge his claim that Aristotle employs a device similar to his own:

> Though there is plenty of room for doubt as to precisely what Aristotle's view was, it is safe to say that he tried to solve our problem by distinguishing two senses in which a man may be said to know (or believe) that one thing is better than another; one sense makes *P2* true, while the other sense is needed in [*P3*]. The flavour of this second sense is given by Aristotle's remark that the incontinent man has knowledge "in the sense in which having knowledge does not mean knowing but only talking, as a drunken man may mutter the verses of Empedocles."[15]

It is true that Aristotle distinguishes between two senses in which one "has knowledge," but, as we have seen, he is concerned with whether we know the *minor premise* of the practical syllogism, not the conclusion. He is concerned with *perceptual* knowledge (cf. 1147b9–10), involved in acts of insight, not with a comparative value judgment, e.g., that *x* is better than *y*. One can, of course make inferences from Aristotle's claims about the status of conclusions in the form of comparative judgments concerning the merits of committing, or not committing, the act in question," but Davidson himself admits that he is going "beyond Aristotle" in doing so.[16] The fact is that Aristotle does not share Davidson's worries about logical contradictions among one's preferences. According to Davidson Aristotle's competing practical syllogisms lead to a "flat contradiction," since one has the conclusion that it is better not to taste the coconut cream pie than to do so, and the other is that it is better to taste than abstain. But this is not the problem with which Aristotle is preoccupied. He *does* contend that the major premise governing the act of weakness, viz. "Sweet things are pleasant," is not opposed (*enantia*) to the right rule, viz. "Such and such things ought not to be tasted," but he adds that the desire for pleasure *is* what is opposed to the right rule (1147b1–3). This suggests that "the opposite" in this context is a *causal* notion rather than a logical concept.

As noted above, Davidson states that "if we postulate a strong desire from which [the agent] acted, then on [Aristotle's] theory, we also attribute to the agent a strong judgment that the action is desirable."[17] But Aristotle is at pains to avoid such a thesis. For him the strength of the conclusion to be enacted derives not merely from desire but also from knowledge, viz. of the minor premise due to practical insight.

Moral weakness of backsliding has puzzled many philosophers, ancient and modern. But the nature of the puzzlement for a given philosopher depends upon specific presuppositions which that philosopher makes about rationality in action. Davidson sees incontinence as involving a "logical difficulty" which can be solved by distinguishing two different senses in which one makes comparative judgments.[18] This difficulty presupposes a contemporary theory of preferences which is essentially alien to Aristotle. One might indeed wonder why Davidson is puzzled about the commonplace fact that sometimes a person chooses *a* over *b even though he judges, all things considered, that b* is better than *a*. For if one ascribes conflicting beliefs or desires to an agent one thereby represents the agent as inconsistent, but one does not seem thereby to offer an inconsistent account of the agent's behavior. Davidson is evidently operating from the assumption that a person's actions are determined by a preference function which is defined by a set of better-than judgments with properties such as transitivity and asymmetry.[19] Given such an assumption, there are obvious difficulties when a preference involved in incontinence does not fit into the agent's "all things considered" preference pattern. But there is no evidence that Aristotle is operating from this sort of assumption. And Aristotle's concern is with why when one is deliberating about how to attain virtuous ends, one's deliberations fail to be carried out and one instead pursues nonvirtuous ends. He is worried not about a "theoretical" difficulty, as is Davidson, but about the *practical* difficulty of why moral deliberation fails to result in action. For he is concerned with the very practical question of how we can cure ourselves of this practical difficulty.

Notes

[1] Henry Veatch, *Aristotle: A Contemporary Appreciation* (Bloomington: Indiana University Press, 1974), pp. 111–118.

[2] Unless otherwise stated, references are to the *Nicomachean Ethics* (abr. *NE*), Bywater's text. References to the *Eudemian Ethics* (abr. EE) are to Susemihl's text.

[3] Some commentators see practical rationality as giving the ends in *NE* VI, 9, 1142b32–33. But the passage is ambiguous, since the antecedent of the relative pronoun in the clause "of which practical rationality is the true apprehension," could be "the means to the end" rather than "the end."

[4] John Cooper, *Reason and Human Good in Aristotle* (Cambridge, MA: Harvard University Press, 1975), p. 64n.

[5] See *NE* VI, 9, 1142b21–26; *Posterior Analytics* II, 11, 94b8–12; *De Motu Animalium* 7, 701a22–23. I argue against this first line of argument at length in "Aristotle on Practical Rationality," forthcoming in *The Review of Metaphysics*.

[6] *Ibid.*, 13, 27.

[7] See *NE* VI, 7, 1141b14–16 and *Metaphysics* I, 1, 981a16–17; VI, 8, 1142a24–25 and 1141b24–29. I criticize Cooper's treatment of these passages in the article cited in note 5.

[8]For an interpretation along these lines see R. Robinson, "Aristotle on *Akrasia,*" in J. Barnes et al., *Articles on Aristotle,* v. 2 (London: Duckworth, 1977). See also the criticisms of this view in W. D. Ross, *Aristotle* (New York: Meridian, 1959), p. 224 and James J. Walsh, *Aristotle's Conceptions of Moral Weakness* (New York, Columbia University Press, 1963), p. 120.

[9]Hardie questions whether *koluomenon* at 1147a31 can mean anything but "external and physical interference" (W. F. R. Hardie, *Aristotle's Ethical Theories,* 2nd ed. [Oxford: Oxford University Press, 1980], p. 282). But the same verb is used for an internal impediment in the next line. Aside from this point, my discussion owes a great deal to Hardie's lucid and comprehensive discussion of moral weakness.

[10]Compare 1147a29 for this construction of the second syllogism. G. Santas remarks (*ad* 1144a31–34) that Aristotle "may have thought of 'rules' as simply summaries of necessary or sufficient means to the final good or some subordinate good"—so that the ultimate premise is always teleological. See "Aristotle on Practical Inference, the Explanation of Action, and Akrasia," *Phronesis* 14 (1969), p. 168. The first syllogism is, of course, suggested by J. L. Austin's amusing "bombe at High Table" example in "A Plea for Excuses." James J. Walsh has a helpful review of the different attempts to interpret the above passage: in general, the two syllogisms either (1) have the same premise but different conclusions, or (2) have different premises only one of which is exercised (*energei*). The second seems most consistent, with the apparent emphasis on the minor premise being in the one case exercised and in the other case either not possessed or not possessed in the right way (1147a33, b9–12), and *pace* Walsh nothing in 1147a31–1147b5 rules it out. Compare Walsh, *Aristotle's Conception of Moral Weakness* (New York: Columbia University Press, 1963), pp. 103–109.

[11]This translation follows most translators and commentators, including Ross, Rackham, and Hardie, in taking *teleutaia protasis* to refer to "last premise"—rather than following Kenny, Vlastos, and Santas in taking it to refer to "conclusion." The latter, somewhat forced translation seems necessary only if one presumes that morally weak persons act on the same minor premises which they would have acted upon if they had acted according to virtue. As the above example indicates, the competing syllogisms can have different minor premises; thus in moral weakness it is possible for a minor premise to fail to be exercised. ("This is sweet" may be exercised to the exclusion of "This is my second piece of pie.")

[12]D. Davidson, "How is Weakness of the Will Possible?" in J. Feinberg (ed.), *Moral Concepts* (Oxford: Oxford University Press, 1970), p. 103.

[13]*Ibid.,* 99, 101.

[14]*Ibid.,* 94–95.

[15]*Ibid.,* 99–100.

[16]*Ibid.,* 104.

[17]*Ibid.,* 103.

[18]*Ibid.,* 110.

[19]*Transitivity:* If s prefers x to y and y to z, then s prefers x to z. *Asymmetry:* If s prefers x to y, then s does not prefer y to x. Other properties may also be presupposed, such as *Completeness:* For any x and y, s either prefers x to y or prefers y to x or is indifferent between x and y.

THE INCOHERENCE OF UNIVERSAL PRESCRIPTIVISM[1]

Joseph Beatty
Randolph-Macon College

By now the universalizability criterion is such a stable article of faith among contemporary moral theorists that merely to ask why it is considered an important test for moral beliefs seems not merely heretic but perhaps reprobate. Its credentials as an essential mark of moral judgments are, it is claimed, patent and varied. Consider: a) the very meaning of "morally ought" is that reasons must be given and reasons necessarily embody principles which apply to all in similar circumstances; b) one's willingness to say that one's principle could be affirmed by everyone in similar circumstances tests one's moral seriousness or sincerity; c) if one's principle is partial to oneself or one's own (family, friends, intimates) it is morally suspect, for morality requires giving all relevantly similar individuals equal consideration and personal affection or affiliation is not morally relevant; d) inasmuch as a moral judgment aims to resolve possible or actual conflicts of interests, it must appeal to a principle which all concerned could accept; e) alternatively, because a moral judgment often limits the freedom or interests of others, it is necessary to justify it by appealing to a common, universal principle which others could accept as binding. While these various formulations (and there are more) have no core or proto-formulation, they do implicate norms of consistency, formal equality or lawlikeness which are then associated with impartiality or fairness.

The recognition, however, that the universalizability criterion, in its formaiity, falls far short of substantive morality is a commonplace in the literature on the subject. This is so largely because the principle which is applied consistently and impartially may employ a (putative) irrelevant or discriminatory criterion for consideration or treatment. Joel Feinberg's comments on *material justice* (supplying "criteria of relevance") apply equally to the universalizability criterion:

> We should not discriminate between persons who are alike in all relevant respects; but which respects are relevant depends upon the occasion for justice; on our purposes and objectives, and on the internal rules of the "game" we are playing. There is no one kind of characteristic that is relevant in all contexts. . .[1]

How one justifies the moral values which underlie one's determination of relevant criteria is an issue which has been widely debated. It is an issue that goes to the heart of the meta-ethical consideration of the relation between 'is' and 'ought' and of what makes reasons *relevant* or *good* reasons. It is also an issue central to the problem of the justification of fundamental moral or social values.

In this paper I intend to show that if we accept the framework of what is perhaps still the dominant paradigm in contemporary meta-ethics for understanding the meaning of moral judgments—Harean prescriptivism—there is no reason at all for accepting universalizability as a necessary criterion of moral judgments. I shall argue that this conclusion follows quite naturally once one understands the implications of the prescriptivist or decisionist starting point. Finally, independently of this dominant paradigm, I will attempt to explain why moral philosophers may have (mis) taken universalizability as a necessary mark of moral judgments.

Winch's Challenge

I begin with a challenge that Peter Winch has made to the scope of the universalizability criterion.[2] For the dominant or mainstream view on the relation between moral judgments and universalizability, Winch cites Sidgwick's view:

> We cannot judge an action to be right for A and wrong for B, unless we find in the natures or circumstances of the two some difference which we can regard as a reasonable ground for difference in their duties. If therefore I judge any action to be right for myself, I implicitly judge it to be right for any other person whose nature and circumstances do not differ from my own in certain important respects.
>
> If a kind of conduct that is right (or wrong) for me is not right (or wrong) for someone else, it must be on the ground of some difference between the two cases, other than the fact that I and he are different persons (p. 151).

Arguably, the mainstream view comprehends both the intelligibility-conditions and the justification-conditions of moral judgments which, in turn, implicate what has been called the "formal principle of *justice* or *fairness.*"[3] According to this principle, similar cases are to be treated similarly, dissimilar cases dissimilarly; distinctions between cases must arise from relevant factors of the objective situation, not from the mere fact that individuals are different (numerically, dispositionally, characterologically).

Winch elaborates his argument for diminishing the scope of universalizability in moral judgments by attention to the phenomenon of moral perplexity arising from a putative conflict between two genuine moral obligations exhibited in Melville's novella *Billy Budd*. In that work, Billy

Budd, a young sailor of high character, is persecuted and, finally, falsely accused of inciting the crew to mutiny by the (evil) master-at-arms, Claggart. The dramatic time is that of the period immediately after the Great Mutiny when there was considerable apprehension that other mutinies on British ships would occur. Accused by Claggart, Billy Budd is outraged at the false charge and is (literally) unable to speak; in his frustration he hits Claggart who falls, strikes his head and dies. Captain Vere is morally obliged to court-martial Billy Budd for the "capital offense" of striking his commanding officer. Yet, he believes that Billy Budd is 'innocent before God' of the 'murder' of Claggart as well as the mutiny of which he was accused. On Winch's interpretation, Vere is faced with a genuine moral dilemma in which both the imperatives ('You ought not to execute an innocent man'; 'You ought to fulfill your duty and execute those who commit capital crimes.') are experienced as morally obligatory but incompatible. Thus, when Vere decides, in opposition to the view of some of the other officers, to give greater weight to the adherence to *law* than to his personal belief in Billy Budd's innocence, he does what he morally ought to do without this 'ought' implying that anyone else in the same or similar situation should act similarly.

Now, according to Sidgwick and the mainstream view, anyone, who, in circumstances like those of Vere, decided to acquit Billy Budd, would have acted morally wrongly. Not so, maintains Winch, for in such situations the universalizability criterion is inoperative or "idle." This is so because both moral demands are singly universal but conflicting. Thus, Winch:

> . . . the admitted universal application of the two 'oughts' which have made a decision necessary cannot be deployed in order to resolve the conflict. Indeed, it is precisely because they are both taken as *uncompromisingly universal* in their application that it has been necessary to ask the question, 'what ought I to do?' (p. 162).

It might be objected that an individual whose moral judgment is non-universalizable falls prey to 'special pleading' and the likelihood of making (irrelevant) exceptions in his own case. Winch retorts that, in the circumstances he is concerned with, the morally sincere agent must reckon not with a (Kantian) sort of conflict between moral obligation and inclination (self-interest) but the (non-Kantian) conflict between two genuine moral obligations. Second, if it is objected that a judgment embodying a decisive reason for Vere which need not be a decisive reason for anyone else is not a moral judgment, given the necessary connection between 'morally ought,' 'reasons,' and 'universalizability,' one could reply that a) such an assertion begs the question at issue or b) when universalizable principles conflict one's decision may appeal to a non-universalizable maxim. Finally, Winch does not wish to associate his argument with some version of subjectivism according to which 'doing what is right' is assimilated to 'believing that what one is doing is right.' It is not the agent's belief, strictly speaking, that makes his decision right in the circumstances described but his serious attention to the moral conflict as well as his weighing of the values involved therein.

This latter procedure of giving more weight or prominence to one principle over another in genuine conflicts *seems* to run a subjectivist risk, however, in the following sense. The agent does appear to be asserting that his decision is right not because of any objective or inter-subjective aspects of the moral situation but, in the final analysis, because he believes (or is characterologically disposed to affirm) that it is right. Why does the agent believe this? To be sure, we could say, in the moment of decision he may consult his own and others' past decisions in similar or relatively similar circumstances. But what accounts for the greater weight he gives to one rather than another principle? *The sort of person he is or wants to be or has already become.* If we allow this to be morally relevant in decision-making then the familiar (and often dismissed) egoist or perhaps subjectivist claim 'I am I' or 'I am more concerned about me or my own good than about you or your good' becomes *morally relevant.* Recently, William Frankena, in the process of distinguishing an ethics of duty from a virtue-based ethics, makes a reflection which bears significantly on the issue before us.

> . . . when a moral agent is faced with the question of what he should do in a certain situation, he must ask what is the right thing to do, not what action would be morally good, because what action would be morally good depends on what motives he has or will act with, and this is irrelevant to the question of what is right. It is irrelevant both because in asking what he should do, he is supposed to be proceeding from the moral point of view and from the right and best motives and because what one ought to do depends on more objective factors about him and the situation he is in, e.g., on whether or not he will be deceiving or injuring someone. Even in an ethics of virtue, an agent must ask what the good person—one with a certain character or motivation—would do if he knew all the relevant facts, not what his own character or motives are or even what he himself would do if he knew all the relevant facts.[4]

Yet, granting Frankena's point, we could still say that a specific moral agent's belief concerning what "the good person" would do involves a reference to his own character and the constitutive ideals thereof. Because of this one's very choice of a paradigmatic individual to model oneself upon in moments of decision will implicate ideals that are constitutive of one's character. What I regard as *right to do* then cannot be detached so easily from what it is *right for me to do*—given my character and its constitutive ideals. If, then, Vere's decisions have a quite inescapable connection with Vere's character and if character and its dispositions *therefore* have to be taken into account in applying the notion of 'exactly the same circumstances,' surely the last vestige of logical force is removed from the universalizability thesis" (p. 169).

The Harean Roots

I shall now maintain that the implications of the view that moral judgments in cases of moral conflict are in large part justified by reference to 'the
sort of person one is' undermine universalizability not merely in situations
where duties conflict, as Winch maintains, but in all moral situations.
Understanding why this is so involves scrutinizing the implications of the
so-called prescriptive or decisionist feature of moral judgments, according
to R. M. Hare. This is appropriate because Winch associates the groundwork of his analysis with that of Hare's (p. 169) and because Hare is singly
responsible in contemporary meta-ethics for the acceptance of the criteria of
prescriptivity and universalizability as necessary (albeit minimal) marks of a
moral judgment.[5] If I am correct then the implications of (Harean) prescriptivity are such as to call into serious question the tenability of universalizability as a necessary criterion of moral judgments.

In maintaining that in genuine conflicts of moral obligations, one's
principle is not universalizable, Winch nevertheless continues to adhere to
the view that in all other situations universalizability remains a criterion of
moral judgments. A clear sign that he remains captive to the very tradition
whose limitations he recognizes is his claim that a moral but (logically)
non-universalizable decision arises because of a conflict between two
genuinely moral, i.e., "uncompromisingly universal" (p. 162) obligations.
If 'moral' here is not to be understood as 'what any other agent ought to do in
like circumstances,' what is its meaning? The alternative suggestion emerging from Winch, relatively unelaborated, is that the 'moral' is that which is
given overriding weight or "precedence" (p. 169) by the agent, that which
"strikes him" (p. 169) as "important" (p. 155) and more important in the
situation than alternatives. Accordingly, an alternative way of filling in
'moral' here would be: that which an agent is willing to *prescribe* (since he
or she conceives it as overriding or more important in the guiding of action).
Moreover, the agent confers such importance upon it (either the situation,
the decision or the principle implicated) because of her view of *herself* or her
way of life. Consider Hare's well-known elaboration of the enterprise of 'the
complete justification of a decision':

> . . . if pressed to justify a decision completely, we have to give a
> complete justification of the way of life of which it is a part. . . . If the
> inquirer still goes on asking, 'But why *should* I live like that?' then
> there is no further answer to give him. . . . We can only ask him to
> make up his own mind which way he ought to live; for in the end
> everything rests upon such a decision of principle. He has to decide
> whether to accept that way of life or not; *if he accepts it, then we can
> proceed to justify the decisions that are based on it* (my italics). [6]

Elsewhere, Hare makes clear that the freedom or autonomy of moral agency and discourse lies in "the logical possibility of wanting anything."[7] That is, there is nothing about features of the world or of human nature which compels us toward certain ideals or interests. Pervasive interests or ideals constitute "ways of life" and, in turn, the character of various sorts of *persons* or *selves*. But, according to Hare, no determinate notion of selfhood or personhood founds our choice; rather our choice or prescription is ultimately unconstrained or undetermined by facts of the world or of human nature. The italicized passage above indicates that once a mode of selfhood or a way of life is adopted and prescriptions flow from it, then we can subject such prescriptions to the universalizability test. "A judgment is not moral," Hare unequivocally says, "if it does not provide, without further imperative premises, a reason for doing something."[8] Thus, according to Hare, all moral prescriptions are ultimately founded on ways of life or some concept or other of what sort of self one is to be. The prescriptions, nevertheless, which flow from that selfhood or way of life may be justified with reference to the universalizability test. In what follows I shall argue that, contrary to Hare's claim, prescriptions are *not universalizable* precisely because they are rooted in this (autonomous) choice of selfhood. Inasmuch as, according to this view, all moral prescriptions are so rooted, all moral prescriptions are non-universalizable.

The Argument

The argument cutting the tie between prescriptivity and universalizability can be stated quite simply. If 1) all prescriptions are rooted in a choice of what sort of person to be and if 2) in order for a judgment to be moral a reason must be provided and if 3) the "reason" ultimately for moral prescriptions is that one desires to be, become, exercise, exhibit a certain selfhood then 4) either the judgment of what sort of person to be which "founds" all subsequent prescriptions is not a moral judgment or the "reason" for that judgment is non-universalizable.

The dilemma for Hare or any ethicist concerned to embrace prescriptivity and universalizability on Harean grounds can be starkly viewed as we scrutinize each of the horns in step (4). If the autonomous choice of a way of life or what sort of person to be is not a moral prescription then the question of appropriateness of justification, and so, of the application of the univer-salizability criterion is moot. But it does seem that one's decision to be or try to be a certain sort of person, which ideal or interest is made concrete in particular prescriptions directly or indirectly, is itself either a *moral* decision or, as Hare himself suggests, is implicated in moral decisions. Yet, Hare might reply that prescriptivity, even *ultimate* prescriptivity (of a sort of selfhood) is a necessary but not a sufficient condition for a judgment's being moral.

. . . I should expect [a moral person] to ask of his own actions, "To what action can I commit myself in this situation, realizing that, in committing myself to it, I am also . . . prescribing to anyone in a like situation to do the same. . .[9]

Suppose, however, we submit the foundational implicit or explicit 'choice of the sort of person one is' to this test. What precisely is universalizable in this "ultimate" decision? Perhaps it is that inasmuch as prescriptions implicate or involve sorts of selfhood, the universalized maxim is: 'All individuals ought to choose to be some selves or other?' But surely this can't be it for, according to the prescriptivist, this is necessary and inevitable; if 'ought' is to imply 'can' (and cannot) then it is pointless to say, 'Everyone ought to act so as to become some self or other'. Perhaps, then, the 'reason' universalized in the ultimate choice yields the following: 'Each person ought to make up his or her own mind'[10] or rely solely on his or her own view of what to be rather than be compelled by "natural" facts. Again, we should insist *either* that this makes little sense in that, according to Hare, we must still *choose* to be the sort of persons who view themselves as merely determined by natural facts and *this choice* is in no logical sense sense determined by natural facts *or* the maxim illicitly imports a substantive moral value—autonomy—into a moral framework in which it is "logically possible to want anything," including heteronomy. Finally, then, it might be argued that since the so-called "ultimate" decision of what sort of person to be is a hypothetical or "background" decision in that whenever we make a particular moral decision in our world we already presuppose some "background" sense of personhood or other, we only subject it to scrutiny *indirectly* by testing the possible universalizability of particular maxims. This construal appears to be in good touch with Hare's claim that it is the *decisions based on* one's adoption of a way of life or mode of personhood which we attempt to justify rather than the so-called ultimate "decision of principle"[11] proper.

This reply, in spite of its apparent authorization by Hare, is unsatisfactory for the universalizability test will certainly be affected by what the agent is willing to accept, given his consideration of what is important or what he deems worthy of being given greatest weight, and this is certainly generated by one's "ultimate decision" of what sort of person to be. Because of this, however, much as the Harean would like "decisions of principle" to be background considerations, they are necessarily rushed into the foreground since they clearly affect the success or failure of universalizability.

Faced, then, with such "dead end" construals as these, the universal prescriptivist could offer (what I take to be) the most promising of the replies so far advanced. In short, he could say, 'Anyone who is faced by a situation relevantly like mine who also desires to be the kind of person I am, ought to give the sort of weight I have to the values at stake and so to decide as I have. If such a person decides otherwise than I have, he has decided wrongly.'

Suppose, for purposes of clarification, a Harean typology according to which there were at least liberal and fanatic kinds of persons. Those then who made ultimate "decisions of principle" to be liberal would say that all those like them whose choice of personhood is bound up with liberalism ought to decide as they have. The troubles here, however, are patent. First, 'liberal' is too comprehensive a category to generate determinate directives with respect to specific moral judgments; such a general category permits innumerable kinds of personhoods weighing values differently. Second, even if there were a determinate "liberal" character with, e.g., a commitment to self-determination or tolerance central to its identity, such tolerance or respect for persons (and their differences) would at least sometimes preclude negative judgments on decisions governed by values similar to or other than their own. In this case the liberal would not necessarily judge that other liberals who judged otherwise than he did in similar circumstances were morally wrong.

But let us suppose a more precise, finer-grained typology than Hare's which is arguably within the moral domain. Thus, consider a Rawlsian, a Nozickian and an Ethical Egoist, each of whom chose tacitly or explicitly 'back there' to be and to remain faithful to the selves they chose to be. (Leave aside the interesting issue of whether *continued* fidelity to one's substantive choice of selfhood is a necessary requirement of the sort of selfhood elected.) Presented with similar circumstances and deciding in the light of their respective principles, does the decision they individually made carry the requirement that all others relevantly like them ought to make the same judgment they did? One *proviso* is important here. I take up only inter-category, not extra-category judgments, since Hare recognizes the possibility of radically opposed moral systems being nevertheless *singly* consistent, e.g., liberals and fanatics. Moreover, because it is logically possible to want anything, one's "decision of principle" to identify oneself as Ethical Egoist, Rawlsian or Nozickian is also logically unassailable. Once this is granted, the judgment that one is morally wrong to make decisions consistent with one's ultimate "decision of principle" is ruled out. If it is morally permissible to make decisions of principle regarding one's ultimate values or what sort of self to be, then it is morally permissible, *prima facie,* to act in accord with those values or that selfhood.

Does universalizability apply, then, to those who might be said to be relevantly similar *re* self and circumstances? Imagine a class of Rawlsians whose commitment to justice is a function of (grows out of) their commitment to a similar sort of personhood. (Note here that it is possible, even likely, that each Rawlsian would expect or anticipate that the other Rawlsians would concur. Stronger, they would, we might say, be surprised, even annoyed and alarmed if the consensus of the others did not materialize. "You call yourself a genuine Rawlsian and you deny that this decision in these circumstances is right?" Or, "I think I'm a Rawlsian but [some or all of] the others don't agree with me when I make what I fervently take to be Rawlsian judgments." But the expectation or anticipation that others relevantly similar will agree is not yet universalizability. "I expect that others relevantly similar with agree [but they may not] is *not* reducible to 'Others relevantly similar ought to [are logically obliged to] concur." Note also that the expectation of agreement is generated primarily because of how one defines the Rawlsian rather than how one defines 'the right.' For, given the foundational "decision of principle," moral rightness cannot be tied conclusively to Rawlsianism rather than Egoism, Nozickianism, etc. Arguably, it is as morally permissible to choose any of the other modes of selfhood as to choose to be a Rawlsian.)

But to return to the question: When one such Rawlsian (R) assesses the moral circumstances presented to her and makes a moral decision based on her belief in the appropriate lexical ordering of values, does she judge that all other R's ought to judge likewise? The proper way to formulate this is, doubtless, hypothetical, viz., *if* there were another R relevantly like me. then that R ought to judge as I do and would be wrong if she didn't. If this hypothetical proposition is denied, Hare would say, one misunderstands or abuses the logic of moral language.

First of all, the locution "relevantly like me" is inherently troublesome. In particular, how is this hypothetical subject "relevantly like me" to be constructed? Must the motives which inclined her to an R "core self" in the first place be similar or identical to mine and continue to be active in compelling allegiance to self-continuity, as they are, let us say, in me? If she is an R by "mere habit" rather than active, deliberative intention, would she be relevantly similar? Suppose we specify that by "relevantly similar" we will mean anything that makes her like me in the morally relevant respects, i.e., not sex, religion, race, social class, geography, humor or its lack, responses of others to her, and so forth. The difficulty here is that all and any of these categories may indeed in large or small part be responsible for the ascendancy or prominence of certain values in the agent. This being so, the very criterion "relevantly similar" threatens to be indeterminate. We could exercise the prerogative of much philosophical inquiry and *specify,* particularly, that R^N is relevantly similar to R *if* R^N's allegiance to values is occasioned and exemplified by similar sorts of motives and reasons. So specified, this would be a "similar character" requirement. But then suppose that R^N's allegiance to Rawlsian "equal liberty" as a principle to which she gives prominence is motivated in large part by *considerable envy* concatenated to other feelings but that R's allegiance to the same principle is motivated in large part by *mild envy* concatenated to other feelings. Presumably, such a person would not satisfy the "similar character" requirement. The Harean might reject such considerations, asserting that they are beside he point, inasmuch as the universalizability test is hypothetical and logical and so is compatible with there being *no* historic similar characters or actions. *If* there were another similar R, Hare might say, she ought to make the same judgment. But if there is no clear way to give a determinate sense to "similar character" or if it is an empty category or if the only subject who could possibly satisfy such a requirement would have to be a sort of 'clone,' then surely much of the import of universalizability as a test for one's own and other's moral judgments is lost. This is so because the sort

of self one has chosen is the foundation of one's moral judgment and such
selfhood indeed affects the category of the "relevantly similar," perhaps
even abolishes it.

There is, however, an even more telling, structurally deeper reason why,
given the decisionist assumption, universalizability is inoperative. Here we
come to the heart of the universal prescriptivist's problem. If I can't will that
everyone ought to decide to be the sort of self I am, since this is a "decision
of principle," how is it that I must will that others similar to me make similar
sorts of decisions? For, presumably, they would only make similar sorts of
decisions if indeed they had a character or selfhood like mine. But no
necessity, logical or moral, compels me to will that others ought to be
similar to me. Is it *unthinkable* that those with similar selfhoods in similar
circumstances nevertheless could will slightly or radically different principles or give weight to other principles than those that strike me as most
important? To say it is unthinkable is to suppose that one and only one
coherent or consistent set of principles would issue from a single sort of
personality. But this claim, to say the least, does not wear its credentials on
its sleeve. Certainly, the phenomenon of conflicts of duties or obligations at
least indicates how one and the same agent could nevertheless hold fast to
inconsistent sets of moral directives. Moreover, the decisionist starting
point permits the possibility that one will the sort of self whose very
complexity involves it in moral obligations of the sort which conflict.

Yet, the universal prescriptivist could still insist on the hypothetical
nature of the universalizability requirement, viz., *if* there is another sort of
self like me . . . . This reply will only be promising, however, if we move
beyond *formal* universalizability to the satisfaction of some *material* epistemic conditions. Do I in fact know myself or the sort of selfhood I have
elected well enough to know that one and only one consistent set of moral
directives follows from it? If I do not, then in prescribing that others like me
decide similarly, I give quite gratuitous directives, since others, consistent
with the sorts of selves they are, may follow *one or the other* sets of moral
directives but not necessarily the one I have prescribed. Since Hare and other
universal prescriptivists indeed assume that one can (logically) will any sort
of selfhood and that no extra knowledge of the constitutive principles of that
selfhood or way of life are needed, universalizability as they employ it is an
unfounded assumption rather than a necessary mark of moral judgments.

Thus, the following dilemma for the universal prescriptivist is generated.
Either a) he claims that one and only one set of moral directives or principles
follows from the sort of self he has chosen, in which case he artificially
limits the scope of "decisions of principle" regarding (complex) selfhood, or
b) he admits the possibility that more than one consistent set of moral
directives is compatible with the sort of selfhood he (and others) have
embraced, in which case universalizability is an unfounded claim. The
universal prescriptivist could attempt to evade the force of b) by universalizing his prescription in the following way: 'If there are other selves
similar to mine in similar circumstances they ought to decide either as I have

or in accord with the alternative set of directives but not otherwise.' Then, assuming there is not a third or fourth consistent set of moral directives, universalizability has been rescued but surely at the cost of determinacy, and so, its action-guiding significance.

Why Universalizability?

If my arguments for the gratuitousness of the universalizability claim following on ultimate decisions regarding selfhood are successful, it is natural to look for an explanation of why philosophers have thought universalizability a necessary test for moral judgments. Necessarily, such an account will be sketchy and, at best, suggestive.

Any account of the prominence of universalizability in modern and contemporary ethical work must not underestimate the Kantian effort to place ethical claims on sounder ground by providing them with a more rigorous (universal and necessary) decision-procedure than either 'intuition' or 'appeal to nature.' Intuition has, at best, private but not authoritative, inter-subjective, validity since when individuals' intuitions conflict nothing about the intuitions as such will successfully decide the conflict. If what confers more validity on some intuitions as over and against others is their touch with some fact of the world or human nature, the ethical justification is metaphysical or naturalist. Kant and Kantians characteristically eschew such 'justification' since a) the relation between nature and ethical value is at best *contingent*, not necessary, and so, incapable of supporting absolutely binding directives, and b) if there were a necessary relation between nature and value the freedom or autonomy of morals so important for moral responsibility (and said to be implicit in the language of 'ought' or obligation) would be lacking. Because of such considerations the Kantian tradition in ethics sought an independent way (independent of subjective apprehension taken by itself or facts of nature) to establish the validity of ethical claims. Universalizability was the result—designed to rescue both the *autonomy* and the *objective* necessity of ethical judgments.

I have suggested above that if one construes the autonomy of morals as universal prescriptivists since Kant have, then universalizability is a gratuitous posit. To be fair, I should add that from the fact that a self deems something important or overriding, it doesn't follow that what it thinks important really is so or that the overriding concern makes for moral rightness, though it may have for the agent a moral significance. I add this lest it be supposed that I have throughout suggested, even espoused, an alternative view of morality, viz., 'the overridingly important.' While I do not see that such a criterion is in any way inferior to 'universalizability,' I mean to suggest only 1) that there are alternatives, not that they are necessarily satisfactory, and 2) that, for the universal prescriptivist, the 'overridingly important' (rooted in "decisions of principle") and 'universalizability' cannot live together harmoniously.

Universalizabilty *seems* most plausibly a criterion of moral judgments when it is radically restricted to certain role behavior (judges, umpires, teachers, public authorities) whose appropriate domain involves the distribution of public burdens and benefits to which the participants in institutions or practices deserve or can claim as their right.[12] What we ordinarily think relevant in the disposition of public authorities in the distribution of (in some sense) public goods is not what sort of selves they have chosen to be, not even why they chose their roles, but a) the objective requirements of their roles and b) the objective facts of the case, e.g., whether individuals do indeed have rightful claims, precedents for awarding merit and demerit, the attention to rules or procedures publicly agreed to. One might maintain that the sort of (social) self that individuals, contracting together in some sense, deem important will—in a way that bears some resemblance to the "decisions of principle"—be regulative. But here, universalizability—as a demand for a certain sort of consistency in the enactment of institutional roles—arises inter-subjectively (at best) as many individuals, tacitly or explicitly, decide on rules and procedures to govern their public institutions. There is no "social self" chosen, although such an entity is a fiction of totalitarian schemes. Universalizability, in this domain, is not a necessary meaning-condition of moral judgments but an instrument employed by many selves desirous of introducing order, consistency and fairness into their social, economic and political interactions.

Notes

*Henry Veatch first stimulated my interest in the issues of rational justification in ethics in general and the work of Hare in particular. For this and for his constant generosity, and encouragement I am most grateful.

[1] Joel Feinberg, *Social Philosophy* (Englewood Cliffs, New Jersey: Prentice-Hall, 1973), p. 102.

[2] Peter Winch, "The Universalizability of Moral Judgments" in *Ethics and Action* (London: Routledge and Kegan Paul, 1972). All page references in the paper refer to this essay.

[3] See R. S. Peters, *Ethics and Education* (Atlanta: Scott, Foresman, 1966), p. 51. See also, R. M. Hare, *Freedom and Reason* (New York: Oxford University Press, 1965), p. 124; Chaim Perelman, *Justice, Law and Argument: Essays on Moral and Legal Reasoning* (Dordrecht: D. Reidel, 1980), esp. pp. 7–22.

[4] William K. Frankena, *Thinking about Morality* (Ann Arbor: University of Michigan Press, 1980), pp. 53–54.

[5] See esp. *Freedom and Reason*.

[6] R. M. Hare, *The Language of Morals* (New York: Oxford University Press, 1969), p. 69.

[7] *Freedom and Reason*, p. 110.

[8] *The Language of Morals*, p. 31.

[9]*Freedom and Reason*, p. 48.

[10]See *The Language of Morals*, esp. pp. 71, 73, 77.

[11]*Ibid.*, p. 69.

[12]But as Billy Budd graphically illustrates, there is no guarantee, even in such public, role-oriented domains, that 'universalizability' will or (morally) should *always* be operative. Would Captain Vere have violated Billy Budd's rights (or others' rights) if he had acquitted him by appealing to 'private conscience'?

HENRY B. VEATCH AND THE PROBLEM OF A NONCOGNITIVIST ETHICS

Sander H. Lee
Howard University

There exist today a number of philosophers, trained in and sympathetic to the Classical approaches to questions in the field of Ethics, who find themselves to be greatly disturbed by the direction they perceive contemporary philosophers have taken in examining these questions. One such philosopher is Henry Babcock Veatch, who has, over the years, become a most persuasive voice in articulating such concerns in a variety of essays and books. In these works, Professor Veatch has argued that neither the analytic nor the phenomenological approaches are capable of yielding workable ethical positions. In this article, I wish to examine some of Professor Veatch's reservations concerning the possibility of a specifically Sartrean ethics in the light of certain claims made by Thomas C. Anderson in his recent book *The Foundation and Structure of Sartrean Ethics.*[1]

In his book *For an Ontology of Morals*[2], Veatch has claimed that an existentialist ethics viewed from a Sartrean perspective would share certain common elements with other non-cognitivist ethical approaches and, thus, would be vulnerable to the major criticisms which he has levelled against all such positions. In the course of clarifying the exact nature of such criticisms, I intend to show how Anderson's interpretation of Sartre might be viewed as a possible way of circumventing these criticisms entirely. Finally, I will examine Anderson's interpretation itself in order to determine if it is, in fact, an accurate reflection of Sartre's own views on these issues.

I.

In his most serious criticism of the non-cognitivist approach towards issues in ethics, Veatch states that, "when moral obligation is regarded not as being ontologically grounded in nature and in natural norms and laws, but rather as grounded either in certain linguistic uses or in the free projects of the human subject, then ethics turns out really not to have any ground at all; and instead of any possibility of moral or ethical justification, one is faced simply with nihilism."[3]

Some defenders of the contemporary approach to ethics, especially those defending Sartre, have attempted to circumvent this criticism by ultimately claiming that, for a Sartrean, ethical values are grounded in the ontological freedom of the individual and that the individual, to the extent that he has an obligation to be authentic, is obliged to choose freedom as his ultimate value.

Such a position is taken by Anderson. While ultimately admitting that for Sartre, "there is no escape from the fact that the choice to value a meaningful and justified life is a free one made without logically compelling reasons"[4] and that "no reasons force him to value consistency and rationality,"[5] Anderson still goes on to argue that Sartre's position "advocates the choice of freedom as man's ultimate value."[6] This choice is seen by Anderson not merely as a hollow expression of faith in a freedom which would then allow individuals to act in any manner they wish, but as, in fact, an ultimate basis for justifying specific moral norms.

As Anderson himself realizes, Veatch heavily criticizes such an attempt to justify a Sartrean ethics in the following manner:

> Supposing that man is free, why should the mere fact that he is so make it wrong for him to pretend that he is not, or to try to conceal from himself his true condition? Is this not to derive an "ought" or an "ought not" from an "is" . . . How, then, from the fact that the existentialist fancies that he has discovered that man has the property of being free can he infer that man is under obligation to make choices in full recognition and acknowledgment of that freedom? Or why, from the fact that a man is free, but tries to hide the fact from his own consciousness, should it be inferred that there is something wrong or morally inauthentic about this? Surely, if the existentialist makes a move of this sort, then his ethics is indeed, if not a natural-law ethics in the usual sense, then at least an ontologically grounded ethics.[7]

In acknowledging Veatch's criticisms, Anderson admits that "Sartre himself would apparently have to agree with this,"[8] yet he still goes on to argue that reasons, albeit "not logically compelling"[9] ones, can still be given by Sartre for choosing freedom as the ultimate moral value, and for holding that specific moral norms can be derived from this value. What kind of argument does Anderson give to support this position? Well, Professor Veatch would undoubtedly be pleased to see that Anderson gives exactly the kind of account which Veatch himself suggests is the only one available to the existentialists, namely, he engages in what Veatch has come to call the "transcendental turn in ethics."[10]

Veatch explains how such a move would operate in the following excerpt:

> Clearly, then, it behooves us to turn our critical attention to precisely this proposal of a transcendental mode of philosophizing, such as might be carried over into the domain of ethics: just what does it involve, and is it feasible as a possible hedge against ethical nihilism? . . . It is supposed to mean that ethical principles, though neither evident in themselves nor susceptible of any direct rational justifi-

cation, may nevertheless be justified indirectly on the grounds that they are principles which we simply cannot dispense with in that primordial ordering of our experience which is supposed to turn it into an experience of a world . . . Thus, to follow a somewhat over-simplified line of illustration, one might say that there is no evidence, either empirical or otherwise, which demonstrates conclusively that we human beings by our very nature as men are subject to moral obligations; and yet . . . phenomenologically we could not be presented with an experience of ourselves in the world, without incorporating moral norms, prescriptions, obligations, etc., into the picture. In other words, while ethics may not be rationally justifiable, so far as we human beings are concerned, it is nonetheless . . . phenomenologically inescapable.[11]

Anderson makes this move in his attempt to defend his interpretation of Sartre's ethics when he states the following:

However, to admit that no compelling reasons can be offered for valuing logic and rationality or for valuing a meaningful existence is not to say that no reasons at all can be advanced. Man's deep longing for justification and the fact that a meaningful life is attainable are certainly reasons that support the valuing of such a life. Likewise, the fact that no matter what he does man is going to create some meaning for his existence, prompts him to value a meaningful life and to create the best possible meaning he can . . . It is also true that no reasons force him to value consistency and rationality. Still, de Beauvoir [states], life "is permitted to wish to give itself a meaning and a truth, and it then meets vigorous demands within its own heart," the demands, I take it, that rationality and consistencey with reality be valued and that freedom be chosen above all else.[12]

Clearly, Anderson here has engaged in exactly the sort of move which Veatch envisioned in his description of the "transcendental turn." The question now arises as to what Veatch thinks is wrong with this move. In order to fully understand this criticism, it is first necessary to explicate his distinction between a "strictly conceived transcendental turn" and a "transcendental turn loosely conceived." The "strictly conceived transcendental turn" as described by Veatch would follow the thinking of Kant, in that "Kant felt the pure forms of intuition and the pure concepts of the understanding, through which our intellect imposes its laws upon nature, were somehow fixed and unchanging — i.e., there could be no experience of any kind save insofar as it comes to be structured through the particular forms of space and time, as well as the particular categories which Kant felt he had been able to derive from the table of judgments."[13]

Thus, if one utilizes the transcendental turn as "strictly conceived" in order to ground an ethics, then one must be willing to concede that there exists exactly one set of correct moral norms which are, in fact, the only proper values available to all those who wish to lead moral lives. All persons, therefore, who choose to view their actions from a moral perspective would be required to view them from the same moral perspective, utilizing the same moral norms in exactly the same manner.

On the other hand, "rather than maintaining that our *a priori* human conceptual scheme, in terms of which we structure our experience, should be something fixed and determinate for all time and for every human subject, the current interpretation of the transcendental turn (i.e., as "loosely conceived") claims that it is a free projection of the subject, and that the subject is ever free to change and to replace it with some other."[14] In other words, the "transcendental turn as loosely conceived" would mandate no specific set of moral norms and, thus, would allow the individual moral agent to constitute his or her values in whatever manner he or she wished in such a way as to continually preserve for oneself the possibility of, at any time, rejecting some or all of those values in order to constitute entirely new ones.

Having made this distinction, Veatch turns to a consideration of the existentialists, and he states, "for the existentialist, a particular scheme of goods and bads, of rights and wrongs, is but one way of our making sense of the world; it is not a way that we have to adopt, or that we cannot but choose to abide by once we have adopted it. On the contrary, the facticity of any one scheme of values is always something that we can transcend and go beyond to an entirely different set of values, thereby bestowing upon our world a very different sense and meaning."[15]

Thus, Veatch claims that Sartre engages in the transcendental turn as loosely conceived, and this claim leads him to make the following criticism:

> The only trouble is . . . that no sooner is ethics conceived and approached in this way than it turns out to be a purely relative matter, incapable of rational justification, and thus doomed to nihilism. Moreover, if to escape this nihilism one places restrictions upon the transcendental turn, demanding that even in its application to ethics it be carried out in the strict Kantian sense, then one immediately sacrifices that absolute autonomy of the human subject or human person, an autonomy which no modern thinker seems ever quite able to bring himself to renege on.[16]

We now see the major criticism which Veatch makes of Sartre on this issue. Yet before we attempt to answer this criticism, it behooves us to pause a moment for reflection upon the interpretation of Sartre which is presented by Anderson. Is it in fact the case that, as Veatch has claimed, Sartrean ethics engages in the transcendental turn as loosely conceived?

If we return to our earlier discussion of Anderson's formulation of Sartrean ethics, we see that Anderson, in fact, seems to be claiming that certain specific rights and wrongs *do* emerge from an acceptance of Sartre and that these rights and wrongs would apply to everyone for all time. If this is the case, and Anderson has interpreted Sartre correctly, then Sartre would be engaging in the transcendental turn not as "loosely conceived," but instead as "strictly conceived." Under these circumstances, Veatch's criticism of Sartre would no longer apply and, as Veatch gives no criticism, at least not in this work, of the transcendental turn as strictly conceived, it would follow that Anderson, and, through his effort, Sartre, would be "home free," at least as far as this criticism is concerned.

So it would seem that our first immediate task is to see if, in fact, Anderson does make the claim that specific moral norms do emerge from the adoption of a Sartrean ethics. We have already seen that Andeson would claim that Sartre's ethics "advocates the choice of freedom as man's ultimate value."[17] But what does Anderson mean by this? Does he mean that the adoption of a Sartrean ethics necessarily implies the adoption of certain specific and unchanging moral values? Let us look at an example given by Anderson:

"A man immersed in poverty, disease, and ignorance obviously has fewer choices and fewer ppossibilities that he can realistically hope to attain than a man blessed with wealth, health, and knowledge. If I value the former's freedom of choice, then I must work to improve his situation so that his poverty, disease, and ignorance are overcome and more goals are in his grasp."[18]

If I choose freedom as my ultimate value, "I must work to improve his situation?" This seems to be like a specific moral norm. Moreover, a page later, Anderson writes:

"I have argued that to choose freedom as the ultimate value means to work to remove restrictions to choice and to the attainment of goals sought, according to Sartre . . . Clearly, then, any repressive political, social, economic, religious, etc., policies or systems that serve to enhance freedom of choice by promoting dissemination of knowledge and by enabling man to attain his goals would be supported."[19]

Finally, two pages thereafter, Anderson states:

It was argued above that to value man's freedom of choice is to seek to provide him with more real possibilities from which he can choose, and that this in turn requires that he be enabled to attain more goals. Now, since man's goals, according to Sartre, are determined and specified by his needs, then to value man's freedom of choice means to value the fulfillment of his needs, especially those which are part of the structure common to all men. Thus, to promote man's freedom in a positive sense would be primarily to assist him in being free for the attainment of those goals that he naturally seeks in fulfilling his basic needs, such as those for food, shelter, warmth, sex, etc., and in continually striving to fulfill his more specifically human needs through pursuits, such as science, art, technology, philosophy, etc. Put simply, it would be to seek continually to develop human existence in all its multi-faceted features.[20]

This is a tall order indeed! It seems that, for Anderson at least, acceptance of a Sartrean ethics engenders a long list of specific moral obligations, obligations which are common to all persons and which are unchanging. Thus, if Anderson's interpretation of Sartre is correct, then Sartre quite clearly can only be viewed as making the transcendental turn as strictly conceived and not as loosely conceived. The implications of this interpretation for Veatch's criticism have been pointed out already. As Veatch's criticism was aimed only at those engaged in the transcendental turn as loosely conceived, it follows that Sartre, by way of Anderson, has escaped this criticism completely.

The following discussion raises the question as to whether Anderson has indeed correctly, or has incorrectly interpreted Sartre's position.

II

It is a very difficult and complicated task to create a credible interpretation of Sartre's ethical views. Sartre did not publish his promised work on ethics, and the attempt to build such an interpretation can often be frustrating since Sartre's comments on ethical and meta-ethical issues are scattered throughout his voluminous writings, and at times seem to be contradictory. Despite these difficulties, however, I do believe it is possible to come to certain conclusions concerning the basic features of a Sartrean ethics, particularly in terms of the issue at hand; namely, whether or not, as Anderson suggests, Sartre claims that we are obliged to view freedom as our ultimate value and, furthermore, whether the advocacy of Sartre's position yields a commitment to specific moral norms.

To begin with, it is quite clear that for Sartre no specific moral values are generated ontologically. It is helpful here to recall these excerpts from Sartre's comments in the final section of *Being and Nothingness* entitled "Ethical Implications":

> Ontology itself cannot formulate ethical precepts. It is concerned solely with what is, and we cannot possibly derive imperatives from ontology's indicatives. It does, however, allow us to catch a glimpse of what sort of ethics will assume its responsibilities when confronted with a human reality in situation. Ontology . . . must reveal to the moral agent that he is the being by whom values exist. It is then that his freedom will become conscious of itself and will reveal itself in anguish as the unique source of value and the nothingness by which the world exists . . . In particular is it possible for freedom to take itself for a value as the source of all value, or must it necessarily be defined in relation to a transcendent value which haunts it? And in case it could will itself as its own possible and its determining value, what

would this mean? . . . What are we to understand by this being which wills to hold itself in awe, to be at a distance from itself? Is it a question of bad faith or of another fundamental attitude? And can one live this new aspect of being? In particular will freedom by taking itself for an end escape all situation? Or on the contrary, will it remain situated? Or will it situate itself so much the more precisely and the more individually as it projects itself further in anguish as a conditioned freedom and accepts more fully its responsibility as an existent by whom the world comes into being? All these questions, which refer us to a pure and not an accessory reflection, can find their reply only on the ethical plane. We shall devote to them a future work.[21]

From these excerpts, we can see that Sartre unquestionably denies that humanity's ontological condition mandates the acceptance of any specific moral norms. Yet, we can also see that Sartre does raise the possibility that freedom could be taken as the ultimate value, although he obviously is aware that such a possibility suggests many confusing and seemingly contradictory implications. To clarify his position on this issue we must turn to other writings of Sartre.

The work of Sartre which most specifically deals with ethical issues is that small book transcribed from a lecture Sartre gave at the Club Maintenant in Paris on Monday, October 28, 1945. This lecture, which Sartre entitled "Existentialism is a Humanism,"[22] has been the source of considerable controversy over the years. There is much that could be said concerning this controversy; however, for the purposes of this short paper, I wish to simply accept the importance of this lecture for an understanding of Sartre's ethical positions. I do believe an argument can be successfully made for this acceptance, an argument which I intend to present in a future paper.

I believe that it would be worthwhile to examine the position taken in "Existentialism is a Humanism." It can be determined that Sartre's existentialism does not yield any specific moral norms. Sartre writes of a group of French teachers in the later 1800s who attempted to set up a secular ethics in which God was abolished "with the least possible expense!" According to Sartre, their argument went as follows:

God is a useless and costly hypothesis; we are discarding it; but, meanwhile, in order for there to be an ethics, a society, a civilization, it is essential that certain values be taken seriously and that they be considered as having an *a priori* existence. It must be obligatory, *a priori*, to be honest, not to lie, not to beat your wife, to have children, etc., etc. So we're going to try a little device which will make it possible to show that values exist all the same, inscribed in a heaven of ideas, though otherwise God does not exist. We shall find ourselves with the same norms of honesty, progress, and humanism, and we shall have made of God an outdated hypothesis which will peacefully die off by itself.[22]

This "little device" to which Sartre refers sounds remarkably like the transcendental turn as strictly conceived. What is Sartre's opinion of such a move? This is what he says:

> The existentialist, on the contrary, thinks it very distressing that God does not exist, because all possibility of finding values in a heaven of ideas disappears along with Him; there can no longer be an *a priori* good, since there is no infinite and perfect consciousness to think it. Nowhere is it written that the good exists, that we must be honest, that we must not lie; because the fact is we are on a plane where there are only men. Dostoevski said, "If God didn't exist, everything would be possible." That is a very interesting starting point of existentialism. Indeed, everything is permissible if God does not exist, and as a result man is forlorn, because neither within him or without does he find anything to cling to. He can't start making excuses himself.[23]

Sartre goes on at great length in this work to emphasize that no set of specific moral norms exists and to claim that, in the absence of such norms, each person must create their own. According to Sartre, this act of creation is not arbitrary or whimsical. He compares the creation of ethical values to the creation of a work of art. "When we speak of a canvas of Picasso, we never say that it is arbitrary; we understand quite well that he was making himself what he is at the very time he was painting, that the ensemble of his work is embodied in his life."[24]

But what of Anderson's claim that for Sartre freedom must be the ultimate value? We saw that Sartre inconclusively mentions this as a possibility at the end of *Being and Nothingness*. In "Existentialism is a Humanism," Sartre discusses this at greater length, and it does appear that he has made up his mind on this issue. He states,

> I declare that freedom in every concrete circumstance can have no other aim than to want itself, if man has once become aware that in his forlornness he imposes values, he can no longer want but one thing, and that is freedom as the basis of all values. That doesn't mean that he wants it in the abstract. It means simply that the ultimate meaning of the acts of honest men is the quest for freedom as such . . . And in wanting freedom we discover that it depends entirely on the freedom of others, and that the freedom of others depends on ours.[25]

Here Sartre unequivocally asserts that freedom is the basis of all values and that one's freedom depends entirely on the freedom of others. Yet, does Sartre mean this as Anderson has interpreted it? As Anderson understands it, this dual assertion yields a host of specific moral norms which apply to all people. In constructing his interpretation, Anderson relies very heavily on the arguments made by Simone de Beauvoir in *The Ethics of Ambiguity,* and there can be no doubt that de Beauvoir takes the positions which Anderson suggests.[26] But what of Sartre's position? Is it the same?

Anderson starts his analysis on this topic by presenting what I think is a fair presentation of Sartre's position in the passage just quoted. Anderson points out that one could choose

> pleasure or fame or even bad faith as the ultimate value of his life. Any of these would, of course, become a value for him, but only because he had freely made it such. As Sartre suggests, once a person realizes that it is only due to freedom that any of these is a value, it is most *consistent* with this state of affairs for him to choose freedom (rather than pleasure, fame, or bad faith) as his ultimate value. His reference to consistency can also be understood in a logical sense. Thus he may be arguing that, since freedom is ontologically entailed in all values as their source, the choice of any and all values logically entails the prior valuing of freedom.[27]

I believe that Sartre is referring to consistency as understood in a purely logical sense[28] and for Sartre no one is obligated to be consistent. However, if one chooses to be consistent, then subsequently the realization that complete freedom is humanity's universal condition, without nature or essence, infers that choice of specific value rests upon a prior choice to value the free activity of choosing. Since it is the activity of creation or invention which constitutes all norms, it follows that one can consistently adopt such a norm only if one also values the process by which that norm was created. As ontology can generate no moral directives, and as man possesses no nature or essence to define his proper conduct, it is only through man's universal condition as a free and responsible activity that values can be constituted.

Thus, if one were to base his actions upon the acceptance of a value freely created, and, simultaneously, to reject the value of the activity of free creation, then one would be in Sartrean "bad faith." To the question, "What if I want to be dishonest?" Sartre answers, "There's no reason for you not to be, but I'm saying that that's what you are, and that the strictly coherent attitude is that of honesty."[29]

Now, how do we interpret Sartre's statement, "Consequently, when, in all honesty, I've recognized that man is a being in whom existence precedes essence, that he is a free being who, in various circumstances, can want only his freedom, I have at the same time recognized that I want only the freedom of others."?[30] Why does the recognition of my own condition as free imply anything at all about my attitudes towards others? Why couldn't I realize my own freedom and, simultaneously, deny the freedom of all others?

The answer to this question lies in Sartre's acceptance of the principle of universalizability. Sartre holds the position that when I choose for myself I am necessarily choosing for all mankind, once again to the extent I wish to be consistent. Sartre states, "If . . . existence precedes essence, and if we grant that we exist and fashion our image at one and the same time, that image is valid for everyone and for our whole age. Thus, our responsibility is much greater than we might have supposed, because it involves all mankind . . . I am responsible for myself and for everyone else. I am creating a certain image of man of my own choosing. In fashioning myself, I fashion man."[31] Sartre continues, "In wanting freedom we discover that it depends entirely on the freedom of others, and that the freedom of others depends on ours. Of course, freedom as the definition of man does not depend on others, but as soon as there is involvement, I am obliged to want others to have freedom at the same time that I want my own freedom. I can take freedom as my goal only if I take that of others as a goal as well."[32]

Does this claim concerning the freedom of others yield any specific moral norms? Anderson believes it does. However, further reading in "Existentialism . . ." suggests that Sartre disagrees. In fact, Sartre specifically discusses the Kantian view of ethics: "Therefore, though the content of ethics is variable, a certain form of it is universal. Kant says that freedom desires both itself and the freedom of others, granted. But he believes that the formal and the universal are enough to constitute an ethics. We, on the other hand, think that principles which are too abstract run aground in trying to decide action."[33]

Thus, according to Sartre, acceptance of freedom as the ultimate value and the goal of freedom for all, both mandated by an acceptance of consistency, do not in and of themselves yield any specific moral norms.

We are now in a position to pass judgment on Anderson's interpretation of Sartre. The following aspects of Anderson's explanation are obviously correct. Sartre does assert that the honest person is compelled logically to view freedom as the ultimate value. Further, the person who chooses to value consistency is logically obliged to view all others as free as well, in that such a person accepts the principle of universalizability.

However, to the extent that Anderson claims that the acceptance of these positions implies that a specific set of universal moral norms are derivable, he is clearly mistaken. As we have seen, Sartre goes to great lengths to clarify that no conclusions concerning how one should act can be derived from the universal aspects of the ethical endeavor, although in some of Sartre's more ambiguous comments, he seems to be implying otherwise. However, a thorough examination of his writings clarifies that Sartre does not believe that these universal conditions contain any specific normative implications. On this issue, Anderson has mistakenly assumed that Sartre's position is the same as that of Simone de Beauvoir. While Sartre and de Beauvoir agree on many fundamental issues of ontology, de Beauvoir has gone far beyond Sartre in her ethical interpretation of that ontology. The fact that Sartre, throughout his life, continued to write a major work on ethics makes it clear that Sartre did not view de Beauvoir's writings on the implications of existentialist ethics as definitive.

Returning then to the issue at hand, we can see that Anderson is in error to imply that a Sartrean ethics makes, what Veatch calls, the transcendental turn as strictly conceived. Veatch is correct in stating that Sartre makes the transcendental turn as loosely conceived. This means that Anderson has not really addressed or dealt with Veatch's criticisms of such a move.

This is not to say that Veatch's criticisms are unanswerable by Sartre and his defenders. Indeed, I hope to formulate such a defense of Sartre's position myself in the near future. I conclude that the attempt to answer criticisms, such as Veatch's, by asserting that Sartre would accept some set of specific universal moral norms is an effort which is doomed to failure.

Notes

[1]Anderson, Thomas C., *The Foundation and Structure of Sartrean Ethics* (Lawrence, Kansas: The Regent's Press of Kansas, 1979).

[2]Veatch, Henry B., *For an Ontology of Morals* (Evanston, Illinois: Northwestern University Press, 1974).

[3]Veatch, *Ontology,* p. 85.

[4]Anderson, p. 52.

[5]*Ibid.* p. 53.

[6]*Ibid.*

[7]Veatch, *Ontology,* pp. 76–77.

[8]Anderson, p. 48.

[9]*Ibid.,* pp. 51–52.

[10]Veatch, *Ontology,* pp. 86–89.

[11]*Ibid.,* pp. 86–87.

[12]Anderson, pp. 52–53.

[13]Veatch, *Ontology,* p. 96.

[14]*Ibid.*

[15]ibid., p. 97.

[16]*Ibid.*

[17]Anderson, p. 53.

[18]*Ibid.,* p. 55.

[19]*Ibid.,* p. 56.

[20]*Ibid.,* p. 58.

[21]Sartre, Jean-Paul, *Being and Nothingness.* (New York: Philosophical Library, 1956), pp. 625–628.

[22]Sartre, Jean-Paul, *Existentialism,* translated by Bernard Frechtman, (New York: Philosophical Library, 1947), pp. 25–26.

[23]*Ibid.,* pp. 26–27.

[24]*Ibid.,* pp. 50–51.

[25]*Ibid.,* p. 54.

[26]Anderson, pp. 46–47.

[27]*Ibid.,* p. 46.

[28]Sartre, *Existentialism,* p. 53.

[29]*Ibid.*

[30]*Ibid.,* pp. 54–55.

[31]*Ibid.,* pp. 20–21.

[32]*Ibid.,* p. 54.

[33]*Ibid.,* p. 55.

THE INTERDEPENDENCE OF RIGHT AND GOOD

John Peterson
University of Rhode Island

I

Consider the following two propositions in ethics:
(1) If a person S does something wrong then S is blameworthy.
(2) If a person S is blameworthy then S does (or did) something wrong.
Since there are evidently other conditions for blameworthiness besides the wrongness of the act performed, (1) is not true. Thus, no one would be held morally responsible for what he did if his act were not voluntary or if he believed that what he was doing was right. By contrast, though, it is widely held that (2) is true. If wrong is not a sufficient condition of blame, blame would seem to be a sufficient condition of wrong. "No one can be blamed unless he does something wrong" is a dictum which almost everyone believes.

Still, the following example casts doubt on (2). Suppose that, being hard-pressed for money, Smith methodically plans to take and then does take a diamond which he believes belongs to his neighbor Jones. Suppose further that, unknown to Smith, the gem really belongs to *him* in the first place and not to Jones. Objectively speaking, no theft has been committed since one can steal only what belongs to another. Yet, though Smith did no objective wrong, no one would deny that Smith is blameworthy in this case since Smith *believed* that the gem belonged to Jones and voluntarily absconded with it nonetheless. This seems to be a counter-example to (2) in which case (2) turns out to be no more defensible than (1). In that case, it seems that the concepts of wrong and of blame are logically independent of each other. In other words, it seems from our example that someone can be blameworthy without doing wrong, just as someone can do wrong without incurring blame.

In the face of this a defender of (2) may do one of two things: first, saying that Smith here went against his conscience, he may count acting against one's conscience as a wrong act, or second, he may claim that Smith's act is wrong for some other reason. But the second possibility is *prima facie* fruitless. If Smith committed no theft and if his going against his conscience is not counted as being a wrong act, it is difficult to see what else is wrong with what Smith did. That seems to favor the first possibility, namely, that of enlisting Smith's contravening his conscience as an objectively wrong act. But this is not even possible, let alone fruitless. For if (2) is true and (1) is false it follows that wrongness is just one among other conditions of blame. If blame is a sufficient condition of wrong then wrong is a necessary condition of blame. But if acting against one's conscience is counted as a wrong act, then wrongness would sometimes be sufficient for blame since acting against one's conscience is clearly sufficient for blame. Therefore, if (1) is false and (2) is true then acting against one's conscience cannot itself be an objectively wrong act. Contravening one's conscience is, *in addition to* wrongness, a condition of blame, at least if (1) is false and (2) is true.

That leads us back to the second alternative if (2) is to be defended. If Smith committed no theft and yet is blameworthy, and if the wrong which according to (2) his blame implies does not consist in flouting his conscience then in what does the wrong consist? To this the answer of common sense is that the wrong in this case is identifiable with Smith's *intent* to steal. Smith did wrong because he willed to steal the diamond even though the circumstances of the case forbade the fulfillment of that will or intent. But if the wrong here of which Smith's blameworthiness is the sufficient condition is Smith's will to steal then it follows that Smith's will to steal is a necessary but not a sufficient condition of his blameworthiness. Otherwise, it could not be held that (2) is true and (1) is false. But the intent to steal is plainly a *sufficient* condition of blame. Smith is blameworthy in this case just because he willed to steal the gem, whatever else may be the case. Hence, the example of Smith cannot be made to conform to (2) by counting Smith's intent to steal as a wrong act. Otherwise, Smith's intent to steal the diamond would wind up being only a necessary whereas it is clearly a sufficient condition of his blameworthiness.

Besides, counting Smith's intent to steal as a wrong act in order to save (2) implies that wrongness is never straightforwardly predicated of human actions. For if it is Smith's intent to steal which is strictly speaking wrong in this case and not any action of Smith's, then intentions must be wrong in at least as straightforward a sense as are the actions which flow from them. Otherwise, (if (2) is true) Smith would not really be blameworthy. Either, therefore, (A), "wrong" is properly predicated of actions and intentions *both* or else (B), "wrong" is predicated of intentions primarily and of actions secondarily. But (A) is ruled out by the logical principle *that if a disjunctive property is predicated in an underived sense of one sort of thing it is predicated of all other sorts of things only in a derived sense.* For example, the disjunctive property of being either healthy or unhealthy is straightforwardly predicated of organisms. If, therefore, non-organisms are called healthy or unhealthy they are so called in a derived sense of the term, as, for example, food is called healthy only because it is conducive to health. Again, being either normal or erratic is predicated in an underived sense of actions or events, as, for instance, a person's actions are called normal or erratic. If, therefore, non-actions or non-events are called normal or erratic they are so called in a derived sense of those terms, as, for instance, a certain person is called normal only because his behavior is normal. Under this principle, then, if the disjunctive property of being either right or wrong is predicated of intentions in an underived sense of the term it follows that it is predicated of actions in a derived sense of those terms. In other words, assuming the truth of (2), (B) and not (A) would be true if the logical principle which has just been enunciated is correct.

But (B) is plainly false. Otherwise, actions such as theft or murder would not be wrong in and of themselves or wrong in any straightforward sense but rather they would be wrong only because they were related in some way to wrong intentions. But clearly and in terms of our example, Smith's intention to steal is wrong only because stealing itself is wrong and not the other way around. To the extent that Smith's intention is called wrong at all it is so called because of what Smith intended *to do* was wrong. But if so, then (2) or the defended assumption that blame implies wrong must not be true after all. For it has just been shown that if (2) is true it must be denied, absurdly, that Smith's intention to steal is called wrong because stealing is wrong.

But if blame does not really imply wrong after all, why has it seemed to so many that it does imply wrong? For (2) has often been compared with (1) as the necessarily true to what only may appear necessarily true. To repeat, almost everyone believes that while you can do wrong without incurring blame, you cannot incur blame without doing (or having done) wrong. What, then, is behind this common-sense intuition if, as has been shown, (2) is not really true? The answer to this can only be that (2) has come to be confused with another proposition which *is* true and which does not imply the outrage that stealing, say, is called wrong only because the intent to steal is wrong. That proposition is,

(3)   If a person S is blameworthy then S is to that extent bad.

Moreover, it seems that (2) has been confused with (3) because wrong has been confused with bad. And wrong has been confused with bad because right has been confused with good. If you once blur the distinction between right and good you also cloud the distinction between wrong and bad. But right and wrong apply to actions while good and bad in the moral sense apply to persons. And a person is good or bad to the extent that he wills or intends right or wrong acts. Thus the more blameworthy a person is the worse he is and the more praiseworthy a person is the better he is. But neither blame nor praise imply wrong or right but rather the presence of a bad will or of a good will respectively. Thus what at first seemed to be a dictum of meta-ethics, namely, (2), that blame implies wrong, turns out to be a false but enticing substitute for the true meta-ethical principle, (3), that blame implies bad—false because it implies (among other things) that theft is wrong because the intention of theft is wrong and enticing because of the all-too-easy confusion of the right with the good.

II

Suppose, then, it be conceded that right and good (or wrong and bad) are distinct concepts in ethics and that confusing (2) with (3) is one result of blurring the distinction between these two concepts. The question then arises as to whether and in what way there is a causal relation between the two. Does a person perform right actions because he is good or, *vice versa,* is he good because he has performed or is performing right actions? In other words, is rightness the effect of goodness or is goodness the effect of rightness? Or is neither the case?

The last-mentioned possibility, namely, that there is no causal relation between rightness and goodness must be at once ruled out of court. For if there were no causal connection between rightness and goodness and if, as was shown, the two are conceptually distinct, then the goodness of a man would have nothing at all to do with how he acted. A man, then, might be called a good man no matter how he acted. Either, therefore, a man is good because his actions are right or else his actions are right because he is good. But from what has already been said in (I) it is clear that rightness is not the cause of goodness or that a person is not good *because* his actions are right. For if right acts are made the condition of goodness then, to be consistent, wrong acts must be the condition of badness. But it was shown in (I) that badness is the condition of blame. A person cannot be blamed even in doing wrong unless he *intends* to do wrong. But then, if wrong acts are the condition of badness and badness is the condition of blame then it follows that wrong acts are the condition of blame. But in (I) we saw that Smith was blameworthy even though he committed no wrong act. In other words, the example of Smith showed that wrong acts are not the condition of blame. Hence, since badness *is* the condition of blame it follows that wrong acts are not the condition of badness or in other words that persons are not bad because they perform wrong acts. It follows, therefore, that persons commit wrong acts because they are bad and that they perform right acts because they are good. And from this it follows further that in the causal order right depends on good even though in the conceptual order right, as was said, enters into the definition of good. In sum, a man performs right actions because he is good but what is *meant* by calling him good is that he intends to act rightly, that he has an inclination toward right actions. And so right and good are interdependent, good depending on right as a *definiendum* depends on its *definiens* and right depending on good as an effect depends on its cause.[1]

Note

[1]This may appear contradictory since, if the *definiens* is a condition of the *definiendum* it is apparently being said here that right is both a condition of and the result of good. This objection may be met by first distinguishing the definition of complexes from the definition of simples and then by insisting both that *good* is a simple concept and that it is only in the case of complex concepts that the *definiens* is a condition of the *definiendum*. The *definiens* of *good*, then, would be in terms of the results of good and not in terms of a condition of good.

PART III

ETHICS AND LAW

INJUSTICE AND TRAGEDY IN ARISTOTLE

David F. Forte
Cleveland-Marshall College of Law, Cleveland State
University

Aristotle was no stranger to the moral quandary of misfortune, cruelty, and pain. Although he reasoned that the ultimate good for man is happiness, he nonetheless confessed that misfortunes and suffering could rob even the most virtuous and courageous man of happiness. Yet Aristotle did not find pain to be such a universal evil that anyone who suffers has a moral and legal call on the assistance of others for relief. On the other hand, the fact that some suffering cannot be relieved and may prevent a man from reaching his true end did not push Aristotle into finding the human condition absurd.

In approaching the human condition, Aristotle treats the "problem of pain," as C. S. Lewis puts it, according to various ethical categories. Aristotle finds that some types of human suffering incur legal obligation on the part of others for relief. Other pain calls upon the moral obligation of benevolence. Some kinds of suffering ought to be left untouched, in some cases because the pain is morally appropriate, and in others because the sufferer is better off left alone, as it were, to work his own way through the pain. Some human sufferings can be dealt with by the community. Still and all, there are some pains which are neither deserved nor relievable, and these can only be endured. In one way or another, Aristotle treats of these kinds of human suffering in the *Ethics, Rhetoric, Politics,* and *Poetics.*

Central to Aristotle's moral taxonomy of pain are his conceptions of injustice (and justice) on the one hand, and of tragedy on the other. Both injustice and tragedy impose undeserved harms on a person. When one man voluntarily and without moral cause harms another in his rightful enjoyment of his person or goods, a legally enforceable moral obligation is incurred by the wrongdoer to restore the innocent victim to his rightful position and to have the culprit's own illegal gain reduced accordingly.[1] Similarly, if the community in distributing its common store of benefits fails to do so proportionately according to the standard of distribution, the one who receives less than his due share has a call upon the community to make up for the lack.[2] The obligation to right such wrongs is normally in the positive law, but the law may be perfected in terms of justice by the judge's use of equity in individual cases.[3]

The person who is robbed, or who fails to receive his fair share, or who even is beaten, does *not* experience tragedy. Rather, he is wronged. His harms are rectifiable at least by the commensurable means of money, or by reducing the "gain" of the wrongdoer through penalty.[4] *A fortiori,* when the unjust man incurs retribution because of, and to the degree of his injustice, he suffers a deserved harm. There is nothing tragic in his situation, nor should there be any moral sense of sympathy or benevolence towards him. On the contrary, when the unjust man suffers harm, it is a satisfying spectacle.

Furthermore, when nature or chance or misfortune visits suffering upon an unjust man (even outside of a specific act of punishment for a specific interpersonal harm) a moral balance of suffering appropriate to the character of the unjust man is achieved. Although the concept of justice in such a case is merely metaphorical, the sufferings are considered appropriate.[5] There is no call for rectification, or pity, or benevolence.

Tragic human suffering is quite different. To begin with, Aristotle's notion of tragedy is literally a term of art. It is, in fact, a specific form of the dramatic arts. Although purely didactive, tragedy is not on that account fictional or unrelated to the moral issue of actual human suffering. As Aristotle perceives it, dramatic tragedy is a substitute experience of life, almost a phenomenological mechanism of discovery. Tragedy is an artistic representation of a certain kind of true human suffering, the kind of true-to-life suffering we can appropriately term "tragic" in an Aristotelian sense.

In its classic and famous formulation, Aristotle defines tragedy as "an imitation *(mimesis)* of a noble and complete action, having the proper magnitude; it employs language that has been artistically enhanced by each of the kinds of linguistic adornment, applied separately in the various parts of the play; it is presented in dramatic, not narrative form, and through the representation of pitiable and fearful incidents achieves the catharsis of such pitiable and fearful incidents."[6]

Although *mimesis* is traditionally translated as imitation or representation, it is universally recognized that the term is greatly more freighted.[7] "Re-enactment" or preferably "re-creation" more accurately conveys Aristotle's conception, for Aristotle views the arts as reproducing human experience from different materials than those which ordinarily make up the experience. Thus when Aristotle says that *mimesis* is greatest in music,[8] he does not mean that flute-playing is the most imitative of the arts in the narrow sense of a copy of human experience. Certainly, in the ordinary sense of the word, drama imitates or mirrors human experience more closely than does flute-playing. Rather, Aristotle means that flute-playing is more re-*creative* in that the act of creation is greater in turning the drastically different materials of tones, rhythms and sequences into the human experience of virtue. And he is insistent that virtue, not amusement, is the true purpose of music.[9]

Music, like tragedy, is didactic.[10] It develops the character by helping one to form the habit "of right judgment and of taking pleasure in good morals and noble actions."[11] In both cases, ". . . to have the habit of feeling pleasure (or pain) in things that are like to reality is very near to having the same disposition towards reality."[12] In that sense, music and tragedy re-create moral qualities. They are not mere substitutes for sensate experiences.[13] And both effectuate their purposes through catharsis.[14]

Dramatic tragedy, then, re-creates through a noble action (not a neutral or immoral act) the kind of experience which excites pity and fear in the observer. For Aristotle, pity and fear represent "the kind of pain excited by the sight of evil, deadly or painful, which befalls one who does not deserve it." It is "an evil which one might expect to come upon oneself or one of this friends," particularly if "it seems near."[15] Pity is the emotion signifying sympathetic moral engagement with the sufferings of another.

We can feel pity for the victim of injustice as well as for the victim of tragedy, for the one wronged by injustice also receives undeserved harm; and certainly injustice can happen to any of us. In concert with the feeling of pity in all moral situations, the witness to the undeserved suffering has to be a person of certain sensibilities. One who is utterly ruined cannot feel pity because he has nothing more to fear for himself. He cannot put himself in the position of the sufferer, in reality or on the stage. Nor can the witness be one who was born with a silver spoon in his mouth, for he cannot conceive of bad things ever happening to him.[16]

No, the witness must be one of an ordinary but not distorted sensibility. He must have experienced some suffering, have had some years behind him, and/or has had the benefit of proper education, or is part of a family. The witness must be basically virtuous, though certainly not perfect, and of course the object of the pity must also be basically a virtuous person[17] for if the witness regarded all persons (presumably including himself) as corrupt, then misfortunes would not be undeserved. They would, in a larger sense, be just.

But in the case of tragedy, the kind of pity we feel has a special moral quality. In the tragic situation, we feel pity not only for one who is undeservedly harmed, but for him whose fall occurs while in pursuit of a noble or worthwhile action, and whose bad end comes not from the injustice of another person, but from a flaw within himself. All these elements must be present in the tragic hero: undeserved harm, a noble purpose, and an internal flaw.

Aristotle is clear about what is *not* tragedy. A tragic plot is not one where a good man is struck down out of the blue, so to speak, by misfortune. That merely shocks us.[18] It does not engage us morally in the situation, that is to say, we do not have that sympathetic experience which is pity. Instead, the catastrophe horrifies us. Nor should evil men go from misery to prosperity. "This is the most untragic of all plots."[19] There is no moral lesson in this. Instead we are indignant at the undeserved good that the corrupt man obtains.[20] No personal pity or fear is awakened in us. Nor is it tragic when a bad man comes to a bad end. That might tally with our moral sense of justice, but again no pity or fear by the observer is involved.

In fact, when we study Aristotle's three examples of non-tragic plots, we see that in each case, the suffering, whether relieved or not, is part of justice or injustice. We are shocked at the injustice of the destruction of the good man or the triumph of bad man. Tragedy is something else again. The true tragic plot concerns "the sort of man who is not conspicuous for virtue or justice, and whose fall into misery is not due to vice and depravity, but rather to some error . . . ."[21] In other words, it concerns a man like ourselves, a dramatic character true to life. Though like ourselves, the hero, in terms of degree, is given greater "authority, passions, and powers of expression"[22] for dramatic and didactic effect.

But what is this flaw that permits the basically good man to fall into misery? In the tragic situation, the fundamentally good person is in pursuit of a noble or good end. Yet things go awry because of some internal imperfection. It is not, as has sometimes been thought, a moral taint, the classical equivalent of original sin. Rather, that imperfection *(hamartia)* seems to be, not a moral flaw, but a form of ignorance, a lack of knowledge of realizing one's human limits in a world where chance and misfortune exist. Aristotle holds that when a person (the hero) acts in ignorance, when he "makes a mistake," the responsibility for the unhappy result lies with the agent.[23] It may mean being imprudent or putting oneself at risk. It may mean acting outside of the mean. It signifies the incompletely educated person who does not yet know, through study and contemplation, how to pursue virtue in a world of chance and vagary and how to handle those chance unfairnesses that come one's way. In the tragic play, the hero comes to realize his mistake in a stunning moment of discovery or reversal, Aristotle's favored dramatic devices.[24]

Tragedy then recreates and illuminates in dramatic form a human dilemma which can also be approached through philosophical reflection.[25] If the tragedy is well done, the audience is aroused to pity and fear. It participates in the experience of the hero with the sure knowledge of "there but for the grace of God (or the gods) go I." When the flaw is exposed through the oncoming misfortune, the audience experiences catharsis, which Aristotle defines as a release, a kind of elation.[26] In fact, it is the emotional equivalent of recognition and enlightenment, for since the flaw is ignorance, its cure is indeed enlightenment. This is why Aristotle so emphasizes the theatrical device of discovery which, if properly used, does not even need to involve the hero in a bad end.[27] If we learn from art, and if drama is an emotional as well as a didactic form of art, then the taking in of the lesson would have to be likewise accompanied by an emotion, which Aristotle calls catharsis.[28] To be relieved of the confusion that resulted in pain is to understand, to have a burden lifted, and to experience the real pleasure at knowing why such things happen. The audience is educated. It absorbs some measure of practical wisdom *(phronesis)*.[29] It actually grows in virtue through this manufactured life experience. The emotions stabilize around the proper mean.[30] The audience has lived through the kind of painful experience which, if intelligently reflected upon, develops virtues and leads one closer to the true happiness which is man's end.

The art of tragedy then re-creates a good action engaged in by actual human beings. It excites pity and fear. And by vicariously experiencing such suffering, the observer is enlightened.[31]

We can now see how the notions of injustice and justice versus tragedy lead Aristotle to categorize the varieties of pains and sufferings that the human person undergoes and what the moral response to each must be. We start with his fundamental division between deserved harms and undeserved harms.

For Aristotle, all deserved sufferings concern the pain that a malefactor receives through the workings of justice, actual or metaphorical. One deserves certain pains either as rectifications for one's own acts of injustice, or more metaphorically because they constitute a kind of justice accruing to one's bad character. There is no nobility in suffering one's just punishments, for "a just punishment is more disgraceful than an unjust punishment."[32] Aristotle leaves little room for creditable benevolence or mercy to one's enemies: ". . . to take vengeance on one's enemies is nobler than to come to terms with them; for to retaliate is just, and that which is just is noble."[33] If anything, the implication is that there is here a moral compulsion to inflict pain upon those that deserve punishment.[34]

Undeserved harms are more complex. Some are the results of acts of injustice. In such cases, the cure lies through the mechanism of legal justice or equity. Other harms are tragic and arise from the limitations of our own human nature. Such undeserved sufferings are the lot of the ordinary virtuous man who is neither depraved nor perfect, who is neither utterly ruined nor incurably spoiled, but who is imperfectly developed in virtue. In such cases the cure is not legal. Rather, one becomes enlightened through education, art, philosophy, or perhaps the experience itself. One's character becomes ennobled and gains, at the very least, the virtue of courage. ". . . since the signs of virtue and such things as are the works and sufferings of a good man are noble, it necessarily follows that all the works and signs of courage and all courageous acts are also noble."[35] For the victim of tragedy, suffering is a necessary part of human development, provided one learns from it either reflectively or dramatically. One does not seek to remove the pain involved in tragedy, for it is necessary to the moral development of the person. One seeks only to reflect and understand and educate.

Of another category altogether are those undeserved pains which come not from the unjust acts of another person, nor from our own failings, but from the "slings and arrows of outrageous fortune." In a metaphorical sense, a good man's fall into such misery is deeply unjust and shocking to us. It shocks us that the world should run counter to the moral end that is in the nature of man. Aristotle is honest enough not to deprecate the frequency in which such misfortunes occur. Even the man in possession of the noble virtue of courage may be so struck down by repeated blows of ill fortune that he cannot attain happiness, his true end, except perhaps by long and arduous activity of the soul.[36] Even acts of personal injustice may not find their cure in justice, as when it is impossible to requite the harm.[37]

If justice and equity can treat some acts of injustice and if education can help us deal with tragedy, how do we deal with straightforward misfortunes, including those unjust acts that cannot be rectified? First of all, Aristotle distinguishes between natural misfortunes, which operate more or less predictably from natural forces, and chance misfortunes, which strike without warning and without reasonable foreseeability.[38] For Aristotle, the art of politics can be something of a systemic cure for natural misfortunes.[39] Not only can a proper political order encourage all the virtues including justice and courage, but it can also help avoid those kinds of misfortunes that are predictable in nature[40] by the prudent development of public works, military defense, agriculture, and a sound economy.[41] As a form of organized friendship seeking the good of all, politics can be an instrument permitting individuals to attain virtue and happiness, particularly by limiting the effects of natural misfortunes.[42]

But the best constitution cannot wipe out all chance. For those unforeseeable misfortunes, there seems to be no cure available in law or politics. Instead, Aristotle relies on the virtue of benevolence to offer succor.[43] He calls it a species of good fortune. We should have a friend "who shares our joy in good fortune and our sorrow in affliction . . ."[44] Yet even here, Aristotle maintains that the compassionate response only occurs when pity is aroused, when one who is morally sensitive sees in another person some undeserved suffering that might befall oneself. But if the suffering is so extreme, it can create terror, not pity, and leave us in a state of shock, unable to render aid.[45] The truly shocking pain can only be endured. There is no legal mechanism of justice available. It comes not from a tragic flaw. It is not even the subject of benevolence as it is too terrible to excite pity.

In sum, Aristotle tries to attack the problem of suffering by mechanisms of legal justice in cases of injustice, of education (much of it self-education) and enlightenment in cases of tragedy, of politics in cases of natural misfortune, and of the moral virtue of benevolence in cases of pitiable chance. But life is too full of luck, good and bad, for Aristotle to pretend to square the circle. Though ignorant of Job, when Aristotle confronts the kind of suffering which was the lot of that great character of religious literature, Aristotle can give no answer. His magnificent philosophy does not help us in such an instance. For us to contend with that all too common form of human misery, we must needs turn to a different vision.

Notes

I am, of course, primarily indebted to Professor Veatch for his Aristotelian inspiration. But I am also grateful to Rev. Joseph Owens and Fred Miller for their research suggestions and to Professor Robin West of Cleveland-Marshall College of Law for her intellectual and editorial critique. The views herein are my own.

[1]*Ethics*, V, 4 (J.A.K. Thomson trans., rev. ed. 1976, reprint 1980).

[2]*Ethics*, V, 3.

[3]*Ethics,* V, 10.

[4]*Ethics,* V, 4.

[5]*Rhetoric,* I, 12 (J.H. Freese trans., 1926, reprint 1975).

[6]*Poetics,* 6 (L. Golden trans., 1968, ed. 1981). The translations by Bywater (1920), Buckley (1872), Dorsch (1965), Grube (1958), Butcher (1948), Potts (1953), and the amplified version of Cooper (1913) are similar. Else's translation (1957), of course, radically alters the catharsis phrase.

[7]H. B. Veatch, *Aristotle: A Contemporary Appreciation* 122 (1974); W. H. Fyfe, *Aristotle's Art of Poetry* 1–2 (1940); L. J. Potts, *Aristotle on the Art of Fiction* 67 (1968); L. Cooper, *The Poetics of Aristotle: Its Meaning and Influence* 75–76 (1963); L. Abercrombie, *Principles of Literary Criticism* 86 (1960); F. L. Lucas, *Tragedy* 26 (1957); G. M. A. Grube, *Aristotle on Poetry and Style* xix-xx (1958); L. Golden, *Aristotle's Poetics* 93 (1968, 1981 ed.); G. F. Else, *Aristotle's Poetics: The Argument* 320 (1957).

[8]*Politics,* VIII, 5 (T. A. Sinclair trans., 1962).

[9]*Ibid.*

[10]The kind of pleasure we receive from art does not arise from the fact that the object in the real world is somehow itself pleasant, but rather, our pleasure arises from "the inference that the imitation and the object imitated are identical, so that the result is that we learn something." *Rhetoric,* I, 11.

[11]*Politics,* VIII, 5.

[12]*Ibid.*

[13]*Ibid.*

[14]*Politics,* VIII, 7.

[15]*Rhetoric,* II, 8; see also *Rhetoric,* II, 5.

[16]*Rhetoric,* II, 8. ". . . it is those who are between the two extremes that feel pity." *Ibid.*

[17]*Ibid.* Because the emotion of pity derives from a moral sympathy with one who suffers, and because one who feels pity must himself be a person whose life experiences are neither excessive nor deficient in suffering, it is hard for me to accept totally Jacob Bernays' otherwise brilliant thesis that tragedy is, for Aristotle, a kind of quasi-medical treatment designed to cure persons afflicted with such feelings. Bernays, *Aristotle on the Effect of Tragedy,* in 4, J. Barnes, M. Schofield, & R. Sorabji, *Articles on Aristotle* 159 (1978). Bernays suggests that the cure was designed for those people with a kind of "diseased" nature, i.e., those whose constitutions impelled them towards such emotions. *Ibid.* at 160. However, as we have just seen in the *Rhetoric,* Aristotle's description of the person in whom pity and fear arise is that of a healthy personality, one without distorted sensibilities. For Aristotle, pity and fear taken together are mechanisms of moral sympathy, not aberrations of the soul. After making pity and fear such important emotions in the moral constitution of man, it is difficult to see (without a more expansive treatment by Aristotle) that so many people would be so morbidly afflicted with such emotions that an entire art form so central to the culture has to be singlemindedly structured to keep these unbalanced creatures in check. It seems significant that in Aristotle's entire discussion of pity and fear in the *Rhetoric,* where the manipulation of the emotions is so central, Aristotle nowhere mentions the pathological forms of these emotions. Finally, as

William Fortenbaugh makes clear, the emotions for Aristotle are only understandable cognitively. Fortenbaugh, *Aristotle's Rhetoric on Emotions,* in 4, J. Barnes *et al., Articles on Aristotle,* 142–144 (1978). "Emotional responses can be intelligent and reasonable actions." *Ibid* at 147. Bernays' theory makes pity and fear more of an animal drive and threatens to collapse at least part of Aristotle's tripartite division of the soul into a bipartite structure. On Bernays' view of catharsis, see note 28 below.

[18]*Poetics,* 13. ". . . those who are panic stricken are incapable of pity, because they are preoccupied with their own emotion." *Rhetoric,* II, 8.

[19]*Ibid.*

[20]*Ibid.*

[21]*Ibid.*

[22]N. Frye, *Anatomy of Criticism: Four Essays* 34 (1957).

[23]*Ethics,* V, 8. "For those who commit these injuries and mistakes are doing wrong, and their acts are injuries; but this does not of itself make them unjust or wicked men, because that harm that they did was not due to malice; it is when a man does wrong on purpose that he is unjust and wicked." *Ibid.* See H. House, *Aristotle's Poetics* 95 (1956, reprint 1978). See also Aristotle's definition of involuntary acts as those done with important facts unnoticed. *Rhetoric,* I, 13. See Furley, *Aristotle on the Voluntary,* in 2, J. Barnes *et al., Articles on Aristotle* 47–60 (1977).

[24]*Poetics,* 16. Professor MacIntyre asserts that Aristotle misread the true nature of Greek tragedy in which the practice of the virtues was in an irremedial conflict. Instead, Aristotle improperly substituted the notion of the internal flaw. A. MacIntyre, *After Virtue* 147–48 (1981). Whether the criticism be correct or not, it is irrelevant for the purposes of this essay, which seeks to fathom Aristotle's notions of the moral aspects of suffering, not whether his description of Greek tragedy was correct. I do not speculate on how Aristotle would have treated the instance of suffering due to an irreconcilable conflict between two or more valid duties in virtue, because such a fancy carries a highly improbable assumption: that his general moral theory and his structure of evaluating human suffering would have remained unchanged.

For a modern Aristotelian solution to the dilemma of two "conflicting" duties, see J. Finnis, *Natural Law and Natural Rights* 176 (1980).

[25]*Ethics,* VI.

[26]*Politics,* VIII, 7. I am following the traditional view that the experience of catharsis is lodged in the audience and not, as Professor Else maintains, in the events of the drama itself. G. F. Else, *supra* note 8, at 229, 423.

[27]*Politics,* 16.

[28]As Bernays points out, in the *Politics,* Aristotle notes that persons of certain kinds of dispositions can be excited to a frenzy by sacred melodies but that these same persons can by the same music be restored "as though they had found healing and catharsis." *Politics,* VIII, 7, quoted in Bernays, *supra* note 18, at 156–57. Likewise, "pity and fear, or again enthusiasm, exist very strongly in some souls, and have more or less influence over all." Aristotle goes on to say "Those who are influenced by pity and fear, and every emotional nature, must have a like experience, and others in so far as each is susceptible to such emotion, all receive a sort of catharsis and are relieved with pleasure." *Ibid. A fortiori,* dramatic tragedy is a cure, like some melodies, for the emotions of pity and fear.

In some ways, Bernays' thesis proves too much. He tries to distinguish those who are "piteous and fearful by disposition" from "the man who is feeling pity and fear." Bernays, *supra* note 17, at 162. But Aristotle makes no such distinction. Whereas only some people are afflicted with religious frenzy, pity and fear have "more or less influence over all." Likewise, catharsis is beneficial to ". . . those who are influenced by pity and fear . . . in so far as each is susceptible to such emotions. And in the *Rhetoric,* one influenced by pity and fear is anyone who has had an ordinary undistorted life experience. We should also keep in mind that pity and fear are necessary emotions for moral engagement. How can they be called a disease when their nature is associated with moral sensibilities and they are experienced by virtually the entire population?

I suggest that the Bernays thesis of catharsis as healing and my view that it is associated with enlightenment are not in contradiction. What exactly is the "disease" that dramatic tragedy is designed to cure? The thesis of this article is that it is ignorance, a lack of understanding of how to handle life's uncertainties, an insufficient development of practical wisdom. The audience experiences pity and fear because it sees itself in the hero; it is morally and emotionally associated with the hero's predicament. It is the reversal, the coming to knowledge, that creates the catharsis and the accompanying pleasure.

> And since learning and admiring are pleasant; all things connected with them must also be pleasant; for instance, a work of imitation, such as painting, sculpture, poetry and all that is well imitated, even if the object of imitation is not pleasant; for it is not this that causes pleasure or the reverse, but the inference that the imitation and the object imitated are identical, so that the result is that we learn something. *Rhetoric,* I, ll.

Catharsis is indeed a kind of healing. It does purify the emotions. But we must keep our eyes on what the flaw or disease actually is. It is ignorance, and pity and fear are the symptoms of the illness. Dramatic tragedy does not treat the symptoms. It treats the illness and thereby relieves the symptoms while providing the audience with the kind of pleasure that accompanies healing.

[29]*Ethics,* VI, 5. The poet (artist) who properly constructs the drama achieves excellence through technē, *Ethics,* VI, 4, but the audience, which is the beneficiary of the artistic event, is educated in the virtue of practical wisdom.

[30]Politics, VIII, 7; *Ethics,* II, 6.

[31]The notion of art as learning is central to Aristotle's thought. L. Golden, *supra* note 7, at 92.

[32]*Rhetoric.,* I, 9.

[33]*Ibid.*

[34]In Aristotle, there is no pity for one who receives his just deserts. Indeed, since pity is a form of moral sympathy naturally excited in the ordinary person by the sight of undeserved suffering, it would follow that a situation which fails to bring about that emotion is a situation without a moral justification for rendering aid, whether it be through benevolence, justice, or mercy.

[35]*Ibid.*

[36]*Ethics,* I, 10.

[37]*Rhetoric,* I, 14.

[38]*Ibid.,* I, 10.

[39]*Politics,* VII, 2.

[40]*Rhetoric,* I, 10.

[41]*Politics*, I, 9.

[42]*Ethics*, VIII, 9.

[43]*Ibid.*, IX, 7.

[44]*Rhetoric*, II, 4.

[45]*Ibid.*, II, 8.

CONCEPTIONS OF THE COMMON GOOD AND THE NATURAL RIGHT TO LIBERTY

Douglas B. Rasmussen
St. John's University

Though the title of this essay is "Conceptions of the Common Good and the Natural Right to Liberty," it might, perhaps, be more appropriate to state the concern of this essay in terms of a question—"Can Lockean political conclusions be rendered consistent with the Aristotelian claim that man is a social and political animal whose well-being cannot be achieved outside the *polis?*" In particular, can the Lockean belief that the state should *confine* itself to the protection of individual rights—specifically, the natural right to liberty in all its forms[1]—be rendered consistent with the Aristotelian contention that the state should promote the common good of the political community? On initial consideration, the answer to these questions seems "no," and upon final consideration, the answer to these questions might remain "no." Yet, there are times when there seems to be a way to reconcile these political traditions (at least regarding the points of conflict these questions illustrate), and I would like to share with you my thoughts on how this reconciliation might be accomplished. I will begin by stating in summary fashion what is involved (and not involved) in two central claims of the Aristotelian tradition. These claims are: (1) man is a social and political animal, and (2) the function of the state is to promote the common good of the political community. I will next briefly sketch part of an argument that has been advanced for the claim that men have a natural right to liberty. My purpose will not be to establish that in fact such a right exists, but only that the protection of the right to liberty is a very plausible interpretation of what it means for the state to promote the common good of the political community. Moreover, it will be argued that if there is such a natural right to liberty, then it would set severe limits on the procedures that the state may employ in promoting anything else which is claimed to belong to the common good of the political community. I will finally consider arguments that attempt to characterize the common good of the political community, and thus the state's function, as something more than the protection of individual rights. I will show that these arguments do not work and involve a failure to consider the differences between the state and the community—differences which are hidden by an ambiguity in our understanding of the term 'polis'.

(1) *Man is a social and political animal.* In terms of his natural origins, man is certainly not an isolated entity in a state of nature. Rather, man is

always born into a society or community,[2] and thus it is fundamentally erroneous to attempt to conceive of man as an entity who takes it upon himself to join society. Man has no option to join society; he belongs! Yet, man's involvement in society is even more basic. Though man at birth can be said to possess by nature certain potentialities, the actualization of these potentialities cannot be properly attained in isolation. Man needs association and companionship with others if he is to have any chance of flourishing. It is only through cooperation and collaboration with others that human beings come to adequately provide for their basic needs and highest aspirations. Man's fulfillment and well-being must involve life in society—viz., the attainment of those goods that only a community or association of individuals could ever provide. Thus, man is a social and political animal in the sense that he naturally needs to associate and cooperate with others in order to succeed at being human and in the sense that his natural origin is within society, not some state of nature.

Yet, the fact that man is a social and political animal does not require that he be regarded as no more than a part within a greater social whole. Man's need for others does not mean that he is no longer an individual substance. On the contrary, individual human beings are ontologically prior to their community. They constitute it and serve as the foundation of its being. Human communities or societies are not substances in their own right and have no ontological priority over their members.[3] Further, the fact that man is a social and political animal and thus needs others in order to attain greater knowledge and material well-being, not to mention love and friendship, does not in any way make the attainment of well-being anything less than something the individual must do for himself. One can, of course, be told truths, endowed with wealth, and given affection; but these will not in themselves lead to fulfillment. A person must still use his own intelligence and choice to fashion a worthwhile existence. Presence in the community does not remove the necessary connection between self-fulfillment and individual responsibility. As Henry Veatch has noted: "Never can a human being possibly be what he ought to be, or make of himself what he ought to, without doing so fully by his own deliberate choice and in light of his own understanding of his natural end, and what that end calls for in the way of day-by-day conduct and behavior."[4] Man's fundamental need for social and political life does not come from what he can receive from others, but rather from what he can do *with* others.[5] It is the greater possibility for growth and achievement that social and political life affords that constitutes its extreme importance for man. Community life not only does not change the need to be author of one's own actions; it intensifies it. Thus, man is indeed a social and political animal, but he is also an individual substance who must use his own intelligence and choice to achieve his natural end.

(2) *The function of the state is to promote the common good of the political community.* Since the political community is not an entity in its own right, there can be no good for it just *as such.* This is, however, not to say that the common good of the political community is simply the sum total of

individual, personal goods. Rather, the common good of the political community is that general condition[6] of things as might make possible the flourishing of each and all. As Mortimer Adler has observed, "each man as a person is an end not a means, and in relation to human beings the state is a means not an end, the good that is common to and shared by all men *as men* (the *bonum commune hominis*) is the one and only ultimate end or final goal in this life. The good that is common to and shared by all men as members of the political community (the *bonum commune communitatis*) is an end served by the organized community as a whole, and a means to the individual happiness of each man and all."[7] The common good of the political community must be in accord with the well-being of each and all. It cannot be in conflict with any requirement of an individual human being's fulfillment. Furthermore, it is important to note that the locution "each and all" provides the key to a proper understanding of the common good. The "each" provides a check on "all", and the "all" provides a check on "each". The good of an individual[8] human being cannot be sacrificed for the sake of the community good, and the community good cannot be made subservient to the good of some individual. Thus, the function of political action is for the sake of the common good, and this is in turn understood as representing those political conditions that allow for the possibility of human excellence by individuals within the community.

The crucial question, of course, is how do we determine what political conditions ought to exist in a human community so as to make possible the flourishing of individual human beings, and it is with this question that the possibility of reconciling Lockean political conclusions with the Aristotelian concern for the common good appears. For what is the claim that men have a natural right to liberty, but a claim about what political conditions ought to exist in a human community so as to allow man an opportunity to attain well-being? Let us briefly consider, then, an argument for the natural right to liberty.

The benefits of human social life cannot be denied—man can live best, flourish, only among others. The goods that a person obtains from social intercourse—love, friendship, knowledge, and trade—make life in a community more desirable than life alone. Yet by the same token these goods indicate, delimit and define what kind of social interaction is valuable to man—namely, an interaction with people who are rational, productive, and free. A society that takes from the individual the product of his effort, or enslaves him, or attempts to limit his freedom of mind, or compels him to act against his own judgment, prevents a person's attainment of his natural end.[9] If men are to live together in a peaceful, productive, and cooperative society, they must deal with one another by means of reason—that is, by discussion, persuasion, and voluntary uncoerced agreement. In a moral human community, physical force (or the threat thereof) may be used only in retaliation and defense, and only against those who initiate (or threaten to initiate) its use. The individual human being's natural right to liberty must be the central and primary principle behind the community's laws, for it indicates the fundamental precondition to be met if a person's life among others is to indeed be one that will have any possibility of self-actualizing. "The choice to learn, to judge, to evaluate, to appraise, to decide what he ought to do in order to live his life must be each person's own, otherwise he simply has no opportunity to excel or fail at the task. His moral aspirations cannot be fulfilled (or left unfulfilled) if he is not the source of his own action, if they are forced upon him by others."[10]

Since the requirements for human fulfillment are determined by the nature of man, and since this must be understood as applying to every man—past, present, and future—the good for man has to be defined in terms of abstract principles covering a wide variety of concretes.

> It is up to every individual to apply these principles to the particular goals and problems of his own life. It is only such principles that can provide a proper common bond among all men; men can agree on a principle without necessarily agreeing on the choice of concretes. For instance, men can agree that one should work, without prescribing any man's particular choice of work.

> It is only with abstract principles that a social system may be properly concerned. A social system cannot force a particular good on a man nor can it force him to seek the good: it can only maintain conditions of existence which leave him free to seek it. A government cannot live a man's life, it can only protect his freedom. It cannot prescribe concretes, it cannot tell a man how to work, what to produce, what to buy, what to say, what to write, what values to seek, what form of happiness to pursue—it can only uphold the principle of his right to make such choices.

> It is in this sense that the "common good" . . . lies not in *what* men do when they are free, but in the fact *that* they are free.[11]

The Lockean claim that the state should confine itself to the protection of the natural right to liberty can thus be regarded as nothing more nor less than the promotion of the common good of the political community. In other words, the common good of the political community is a condition determined by an individual's natural right to liberty and which governs the procedures that individuals use in fashioning a worthwhile existence for themselves. When understood in this way, the common good of the political community governs what procedures in social living are just and unjust and not what is the specific result that should be attained by those procedures. The common good of the political community is thus not to be substituted for an individual's natural end. Though they need not be in conflict, at least when correctly interpreted, they are not the same and should not be conflated. Living a good human life remains something an individual must do for himself. Government should only promote the political condition which makes this possible.

Yet, no sooner is it said that protecting the natural right to liberty is the common good for the political community, but comes the reply that this proposed reconciliation of Lockean and Aristotelian political traditions regarding the function of the state is an over-simplification. Though the state may have the function of protecting liberty and though the protection of this right promotes the common good, there is more to promoting the common good of the political community than protecting liberty, and so there is something more for the state to do. Before considering what this "something more" could be, there are two things that should be realized.

First, the common good of the political community must be something which is good for each and every member of the political community. So, whatever is claimed to belong to the common good must not only be truly good, it must be sufficiently universal. Liberty seems to fulfill this requirement. Anything else that allegedly belongs to the common good of the political community must fulfill this requirement also. Second, even if the common good of the political community can be shown to consist of something more than protecting the right to liberty, it cannot be claimed to be something *supraordinate* to this right; for if man has this right, it governs what means or procedures may be employed to achieve any alleged additional feature of the common good of the political community. The government ought not employ procedures inconsistent with this basic[12] right. If the common good of the political community should prove to contain, as a matter of principle, contradictory features, then its attainment in a political community would be impossible and would, therefore, no longer be something that the state should attempt to achieve. Yet, there seems little reason to suppose that the common good of the political community must suffer such a fate.

Many times it is claimed that the state is needed as an authority to supervise those cooperative endeavors that characterize community life. The argument for this claim can be summarized as follows: it is impossible for man to attain his natural end independently of community life. Community life by its very nature requires that men cooperate and collaborate in common enterprises. Yet, common enterprises require that there is someone in authority so as to make sure everyone "pulls his own weight"—otherwise there will be shirkers and the aim of the common enterprise will not be achieved. Thus, the state is needed as an authority who will make sure that everyone "pulls his own weight" in the common enterprise. As Ives Simon notes:

> . . . unity of action depends on unity of judgment, and unity of judgment can be procured either by way of unanimity or by way of authority; no third possibility is conceivable. Either we all think that we should act in a certain way, or it is understood among us that, no matter how diverse our preferences, we shall all assent to one judg-

ment and follow the line of action it prescribes . . . . But to submit
myself to a judgment which does not, or at least may not, express my
own view of what should be done is to obey authority. Thus, authority
is needed to assure unity of action, if and only if, unanimity is
uncertain.[13]

Common enterprises in society, Simon claims, would seldom if ever take
place if one had to achieve unanimity. So, there must be an authority whose
judgment is final, and in the human community this must be the state.

Let us consider this argument. It is true that if common enterprises are to
succeed, there must be cooperation and coordination among participants.
However, it by no means follows from this that there must be directors or
planners to make sure everyone cooperates. Cooperation and coordination
of activities in a common enterprise can arise out of the voluntary interaction
of the participants in accordance with how they perceive their well-being.
Coordination of action does not imply unity of judgment. It is what F. A.
Hayek calls "the constructivist fallacy" to assume that all common enterprises require directors or central planners.[14] Indeed, the entire system of
division of labor, specialization, and market exchange is an example of a
common enterprise that is highly coordinated but has no planner. In fact, the
entire system is so coordinated that it is doubtful that such coordination of
activities could be achieved by some director or even a group of directors.
This is not to say, however, that there are no common enterprises that
require directors, authoritative coordination, or planners. One need only
consider such activities as playing in an orchestra or on an athletic team in
order to see the need for some authority and planning. Yet, examples such as
these do not show that the *kind* of authority necessary for common enterprises is that which comes from the state. Indeed, the very examples of an
orchestra and athletic team indicate that common enterprises can have
authorities that do not involve the state. So, the argument which attempts to
show that the state is needed as an authority to coordinate and supervise
common enterprises does not work.

The examples of an orchestra and team may, however, be used in another
way—namely, to suggest an analogy between them and a human community. Just as orchestras and teams require that there be someone in
charge, some authority, so does a human community. Thus, the state's
function is to direct and coordinate activities within the community in order
to attain those social/political conditions that make possible the flourishing
of individual human beings. Now it must be admitted that there is a point to
this analogy, but what it shows is hardly anything someone from the
Lockean political tradition would wish to deny. What the analogy shows is
that a human community needs law—namely, a system of rights and duties
that allow each and every member of the community to seek fulfillment.
Establishing law is, however, the very point of protecting the natural right to
liberty in its various forms. A legal system that implements and protects this
right is necessary if the human community is to succeed, but what is denied

is that this analogy shows that the state needs to do more than this in order to promote the common good of the political community.[15]

Regrettably, the foregoing argument is not clearly recognized in the Aristotelian political tradition. This lack of recognition is due, at least in part, to a failure to come to grips with an ambiguity in the use of the term 'polis'. 'Polis' can be understood in a broad or narrow fashion. Broadly, it means "a community, a complex system of human relationships, voluntary as well as coercive, personal as well as public."[16] Narrowly, it means "an association of citizens in a constitution."[17] In other words, the polis can be understood as either a human community or a state.

The failure to note this difference is also responsible for the claim advanced by some Aristotelians that the essential function of the state is one of coordination, rather than the use of coercion to enforce laws for protecting individual rights. Yet, we have already seen that it is not necessary that coordination of common enterprises be the result of some planner or authority, and it is certainly not the case that coordination of common enterprises is a unique function of the state. Human beings throughout the community work in concert through voluntary association without the direction of state authorities. Though it is true that the state coordinates and is an authority, what differentiates state coordination and authority from other forms is that the state possesses a *legal* monopoly on the use of physical force. The use of coercive power to enforce law is what ultimately differentiates state authority and direction from other forms of authority. The unique character of the state will not be noted, and indeed cannot be, if one fails to differentiate between the community and the state. One sees only the similarities between the orchestra or team and the state, while ignoring the differences.

The function of the state within a human community is an important one, for it must use its coercive power to enforce laws which protect a human being's natural right to liberty. It seems that this Lockean view of the state's function is consistent with the Aristotelian view that the state should promote the common good of the political community. Whether there is more for the state to do is a most difficult question, but it can be said for now that those who wish to amplify the state's role must consider the issues raised here.[18]

Notes

[1]This involves both the right to life and the right to property. Both of these rights are rights to action—that is, the right to take all the actions necessary for the support and furtherance of one's life, and the right to the action of producing or earning something and keeping, using, and disposing of it according to one's goals. To have a right in this sense morally obligates others to abstain from physical compulsion, coercion or interference. It is also to morally sanction the freedom to act by means of one's voluntary, uncoerced choice for one's own goals. See Ayn Rand, "Values and Rights," in John Hospers' (ed.) *Readings In Introductory Philosophical Analysis* (Englewood Cliffs, N.J.: Prentice-Hall, 1968), pp. 381–381. Also, see Eric Mack, "Individualism, Rights, and the Open Society," in Tibor Machan's (ed) *The Libertarian Reader* (Totowa, N.J.: Rowman and Littlefield, 1982), pp. 3–15.

[2]Though the terms 'society' and 'community' do not always mean the same thing, the differences in their usage do themselves differ; so there is little advantage in attempting to work out all their various meanings here. I will follow John Finnis' procedure regarding this difficulty: "what is here said of 'community' might equally be said of 'society'." *Natural Law And Natural Rights* (Oxford: Clarendon Press, 1980), p. 135.

[3]This is not to deny that there may not be human groups which possess a kind of unity which cannot be explained by the mere physical existence of the individuals who compose them. Yet, a human group is a noetic and moral entity and is entirely dependent on its members' intentions and actions for its unity.

[4]*In Defense of Natural Law* (forthcoming), p. 111 of manuscript.

[5]I owe this insight to Douglas J. Den Uyl.

[6]According to John Finnis, the common good of the political community is one that "neither asserts nor entails that the members of the community have the same values (or set of values or objectives); it implies only there be some set (or set of sets) of conditions which needs to obtain if each member is to attain his own objectives." *Natural Law And Natural Rights,* p. 156.

[7]"Little Errors in the Beginning," *The Thomist* 38 (January 1974): 39.

[8]It should be noted that there is little reason to confine the meaning of 'individual goods' to only apparent goods. Yet, see Mortimer Adler's *The Time of Our lives* (New York: Holt, Rinehart and Winston, 1970), p. 181 for an example of this definition of 'individual goods'. Furthermore, since man is a unified being, he cannot be divided into metaphysical aspects which can be treated differently—viz., one which can be made to serve the state or community and one which cannot. Yet, see Jacques Maritain, *The Person and the Common Good* (Notre Dame, Indiana: Notre Dame University Press, 1966). For a discussion of the legal relationship between the right to liberty and actions taken in emergency situations, see Tibor R. Machan, *Human Rights and Human Liberties* (Chicago: Nelson Hall, 1974), pp. 213–222.

[9]Yves R. Simon claims that "state coercion can have a pedagogical function." *Philosophy of Democratic Government* (Chicago: University of Chicago Press, 1951), p. 110. Yet, see Douglas J. Den Uyl's "Freedom and Virtue" in Machan's *The Libertarian Reader,* pp. 211–225, for a criticism of this kind of claim.

[10]Machan, *Human Rights and Human Liberties,* p. 119.

[11]Ayn Rand, "From My 'Future File'," *Ayn Rand Letter* 3 (September 23, 1974): 4–5.

[12]The natural right to liberty recognizes that a person is not a natural resource whose talents and abilities can be forcibly used for the benefit of others. See Fred Miller, Jr., "The Natural Right to Private Property" in Machan's *The Libertarian Reader,* pp. 275–287.

[13]*Philosophy of Democratic Government,* pp. 19–20.

[14]See Hayek's discussion of this fallacy in *Law, Legislation and Liberty,* Vol. 2 (Chicago: University of Chicago Press, 1977), passim.

[15]Traditionally, such things as money, roads, postal service, dams, and bridges were regarded as common enterprises that require government direction and supervision. Yet, it is not at all clear that these could not be provided by the market. See, for example, Walter Block, "A Free Market in Roads," and Tibor R. Machan, "Dissolving the Problem of Public Goods: Financing Government Without Coercive Measures" in Machan's *The Libertarian Reader.*

[16]Fred Miller, Jr., "The State and the Community in Aristotle's Politics," *Reason Papers* 1, (Fall 1974): 63.

[17]*Ibid.,* p. 64.

[18]This essay is taken, with certain additions and modifications, from a chapter in a forthcoming book, tentatively titled *Towards A Philosophy of Freedom,* which I coauthor with Douglas J. Den Uyl.

THE STATE: ETHICS AND ECONOMICS

Wilfried Ver Eecke
Georgetown University

In his book on Aristotle, Henry Veatch draws attention to a number of important features of man and the study of human affairs. He presents these features in such a lucid way that they appear to be self-evident. But what appears self-evident when presented by one author is often overlooked, forgotten or contradicted by other authors.

In this paper, I will first recapitulate a number of important features of Aristotle's philosophy as Henry Veatch presents it. Secondly, I will show that the mainstream of economic theoreticians disregard the above-mentioned Aristotelian insights. Thirdly, I will show how the difficulties with the concept of "merit good" in economic theory could be resolved by paying attention to Aristotle's basic insights.

1. Aristotelian Insights.

Man is a complex being with a variety of desires. But man's specific nature is rational.[1] Some desires will, upon reflection, be clarified as of secondary importance, others will be thought of as of primary importance; yet others will be considered base or noble. Man, as a rational animal, therefore has the freedom to judge the relative value of his desires and their objects. He can select what is a worthwhile object to strive for. The selection of such a worthwhile object of desire is the selection of "a proper telos or a final cause of human behavior."[2]

Human life and action can therefore be explained fully only by including a reflection on man's effort to choose the proper objects of his desire, the effort to choose the proper goals for his life. Such a reflection is, as Henry Veatch stresses, more than a mere study of human nature as physics. It is the study of appropriate ends, i.e., ethics.[3]

Finally, Aristotle points out that integral to the fullness or perfection of any individual life is a life lived in society or a life of political association.[4] Politics will, therefore, have an ethical function in Aristotle's philosophy. Let me quote Henry Veatch on this point: "Most of us nowadays are inclined to assume that the purpose and function of the state is to make available to us various so-called external goods, hopefully in ever-increasing amounts, and so to provide us with ever-higher and higher standards of living. But not so Aristotle, for his constant message is that the aim of the state is not so much to provide men with goods as to make them good men. And by 'good' Aristotle means 'morally good.'"[5]

Some of the essential features of Aristotle's view of man and his affairs can thus be summarized as follows:

a) Man has right and wrong desires.[6]

b) As a rational being, he can discern between right and wrong.

c) The systematic effort to help in such discernment is ethics.

d) Politics is an integral part of the human good and therefore has an ethical function.

2. Economists and Their Views.

The Scottish philosopher Adam Smith has set forth the philosophical framework for the Western economic profession. In his book, *The Wealth of Nations,* two important ideas emerge. The first idea is that the wealth of a nation consists in productive capacities (machinery) and the concomitant division of labor. The second idea is that ideally social life should be divided between an economic domain and a political domain. In the economic domain, the first rule is that there should be absence of political interference. As a consequence, Adam Smith argues that one will witness the emergence of "the obvious and simple system of natural liberty."[9] This system of natural liberty is the economic domain which he describes as follows:

> Every man, as long as he does not violate the laws of justice, is left perfectly free to pursue his own interest his own way, and to bring both his industry and capital into competition with those of any other man, or order of men.[10]

The political domain is reduced to three functions:

> According to the system of natural liberty, the sovereign has only three duties to attend to . . .: first, the duty of protecting the society from the violence and invasion of other independent societies; secondly, the duty of protecting, as far as possible, every member of the society from the injustice or oppression of every other member of it, or the duty of establishing an exact administration of justice; and thirdly, the duty of erecting and maintaining certain public works and certain public institutions, which it can never be for the interest of any individual, or small numbers of individuals, to erect and maintain.[11]

In the discussion of these political functions Adam Smith regularly points towards their commercial usefulness. About national defense, he writes: "An industrious, and upon that account, a wealthy nation, is of all nations the most likely to be attacked; and unless the state takes some new measures for the public defense, the natural habits of the people render them altogether incapable of defending themselves."[12] About the system of justice he writes:

> Commerce and manufactures can seldom flourish long in any state

which does not enjoy a regular administration of justice, in which the people do not feel themselves secure in the possession of their property, in which the faith in contracts is not supported by law, and in which the authority of the state is not supposed to be regularly employed in enforcing the payment of debts from all those who are able to pay. Commerce and manufactures, in short, can seldom flourish in any state in which there is not a certain degree of confidence in the justice of government.[13]

Finally, about the third function of the government, the erecting and maintaining of certain public works, he writes: "After the public institutions and public works necessary for the defense of the society, and for the administration of justice, both of which have already been mentioned, the other works and institutions of this kind are chiefly those for facilitating the commerce of the society, and those for providing the instruction of the people."[14]

Thus Adam Smith assigns to the political domain predominantly economic responsibilities. Governmental responsibilities for the education of all people remain a remarkable exception. Indeed, Adam Smith defends the idea that "Though the state was to derive no advantage from the instruction of the inferior ranks of people, it would still deserve its attention that they should not be altogether uninstructed."[15] As the economic profession does not often refer to Adam Smith's argument about education it is fair to say that the economic profession comes to see the state ideally as subservient to the economic order.

The understanding of the essence of the economic order underwent a crucial correction towards the latter part of the nineteenth century. Whereas wealth was identified by Adam Smith mainly as productive capabilities, there was a group of economists (Jevons, Menger, Walras), which connected the production of wealth with the idea of marginal utility.[16] Wealth is not any product; wealth is a product that is demanded, and that is thus useful. Increased wealth is a production of goods that are marginally cheaper or marginally more desirable than the ones which used to be produced. This conception of wealth was introduced because, during the nineteenth century, Europe witnessed for the first time the phenomenon of overproduction. Wealth could therefore not be just production. It had to be appropriate, useful production. Thus emerged the marriage between economic theory and utilitarian philosophy. This marriage had originally the great advantage of stressing the fact that the purpose of economic activity was to benefit people. The purpose of economic activity was indeed to maximize utility, not to maximize the number of machines or the productive capabilities of the country. And, as Joan Robinson stressed, this changed view of the goal of economic activity could not fail to alter the economists' view of wages. Whereas wages used to be considered a cost factor which made accumulation of capital that much more difficult, now wages are seen as a crucial part of economic activity. It gives workers the means to vote with their dollars for what they consider useful. Consumption by workers, further-more, is seen to contribute to the national welfare because it increases utility.[17] The other side of the marriage of economic theory and utilitarianism is that the wishes of consumers must be accepted as sovereign. Utility is what individual consumers consider useful and what individual consumers desire. By accepting the maximization of utility as the goal for economic activity, economic theory deprives itself of the right to distinguish between right and wrong desires, because what is wanted is useful and contributes to the goal of economic activity. Economic theory, furthermore, has reduced, since Adam Smith, the rightful functions of the state vis-a-vis the economic domain. Economic theory cannot therefore easily appeal to duties or rights of the state to put limits on the wishes of the consumers. Contemporary economic theory ends up disregarding the crucial Aristotelian insights enumerated in part 1 of this essay. I want to argue that the difficulties with the concept of "merit good" in contemporary economic theory are related to the disregard of the above-mentioned Aristotelian views.

3. The Concept "Merit Good" and Its Problems

Modern Western economic theory takes the wishes of individuals as normative. The free market is the mechanism by which individuals are able to express their wishes. Goods transacted in the market-place, for example, foodstuffs, automobiles and houses are called private goods. Unfortunately, there are goods which have technical characteristics such that they cannot optimally be handled by the market. Such goods, for example, bridges, street lights and national defense, are called public goods. The problem with public goods is that if one person buys them, other persons can also enjoy them, without the first person suffering any loss. This is different from private goods, because my neighbor cannot eat the bread I bought without my suffering a loss. Public goods can therefore be enjoyed by many whereas private goods can only be enjoyed by a single individual. Individuals can buy private goods. Groups of individuals must first come together, reveal their interests and their willingness to pay before they can buy a public good. Furthermore, a group might not be able to collect payment from its members for the purchased good. Economic theory thus recognized the difficulties with the provision of public goods. One solution proposed by economists goes by the name of "voluntary exchange theory of taxation."[18] The solution appeals for help from the state and the state is supposed to use its power of taxation, but it should use it in such a way that any rational individual would prefer to pay his taxes and receive the public good rather than not to be asked to pay taxes and thus not to receive the public good. The solution works as follows. The state is supposed to ask its citizens how much they value a particular service or good, for example, a new bridge, free swimming pools, or police protection. If the sum of the declared value for all citizens together is greater than the cost, then the state is supposed to provide the good or the service. The state is then supposed to use its power of taxation to raise the money to pay for the good or service. The state is supposed, however, to charge each person according to his declared utility in the good or service. As the good or service is to be provided only if it is worth more to the citizens than it actually costs, the state does not have to charge more than what the citizens declared they were willing to pay. The state might even be able to charge less. Thus the citizens receive what they declared they wished; hence the name for the solution to the public goods' problem: "The voluntary exchange theory of taxation". It is clear that the state performs only a subservient role in the provision of public goods and that the wishes of the consumers (citizens) remain sovereign.

When surveying the different economic activities of the state, Richard A. Musgrave discovers still another classification of economic good: "merit goods." He gives as examples: publicly furnished school lunches, subsidized low-cost housing, free education.[19] A merit good is a good that is in the eyes of the appropriate authorities so meritorious that these authorities feel that the consumption level of these goods is not high enough if it is regulated by the market. The authorities therefore refuse to accept the wishes of the consumers as sovereign; instead they act in order to change the level of consumption that consumers would freely opt for. The government can do so by subsidizing a good, by providing it freely, or by making its consumption obligatory.

If we accept the Aristotelian view that one can objectively make distinctions between desires that are important and those that are not important and if one also accepts the further idea that the state has the duty to make the good life possible, the idea of "merit good" would be a natural idea. Contemporary economic theory has, however, deprived itself of the intellectual tools needed to justify "merit goods" even though Musgrave discovered that they are part of the economic activities of the state.

Musgrave clearly sees the dilemma. He asks the question: "Does the satisfaction of merit wants have a place in a normative theory of public economy, based upon the premise of individual preference in a democratic society?" His answer is worth quoting: "A position of extreme individualism could demand that all merit wants be disallowed, but this is not a sensible view."[20] Musgrave then tries to find arguments for merit goods provision. But clearly, such arguments must fail because of the methodological restrictions of contemporary economic theory. Let us analyze the three arguments provided by Musgrave. Musgrave's first argument for merit goods is that those goods may involve public goods aspects.[21] We already know that the state has to provide help with public goods. But if the state provides help because there is a public goods aspect involved, the state must respect consumer preferences. This first argument therefore justifies public goods' provision, not merit goods' provision. Musgrave's second argument is that there is a role for leadership in a democratic society. Consumers may be forced or enticed to consume certain goods and services in order that they may learn about the real benefits of these goods (e.g., education). The trouble with this argument is that it justifies temporary interference with

consumer wishes, whereas merit goods typically are based upon legislation
which is not tied to such a learning process. Educational subsidies are not
restricted to two or three years of one's life until one can appreciate the
benefits of education. Similarly, subsidies for housing or free lunches in
schools are not given until people realize how beneficial it is to live in a
house or to have a lunch. This second argument, therefore does not justify
merit goods either. Musgrave's third argument is not worked out. He simply
mentions that consumers might not have the knowledge required for a
correct choice or they might not make a rational appraisal. Thus, says
Musgrave, "There may arise a distortion in the preference structure that
needs to be counteracted."[22] He immediately adds, however, that: "Interference with consumer choice may occur simply because a ruling group
considers its particular set of mores superior and wishes to impose it on
others." Thus Musgrave does not give a criterion to distinguish between
justified merit goods and arbitrarily imposed merit goods. Still he wants to
preserve the concept of merit good.

In his article, "Merit Wants: a Normatively Empty Box," Charles E.
McLure, Jr., addresses Musgrave's ambiguous attitude towards the concept
of merit goods. He argues that even though there might be "cases that do
involve violation of consumer sovereignty" (p. 475), the concept of merit
good has "no place in a normative theory of the public household based upon
individual preferences" (p. 474).[23] McLure's position is thus that actual
cases of merit good interventions might exist (pp. 475, 483), but that these
"interferences can have no normative justification in a system such as
Musgrave's" (p. 483).

The view of McLure seems very consistent.[24] It argues that if you accept
the wishes of the consumers as sovereign, you cannot justify interference
with these wishes. You can therefore not justify merit goods. Musgrave has,
however, the honesty of pointing out that there are economic activities that
cannot be classified among the two concepts that explicitly respect consumer wishes: private goods and public goods. He even senses that the
concept of merit good is a necessary concept for economists to be able to
classify all economic activities. Furthermore, he senses that the search for
justification is necessary. John Head, a very well-known public finance
theoretician, calls Musgrave's concept of merit good one of the central
contributions made by Musgrave in his book *The Theory of Public
Finance*.[25] Economists are thus perplexed when confronted with the concept
of merit good.

4. A Possible Solution for the Problems Connected with the Concept of Merit Good.

Merit goods are goods that are so meritorious that the government is
willing to impose its judgment about the level of consumption of a good or
service even against the free choice of the consumers/citizens. This is the
case with free, obligatory education, freely provided school lunches and the

like. These examples give the false impression that the concept of "merit goods" applies only to a very few governmental activities. If a merit good is any service imposed against the wishes of one or more consumers, it is clear that there is a long list of governmental activities that must be classified as merit goods. Let us enumerate some. First of all, there is the judicial system with its arrests and its imprisonments. It is difficult to see how one can argue that arrests and imprisonments are submitted to voluntarily. Second, there are the anti-trust laws and the laws against unfair trade practices. Third, there are the different regulatory agencies such as the Food and Drug Administration. It is difficult to see how one can argue that everybody accepts voluntarily all these different laws, or regulations/rules. But if they are not freely accepted, they must be classified as merit goods. The inability to justify merit goods therefore means that the economic profession is without normative tools for a large part of the public finance sector.

The root of the problem is that the marriage between economic theory and utilitarianism forces economists to accept as given the set of wishes of the consumers/citizens, even if that set of wishes is self-contradictory. But if a society wishes to have an efficient free market, then cartels, trusts, import restrictions and subsidies to failing industries must all be prohibited whether or not that is the wish of all consumers/citizens. If a society does not promulgate and does not enforce such prohibitions, that society lives with contradictory wishes and does not get what it wanted in the first place — an efficient free market. If the society, however, does promulgate and does enforce such prohibitions, then such a society gives the state a right and a duty that contemporary economic theory is not able to see. Such a society, indeed, gives the state the right and the duty to distinguish between acceptable desires and unacceptable ones. We thus are able to demonstrate that economic theory must accept some of the essential distinctions made by Aristotle and enumerated in the first part of this essay.

It is encouraging to see that some classic economic authors have disregarded the methodological restrictions imposed on contemporary economic theory and have gone the route of giving the state the positive task of distinguishing between acceptable and unacceptable desires of the consumers/citizens. Let me quote from Henry Simons' *Economic Policy for a Free Society*. As part of a well-thought-out program, Henry Simons proposes that the state should be responsible for the "outright dismantling of our gigantic corporations" (p. 58). And to the possible objection that the owners of these corporations might not accept such a governmental action, he argues that efficiency does not justify such gigantic corporations (p. 59) and that "their existence is to be explained in terms of opportunities for promoter profits, personal ambitions of industrial and financial 'Napoleons,' and advantages of monopoly power" (pp. 59–60). [26]

Simons further proposes to abolish tariffs and industrial subsidies. He does not hesitate to point to the moral implications of this governmental duty. Thus he writes: "A nation which wishes to preserve democratic institutions cannot afford to allow its legislature to become engaged on a large scale in the promiscuous distribution of special subsidies and special favors" (p. 70). "Tariff legislation is politically the first step in the degeneration of popular government into the warfare of each group against all. Its significance for political morality is, moreover, quite patent. Against the tariff, all other forms of 'patronage' and 'pork-barrel legislation' seem of minor importance." (p. 70).

Musgrave and Head are correct in stressing the importance of the concept of merit good. McLure is right in pointing out that there is a deficiency in the justification given for that concept. I indicated that such a justification can only be given if the economic profession is willing to accept the basic Aristotelian distinction of acceptable and unacceptable desires and if it is furthermore willing to assign to the state the task of restricting the unacceptable wishes of its consumers/citizens. I pointed out that there is a logically binding argument for such a view in economic theory even though contemporary economic methodology precludes it. It is encouraging to see that a classic author like Henry Simons does not hesitate to incorporate such a view.

Notes

[1]Henry Veatch, *Aristotle:A Contemporary Appreciation.* (Bloomington: Indiana University Press, 1974), p. 95.

[2]*Ibid.*, p. 98.

[3]*Ibid.*, pp. 98, 100.

[4]*Ibid.*, p. 119.

[5]*Ibid.*, p. 120.

[6]*Ibid.*, p. 108.

[7]Adam Smith, *The Wealth of Nations.* (New York: The Modern Library, 1965), pp. 3–12.

[8]*Ibid.*, p. 651: "All systems, either of preference or of restraint, therefore, being thus completely taken away."

[9]*Ibid.*

[10]*Ibid.*

[11]*Ibid.* Elsewhere (p. 767), Adam Smith adds, "supporting the dignity of the chief magistrate."

[12]*Ibid.*, p. 659.

[13]*Ibid.*, p. 862.

[14]*Ibid.*, p. 681.

[15]*Ibid.*, p. 740.

[16]For a brief description of the lives and contributions of these authors, see Joseph A. Schumpeter, *History of Economic Analysis,* Part IV, Ch. 5; particularly pp. 825–29.

[17]Joan Robinson, *Economic Philosophy.* (New York: Doubleday & Co., 1964), p. 52.

[18]Richard A. Musgrave, *The Theory of Public Finance,* (New York: McGraw-Hill, 1959), pp. 73–ff.

[19]*Ibid.,* p. 13. The opposite of a merit good is a demerit penalty taxation. As the economic arguments about merit and demerit goods are similar, I will talk in the rest of the paper only about merit goods.

[20]*Ibid.,* p. 13.

[21]*Ibid.,* Musgrave's term for public goods is social goods (wants).

[22]*Ibid.,* p. 14.

[23]The author repeats that claim, pp. 475, 478, 482, 483.

[24]Charles E. McLure, Jr. "Merit Wants: A Normatively Empty Box," in *Finanzarchiv,* 27 (1968), pp. 474–483.

[25]John Head, "On Merit Goods," in *Public Goods and Public Welfare.,* (Durham: Duke University Press, 1974), p. 214.

[26]Henry C. Simons. *Economic Policy for a Free Society,* (Chicago: University of Chicago Press, 1973). It is clear in the text that Simons considers all these wishes and motives as undesirable.

PART IV

ETHICS AND RELIGION

CONTEMPLATION IN ARISTOTELIAN ETHICS

Francis H. Parker
Colby College

In his book *Rational Man*, published in 1962, Henry Veatch wrote the following:

> . . . Aristotle unequivocally proclaims that the true end of man must needs consist precisely . . . in contemplation (*theōria*) — that is to say, in knowledge for its own sake . . .

If this was Aristotle's position, then we have no alternative but to "lay hands on our father" Aristotle and to come out in flat disagreement with him on this particular matter. The basis of our disagreement is simply our unshakable conviction that living is not for the sake of knowing, but rather that it is toward intelligent living that all our powers and capacities are ultimately directed, including our powers of knowledge . . . In short, knowledge for its own sake can never be the be-all and end-all of human existence, nor can the chief good of man ever consist in the mere possession or even the exercise of knowledge. (pp. 65, 67)

Later, however, in his book entitled *Aristotle: A Contemporary Appreciation*, published in 1974, Professor Veatch is no longer unshakably convicted of philosophical parricide:

> It has been thought by many to be ironical, if not a simple inconsistency [he there writes], that having set forth with such care and detail . . . what he takes to be the nature and requirements of the moral life . . . Aristotle then appears — or at least so it has seemed to many — to take it all back in the tenth and last book of his *Ethics*. For there he seems to be saying that the good life or the happy life for a human being must consist finally not in moral and political action at all, or in the exercise of virtues like courage, temperance, generosity, justice, magnanimity, *et al.*, but rather simply in a supreme and, so far as possible, wholly uninterrupted activity of theoretical knowledge and pure contemplation. . .

> . . . Yet has he perhaps over-reached himself and betrayed what one might well call the earthy, naturalistic, down-to-earth bias of his philosophy as a whole and of his ethics in particular? Or is it that he is

exploiting various hidden potentialities of that philosophy which he himself glimpsed perhaps none too clearly, but which many of his commentators and interpreters have altogether failed to see? We leave the question open. (pp. 124, 127)

"Veatch's Progress," we might entitle this development, since during those twelve years "case closed" improved to "open question." I'd like to give myself credit for this progress, slight though it may be, since half of the later book was dedicated to me; but it may well be that it was the *other* half. And I hope there has been further progress since 1974, though it would have to be in the last three and a half years because in the fall of 1979, while a Visiting Professor at Colby College and while generously helping me with some lectures on Aristotle's ethics, Henry was quite unsuccessful in his charitable attempt at masking his disapproval of my encomium to Aristotelian contemplation.

The place of contemplation within the total context of Aristotle's ethics — the relation of the contemplative, the *sophos* and *theōros*, to the *phronimos* and *sōphrōn*, the practically moral man — does seem to be regarded as a problem; and commentators' views regarding this apparent problem have run the gamut from Ackrill's mild "Aristotle does not tell us how to combine or relate these two ideas"[1] through Nagel's [Aristotle] "exhibits indecision between" a "comprehensive" and "an intellectualist (or perhaps spiritualist) account of . . . *eudaimonia*"[2] to Sullivan's outrage that ". . . in chapters 7 and 8 of Book 10 [of the *Nicomachean Ethics*] Aristotle completely contradicts," "so desperately contradicts himself."[3] Some of these who see a problem here feel compelled to try to solve it, sometimes in quite ingenious — if implausible — ways. Ackrill, for example, suggests Rule-Utilitarianism: ". . . the ultimate justification for requiring and praising the sorts of acts and attitudes characteristic of the good man is that general adherence to the rules and standards he subscribes to would . . . maximise the amount of *theōria* possible in the community . . . The theory that the *ultimate* objective of morality is the promotion of *theōria* is quite compatible with saying that its more *immediate* objective is a balanced satisfaction of many human needs and desires."[4] Such a Rule-Utilitarian solution, though not I think formally inconsistent with Aristotle's philosophy, is in its modernity quite alien in spirit; and Ackrill's equation of the promotion of *theōria* with "encouraging and sustaining Institutes of Higher Learning,"[5] while generously including the Academy and the Lyceum, is not primarily what Aristotle means. Amelie Rorty, on the other hand, solves the apparent problem by identifying, *via* friendship, the *object* of contemplation with the morally good human life itself: the *sophos* contemplated himself as *phronimos*. "We can contemplate the moral life . . . as well as the starry heaven above," and she claims that "It is only in a corrupt polity that the contemplative life need be otherworldly."[6] The *sophos* as *theōros* is thus turned into "the contemplator of Humanity."[7] Although Rorty rightly points to "the mutual mirroring of friends observing (*theōrein*) [*N.E.* IX, 9 1169b33] one another's virtues,"[8] and although she might also have cited the great-souled man's almost ridiculous admiration of his own moral virtue (*N.E.* IV, 3), it is perfectly clear that for Aristotle it is God, not man, who is the object of contemplation.

Now after all this breast-beating and cart-wheeling by all these experts on Aristotle I find myself slightly fearful and more than slightly embarrassed to confess that I have never been troubled by any *philosophical* problem at all, and not much by any verbal one, regarding the relation between contemplation and the life of moral virtue. I have learned more philosophy from Henry Veatch than from anyone else, but on this point I've just been too thick-headed to learn from him. It's true that there are some apparent verbal inconsistencies and discrepancies within the *Nicomachean Ethics* and between parts of that work and some parts of Aristotle's other ethical writings, but that's hardly surprising considering the age and adventures of these texts. *Veatch* should look so good when *he's* 2300 years old! And this verbal problem should not cause any philosophical problem; it doesn't to my undergraduate students — though they may disagree with Aristotle, especially about the value of contemplation. They easily see that for Aristotle happiness consists in acting out *all* human excellences and therefore *also* that special excellence which is the highest and most divine. Though my students tend to be of two minds — their scientistic mind clashing with their religious one — about whether humans do in fact possess any such divine, more than natural, excellence, they never at all question the fact that *if* humans *do* have a divine excellence which sets them apart from the other animals, why then of course the activity of that excellence will be the highest and best part of happiness, though certainly not the whole of it. Even in wintry Maine students feel a natural urge — or is it a supernatural urge? — especially on a warm April day, to bask in the sun and contemplate first and last things without at all feeling that this activity is incompatible with their total human flourishing.

I have neither the competence nor the time to prove that this was in fact Aristotle's own view by citing every chapter and verse, nor do I think this necessary for philosophical and ethical purposes. However, I would fail in my filial piety to both Aristotle and Veatch if I cited no verses at all. The especially sticky points are in Bk. I, Ch. 7 and Bk. X, Chs. 7 and 8 of the *Nicomachean Ethics*. In I, 7 Aristotle says that the "human good is an activity of the soul in accordance with virtue, and if there are more than one virtue, in accordance with the best and most complete."[9] This conjoined with the tenet that *sophia* is the "best" virtue seems to imply that *theōria* is identical with, is the whole of, the human good and not merely a part of it; and this is stated explicitly in X, 8: "Happiness extends, then, just so far as contemplation does . . . Happiness, therefore, must be some form of contemplation."[10] But other passages and the total context wash away this verbal stickiness by showing beyond any reasonable doubt that Aristotle means *both* that *eudaimonia*, the human good, is a whole of parts which are the activities of all the various virtues and *also* that one of these parts, *theōria*, which is the activity of the virtue of *sophia*, is the "best" or "highest" part in the precise sense that it alone of all the parts is divine — or at least is intentionally united with the divine. As Ackrill says,[11]

> The only proper conclusion [from Bk. I, Ch. 7] would be: "if there are more than one virtue, then in accordance with all of them." This is precisely how the conclusion is drawn in the *Eudemian Ethics* (1219a35–39): ". . . *eudaimonia* must be the activity of a complete life in accordance with complete virtue." The reference to whole and part makes clear that by "complete virtue" here is meant all virtues . . . total virtue, the combination of all virtues.

Thus there is no inconsistency. *Eudaimonia* includes both the practical moral life of the *phronimos* and also the theoretical contemplative life of the *theōros*, but of the two *theōria* is the higher.[12]

This brings me to the final point: the connection between Aristotelian contemplation and religion. Some attention should first be paid to Aristotle's word for contemplation: *theōria*. Though the etymology of this word is uncertain, *theōroi* were sacred ambassadors sent by the state to consult a divine oracle; and it is very likely that Aristotle etymologized — either sincerely or punningly — that the words *theōros* and *theōria* derive from *ōreuō* = to attend to, and *theos* = God.[13] This would make attention to God the very definition of *theōria*. It should next be noted that the conclusion of the *Eudemian Ethics* is absolutely unambiguous on this point — although also tantalizingly brief. "What choice, then, or possession of the natural goods . . . will most produce the contemplation (*theōria*) of God (*theos*), that choice or possession is best," Aristotle there writes[14]; "this is the noblest standard . . . the contemplation and service and worship (*therapeuein*)[15] of God. . ." Finally, I just must quote the famous passage in the *Nicomachean Ethics* — as Henry did both in *Rational Man* and also in *Aristotle* — though to put it in its theological context I will first quote from the *Metaphysics*, Bk. XII, Ch. 7:[16]

> Such, then, is the Initiating Principle upon which the phenomena of sky and earth depend. It enjoys such a life as we may enjoy in our best moments, and it lives perpetually in that state (as we cannot do), for actuality in that state is pleasure as well. Now thought in its intrinsic nature deals with what is intrinsically best, and where thought is most completely present its object is most completely present. Therefore thought in the most complete sense thinks itself, because it participates in the object it is thinking of . . . Perfect thought apprehends and thinks its object in such a way that the thought and its object become one, and the thought thus becomes its own object . . . Hence . . . the divine . . . contemplation is at once its best and most pleasurable state. If, then, God is perpetually in that condition of contemplation to which we occasionally attain, it is wonderful

enough; if in an even higher condition, it is still more wonderful.

"Such a life as this is superior to anything merely human," Aristotle then goes on to say in the *Nicomachean Ethics* passage,[17]

. . . for it is not in so far as he is man that he will live so, but in so far as something divine is present in him. To just the extent that this divine element is superior to our composite human nature, its proper activity is superior to ordinary virtuous conduct. If reason is divine in comparison with man, the life according to it is divine in comparison with human life . . . We must not follow those who advise us, being men, to think of human things, and, being mortal, of mortal things; we must, so far as we can, make ourselves immortal, and strain every nerve to live in accordance with the best thing in us, for though this best part of us be small in bulk, it surpasses all the rest in power and worth.[18]

Although I have not been given the grace to be a Catholic — not even a Roman, let alone an Anglo- — I'm convinced that this passage is genuinely religious in both content and tone. It's even Christian, by means of the *eternal logos*, for, as St. Paul writes,[19] "I live; yet not I, but Christ liveth in me . . ." Or, as Quakers say, "There is that of God in every man." "At this point philosophic contemplation merges with religious prayer and meditation," as John Wild wrote in his Aristotelian days[20] — and *he* was *both* a Catholic and an Anglican. "This is the highest and most perfect *part* of our human happiness," Wild concluded, "for *in it*, that which is most divine *in us* contemplates that which is truly divine." For both the Aristotelian and the Christian, the *ultimate* goal — though not the *only* one — is to know God and to enjoy Him forever. The rest is history — the history of contemplative and mystical religion in the Western world.

Notes

[1]J. L. Ackrill, "Aristotle on *Eudaimonia*," Ch. 2 in *Essays on Aristotle's Ethics*, Amelie Oksenberg Rorty, ed. (Berkeley: University of California Press, 1980), p. 15.

[2]Thomas Nagel, "Aristotle on *Eudaimonia*," Ch. 1 in *Essays on Aristotle's Ethics, op. cit.*, pp. 7, 8.

[3]Roger J. Sullivan, *Morality and the Good Life* (Memphis: Memphis State University Press, 1977), pp. 171, 173.

[4]J. L. Ackrill, *Aristotle the Philosopher* (Oxford: Oxford University Press, 1981), pp. 140, 141.

[5]*Ibid.*, p. 141.

[6]Amelie Oksenberg Rorty, "The Place of Contemplation in Aristotle's *Nicomachean Ethics*," Ch. 20 in *Essays on Aristotle's Ethics, op. cit.*, p. 378, where she also says that this

interpretation "is not the one that Aristotle himself advances as a resolution of the tensions of the *Ethics*" — though *N.E.* VI, 5, 1140b 8–10 does make *phronesis* the object of *theōria* (as pointed out to me by William S. Cobb).

[7]*Ibid.*, p. 388.

[8]*Ibid.*, p. 389.

[9]1098a16–18, Ross translation.

[10]1178b29–32, Ross translation.

[11]*Essays on Aristotle's Ethics, op. cit.*, pp. 27–28.

[12]As Trond Berg Eriksen shows in his *Bios Theoretikos* (Oslo: Universitetsforlaget, 1976), p. 202, ". . . the morally acting man must look at the *phronimos* for a paragon of right action. The *phronimos* must look at the *sophos* for a paragon of human freedom. And the *sophos* must contemplate the life of God to share in the supreme perfection. To the *scala naturae* there corresponds, then, a *scala humana.*" Eriksen also presents an interesting speculation, culminating on p. 210, as to Aristotle's reason for holding this composite view of the human good. Kathleen V. Wilkes' explanation reminds me of Pascal:

> His psychology tells us that man is hybrid — caught in a constant tug-of-war between the claims of his divine and his hylomorphic nature; his theology tells us that the divine element is not commensurable with the hylomorphic (see 1154b20 ff.). The contemplative life is fully attainable only insofar as man can become godlike, and the constant and irremovable block to this is that he is biologically an animal. But the mixture of the divine and the animal is not a stable one; there could be no compromise effected between such disparate elements. No man may attain full divinity, but once he has tasted it in part he is, as it were, foredoomed to try for the impossible. Frustration is then evidently a permanent fact. The indecision in Aristotle's ethics arises directly from the bilateral nature of Aristotle's man and cannot be evaded. ("The Good Man and the Good For Man," Ch. 18 in *Essays on Aristotle's Ethics, op. cit.*, p. 352.)

There is also an interesting discussion of this whole problem in John M. Cooper, *Reason and Human Good in Aristotle* (Cambridge: Harvard University Press, 1975) Ch. III; Cooper contrasts the "intellectualist" view of *eudaimonia* in the *Nicomachean Ethics* with the "mixed" view in the *Eudemian Ethics*. My own view as expressed in this present essay agrees completely with that expressed by Joseph Owens in his admirable review of Cooper's book in the *Canadian Journal of Philosophy*, vol. VII, no. 3 (September 1977), especially pp. 630–635.

[13]Stephen Toulmin first brought this etymology to my attention; and I have been greatly helped in this matter by Dorothy Koonce, Professor of Classics at Colby College. The authority on Greek etymologies, Hjalmar Frisk, says (in *Griechisches Etymologisches Worterbuch* [Heidelberg, Carl Winter, 1960], p. 669) that the word *theōria* derives from *thea* = sight or spectacle; but he also notes that Koller in *Glotta* 36, 273 ff. derives it from *theos* = God. Professor Koonce believes that Frisk is right about the true derivation of the word; but she also believes that it is highly probable that Aristotle had the God derivation in mind and was exploiting it. The Greeks were crazy about etymologies, she says.

[14]*Eudemian Ethics*, 1249b16–21.

[15]The word "worship" is used for *therapeuein* by W. F. R. Hardie (*Aristotle's Ethical Theory* [Oxford University Press, 1968], p. 341) following W. D. Ross (*Aristotle* [London, 1923], p. 234). Scholars who see God as the object of contemplation and who see the connection between Aristotelian contemplation and religion seem to be in ample supply. Here are just two more:

"Nor does Aristotle fail to relate this supreme value, *eudaimonia*, to the highest level of being, i.e. to god conceived of as unmoved mover." (Hellmut Flasher, "Critique of Plato's Theory of Ideas in Aristotle's Ethics," Ch. 1 in *Articles on Aristotle*, edited by Jonathan Barnes, Malcolm Schofield, and Richard Sorabji, vol. 2, *Ethics and Politics* [London: Duckworth, 1977], p. 15.) ". . . you cannot set off the religious inspiration of the one [the *Eudemian Ethics*] against the rationalism of the other [the *Nicomachean Ethics*] . . . In both works, Aristotle envisaged only *theōria tou theou*; the two differ only in this, that whereas the end of the *Eudemian Ethics* describes the object of contemplation, God, and leaves us to discover the human faculty in question, the *Nicomachean Ethics* describes the speculative activity of *nous* and leaves us to find its divine object." (Pierra Defourny, "Contemplation in Aristotle's Ethics," Ch. 10 in *Articles on Aristotle*, vol. 2, *op. cit.*, p. 112.)

[16]1972b14–25, Wheelwright translation with minor changes.

[17]X, 7, 1177b26–35, a combination of the Ross translation and the Wheelwright translation, slightly modified.

[18]Here it is rightly customary to refer to the *De Anima*: "When mind is set free from its present conditions it appears as just what it is and nothing more: this alone is immortal and eternal . . ." (III, 5, 430a23–24, translated by J. A. Smith.)

[19]Letter to the Galatians, 2:20, King James version.

[20]John Wild, *Introduction to Realistic Philosophy* (N.Y.: Harper and Brothers, 1948), p. 173.

RELIGION, GRACE, AND THE LAW ON THE HEART

Donald F. Dreisbach
Northern Michigan University

Religion is often seen as having to do with ethical knowledge, with discovering or revealing, as well as maintaining, ethical norms. I think this view is incorrect. Religion is, I contend, only in a secondary way concerned with coming to know the good; it is primarily concerned with doing it. One must, of course, be cautious when making generalizations about religion, since there are many religions and different religions may well have quite different approaches to the problem of ethics. Even within one particular religious tradition there may be more than one approach to knowing and doing the good. But in general, from the Pali Canon to the writings of Mencius and to the letters of St. Paul, the most important ethical issue, although not necessarily the most important issue of all, is how human beings might be brought to do the good. However, I will confine my comments to the Christian tradition or, more precisely, to a small part of it, to some of the writings of St. Paul.

We might first ask what Paul thinks is the source of ethical knowledge. In his Epistle to the Romans, he writes of the "Gentiles who do not possess the law [but still] carry out its precepts by the law of nature," Gentiles who "display the law of nature inscribed on their hearts." (Rom. 3: 14, NEB) Here Paul is saying that at least some pagans know how to behave, that one can know the good without depending on the authority of the Bible or Church or, for that matter, without studying Kant or Aristotle or Nietzsche. And this does seem to be true. There have been noble pagans and atheists and disappointing Christians, great gouls completely ignorant of ethical theory and dismal souls residing in philosophy departments.

Paul's assertion about the law on the heart seems to imply that the Church should get out of the ethics business altogether. Indeed, it implies that philosophy should get out of the ethics business. But I doubt that Paul was recommending increased unemployment for philosophers, or for preachers. Paul himself was quite willing to make ethical assertions and to give ethical advice. His belief in a law written on the heart does not imply that he was an extreme intuitionist, that he believed all talk or thought about ethics was useless. In fact, Paul's law on the heart strikes me as not altogether unlike a natural end, or at least a natural orientation, for human existence. Few philosophers who believe in a natural end for human beings have chosen to remain silent.

There is really nothing odd about believing that ethics is based on some sort of natural inclination or intuition and at the same time believing that ethical thought and study are helpful. We quite normally believe this about the arts. That is, human beings seem to have a natural inclination to enjoy song and story, pleasant sounds and pleasing and colorful shapes. Hence we take delight in music, literature, and art. But this natural delight by no means puts the critics out of business, nor does it obviate the need for university courses in these subjects. By thinking and talking about the arts, our natural sensibilities are refined and our tastes broadened. We find more and different things to enjoy, and so the range of our enjoyment broadens. We might also acquire some understanding of why we take delight in a symphony by Beethoven or a painting by Van Gogh, and this understanding is itself enjoyable and provides the added, also pleasurable, sense that we have a right to our enjoyment.

The situation in ethics is similar. The study of ethics might refine and enlarge my natural inclination to the good and give me some understanding of why I find some actions to be admirable and some reprehensible. The study of ethics might also equip me to defend my choices against those who would persuade me to adopt others. But in this I think religious ethics is no different from secular ethics. Both are forms of thought and discussion by which our natural sensibilities are broadened and deepened.

Although as far as the intellect is concerned and as far as argument and reflection help us to refine and deepen our ethical sensibilities religion has no special advantage over a purely secular ethics, it does have a kind of persuasiveness or vitality that secular thought usually lacks. This is simply because religion generally deals in symbol and story much more than in dry argument. These symbols and stories have a power to awaken our sensibilities and to elicit from us an emotional response. Although there may be good arguments which direct me to aid my fellow human beings when they are in need, Christianity's picture of God's universal fatherhood and therefore of my relation of brotherhood or sisterhood to all other human being is more likely, especially amid the distractions of everyday life, to awaken or sharpen my natural sympathy and rouse me to action.

But the fact remains that, with or without religious symbols to enliven my moral sensibilities, I often fail to do that which I know I ought to do. It appears to be this phenomenon which Paul is describing when he says: "The good which I want to do, I fail to do; but what I do is the wrong which is against my will; and if what I do is against my will, clearly it is no longer I who am the agent, but sin that has its lodging in me." (Rom. 7: 19–20, NEB)

Certainly this is a puzzling statement. Paul here is speaking in a mythological way, treating sin almost as a magical power that takes control of the self and overpowers the will. In fact, as Paul describes the situation I have no responsibility at all for my misdeeds, since it is not I, but sin, that commits them. Surely this is not what Paul really wanted to say. But whatever the hermeneutic difficulties, it is clear that Paul is very much concerned with that which keeps us from doing that which we know we ought to do.

It is quite surprising how few philosophers have concerned themselves with this issue, with the leap from knowing the good to actually doing it. Perhaps the ghost of Plato still haunts us, persuading us that to know the good is to do it, although Plato himself seemed at times to be dubious about this. Or perhaps academic division of labor leads us to think that problems concerned with doing, as opposed to knowing, are the domain of the psychologist or, ultimately, the police officer.

Some philosophers, of course, have considered this problem of turning moral knowledge or moral sensitivity into right action. Aristotle saw the main block to right action to be fear and other emotions, and so advised us to form good habits or virtues. Nietzsche saw the problem to be the destructive power of a morality of mere convention, and so advised us to philosophize with a hammer. Marx argued that class conflict distorts our view of ourselves and our relations with others, and so advised us to transform the socio-economic situation. And there may have been other philosophers who have tried to give us concrete advice regarding action. But the usual aim in philosophic ethics, including much philosophy that calls itself practical, is to understand ethics, or even to advise us as to what we ought to do, but not to advise us as to how we might bring ourselves to do it.

The three philosophers named above describe the human situation in ways rather similar to Paul's. That is, just as Paul sees the self in bondage to the power of sin, so Aristotle, Nietzsche, and Marx see the self in bondage to, respectively, fear and other emotions, social convention, and economic class interests. These problems are, I think, not unrelated to Paul's notion of sin. Yet Paul is concerned with something that is broader and more insidious. Even if all men formed good moral habits and if the power of convention and of class were broken, there would still be a force that pushed me away from doing the good that I know. This force is, I think, at least a part of what Paul meant by sin.

This force that I am talking about, this power of sin, grows out of the fact that human beings just naturally want a life that is meaningful and valuable. I have here rather dogmatically asserted that human beings have all sorts of natural drives or inclinations, and have not offered much of an argument. But is it not inconceivable that a sane human being would pursue a life that is meaningless or senseless, or one that is bad, bad not by some external judgement but bad in the eyes of the one who lives it? Is this not as inconceivable as someone who would pursue a life of disease instead of health?

But this drive to endow my life with meaning and value might conflict with my natural inclination to be moral. If I perceive my wealth, the number of dollars in my bank account, as a measure of my worth, as a measure of the value of my self (and in a capitalistic society it is very difficult completely to avoid this), it is much harder for me to practice the virtue of generosity. Any response to the legitimate needs of others is going to cost me, and so not only diminishes my bank account but also my value as a person. And in those instances when I am generous, my motive may well be to appear generous rather than to be generous. That is, I want to be perceived as one who is wealthy and powerful enough to give money away, and I also want to demonstrate that I am better than those who benefit from my generosity, thus making use of the needs of the poor.

Generosity is of course only one example. All of my relations with others are colored by my desire to make myself valuable and significant, so human relations often become a power struggle, or a barter arrangement. I want others to recognize and confirm my meaning and value, and others want that from me. So I strike a bargain: I will admire them if they will admire me.

Even my relations with myself are colored by this drive to establish worth and meaning. Activities that tend toward a fulfillment of myself as a full human being, such as taking a walk in the woods or talking to a friend or listening to a symphony, come into conflict with a drive to do things by and through which my value and significance, both in the eyes of others and in my own, will be increased. Even goods, such as being a productive worker or an upstanding citizen, might be chosen not because they are good but because they increase my stature. Even in keeping the law, I sin.

I am not claiming that the natural desire for a meaningful and valuable life is in itself sinful. The desire itself is neutral, but its presence may tempt us to neglect moral principles. And the concept of sin is only partially a moral one; it designates less a transgression of ethical norms than a separation or estrangement from God. In the state of sin I am on my own, dependent upon personal or worldly power rather than on God. Sinfully seeking a life of meaning and value therefore implies that I must rely on my own efforts to establish this meaning and value. The Church responds to this situation by being the mediating vehicle of grace, grace to which the self, the full person and not just the intellect, can faithfully respond. That is, through preaching and the sacraments the self's estrangement from God, and with that the self's need to be the ground of its own value, is at least fragmentarily and momentarily overcome.

This all sounds quite mythological, even magical. Let me describe the situation in other terms. The Church's primary message, the message of the New Testament reduced to a few words, is that God loves us. It is this that is, or ought to be, preached, and it is this that is manifested in the sacraments. Now, if I can accept this message of God's love, if I can, in Tillich's terms, accept my acceptability to God in spite of my unacceptability to myself, the sense and value of my life is thereby established. What greater sense of meaning for my life could I want or hope for than that provided by God's loving me. And if the basis for my life is established by God, I do not have to rely on my own power, exercised in my relations with others, with the world, and with myself, to establish my importance and power. Hence I am free to follow my natural inclination to be generous, to be kind, to take time to listen or to help, to obey the law inscribed on my heart. This does not mean that I stop having relationships with others and the world; it means that these relationships are no longer power struggles. I am freed from the temptation to use others, or, for that matter, the world or even myself, as an instrument by which I establish my own worth, since God has already established that worth, and so I am free for relationships that are genuinely free and loving. And this is what I take to be the primary contribution of the Christian religion to the ethical life, not the giving of law but the preaching of God's love which makes it possible for me to follow that law, or which really frees me from a sense of law imposed on me, frees me to be my own better self.

Let me note in passing that I do not see the power of the Church's proclamation as depending on a metaphysical proof for the existence of God. Language has just in itself the power to transform one's self-understanding. One does not require an argument to feel changed upon receipt of a love letter, or a curse.

And I of course do not think that it is only through the New Testament message that we ever feel loved. We have friends and relatives who love us, and we have jobs or other ways in which meaning and value are established. But these sources of value and meaning are fragile; friends die or fade away, jobs are lost or become boring. The sense of value derived from the Church's preaching transcends these changes within our experience.

There is a strand within our culture, one among others, that holds that a human being is valuable just in and of him or herself. Hence it would not surprise me to find that some people do have a sense of their worth, quite independent of position, friends, lovers, and equally independent of the preaching of the Church. But this cultural strand of self-reliance derives, I suspect, from either Christian or Stoic roots. Certainly it is not self-evident that a human life is valuable, quite independent of any relation to the world or other people. And maintaining without any support the conviction of one's own worth in the face of life's demands and disappointments might be extremely difficult. It is difficult enough with the support of the Church.

I said earlier that different religions might have quite different relations to ethical issues. Indeed, this strikes me as one of the most significant ways in which religions differ from one another. Theravada Buddhism, for instance, has a quite different strategy for freeing one from bondage to a desire for worldly power. It teaches that the world is suffering so that becoming more tightly bound to it just increases one's suffering. It also teaches that there is no real self anyhow, and that attempts to establish one's value and meaning are really attempts to establish the reality of an illusion. Hinduism, with its doctrine of Atman being Brahman, teaches that the self already is God, and so needs no further worldly support. Other religions would, I assume, have different strategies. But I would expect that most religions contain some attempt to free the self from its bondage, from its responsibility to establish one's own meaning and value, and so help to make an ethical life possible.

THE DIVINE COMMAND THEORY AND
OBJECTIVE GOOD

Bruce R. Reichenbach
Augsburg College

A central issue in the continuing discussion of the relation of ethics to religion concerns the divine command theory of ethics. Repeated are a number of charges: the divine command theory makes the standard of right and wrong arbitrary;[1] it traps the defender of the theory in a vicious circle;[2] it violates moral autonomy;[3] it is an infantile relic of our early deontological stage of moral development, a stage now superseded by an adult teleological ethic.[4] In what follows I will evaluate these objections with an eye to noting the relation of ethics to an ontological ground. I will then briefly suggest how Henry Veatch's view of good as an ontological feature of the world provides a context in which the divine command theory can be reasonably justified.

My intent is not to present an argument to establish the truth of the divine command theory, in the sense of showing that ethics is logically dependent on religion, either for its particular moral judgments or for the moral concepts appealed to. Rather, I will attempt to respond to criticisms of that theory. Of course response to such criticisms will not by itself show that the theory is true; that would depend on whether a reasonable case can be made for it. However, my effort does serve to remove certain objections to the theory, objections which purportedly evidence its indefensibility.

There are numerous versions of the divine command theory: in the course of our presentation we shall have occasion to refer to several of them. What they all have in common is the belief that certain acts are obligatory, forbidden or permitted either wholly or partly because God wills or commands them to be such.[5] This analysis of the divine command theory leaves open the question as to why God wills as he does; as we shall see, a variety of possible answers are provided to this question.

The Arbitrariness of God's Will

The charge that the divine command theory entails that moral standards are arbitrary is a common one. For example, Patrick Nowell-Smith writes, "To make morality dependent on religion in this way is to assume first that law is a product of the arbitrary will of a lawgiver."[6] Similarly, A. C. Ewing comments, "If what was good or bad as well as what ought to be done were fixed by God's will, then there could be no reason whatever for God willing

in any particular way. His commands would become purely arbitrary."[7]
Thomas Mayberry puts the argument in the form of a dilemma.

> One must face the objection that God's commands, on this view, lose
> their moral force, since there is no criterion by which they can be said
> to be morally right or justified. On the one hand, it seems that God
> must have had or be in a position to give a moral reason for issuing a
> given command; otherwise, his command would have been arbitrary.
> On the other hand, if he can issue a morally obliging command
> without having a moral reason, he must be able to make an action right
> just by commanding it. In the one case, he uses an independent
> criterion; in the other case, he acts arbitrarily; to issue a command
> without being able to give a justifying reason is to issue an arbitrary
> command. Our concept of God is such that it seems inconceivable that
> God would issue arbitrary commands.[8]

Mayberry's demand that God, as a rational being, must have a reason for
requiring or forbidding or permitting certain actions is consistent with the
more general thesis that the standards or principles of moral conduct,
whatever they may be, need rational justification. As Alan Gewirth writes,
"The question whether a moral principle can be rationally justified has long
had a central place in philosophical ethics. On its answer depends the
possibility of construing the difference between what is morally right and
what is morally wrong, or objective and universal, and hence as knowable
by moral judgements on which all persons who use rational methods must
agree."[9] When applied to the divine command theory, this means that "we
would not and should not think that our ethical beliefs were justified by
being shown to rest on and follow from certain religious or theological
beliefs unless we thought that those were themselves in some way rationally
justifiable."[10]

What kind of justification lies open to the divine command theorist?
Mayberry suggests that the only option open to the theorist, if he is to avoid
arbitrariness, is to opt for justification in terms of an autonomous ethic—
which is in effect to abandon the divine command theory. But might there
not be something about certain states of affairs in the created world or about
the nature of God which provides the needed justification and thus enables
the divine command theorist to escape the dilemma? Let us consider these in
turn.

A Natural Law Ethic

With respect to the first it might be argued that God has created things
with specific natures and potentialities. Further, being omniscient, he
understands both the natures of the things he has created and what fulfills or
completes their potentialities. In particular, he knows what potentialities
human beings have and how best those potentialities are actualized. This

applies to the individual human person just as well as to the species. On the basis of this knowledge, God wills and commands that which will best complete or fulfill and hence perfect human persons, and these commands provide the criteria for determining the rightness or wrongness of human actions.

Not only would God's commands then be justified and not arbitrary, but their justification would be grounded in the kind of thing a being is and what it would be if fulfilled. As such, God's commands are grounded in objective good. This would mean that moral judgments would then be true or false, depending upon whether that judgment coincided ultimately with what would really fulfill that particular person or bring about his self-realization, i.e., with what would be good in fact for him.

Further, this view also removes the common objection to the divine command theory that it is false to contend, as the theory seemingly does, that one could not determine the good for human persons without some divine revelation which embodied the divine command regarding obligations and prohibitions.[11] On our view the non-believer could in fact discover by reason his moral obligations through an analysis of the nature of human persons, their potentialities, and their fulfilling ends. As such, a non-theistic ethic could be constructed. Such an ethic would then be similar to ethics classically conceived. Ethics would be "the science which . . . enables men to understand how they make the transition from man as he happens to be to man as he could be if he realized his essential nature. Ethics on this view presupposes some account of potentiality and act, some account of the essence of man as a rational animal and above all some account of the human *telos*. The precepts which enjoin the various virtues and prohibit the vices which are their counterparts instruct us how to move from potentiality to actuality, how to realize our true nature and to reach our true end."[12] Divine revelation would be sufficient for ascertaining what is morally obligatory or forbidden but would not be necessary. For the theistic *philosopher*, for example, it might be seen in a confirming role, i.e., confirming what practical reason has determined to be morally obligatory, whereas for the theistic *non-philosopher* it would be the source of knowledge concerning divine commands and moral good.[13]

Two objections might be raised against this position. First, if moral goodness is determined by divine commands which are justified in terms of created nature, how can one make sense of such theological assertions as "God is essentially good," "when God created he saw that all was good," and "God has created the best possible world"? Supposing the latter makes sense (which I doubt),[14] one might suggest that the good referred to in all these statements has nothing to do with moral good, but rather refers to a kind of ontological perfection. The created world is good or best in the sense that, for example, it is ordered rather than chaotic, that it has proper means-ends adaptation, or that it provides an arena for the development of life or of moral values. Likewise the goodness herein predicated of God has to do with his ontological and not his moral perfection, that for example he is eternal and not subject to essential change.[15]

The other objection has to do with whether the kind of justification here envisioned is feasible. More particularly—and for a post-Humean and -Moorean age—can facts provide a basis for determination of moral good? Would not the attempt to justify God's commands in terms of the natural order and the way things would be if fulfilled or perfected be guilty of deriving an ought from an is, or at least grounding an ought on an is? Since we shall have more to say about this toward the end of our paper, we shall postpone our discussion of this critical objection until then.

Finally—and in passing, since Nowell-Smith's charge of "being infantile" scarcely merits reply—it can be readily seen that this justification of the divine command theory (as with those to follow) appeals to teleological rather than deontological justificatory considerations, and hence the divine command theory cannot be smugly subsumed under any simplistic deontological analysis and correlative quasi-Freudian refutation.

Obligation-Creating Properties

An alternative response to the demand for justification is to contend that there is something about certain properties of God or his relation to creation which provides such a justification. Philip Quinn embodies something of this sort in his T2 analysis of the divine command theory.

(T2a) It is necessary that, for all p, it is required that p if and only if God makes the universe and God commands that p.

(T2b) It is necessary that, for all p, it is permitted that p if and only if it is not the case that God makes the universe and that God commands that not-p.

(T2c) It is necessary that, for all p, it is forbidden that p if and only if God makes the universe and God commands that not-p.[16]

The point of this particular formulation of the divine command theory is that it is not merely God's command which makes an action obligatory, forbidden, or permitted, but that there are additional factors which either provide necessary conditions for the rightness of certain actions or in terms of which the commands themselves can be justified. In Quinn's formulation the additional factor is the contingent fact that God is the creator of the universe. Unfortunately Quinn fails to develop what there is about the fact that God creates the world which would provide a justification.

A fuller discussion of this view can be found in Baruch Brody, who argues that God's being our creator can be a reason for obeying God's commands. The analogy he draws is one with children and parents. The fact that our parents have brought us into existence provides a reason why we have special obligations to obey their commands. Similarly, since God is our creator, we owe obedience to him. But what specifically is the relation between God's being creator and the obligation of the created to obey him?

Brody develops his thesis along the lines that one comes to own property and thus have property rights by virtue of mixing one's labor with unowned objects. God, by virtue of the fact that he is the creator, owns the entire universe. Consequently he has property rights over it. Human beings were created and appointed stewards over that property, with certain obligations and restrictions with regard to their use of that property. God "allows men to use for their purposes the property that they mix their labor with, but he does so with the restriction that they must not use it in such a way as to cause a great loss to other people."[17] As stewards, obedience to those property obligations and restrictions imposed by the owner is expected. The ground for the divine commands, then, is found in the fact that God as creator is owner of the creation and that as divinely appointed stewards over that property we are obligated to obey his commands.

But, it might be objected, does not this view again attempt to ground obligation in certain facts, this time certain contingent facts about God being the creator and owner of property? In what sense does having a certain property (being creator) entail that one ought to be obeyed? Brody himself admits that we are not obligated to obey all the commands of our creators (our parents), only in "some cases." Indeed, one could make the case that we are obligated only to obey those commands of our parents which are moral. Similarly, we are obligated to obey only those commands of God which are moral, and should what he commands not be moral, our obligation to obey him as creator at that point ceases. Similarly, the owner of a piece of property cannot do anything he pleases with that property, despite the fact that he owns it as the result of his labors. Ethical considerations impose limits on his use of that property. Likewise God cannot use his property in just anyway he pleases; his use of what he has created is subject to moral limitations. Brody himself seems to want to impose moral limits on the extent of God's property rights when he queries whether it would be consistent with God's being all-just to allow or order the life of a piece of property (human or animal) to be taken by another.[18] But then this justification is inadequate by itself; the obligation to obey does not follow simply and solely from the creator-created relationships. Again the spectre of deriving values from factual states of affairs haunts the attempted justification of the divine command theory.

Brody's appeal to an all-just God indicates that something more than merely the creator-created and property-owner-steward relation is required to make this justification work. Something must be said not only about God's being the creator, but also about the essential properties which this creator possesses. It is to this now that we turn.

Essential Properties of God

A third possible response to Mayberry's dilemma lies open to the divine command theorist. Instead of introducing ethical considerations based on contingent states of affairs, he might contend that the justification for God's commands being good is that they are commanded by a good God, by a being who is essentially and necessarily good. Philip Quinn has embodied this formulation in the following argument:

(46) Necessarily, if God is perfectly good, then for all actions a and for all agents p, if a has the property of being commanded by God, then a is what p ought to do.
(27) Necessarily, God is perfectly good.
(47) Necessarily, for all actions a and for all agents p, if a has the property of being commanded by God, then a is what p ought to do.[19]

God's commands would accord with his nature, which is essentially and necessarily good. Since God could not command anything which was contrary to his nature, God could not require or prohibit anything which was contrary to his essential goodness. Thus, rather than being arbitrary, God's commands are grounded necessarily in his own being, which is good. And as grounded in his nature, they are not independent of God. Consequently, one could adequately reply to Mayberry's dilemma by contending that God can justify his commands in terms of his own nature.

Mayberry might reply to this by restating his dilemma as follows: either God can justify the goodness of his nature, which would require appealing to an independent standard of good, or else God cannot justify the goodness of his nature, in which case that he is good is arbitrarily decided. Two responses might be given at this point. First, the series of justifications must come to an end somewhere; otherwise one is caught up in an infinite regress. But if the ethical autonomist can draw the terminus at some fundamental fact about what humans desire or human language or human intuition requires, the divine command theorist can draw it at some fundamental fact about the nature of God. Secondly, one might accept the challenge of requiring a justification for contending that God is good, and in turn choose to follow the example of someone like Thomas Aquinas and give reasons why God is good. We shall have more to say about this shortly.

Circularity and the Divine Nature

Enough has been said to show that Mayberry's dilemma is both hornless and toothless: justification in terms of something other than an autonomous ethic is at least possible. However, we still must face A. C. Ewing's objection that the divine command theorist's argument is caught in a vicious circle. The divine command theorist who grounds God's commands in his goodness, Ewing writes, exposes himself "to the charge of being guilty of a vicious circle, since he should in that case have defined both God in terms of goodness and goodness in terms of God."[20] Elsewhere he writes, "Obviously we cannot deduce our ethics from belief in any sort of God: it must be a good God, but how could we possibly reach the conception of a good God without presupposing the independent prior validity of our ethical thought? Without that we could have no notion what goodness meant, or what kinds of things were good, so that the word would be meaningless to us and give us no indication that, e.g., God was a God of justice rather than of injustice. . . ."[21]

Ewing's objection here is couched in the terminology of meaning; his thesis is that one must have a standard of meaning for ethical terms such as "good" independent of God in order to understand what it is to call God good. Unless we know what "good" means independent of God, we are caught in a vicious circle of defining "God" and "good" in terms of each other.

The introduction of the question of meaning catapults us into the thicket of the problem of meaning, with all its disputes, unclarities, confusions and disagreements. To explore the question of meaning in depth would take us too far afield—so far in fact that we should never return to the substance of our topic. However, in lieu of dismissing or avoiding the issue entirely, it might be profitable to refer to a discussion of this very issue by Patterson Brown. Brown argues that the divine command theorist is not making a claim about the meanings of moral terms such as "right" and "good"; rather he is advancing a claim about the criteria for application of such terms. "My analysis presupposes the doctrine that moral terms have meanings or definitions which, not being descriptive, entail no criteria of application. So that merely knowing the dictionary definition of, e.g., 'good' does not suffice to tell one what is good. A criterion of application, a moral standard, is needed as well."[22]

Brown here is making a distinction between the meanings of terms and the criteria or rules for their application. He contends that though it is usually the case that giving the meaning of a word includes giving the criteria for the application of that word to events or things in the world, there are some words for which this is not the case. Thus, whereas to give the meaning of "chair" and "to drink" is to include the criteria for the application of these terms, to give the meaning of terms such as "millimeter" ("one thousandth part of a meter") or of "meter" ("a unit of length in the metric system") fails to provide the criteria for application to the physical world. The criterion is supplied by markings on a certain platinum-iridium bar in Paris. Similarly, to give the meaning of value terms like "good" and "right" is not to provide the criteria for the application of these terms.

> Moral words have meanings which do not provide criteria for their application, and yet they are properly applied to things, events, and so on in a systematic way. One can all too easily know the intertwining dictionary entries for 'good,' 'right,' 'obligatory,' 'commendable,' 'evil,' 'wrong,' 'prohibited,' 'condemnable,' etc., and yet be confused about or simply ignorant of standards for their application. Knowing the meanings of moral terms does not suffice in a search for what is moral. One must in addition have moral stands. . .[23]

Whether or not Brown is correct when he contends that to give the meaning is not necessarily to give the criteria for application, he is correct in holding that there is a distinction between meaning and criteria of application, and that the divine command theorist is not intending to provide the meaning of the terms "right" and "good" when he provides an analysis of the sort found in T2 above. Indeed, were he trying to do so, then to say that what God wills is good is to say "What God wills is what God wills," which is a tautology.[24] And if to say God is good is identical to saying that what God wills is good, then that God is good is likewise a tautology.[25] Rather, T2 provides the criteria for determining whether an action is required, forbidden or permitted, and this in terms of the commands of God, either *simpliciter* or along with other theological or factual considerations. Those who contend that divine command theories claim or necessarily entail that "God's commands are *definitive* of moral obligation, that 'I ought to do x' simply *means* 'God commands me to do x'",[26] are wrong. Divine command theories "ought not to be construed as expressing truths of meaning,"[27] but rather as providing criteria for determining rightness of actions. Being commanded by God might be a sufficient reason for something being obligated, but it is not the meaning of "being obligated."

However, this move does not free us from the fundamental charge leveled by Ewing and others, namely, that it is not the commands of just any being which can legitimately or reasonably be taken as providing the criteria for right actions. It is only the commands of a good being which can be so considered. Ewing's objection, of course, is not novel. Precedents can be found in G. E. Moore[28] and before that in Plato.[29]

The point here is that if any given set of commands is to be justified in terms of the nature of the commander, the nature of the commander must be good. But then in terms of what is the goodness of the commander determined? It cannot be in terms of its own commands, for this truly would be circular. If it be in terms of some other standard of goodness, then the divine command theorist is forced to admit to an autonomous standard of good, to an autonomous ethic. The other option is that there is something about the being itself and the properties which it possesses essentially in virtue of which it is good. That is, because it possesses certain properties essentially, it is the sort of being whose commands can be taken reasonably as providing the criteria for right action. The properties which are commonly appealed to are God's love, benevolence, perfection, and desirableness.

According to the first two options, God is viewed as being essentially a loving and benevolent being, a being who necessarily always seeks the good for his creation. Since what God commands is necessarily connected with his will, and since his will is necessarily connected with his nature as loving and benevolent, that which is commanded as being obligatory or forbidden is necessarily grounded in God's very being or nature.[30] Since God is by nature loving and benevolent, God is good—the sort of being whose commands can provide the criteria for determining human moral action.

The latter two properties are those appealed to by Thomas Aquinas.

According to Aquinas, God is good, first, because he is pure act. Whatever has actuality is perfect in the way and to the extent that it has actuality. God, as the uncaused necessary being, as the being in whom essence and existence are identical, is pure act, having no potentiality. Thus he as pure act is perfect in the way in which he is pure act (in his essence) and to the extent to which he is pure act, i.e., necessarily and completely. God, by virtue of being perfect, is necessarily good.[31] Secondly, insofar as God is the first producing cause of all creation, he is the end which all seek; all effects seek after God as their end in that all desire their own perfection, which is the likeness of divine perfection. God thus is desirable and hence good.[32]

But what is there about the fact that God is loving, benevolent, perfect or desirable which provides the ground or justification for the divine commands? Simply because God possesses these properties does not, in itself, suffice to justify he divine commands. This is because it is not necessarily the case that an object which has certain properties necessarily is identical to or the ground for another *qua* having those particular properties. For example, the number two is necessarily the only even prime; it is also necessarily the predecessor of the number three. But the number two is not the predecessor of the number three *qua* being the only even prime. Similarly, Venus is the evening star; but it is not the morning star *qua* being the evening star. Given this, one might then query whether it is similarly the case that though God is both necessarily perfect, loving and desirable, and the author of the divine commands, it is in virtue of his being the former that he is the latter. To show that this case is different from the cases of the number two and Venus, the divine command theorist must show what connects these necessary properties with the divine commands. The mere possession of these properties will not, in itself, suffice as justificatory.[33]

Now it might be thought that the connection has to do with the fact that these divine properties are moral properties. As such, since God is *essentially* perfect and loving in a moral sense, it would necessarily be the case that his commands would be morally perfect. Indeed, this is the basis for the justification which Ewing, Nowell-Smith and Mayberry have in mind in their objection. For them divine commands can be justified only in terms of some prior moral good. But in fact the good which, for example, Thomas Aquinas derives from God's perfection and desirability is not moral, but ontological, good. But how is this ontological good to be linked to moral good? If it is by a standard invoking God's own commands, the appeal would be circular: justifying God's commands in terms of moral goodness, and establishing that moral goodness in terms of his commands. But if it is by appeal to a standard other than God's commands, some sort of autonomous moral good is invoked, which way is not open to the divine command theorist.

But what then is the connecting link between these divine properties and the divine commands? One possibility is to conjoin these properties with God's being the creator of the natural order and with his knowledge. The connection then is that God created the natural order with certain potentialities which need fulfilling. God, as loving, wills that human beings obtain their fullest self-realization, given the kinds of beings they are, both in terms of their being human and in terms of their being specific individuals. As omniscient, God knows both the natural order and individual human persons. On this basis he issues divine commands which, if followed, would lead to the fulfillment and realization of individual human potential. Thus, it is in terms of God *qua* being the omniscient and loving creator of the universe that is a justification for the divine commands. But this returns us to the first justification given above. Indeed, it would seem that both the second and the third alternative justifications are contingent upon the meaningfulness and truth of the first justification.

If so, we must return to the objection against this first justification which we posed initially but delayed. This view justified the divine commands in terms of the *telos* of created natures. But this objectivist conception of ethics is viewed by most contemporary ethicists as "a frankly irrational position."[34] Yet is it irrational, as is claimed? Some contemporary ethical theorists are not so certain—and this brings us to Henry Veatch's thesis that ontological considerations can provide a ground for moral goodness.

Goodness as a Consequential Property

In his writings Henry Veatch frequently observes that contemporary ethical theorists have little sympathy for ethical theories which assert that ethics and ethical judgments have anything like an objective or ontological basis. "Neither goodness nor rightness is ever an objective feature of the world."[35] Yet, as C. S. Lewis has pointed out, modernity is not tantamount to truth. Thus we find Veatch looking back to Aristotle and Thomas Aquinas for his insights into the possibility that the good is grounded in objective fact.

Veatch argues that goodness is not merely grounded in, but can be "defined directly in terms of certain of the features or properties of the real world. . . . Value or disvalue . . . pertains to things as they are in themselves, and thus are possessed of a proper ontological status of their own."[36] He analyzes goodness in terms of Aristotelean act-potency distinction. All actuality is correlated with potency, such that actuality is what a given potentiality is a potentiality for. Actuality is the fulfillment of potentiality; it is realization of the capacity or ability manifested in being the potentiality for something. The actual, then, is the completion or perfection of the thing, for in becoming actual vis-a-vis its potentiality it has reached its *telos*.

Since goodness lies in the completion or fulfillment of the existent potentialities, goodness is in some sense a property of things in the world. However, it is not like many other properties. ". . . goodness is not a property of things in the usual sense of property at all. To say that a thing is good is not like saying that it is round or square, or pink or blue, or late or early, or above or below. . . . Instead, it seems to be what some . . . call a consequential or supervenient property."[37] That is to say, it is a property that a thing has in virtue of other properties which it possesses. "The properties of a thing can be the sources of its goodness or value . . . just insofar as they are properties that evidence the perfection or complete actuality of the thing in question."[38] Goodness then is a property that a thing has insofar as it has actualized its potential.

However, there must be a subjective dimension to the good as well. "Goodness is no mere objective property of things which can both be and be conceived quite apart from such feelings of approval . . . and such tendings toward it as are characteristics of potency with respect to their actualities."[39] Neither is the good to be identified merely with what is desired, as in Mill's utilitarianism. The good is not made good by being desired; rather, the good is the desirable. "Goodness as such is neither an objective property that can either be or be understood apart from all reference to such subjective responses to it as desire, approval, commendation, etc.; nor is goodness to be simply equated with our subjective reactions to the object, being itself nothing objective at all."[40] Rather, good is the actuality of the potentialities found in the thing itself, the actuality which is the end or *telos* of those potentialities and as such desirable by that thing. The good, as Aristotle claimed, is that which all things seek as the completion or fulfillment of their nature, and, as Thomas Aquinas argued, that toward which we have a natural inclination.

In sum, his point is that "the worth or excellence of things is . . . an objective characteristic of things with which our likings and desires must needs be brought into conformity. . . . The goodness of things is an objective feature of such things, and as such can provide an objective ground or reason for their being desired."[41]

How, then, can this be applied to the divine command theory? The answer is simply that if a justification for God's commands is to be required, and if the divine command theorist is to reject justification in terms of some autonomous ethic, he must provide some sort of justification in terms of ontology. Veatch's claim is that not only is this possible, but modern Kantian, Utilitarian and Prescriptivist attempts at justification having failed, this is the only way a reasonable justification can be given for ethical principles. Should he be correct, then the divine command theorist, in appealing to an ontological ground to justify God's commands, has provided a response to the objections raised at the outset. Adequate justification for the divine commands can be found in certain objective facts about God himself (that as loving he wills our fulfillment and as omniscient he knows what will fulfill us) and his creation (what in fact will fulfill particular persons, given the kind of beings and individuals they are).

But what of the question of the particular relation of fact and value which this justification embraces? We have already noted that the major objection to this kind of justification of the divine command theory is that it grounds the divine commands in certain facts about God and the creation. But is this not to commit a fallacy—if not the infamous Naturalistic Fallacy, at least a logical fallacy of deriving something in the conclusion not contained in the premise? That is, does not this justification attempt the impossible of grounding the *ought* in the *is?* And is not Veatch's ontological ethic guilty of the same? Veatch's response is that this objection presupposes a distinction between fact and value which is overblown. Indeed, if good is, in part, objective, then facts about the world include facts about the good. There are states of affairs which constitute the perfection of a being; these states of affairs, if realized, fulfill the potentialities of that being and in so doing constitute its good. These actualities are describable and empirically ascertainable, and consequently are an objective good. A description of the facts about the world would include this objective good. Consequently, it is legitimate to ground values in facts, so long as these facts themselves contain or are related in some manner to the objective good. Thus, though one cannot ground or derive values from just any set of facts—for example, about what is desired by men—such can be done when the facts include a description of the *telos* state of affairs which is, by virtue of the nature of the being under consideration, what the being ought to be and which, if realized, would result in that being's self-fulfillment.

In short, utilizing the kind of approach presented by Veatch provides the divine command theorist with the kind of metaphysical framework within which he can construct the kind of justification demanded by the ethical theorist without appealing to an autonomous ethic. Within this framework there is objective good in terms of the *telos* of created beings, and the divine commands can be seen to be reasonable or justified insofar as they are grounded in that *telos,* that is, insofar as they are commands whose very character is to aid in human self-actualization or self-fulfillment.

Concluding Remarks

Several issues remain, two of which can be briefly discussed here, while the others must be addressed more fully at another time and another place.

First, in appealing to objective good in order to justify the divine commands, have we not in effect departed from the divine command theory? In fact, and more generally, does not any attempt to give a justification for the divine commands concede the very issue to the critic, namely, that the good in terms of which the divine commands are ascertained ultimately must be an autonomous good?

The response, I believe, is negative. In many instances where appeal to some justification is made, this might be true. However, I do not think that the general thesis is necessarily true; neither is the objection sound in the case of an appeal to objective good in the fashion in which we have constructed it. The reason is that the creation is God's creation, and the human *telos* is a *telos* built into creation by God. Thus the objective good in terms of which the divine commands are, in part, justified is not independent of God; it is not an autonomous good, but rather a product of God's creative activity. It is a good created by God. Above we noted that a divine command theory is defined as a theory which holds that certain acts are obligatory, forbidden or permitted either wholly or partly because God commands them to be such. On our interpretation of the theory, God's commands provide the criteria for determining right and wrong actions, and God's commands are justified in terms of the objective good in divine creation. Neither the right nor the good stands independent of God; the first depends upon his commands, whereas the second depends upon his creative act and wisdom.

Secondly, is man's nature determinate enough to enable the ethicist to ascertain the good of man? Man's functions and operations are too diffuse, it is objected, to enable one by means of practical reason to ascertain man's *telos*. It is true that one can speak of general goods like human happiness, well-being, health, preservation of life, and the like, but these goods seem too general to be of much assistance in resolving the concrete moral questions. How does human happiness translate into a resolution of the problem of whether or not to preserve the life of defective neo-natals? How does the general good of the preservation of life resolve the problem of the just distribution of scarce resources? Can ascertaining man's *telos* enable us to determine whether homosexual acts are moral? In short, is the natural law theory of much specific help in resolving concrete questions concerning right actions?

Notes

[1] Patrick Nowell-Smith, "Religion and Morality," *The Encyclopedia of Philosophy* VII (N.Y.: Macmillan, 1967), p. 155; Thomas Mayberry, "Morality and the Deity," *Southwest Journal of Philosophy* I (Fall 1970), p. 122.

[2] A. C. Ewing, *Prospect for Metaphysics* (London: George Allen and Unwin, 1961), p. 41; A. C. Ewing, "Ethics and Belief in God," *Hibbert Journal* 39 (no. 4, July 1941), p. 375.

[3] C. A. Campbell, "Patterson Brown on God and Evil," in *God, Man and Religion: Readings in the Philosophy of Religion,* ed. by Keith Yandell (N.Y.: McGraw-Hill, 1973) p. 343; Nowell-Smith, p. 156.

[4] Patrick Nowell-Smith, "Morality: Religious and Secular," in *Readings in the Philosophy of Religion,* ed. by Baruch Brody (Englewood Cliffs: Prentice-Hall, 1974), pp. 581–589.

[5] Robert Burch suggests that those who hold that morality is what is willed by God, that "God wills morally good things because they are morally good," hold a version or type of the divine command theory. ["Objective Values and the Divine Command Theory of Morality," *New Scholasticism* 54 (Summer 1980), p. 280.] This seems to me an unlikely explication, unless somehow what is willed by God is in turn the criterion by which humans determine moral or immoral actions. Robert Adams seems to agree. "According to the divine command theory, insofar as [facts of wrongness] are nonnatural and objective, they consist in facts about the will or commands of God. I think this is really the central point in a divine command theory of ethical wrongness. This is the point at which the divine command theory is distinguished from alternative theological theories of ethical wrongness, such as the theory that facts of ethical rightness and wrongness are objective, nonnatural facts about ideas or essences subsisting eternally in God's understanding, not subject to His will or guiding it." ["A Modified Divine Command Theory of Ethical Wrongness," in *Religion and Morality,* ed. by Gene Outka and John P. Reeder, Jr. (Garden City, N.Y.: Anchor Press/Doubleday, 1973) p. 328].

[6]Nowell-Smith, "Religion and Morality," p. 156.

[7]Ewing, *Prospect for Metaphysics,* p. 39.

[8]Mayberry, *op. cit.,* p. 122.

[9]Alan Gewirth, "Moral Rationality," quoted in Henry Veatch, "The Rational Justification of Moral Principles: Can There Be Such a Thing?", *Review of Metaphysics* 29 (1975), p. 217.

[10]William K. Frankena, "Is Morality Logically Dependent on Religion?", in *Religion and Morality,* ed. by Gene Outka and John P. Reeder, Jr., p. 313.

[11]C. A. Campbell, "Does Religion Challenge Ethical Autonomy?", *The Hibbert Journal* 47 (1949), pp. 344–345.

[12]Alasdair MacIntyre, *After Virtue* (Notre Dame: University of Notre Dame Press, 1981), p. 50.

[13]This might be conceived along the pattern of Aquinas' doctrine of two-fold truth.

[14]Bruce R. Reichenbach, "Must God Create the Best Possible World?", *The International Philosophical Quarterly* 19 (no. 2, June 1979), pp. 203–212.

[15]Bruce R. Reichenbach, *Evil and a Good God* (N.Y.: Fordham University Press, 1982), pp. 131–139.

[16]Philip Quinn, *Divine Commands and Moral Requirements* (Oxford: Oxford University Press, 1978), p. 33.

[17]Baruch Brody, "Morality and Religion Reconsidered," in *Readings in the Philosophy of Religion,* ed. by Baruch Brody, pp. 596–597.

[18]Brody, *op. cit.,* p. 603.

[19]Quinn, *op. cit.,* p. 18.

[20]Ewing, *Prospect for Metaphysics,* p. 41.

[21]Ewing, "Ethics and Belief in God," p. 376.

[22]Patterson Brown, "Religious Morality: A Reply to Flew and Campbell," in *God, Man and Religion: Readings in the Philosophy of Religion,* ed. by Keith Yandell, p. 380.

[23]Patterson Brown, "God and the Good," in *God, Man and Religion: Readings in the Philosophy of Religion, op. cit.,* p. 386.

[24]Keith E. Yandell, *Basic Issues in the Philosophy of Religion* (N.Y.: Allyn and Bacon, 1971), p. 153.

[25]Burch, *op. cit.,* p. 284.

[26]Nowell-Smith, "Religion and Morality," p. 156.

[27]Quinn, *op. cit.,* p. 41.

[28]"Yet it is obvious that if by a source of obligation is meant only a power which binds you or compels you to do a thing, it is not because it does do this that you ought to obey it. It is only if it

be itself so good, that it commands and enforces only what is good, that it can be a source of moral obligation. . . . However an authority be defined, its commands will be morally binding only if they are—morally binding; only if they tell us what ought to be or what is a means to that which ought to be." G. E. Moore, *Principia Ethica* (Cambridge: Cambridge University Press, 1903), p. 128.

[29]Plato, *Euthyphro* 9d–11b.

[30]Burch, *op. cit.,* pp. 332–333. Robert Adams has a similar view, except that he sees God's property of being loving as being a logically contingent property; he leaves open the question whether it is causally contingent as well, i.e., whether God can act contrary to his character. Adams, *op. cit.,* p. 322.

[31]Thomas Aquinas, *Summa Theologica,* Ia, Q3, arts. 2 and 4.

[32]*Ibid., Q5* art. 4; Q6, art. 1.

[33]This objection was suggested to me by Thomas Sullivan.

[34]Campbell, *op. cit.,* p. 378.

[35]Henry Veatch, "Language and Ethics: What's Hecuba to him or he to Hecuba?" *Proceedings of the American Philosophical Association* 44, (1972), p. 49.

[36]Henry Veatch, *The Ontology of Morals* (Evanston: Northwestern University Press, 1971), pp. 105–106.

[37]*Ibid,* p. 109.

[38]*Ibid.*

[39]*Ibid.,* p. 113.

[40]*Ibid.,* pp. 116–117.

[41]Veatch, "Justification of Moral Principles," pp. 235, 238.

[42]I am using God here as a proper name, and not as a title.

[43]Thomas Aquinas, *Summa Theologica,* Ia, Q25, art. 5, ad 2.

PART V

ETHICS AND EDUCATION

THE NEW SOPHISTS: EMOTIVISTS AS TEACHERS OF ETHICS

Ronald Duska
Rosemont College

I was delighted to accept Rocco Porreco's invitation to participate in this symposium since it affords me an opportunity to pay tribute to a philosopher who more than any other taught me what philosophy is, Henry Veatch. Still, if I was delighted at the chance to pay homage to Professor Veatch, I was simultaneously discomfited by the fact that it would be embarrassing not only for me but also for Veatch, as my former teacher, if I had nothing worthwhile to say. The uneasiness was increased when Professor Porreco suggested I talk about Ethics and Education. It is difficult enough finding something significant to say about ethics. It is well nigh impossible trying to talk significantly about education along with ethics. Debates such as whether virtue can be taught are almost as old as philosophy itself and I have precious little to add to those issues. However, I have rarely been noted for my prudence and with my usual optimism if not downright foolhardiness I decided to use this occasion to reflect on two things I encounter as an ethics teacher that make me downright angry. Whether the reflections are worthwhile or not is problematic. If this paper is a mere wind egg, one ought not to hold Veatch responsible. After all, is someone responsible for those before whom he casts his pearls? But enough of that . . . on to the object of my wrath!

To begin, I am angry with the fact that students today, for the most part, are emotivists, i.e., they believe that good and bad are really only a matter of what they feel. They are thoroughly convinced that what one feels is good is good and that what one feels is bad is bad. Think of how often they resolve an argument by using some barbaric phrase such as: "True for me," "Good for me," "Do your own thing," "If it feels good, go for it," or finally that abomination of toleration, "Everyone's entitled to his own opinion." Such talking and thinking would seem to indicate that students are by and large emotivists for whom morals are a matter of personal opinion based on personal feelings, and that they rarely if ever recognize objective standards of true or good.

Secondly, since I don't believe that students come out of the womb as emotivists, I am convinced that they are taught emotivism by their culture and I am angry at that. I am even angrier that we teachers of ethics have been seduced by that emotivist culture into adopting a teaching method in ethics that reinforces the emotivism. I have often in jest (I'm not sure I want to

[235]

continue to joke about it) threatened to write an ethics test entitled *How to Do Whatever You Always Wanted to Do Without Feeling Guilty About It.* But in all seriousness, doesn't the way we teach ethics today seem to call for just such a work? We set up problems so that no resolution seems possible. Irreconcilable dilemmas and incompatible theories are presented to students who are left with no grounds on which to choose between them. We dig pits of scepticism and let our students fall into them if we do not lead them into them. Such an approach to ethical issues must reinforce, if it does not create, the impression that there are no answers to ethical issues, and that our babbling about them is pure sophistry. Ethics teachers can argue any side of any issue with the agility of a Protagoras. We are indeed the new sophists. We come across as insincere pedants.

Even if we are not believers in "emotivism" and are not "sophists" it seems that the way we teach ethics belies our beliefs and reinforces the respectability of the emotivism of the culture. We might not be willing to accept such an indictment of our methods, but what effects do all our distinctions and precisions have? What effect does the standard disclaimer that "Ethicists take no responsibility for their students' morals" have? (Socrates would be appalled!) What effect does bending over backwards to present every viewpoint, even the most ludicrous, have? We wish to be detached, objective, "scientific" presenters of incompatible theories and so never take a stand, at least in the classroom. Does not all of this have the effect of reinforcing emotivism? The question then arises whether such an approach is justified? That leads to an intriguing question, somewhat meta-meta-ethical: if what we're doing is inappropriate, what *should* ethics teachers do?

One could do worse in answering the question of what ethics teachers should do, than to reflect on what Henry Veatch does and thinks they should do. For Veatch, ethics or ethical study should make a better person, i.e., a person who knows the good and does the good. Veatch argued against emotivism in general and twentieth century emotivists in particular. He maintained that Charles Stevenson, the foremost emotivist, and those philosophers in agreement with his position, with their talk about the language of morals and with their refusal to do what they called moralizing simply covered a basic nihilism with respect to morals. Whenever it occurred to one of Veatch's students, that Hare's decision of principle was as groundless as a Sartrean choice, and that for all his talk of reason in ethical matters, Hare like Stevenson was still a nihilist, Veatch would smile knowingly. The student was discovering what Henry saw clearly. *Rational Man* and *For An Ontology of Morals* maintained that a large part of contemporary ethical theory is—subjectivist, emotivist, and nihilist. Ethics, meta-or normative, whatever the difference, as done in the twentieth century was baseless and ethical theories needed grounding in the nature of man, not in an autonomous subjective decision based on nothing. What Veatch taught, and tried to show his students among other things, was the bank-ruptcy of what I have called "emotivism."[1]

It is somewhat disconcerting then to find one's own students locked in the grip of a theory one has been taught and believes is bankrupt. But if emotivism is bankrupt, and a teacher of ethics should enrich one's students, how should one teach ethics? Most of us who teach ethics present a chapter showing the shortcomings of emotivism, relativism or subjectivism. But this approach has little effect on the students taught.

For example, in a standard approach, a teacher gets students to agree that a certain moral statement is true, e.g., "The holocaust is immoral". The teacher then shows that if truth is subjective or a matter of feeling, the opposite statement, "The holocaust is moral", is also true and Hitler in holding that was as right as they were. The students cannot accept this and thus the logic of the situation and the horrors of the Holocaust convince them of the shortcomings of emotivism. But only for a moment. Having agreed that the objection is valid, the students quickly return to their emotivist position, an emotivism so deep and pervasive that their emotivist responses are almost second nature—like knee jerk reflexes. By the end of the period the students will again staunchly maintain that we have no right to judge another's actions or opinions because it all depends on how one feels about it.

But why don't the standard attacks on emotivism work and what should we do as teachers to combat the emotivism of our culture? We need to recognize that the attacks on emotivism are epistemological and logical in nature. Such an attack may have an effect on a graduate student interested in meta-ethics. But for all sorts of reasons I suspect this is precisely the wrong way to go about it with undergraduates. It resembles Descartes' investigating the possibility of knowing before getting on with knowing. Rather than worrying about "Who's to say?," what would happen if we just got on with saying and defending what we're saying? What would happen if we took a substantive ethical position and began to defend it? Such a defense would indicate that we think *we* have the authority *to say* until someone has better reasons than ours. What I am suggesting is that instead of the dialectic method of pro and con arguments being defended equally vociferously and dispassionately, we take a stand based on our considered beliefs and defend it. In this way we put ourselves on record as an example of an anti-emotivist. Rather than simply approaching the issue as the disinterested observer who acts like a total skeptic, why not approach an issue as a defender of a position one believes to be true and defensible? Philosophers do it in journals of applied ethics. Why not in classrooms or in textbooks?

I suspect there are two reasons we don't. First, it smacks of dogmatism. Second, to take a stand on a moral or value issue is to confront head on the emotivism of our culture, a culture that dichotomizes facts and values, beliefs and attitudes, science and ethics . . . a culture that in the name of pluralism and tolerance will simply not accept ethical judgments as having the same sort of warrant that scientific judgments carry.

The dogmatism (at least in theory) is easy enough to take care of. One presents one's position with sufficient rational defense and fair consideration of objections. Most first rate philosophers do this in their writing. The second reason however is a lot more difficult. Our culture is influenced by Cartesian and Humean approaches to knowledge. Such approaches make science the result of cognitive states and ethics the result of affective states. Further the only defensible cognitive states are empirically derived states. A common approach to value issues is the following. "I am a scientist and I don't make value judgments, those are matters of personal opinion."

Most intellectuals will take a stand, i.e., teach positions based on what they call facts, meaning empirically observable data. They recognize the realm of facts as yielding objective knowledge. But values for them are not observable and not objective for they depend on feelings or emotions, and are considered subjective and each person has an autonomy or freedom over their own. Value disputes, then, are merely disputes about personal opinions, personal attitudes or personal stances. Science is, after all, so the line goes, value free, and hence occupies the ideal objective stance.

This distinction as we might suspect is found in Stevenson under the labels of "beliefs" and "attitudes." Emotivists, for whom Stevenson is the exemplar, reduce ethical disagreement to two kinds: disagreement in attitudes and disagreement in belief. I may have the same attitude toward something as you do, e.g., we both disapprove of euthanasia, but not believe I am in the presence of an act of euthanasia. Or I might approve of euthanasia, and believing I am in the presence of an instance of euthanasia approve of it while you disapprove of it, not because it is not an instance of euthanasia but because you have a negative attitude toward it.

According to emotivists, since disagreement in beliefs can be resolved by factual considerations, a teacher of ethics might do something in that vein in addressing students, but there he is really only giving scientific input. Attitudes are private and either attach to certain facts or beliefs or do not. That is simply a matter of personal preference, physiology or taste. There is no way attitudes can be taught. Because of this distinction between attitudes and beliefs, Stevenson can say, "Any statement about *any* matter of fact which *any* speaker considers likely to alter attitudes may be adduced as a reason for or against an ethical judgment."[2] But because a fact moves someone else doesn't mean it will move me. The only thing that makes a given fact *relevant* is my *decision* (?) or *propensity* (?) to make it count. Reasons, facts or beliefs adduced in defense of attitudes are virtually useless as a support of a moral position because which reasons count depend on my attitudes which are purely personal. If I am inclined to be moved by these beliefs, fine . . . if not, fine also. . .The dichotomy between beliefs and attitudes leads to the belief of Stevenson and most contemporary ethical theorists that facts can resolve disagreements in beliefs but facts, reasons and beliefs leave disagreements in attitudes unaffected. Beliefs can be taught and verified scientifically. Science deals with facts and thus can bring facts to bear in support of beliefs, but morals are based on attitudes and what facts or beliefs move what attitudes is a matter of pure chance and personal preference. Morals cannot be taught, only preached.

What I wish to claim is that this dichotomy between attitudes and beliefs is misguided, but its wide acceptance leads us into a style of teaching ethics that reinforces the emotivism it reflects.

Why is it misguided? Simply because attitudes and beliefs are not as distinct and separate as modern perspectives makes them out to be. Suppose we assume that attitudes (feelings) or emotions and beliefs (cognitive content) are not opposites or radically different but that they are interrelated. A belief could be a function of an attitude and an attitude could be a function of a belief. But how is this possible? Simple enough. I want to propose that we construe the act of believing or knowing a fact as the result of adopting a certain epistemic attitude [a certain intention(?)] toward the world! But is this plausible?

Aren't statements of fact primordial? Aren't facts just there? Do they really require attitudes? Yes they do! For example, in working on the distinction between attitude and belief statements in a Logic course it becomes clear the dichotomy only holds if you don't think too deeply. Take a statement like, "The U.S. won World War II." That seems to be a clear-cut factual belief until you began to ponder what counts as winning. Let us ask some embarrassing questions. Who agreed to count 1939 to 1945 as the terminal dates of the war? Who decided when the war began? Who decided there was a second world war and not just an interrupted first world war? Does war have to begin with a declaration? Events don't break up as easily as historians would like. Historians break them up and adopt a stance wherein they pay attention to what they take to be important and disregard what they take to be unimportant. One of the more interesting reflections on who won World War II was made by a student who looked at industrial success as a mark of winning. As he put it, "The Japanese may have surrendered, but it is not all that clear that they lost." Beliefs, then, even factual ones thoroughly involve attitudes. This holds not only in social sciences but also in natural sciences. Is this desk I'm writing on mostly solid or mostly empty space? That depends on what perspective one adopts, one's attitude.

But if we see that beliefs are often a function of attitudes we also need to recognize that attitudes are often a function of beliefs. Stevenson's approach leads us to think of attitudes as purely internal states. But since Wittgenstein this seems inadequate.

Suppose, with Wittgenstein, we quit thinking of attitudes as purely internal affairs and see them as learned, socially taught, publicly verifiable and acceptable responses to the world, in short, forms of life. For example, rather than viewing pride as an entirely internal feeling, suppose we view it as a response learned by learning what our society calls pride and our society's requirement for pride-feelings. The man surveying the Pacific Ocean *cannot* feel proud of it unless he believes he made the ocean. Why? Because the requirements for pride are set by the society. We feel proud of an achievement. Thus for the man who believes he made the ocean, that belief is a relevant reason for justifying his prideful attitude. His beliefs and society's conditions for pride must blend together to make sense and society's conditions determine what count as reasons in defense of an attitude. We ask the man to justify his prideful attitude by giving relevant reasons that are publicly associated with pride. What this shows is that we are taught attitudes as we are taught beliefs.

Suppose we accept the interdependence of attitudes and beliefs, and suppose we admit that attitudes are learned. Then what would happen if we distinguished not between attitudes and beliefs but between scientific attitudes and moral attitudes? Scientific attitudes would be those learned as a member of a scientific community and moral attitudes would be those learned as a member of a moral community.

When we become members of a community we share a form of life. But the form of life makes no sense unless we learn and share the goals and purposes, and these goals and purposes designate what attitudes there are, and which are acceptable. Suppose we compare learning to be a member of a community with learning to operate in a restaurant. One must know the purpose and practice of "restauranting" in order to operate in one. One needs to know (to have learned) the form of life involved and to share it to survive in a restaurant. You need to know and agree on what waiters are, what hostesses are, what money is, what menus are, what lines are, what tips are, what forks, knives, napkins are, what tone of voice is appropriate, whom to call and when and so on and so on. That is part and parcel of what it means to go to a restaurant. For example, if one doesn't tip the waitress, he has the wrong attitude toward her probably because he has not learned enough about restaurant life. In the very beginning to be a member of a community attitudes are created and formed. But just as we don't teach about going to restaurants as we teach science, so we don't teach the moral form of life as we teach science.

A "scientific attitude" is neither a natural one, nor a primordial one, but, like all other attitudes, it is learned. We *learn* to view things dispassionately, scientifically and disinterestedly. We *learn* to distinguish between facts and values. More importantly, not only do we learn *to* do it but we have to learn *when* to do it, i.e., we have to learn when such an attitude is appropriate. And this by the way is not a scientific but a moral question.

When is a scientific attitude appropriate? Distinguishing between beliefs and attitudes is appropriate when acting like a scientist. It is a part of the scientific form of life. But operating in the scientific community requires different attitudes from operating in the moral community, just as treatment of a waitress in a restaurant requires different attitudes than treatment of one's mother. Both wait on your table, but you don't tip mother. Since the scientific community is not a natural one, nor an epistemolgically privileged one, it need not furnish us with the only proper attitude toward teaching, and indeed it may furnish us with a faulty model with respect to the teaching of morals.

Because of the influence of positivism, I fear, we teachers of ethics have not yet seen that the scientific approach is not always appropriate in teaching. Reinforced by the influence of positivism, Stevenson could rail against moralizing in academia and teachers of ethics or ethicists were intimidated into not doing ethics in the classroom. There are times, then, when the scientific attitude is uncalled for. Dealing morally with people is clearly one such time.

To see the "facts" of a loved one's death, to view a subject as an object, one has to be dispassionate, and being dispassionate is adopting an attitude, taking a stance. But such a position is not always appropriate. One can, I suppose, take a dispassionate view toward a loved one's death, as Mersault in Camus' *Stranger*. But society frowns on such a point of view, expects grief, and calls for the wearing of black, mourning, wakes and ritual. Grief is the appropriate stance or attitude, not scientific objectivity.

Take another example. Is there not something chilling about a psychologist who "studies" his child? Can one respect that position or attitude? It is scientific but inappropriate in the context of parent/child. Still it shows scientific positions as attitudes. But it also shows that "neutral" in one sense is not neutral. One must stand somewhere.

But if it is inappropriate at certain times to adopt a scientific attitude in dealing with people, might it not also be inappropriate to adopt such a stance in the teaching of people? Could it not just be wrong-headed to teach ethics as if we were teaching science?

Education is in one sense teaching one to belong to a community and hence to share attitudes because any community takes a stance toward the world, an attitude. That attitude affects what it sees, what it believes, what it finds orthodox, what it finds heretical and vice-versa. Its beliefs affect its attitudes. There are precious few beliefless attitudes (emotions) and precious few attitudeless beliefs. To learn to view "objectively" or "dispassionately" is a form of life, but it is the scientific form of life, and it too is governed by pro-attitudes toward parsimony and other "scientific" requirements. To learn to view "ethically" or "morally" is a different kind of approach. Since our morals are somewhat different than our science, it is a mistake to think they need to be taught in the same way. If ethics is a teachable subject and if forms of life are learned, our dispassion in the name of objectivity may have the paradoxical effect of creating an emotivism that legitimates radical subjectivity, an emotivism that denies the very moral community necessary for morality.

In summary we have argued that a neutral attitude toward ethical issues is inappropriate in the teaching of ethics, for such an approach would have to be the approach of a god or a beast, one who would stand outside the very community, or, as our students would perceive it, the approach of one who trivializes the very issues he talks about. Moral issues are serious. If we refuse to take a stand and defend our positions we are no better than Protagoras.

One last comment. At this point, Henry Veatch certainly will raise a telling objection. . . . What legitimates your stance or your attitude? The fact that I am a member of a moral community which demands relevant reasons for attitudes and which holds certain attitudes appropriate certainly doesn't make that community's moral perceptions or attitudes correct ones. Have I not just substituted a tribal or societal emotivism for an individual emotivism? Tribes have been wrong as have societies and as have individuals. My response is that I do not wish to claim all the attitudes are appropriate nor all stances equally viable. But to get into this issue is to go beyond the scope of this paper into ethical theory rather than the teaching of morals. I would, however, answer just briefly that any attitude or community would be constrained by natural goods, i.e., the needs any human has, and the requirements of justice and caring for others. Most attitudes, however, that I have seen in ethics recognize these constraints. Still there is one overriding attitude/belief that is insidious and that is emotivism. It is insidious because it glorifies the individual's affective state and trivializes the very reasons that we use in our community to conduct moral discourse. It effectively reduces ethics to might makes right, an egoism that is antithetical to moral community. That these last statements need further explanation and defense is obvious. But that must await another occasion.

NOTES

[1] It should be obvious that I am using the word "emotivism" to apply to other positions such as "subjectivism" and "relativism". The differences for our purposes are minimal. "Emotivism" may indeed be but one species of relativism and relativism is not necessarily subjectivism, since it can be cultural. Nevertheless, I am using "emotivism" in the way I think Alasdair MacIntyre does in *After Virtue,* to designate an ethical theoretical position and attitude toward morality that maintains there is no ground for good or right other than human preference, be that individual or tribal, emotional or otherwise, such as a Sartrean choice or a decision of principle. Veatch would maintain, I believe, that they are structurally similar because they are all basically groundless.

[2] Charles Leslie Stevenson, *Ethics and Language* (New Haven: Yale University Press, 1944), p. 114.

MORAL FORMATION AND THE LIBERAL ARTS

Kevin McDonnell
Saint Mary's College

Henry Veatch has long argued against the many philosophies which posit a wall of separation between facts and values. Regardless of the intellectual merits of his and others' arguments, they have not been widely persuasive. The pervasive acceptance of some sort of fact/value dichotomy, on the other hand, has had important ramifications not only in the arcane world of professional philosophers, but also for the way we live our lives and structure our institutions. Perhaps more than others, institutions of higher education have suffered from the confusions which surround this dichotomy. The resurgence of interest in values education and curricular structure bring out clearly the difficulties inherent in a dichotomy between fact and value.

These difficulties are apparent in the "Summary Recommendations" of the Hastings Center Project on the Teaching of Ethics. One paragraph begins: "The general purpose of the teaching of ethics ought to be that of stimulating the moral imagination, developing skills in the recognition and analysis of moral issues, eliciting a sense of moral obligation and personal responsibility, and learning both to tolerate and to resist moral disagreement and ambiguity." The following paragraph begins: "Courses in ethics ought not explicitly seek behavioral change in students."[1] Is not "learning to tolerate and resist . . ." a behavioral change? How can students develop a sense of moral obligation or personal responsibility without in some way acting differently? There may be a widespread consensus on the value of tolerance, but tolerance is nonetheless a normative value. It is not possible to teach courses in normative ethics without being normative.

While a consensus about such normative issues as tolerance may disguise for a time underlying confusions about values and their origins, no such consensus exists when it comes to the reform of general education. In this area, faculty politics and the demands for individual, departmental, or institutional survival seem to dominate discussion. As Richard Burke has persuasively argued, competing ideals of general education rest on different epistemological assumptions.[2] But few faculty members are willing to take the time to work through the hard intellectual issues involved, much less lead a whole faculty to do the same. The reasons for our problems in dealing with the liberal arts and moral formation, however, have to do not only with the inherent intellectual difficulty of the issues, but also with the peculiar history of American institutions.

Facts and Values in Higher Education

In 1895, the Amherst College catalogue devoted the entire first page of the section on "The Course of Study" to a description of the course in ethics taught by the president of the college to the senior class. But in 1905 ethics had disappeared from its front page billing in the catalogue, and was to be found as merely one among several courses offered in Amherst's philosophy department as an elective for sophomores.[3]

This change in the status of the ethics course is symbolic of the dramatic change in American higher education which took place in the late nineteenth and early twentieth centuries. Understanding the nature of that change is crucial for understanding many of the contemporary arguments about the nature and role of higher education.

Through the middle of the nineteenth century, American higher education was collegiate in structure and religious in orientation. Most schools were modeled on British- or Scottish-style university colleges and were denominationally affiliated. The emphasis in these institutions was on the moral and intellectual formation of students rather than on disciplinary or departmentalized studies. Not just the ethics course, but the entire curriculum and student life of the college was devoted to this goal. Chapel was required and the colleges acted *in loco parentis,* with a very strict sense of parenting. "The entire college experience was meant, above all, to be an experience in character development and the moral life, as epitomized, secured, and brought to a focus in the moral philosophy course."[4]

John Henry Newman surprises the contemporary university scholar with his view that the function of the university is ". . .the diffusion and extension of knowledge rather than its advancement. There are other institutions far more suited to act as instruments of stimulating philosophical inquiry, and extending the boundaries of our knowledge, than a university. Such, for instance, are the literary and scientific academies."[5] By the late nineteenth century, universities in America had absorbed most of the functions of the earlier academies. The current structure of American higher education was well established.

The development of the university model was precipitated by the failure of the collegiate model. It was not thought that the colleges were trying to do the wrong things but that they were ineffective and poorly organized for accomplishing their goals.[6] The response was to make American educational institutions far more complex. Many of the features of the collegiate institutions were retained, while university facilities and faculties were added to them. It is helpful to analyze the complexity of colleges and universities by thinking of them as situated between the collegiate and the university ideal. Virtually all schools in America, whether they happen to be named colleges or universities, embrace both of these ideals. Only a few technical schools and a handful of research institutions are not in the grip of this tension. The collegiate ideal is the liberal education of students. Liberal studies are pursued because they are fitting ways for human beings to live. The university has its own purposes in research and the expansion of human knowledge. Faculty members who feel under enormous pressure to publish lest they perish (perhaps not an unbiased picture of life outside academe) find their students complaining that courses are not preparing them for the job market. Schools which are dedicated to technical or professional studies find their students to have little sense of personal commitment, so they introduce courses in medical or legal or business ethics. The emerging universities of the late nineteenth century did not abandon the functions of their collegiate predecessors. They rather incorporated all of them into the very complex structure of modern higher education.

As schools became more complex, moral philosophy lost the integrating role it once had and nothing emerged to take its place. In the nineteenth century, moral philosophy embraced much of what is now thought of as social science. Moral psychology was one of the origins of psychology as a separate intellectual discipline. The moral philosophy course also incorporated considerations of social ethics which later developed into sociology and economics. The development of the social sciences as independent disciplines involved their separation from the value orientation provided in moral philosophy. This separation came hard because many of the first social scientists were also social reformers. At least partially under the influence of Comte, they saw the human sciences as the ultimate integrating disciplines. Albion Small, who founded at Chicago the first graduate department in sociology, wrote: "Sociology in its largest scope, and on its methodological side is merely a moral philosophy conscious of its task, and systematically pursuing knowledge of cause and effect within this process of moral evolution . . . Science is sterile unless it contributes at last to knowledge of what is worth doing." Three years after Small's death in 1929, William Ogburn said in his presidential address to the American Sociological Association: "Sociology as a science is not interested in making the world a better place in which to live, in encouraging beliefs, in spreading information, in dispensing news, in setting forth impressions of life, in leading the multitudes, or in guiding the ship of state. Science is interested in one thing only, to wit, discovering new knowledge."[7] The social sciences had become value neutral.

As the methods of sociology and the social sciences generally became more positivistic, the outlook for philosophy was hardly any better. Within the structure of the university, philosophy was a department like any other, with no particular claim to primacy. The move to positivism in the social sciences was paralleled by the rise of non-cognitivism in moral philosophy. From a non-cognitivist perspective, moral positions can only be justified in terms of emotions, commitments, or other non-rational factors. These developments put any notions of moral formation in an intellectually tenuous position. Schools, both nonsectarian and religiously affiliated, continued, however, to enforce moral, or at least moralistic, rules. Barnard and Columbia, for example, had parietals in the 1960s. Institutions promoted moral values without a coherent intellectual structure behind them. Their collegiate functions had become so separated from their university-style research that they no longer thought about what, as institutions, they were doing with their students. Students made this point forcefully in the sixties. Now that attempts are being made to develop coherent academic programs, there is great interest in education for values and a renewed search for a coherent and intellectually defensible account of how virtue can be taught. As is so often the case in such discussions, turning to Aristotle is of great help.

Aristotle on Virtue and the Liberal Arts

"The first principle of all action is leisure."[8] This principle is the keystone of Aristotle's treatment of liberal education in his *Politics*. His principle strikes us as paradoxical because we understand leisure in terms of inactivity while Aristotle understands it as the things one does when there is nothing one has to do. Leisure is activity free from compulsion. Aristotle distinguished leisure from recreation or amusement in that these activities served to refresh people so they could return to work. And work is the set of activities which biological nature demands of us.

In the eighth book of the *Politics,* Aristotle attempts to separate those activities which are dictated by necessity from those one would freely undertake—the liberal activities. Most of his discussion concerns music which should be understood in the broad Greek sense to include literature and theatre. Aristotle believes that some musical modes are suitable for recreation while others provide intellectual enjoyment or even moral formation. "Since then music is a pleasure, and virtue consists in rejoicing and loving and hating aright, there is clearly nothing which we are so much concerned to acquire and to cultive as the power of forming right judgments, and of taking delight in good dispositions and noble actions."[9] Music, Aristotle argues, forms character, and does so very effectively because of the way people enjoy its performance. Certain types of music, and he discusses the Greek modes in detail, are suitable to the formation of free people while others are not. Different types of people respond differently to music because ". . . the music will correspond to their minds; . . . A man receives pleasure from what is natural to him."[10] Aristotle therefore thinks that musical education—we might call it education in the humanities—is part of moral education. Morality is not added on to such an eduction; it is inherent in it.

It is clear from other places in the *Politics,* and abundantly clear from other of Aristotle's works, that scientific education also imparts moral formation since it too can be pursued for its own sake. It is difficult to think, therefore, what Aristotle would make of the "two cultures" phenomenon, of the fashion that pits the liberal arts against the sciences. This view holds the sciences suspect both because, paradoxically, they are objective and because they are tied to technology. The humanities, on the other hand, are thought of as subjective and pure.[11] In the *Politics,* Aristotle is very alert to the uses of music. Not only can it be enjoyed for its own sake, but it can be used to rouse or soothe the masses. It can be a tool of propaganda. Contemporary advocates of arts education cannot urge the virtues of its purity on the one hand and its value for advertising and marketing on the other. More significantly, however, confining the adjective "liberal" to the arts misses the human significance of science and scientific education. Science, the effort to understand the world, is a great human achievement. To separate it from the humanities invites distortion of our picture of being human. Liberal studies, from an Aristotelian viewpoint, must include both the arts and the sciences.

The great objection to Aristotle's view of liberal education is that, when he speaks of those who are free from the need to work, he is speaking of those Athenians whose needs were met by the labor of slaves. Not only is Aristotle's whole theory of slavery open to objection, but a theory about the education of the idle rich is simply irrelevant to our present academic situation. Our students do need jobs, and they have a legitimate need for the skills which such jobs require. Some of Aristotle's hard sayings appear to doom his views on liberal education to irrelevance. He argues that "any occupation, art, or science, which makes the body or soul or mind of the human less fit for the practice or exercise of virtue, is vulgar; wherefore we call all those acts vulgar which tend to deform the body, and likewise all paid employment, for they absorb and degrade the mind."[12]

Aristotle's view strikes most modern readers as not only outdated but perverse. An education based on his principles might be thought worse than irrelevant because it would be just the opposite of a moral education. We tend to think of morality as doing what we ought to do. The contemporary paradigm, under the influence of a certain reading of Kant, makes morality a matter of fulfilling our obligations rather than fulfilling ourselves. When we think of ethics for our students entering the job market, therefore, we think of specialized courses in which nurses, doctors, social workers, or business people learn the specific obligations of their professions. The structures of morality affect how we do our jobs more than how we live our lives. As Josef Pieper observes:

> In Kant's view, indeed, the fact that man's natural bent is contrary to moral law, belongs to the concept of moral law. It is normal and essential, on this view, that the good should be difficult, and that the effort of will required in forcing oneself to perform some action should become the yardstick of the moral good: the more difficult a thing, the higher it is in the order of goodness.[13]

If Aristotle's ethics can be faulted for inadequate concern with our working lives, current ethical discussion can be faulted for its exclusive and obsessive concern with such issues. While our students should be formed with a sense of virtue suitable for their professions, the virtues of the professions alone are not enough.

Henry Veatch has argued that the key conflict within the contemporary moral paradigm is between self-regarding actions which are not moral and other regarding actions which are.[14] "Why should I be moral?" becomes a crucial question in any such system. The assumption is that one has desires which one will naturally fulfill unless morality in the form of some constraint interferes. On this account, therefore, morality is an external interference on the way we would naturally live.

Thinking of morality in this way raises just the difficult pedagogical and philosophical questions which the Hastings Center Project glosses over. If morality is an external imposition, how are we to teach it to students without interfering with their freedom to pursue their natural inclinations? Once morality is conceived as outside the self in this way, then it is an imposition of some external authority, be it teacher, state, society, or establishment. If we take refuge in "laying out the options" and tracing the consequences of different decisions, can we change the way our students will act? There is no good reason to think that students who are simply exposed to a number of philosophical theories about morality are going to be better, or even different, for the experience. If we will not or cannot change the way our students behave, then our courses are not doing in the post-Watergate and post-Vietnam era what they are supposed to do. Our unfortunate choice, if we accept the contemporary paradigm, is between impotence and incoherence.

Rethinking Moral Education

The problems of the contemporary paradigm force us to reconsider the Aristotelian view that morality is about the way we live our lives. To make this view sensible and credible we need to separate it from Aristotle's culture and wed it to our own. Many of the professions for which our students are preparing are not mere jobs, burdens imposed by the necessity of earning a living. They are professions incorporating values that their practitioners profess. The moral standards for physicians or accountants are not side constraints dissuading them from taking advantage of their sick or ignorant clients. Just as the physician does not deliberate whether or not to heal, so the accountant does not deliberate whether to be accurate or honest. Management, marketing, nursing, medicine, accounting, law and many others are not just collections of skills or techniques. They shape and are shaped by the lives of their practitioners. While Aristotle reminds us that people are not just workers, we must remember that they are also workers.

The departmentalization of knowledge which came with the university structure of higher education makes it difficult to integrate ethical considerations into other professions. It leads people to believe that, as chemistry is what chemists do, so ethics is what ethicists do. Ethics it is thought should be a discipline as specialized and developed as any other, and academic philosophers have done their best to oblige. Now that normative or first level ethics is back in vogue, philosophers are invited almost as missionaries to visit the faculties of business, law or medicine. If these visits end with physicians as expert in the interpretation of the categorical imperative as they are at appendectomies, then philosophers' visits will have been wasted. The task of ethics is to help people think about what they are doing, not to add another discipline for them to think about. The teaching of ethics needs to be, as far as possible, internal to each discipline and profession.

Finally, if moral virtue is recognized as internal to the arts and sciences, a certain seriousness of purpose may return to some disciplines and be respected for what it is in others. We have come to expect science students to be dedicated and serious about their enterprise, and I think we should recognize this, when genuine, as a moral virtue. By the same token we have disparaged the humanities for the sometimes less-than-serious attitudes of some of its participants. Such attitudes might change if teachers and students came to realize the moral importance of what they are about. Not only whether they read and write, but what they read and write, are forming them as human beings. Morality is not the icing on the humanities nor is it censorship. It is part and parcel of what we are doing.

These remarks are more by way of ideals than proposals. An important implication of the position I have developed is that higher education, whether or not we like to admit it, is inevitably involved in the moral formation of students. The only real question is the kind of formation we are providing. The failure of the model of moral education with which colleges and universities have been working is, on both historical and intellectual grounds, irremediable. Higher education will change. How it changes will depend to some extent on how well those of us involved in the enterprise think about what we are doing. I hope this paper is a small contribution to that end.

NOTES

[1] *Ethics Teaching in Higher Education,* ed. D. Callahan and S. Bok (New York: Plenum Press, 1980), p. 300.

[2] "Two Concepts of Liberal Education," *Academe* 66 (1980), p. 356.

[3] Douglas Sloan, "The Teaching of Ethics in the American Undergraduate Curriculum, 1876–1976," in *Ethics Teaching in Higher Education,* p. 9.

[4] *Ibid.,* p. 7.

[5] John Henry Newman, *On the Scope and Nature of University Education* (New York: E. P. Dutton, 1915), p. xxxvi.

[6] Henry P. Tappan, "University Education," in *American Higher Education: A Documentary History* (Chicago: University of Chicago Press, 1961), pp. 489–491.

[7] Quoted in Sloan, p. 18.

[8] Aristotle, *Politics* 1337^{b}32.

[9] *Ibid.*, 1340^{a}17.

[10] *Ibid.*, 1342^{a}25.

[11] C. P. Snow, *The Two Cultures* (Cambridge: Cambridge University Press, 1959), pp. 1–25.

[12] Aristotle, *op. cit.*, 1337^{b}10.

[13] Josef Pieper, *Leisure - The Basis of Culture* (New York: New American Library, 1952, p. 29.

[14] Henry B. Veatch, "Is Kant the Gray Eminence of Contemporary Ethical Theory?" *Ethics* 90 (1980), p. 219.

THE POVERTY OF MORAL EDUCATION TODAY: WHERE HAS ALL THE CONTENT GONE

William Casement
Biscayne College

During the past two decades Henry Veatch has acted as a conscience for moral philosophers. He has invited us to step back and look critically at the very foundation of contemporary ethical theory. He has warned us that the foundation is shaky, and that considerable repair is necessary. Further, he has given us direction regarding how the repair operation should be conducted.[1] I wish to pick up on this lead from Professor Veatch, particularly as it may be followed out in the connection of ethics with education. What I am concerned with is finding the proper means for moral education. This involves investigating the foundation on which contemporary views of moral education rest, and, having exposed it as faulty, pointing the way toward a corrective.

In recent years moral education in the United States has undergone a dramatic alteration. Traditional approaches to teaching morality have been abandoned, and various new models proposed. At the elementary and secondary school level two of these new models, values clarification and the cognitive-developmental model, have raced ahead of the field and captured the allegiance of many thousands of teachers. Higher education has been slower to catch on, but the new models are invading this territory as well. Together the new models comprise what is probably the most dominant force in moral education today. It is a new trend, a new concept of what moral education is all about.

While the new models are dissimilar in many ways, they share in the notion that mature moral decision-making is characterized by autonomy. They equate autonomy with the absence of values learned from other people. Moral decision-making, it is held, must be done without the influence of what other people hold to be right and wrong. The new models aim at teaching students the *how* of moral decision-making, that is, the process one employs, and they reject the teaching of values per se, the *what* of morality, or what is often referred to as content. The working assumption is that in mature moral decision-making, that which is characterized by autonomy, process determines content without the influence of content borrowed from other people. Here, then, is the new trend in moral education — distinguish between process and content, and teach the former but not the latter. Proponents of the new models believe that this can be done, and that if it is, students will be on their way toward moral decision-making at its highest level.

[251]

If the new models for moral education could deliver what they promise, they would indeed be worthy of the attention and adulation they have received. But, what if it turns out that the new models don't work? What if values learned from other people are a significant component in moral decision-making, and the emphasis the new models have placed on autonomy is misconceived? If this is the case, it will again be time for a shift in emphasis in the basic goal for moral education. Rather than beginning with the conviction that teaching content is not a proper part of moral education, educators will turn to searching for a proper way to teach it.

My aim in what follows is first to show that the new models for moral education have mistaken the nature of mature moral decision-making. What they fail to acknowledge is that values learned from other people are an important element. Secondly, I will claim that since such values are important in moral decision-making, programs of moral education should concentrate on them. The humanities curriculum provides a ready-made way for doing this, although the potential of the humanities in this regard seems to have been forgotten or ignored by many educators.

Values Clarification

The philosophical basis of values-clarification is a rather unsophisticated value relativism. Values, it is claimed, arise in experience, and because of variances in time and place, no two people will have the same experience. It is accepted, then, that values will vary from person to person. If all values are relative to an individual's own experience, it follows that in determining what is right and wrong for himself, a person should not rely on the values of others. Teaching values or content in a program of moral education would be inappropriate as what this would amount to is forcing one person's values on someone else.[2]

Rather than teaching values at all, values clarification purports to teach students the "process of valuing." Within this process the component of choosing is the focal point. Choosing, it is held, must be done freely, from among alternatives, and after thoughtful consideration of consequences.[3] The concern for autonomy, or freedom, is the key here, and while no exact explanation of the nature of freedom is provided by values clarification, its meaning becomes clear when we consider the methodology designed to promote it.

The teacher's role is to make students aware of various value issues, and to ask questions in such a way that students are forced to engage in moral decision-making. The critical element is that the teacher is responsible for maintaining an atmosphere of neutrality. That is, he must ensure that students make their choices without being influenced by the choices of others. The teacher never shows favoritism toward or against any values a student might express, and instructs students to make their choices without regard for what teachers or classmates might choose.[4] The emphasis on neutrality even extends to matters of discipline. Students are told that they must follow certain rules while in school, but that the reason for doing so is simply that they will be subject to punishment if they refuse. Whether or not they accept the rules as actually representing what is right, and will follow those rules when in situations outside of school, is up to them to decide.[5]

The extreme emphasis on maintaining an atmosphere of neutrality reveals the concept of freedom inherent in values clarification. Choosing freely means doing so without modeling after anyone else's choices. Any move in this direction would be a denial of freedom and surrender to the relativity of someone else's experience. Mature moral decision-making is done without being prejudiced by what is or is claimed to be right and wrong for other people. But herein lies the difficulty with the values clarification position. Are people being asked to make choices in a vacuum?

What will one's choices ultimately be based on if content learned from other people is to be ignored? What makes a choice right for one individual if what makes choices right for others has no bearing? Values clarification's only answer is to consider the consequences of any possible choice. This is an attempt to establish a grounding for moral choices, or as contemporary philosophers might say, to show how there can be good reasons in ethics. But this advice leaves us with further questions which values clarification fails to answer: How does one evaluate consequences? A standard is needed. And where would such a standard come from? Presumably it could not be acquired from other people, as this would run counter to the relativity upon which the values clarification model is based. In what way, then, could it be acquired? As values clarification is silent about this matter, perhaps we are to assume that there is no standard, at least in terms of logic and reason. Perhaps the values clarificationists mean to say that the proper grounding for our moral judgments is irrational, that is, it lies in our impulses or what we might term feelings and habits. As the values clarifications fail to explain what the proper grounding is for our moral judgments, we are left with conjecture and concern.

Our main concern here is with how this philosophical short-sightedness impacts on the claim of the values clarification model to provide an adequate program of moral education without teaching content. Students will be told to make their judgments without regard for the judgments other people make. Their only alternative is to look within themselves to find a rational or irrational basis for their judgments. But, what will they find within, be it rational or irrational, which has not come from, or been influenced by, the values they have observed other people to express and live by? Is it not common sense to realize that we all take in considerable content, especially as young children? Here is the source of the values we carry with us, and it has a significant bearing on our impulses. That is, what we assimilate cognitively has a bearing on our affective side.

The point here is that when students are forced to choose, even if they attempt to follow the dictate of values clarification not to look to the choices of others, and even if they believe they are successful at this, they will still be influenced by the values of other people. We have been assimilating content virtually since birth. Do the values clarificationists expect that students will suddenly snap a switch and turn off their personalities? Unless they do, it seems they should admit the importance of content learned from other people, and proceed to alter their program of moral education accordingly. But what if they were to suggest that students are capable of turning off the influence of content learned throughout their life history? Is this not a possible defense against the suggestion that because students have learned values from other people they will be inclined to employ them in moral decision-making?

The values clarificationists do not make such a claim, but if they did they would still be faced with the difficulty of explaining the basis for making moral judgments. And, of course, they have no such explanation. Still, this does not mean that such an explanation cannot be proffered. Values clarification is only part of the story in the latest trend in moral education. The other new model, the cognitive-developmental model, provides a supplement for precisely what values clarification has been shown to be lacking. The claim is that students can in fact be brought around to the point where they can turn off whatever values they have accumulated through their life experiences of watching and listening to other people. In doing this they not only preserve autonomy, but also discover the content-free grounding for moral decision-making which values clarification lacks.

The Cognitive-Developmental Model

While originating in the work of Piaget, the cognitive-developmental model for moral education is today associated with Lawrence Kohlberg. Kohlberg's version of the distinction between process and content in moral decision-making employs the notion of cognitive structures. Structure refers to the pattern one's thinking follows, and it is structure which determines content.[6]

Kohlberg's celebrated stage theory identifies six basic structures which are arranged hierarchically.[7] At stages 1 through 4 the structures operate in such a way that content from other people is assimilated and employed in determining what one's own content will be. At stages 5 and 6, however, one moves beyond this to the level of autonomy. At stage 6, the highest level of moral reasoning, the structure operates on purely formal terms, and values learned from other people are not allowed to prejudice one's choice. A moral decision is seen as a choice between competing values, with the standard of choice being something other than one of the competing values or any other value, and which stands outside the competition as an objective arbiter. Kohlberg identifies stage 6 reasoning with Kant's categorical imperative and Rawls' original position and veil of ignorance. What stage 6 amounts to is the principle of universalizability,[8] asking what I would want to see done if I were in someone else's shoes. If I would consider a choice to be right regardless of what shoes I might discover myself to be wearing, then I have found what is truly right.

Kohlberg's classroom program is built around his stage theory. Students are engaged in group discussions of moral dilemmas, and when they hear reasoning one stage above their own they are attracted to it because they are able to recognize it as philosophically more adequate. Very gradually they are enticed to advance to the next stage. Kohlberg makes no attempt to establish a neutral atmosphere in the classroom as the values clarificationists do. He is willing to have students hear the values others express. Presumably this is because he recognizes that in order to reveal to one another the reasoning they employ, students must also reveal the values that reasoning yields. All of this, of course, is done with the aim of advancement toward the autonomous level. Kohlberg is confident that the ideal of moral reasoning toward which students are striving is both free of the influence of other people's value biases and still capable of making unimpeachable determinations of right and wrong. This is where the values clarification model was seen to be lacking. It presents the highest level of moral reasoning as free of values learned from other people, but offers nothing in the place of such values to provide the grounding for moral judgments. Kohlberg, on the other hand, replaces values learned from other people with the principle of univeralizability. The question which immediately looms, then, is whether this principle is capable of carrying the load which is assigned to it.

The idea that the mere universalizability of a possible moral choice provides us with an adequate grounding for that choice has long been suspect by philosophers not of the Kantian persuasion. Is it not possible, one asks, to show two contradictory positions to be equally universalizable? If this is the case, something other than that formal principle will be required in order to decide between the contrary positions. Let us consider the capability of the principle of universalizability in light of one of Kohlberg's own examples of its application.

Kohlberg has claimed that capital punishment is wrong and that stage 6 reasoning demonstrates why.

> Would persons in the original position contract into a system of capital punishment? For one thing, we can be absolutely certain that whatever appeal the idea of retributive punishment may have in the abstract vanishes altogether once we put ourselves into the original position. For no rational person who thought that he himself might be the object of retribution would contract into a penal system founded thereon, particularly when the retribution is to be exacted in the form of death. Even if such a system would promote the validation of the social order in the mind of the average citizen, this objective is simply not worth risking one's life for.[9]

The argument here follows a Rawlsian line and claims that no rational man would contract into a society in which it might turn out that he would be sentenced to death. In other words, if we put ourselves in the shoes of a criminal who was found to be liable to the death penalty, we would be against it. But, is it not possible for someone to claim that he is in favor of capital punishment even if it is possible that it might be applied against him? In other words, is the pro-capital punishment position not as universalizable as the anti-position? Kohlberg would say no, and claim that the pro-position would not be within the bounds of rationality. A rational man would always prefer to secure his life over the prospect of possibly losing it. But why? It seems to be a precondition of rationality that it includes adherence to the value of the preservation of life. Without this value, rationality would be weighted neither toward nor against capital punishment. But if this value is part of the essential equipment of stage 6 reasoning, then the stage 6 structure involves more than a purely formal principle. While Kohlberg claims to be working from a purely formal principle, without realizing it he has supplemented this principle with an established value.

The significance of this point for the main topic of our discussion is that there must be more to mature moral decision-making than Kohlberg recognizes. In order to function effectively, the formal structure of stage 6 must be supplemented with values. The implication for Kohlberg's new model for moral education is similar to the implication values clarification was found to be facing when its ideal of moral decision-making was exposed as insufficient without the influence of values derived from outside the autonomous "process of valuing." If values are needed as part of the input into mature moral decision-making, then people will supply these values. And where will the values come from? Undoubtedly from one's own life experiences. And this will include values assimilated from other people. These values may enter our moral decision-making at either the cognitive or affective level, but in either event the point remains that the values we have learned from other people will come to have a bearing on our moral judgments. In sum, the workings of stage 6 are not so different from those of stages 1 through 4 as Kohlberg would have us believe. He errs in thinking that while content learned from other people is a component in moral decision-making at these lower stages, this ceases at the highest stage.

Teaching Content Through the Humanities

The claim has been made here that the new models for moral education have misconceived the nature of mature moral decision-making. They assume that exclusion of the influence of values learned from other people is desirable because it leads to autonomy. And they assume that it is feasible, that is, that moral judgments can be made in the absence of any predisposition established through the assimilation of values. The new models fail to recognize that the autonomous and supposedly content-free versions of the moral decision-making process they present as ideal are in fact inoperable without the influence of previously established values. But, if this is the case, the educational programs the new models have built upon the faulty ideal become suspect. We should recognize their attempts at moral education without teaching content to be misguided. If all arrows point to values learned from other people as a significant factor in moral decision-making, we should ensure that programs of moral education concentrate on this. If the values of other people are important, we should ensure that students be given maximum exposure to them.

The place to begin is with the recognition that one's life experiences naturally occasion the assimilation of content. However, we must recognize that life experiences are often narrow or provincial. They should be enhanced considerably through a proper educational program. It is in this regard that the teaching of the humanities should be given a leading role. Through the study of the humanities students will be exposed to a wider and deeper variety of content than through their everyday life experiences.[10]

To conceive of the humanities as a vehicle for moral education, no less as a corrective or substitute for the popular new models, may at first seem far fetched. Even among humanities teachers themselves, many do not conceive of their enterprise as the teaching of morals. Rather, they see themselves as teaching certain skills, whether they be basic skills for the novice or precise, refined skills for the budding expert. And, if not on skills, or perhaps in addition to skills, the emphasis of humanities teachers is often on aesthetic concerns. We study the humanities to appreciate beautiful works, to have fun, to be inspired. What is missing in such a picture of the humanities is a proper recognition of the moral values with which they abound. And it is precisely this which is the key to moral education.

Let us consider literature. We may read literature to improve our reading skills, and we may read it for enjoyment, but we may also read it with an eye on the messages therein about how sundry human beings have lived their lives. Sometimes the messages are explicit recommendations to the reader about the right way to live, for instance, a poem which extols courage or compassion. Sometimes the messages lie beneath the surface, and the reader, instead of listening to a direct exhortation, observes the choices another person makes through that person's actions. And, further, the reader is privy to the outcome of those choices and actions. They can be recognized as promoting happiness or grief, as designating virtue or vice. In a sense what we are doing in reading literature at this level is reliving the lives of its characters, experiencing vicariously what they have experienced. From their struggles and decisions, triumphs and tragedies we draw content. Our life experiences are, then, greatly enhanced. The store of values we possess that is available for infusion into the process of moral decision-making will have been enlarged and refined.

What has been said about literature also holds for history, that is, if history is taught as more than a subject of facts and figures. The concern is not about how many people died at some great battle, or with tracing the Hapsburg bloodline. In the study of history we may go beyond this and focus on the people themselves who lived the lives which contributed to the facts and figures. For instance, we ask how did a particular individual or even a whole army think and act in the face of imminent defeat and death in battle. Or what were the people really like who bore the Hapsburg pedigree? In history, as with literature, we observe what others have chosen to do with their lives and what the outcomes have been. We enrich our store of content.

Literature and history, then, provide a vehicle for teaching content. But, this is not all there is to it. The picture presented so far, in spite of whatever glossiness may have been attached to it, is brief and incomplete. The hard questions have yet to be tackled, the sorts of questions which would legitimately be asked by those holding rival views on the humanities, and perhaps by the values clarificationists and Kohlbergians. Someone would undoubtedly want to ask why this enlarged content drawn from the study of the humanities is superior to that of one's everyday here and now experiences. Are not the values of people from different times and places relative to those times and places? Here is the relativism with which the values clarificationists, as well as many others, are so smitten. The answer is that by observing a diversity of people we may in fact come upon a diversity of values. However, not all of these need to be accepted as right. By sorting out one from the other we dig beneath the surface to a common core. The search is for a content which holds for man as man rather than man in certain times or places. Whether this universal element exists will undoubtedly stir debate, and will not be argued here. Rather, we will turn briefly to a second question which follows in its wake.

If in fact the universal element does exist, will not a considerable amount of sorting of competing messages be required — and considerable skill need to be exercised at this — before this element can be revealed or at least revealed very fully? This is of course the case, but there is a means available for attempting it. In order to sort out the many competing messages we will be exposed to through literature and history, as well as our everyday lives, we should turn to the study of philosophy, particularly to that branch of philosophy called ethics or moral philosophy. This is not to say that moral philosophers are in basic agreement about a universal element in humanity and about the right way to live, but only that by participating in philosophical discourse one may begin to make sense of competing messages.

These questions and related ones are worthy of continued attention, but this must be left for other occasions. The main point has been made. The study of the humanities provides a means for teaching content. This is precisely what the new models for moral education were shown to be lacking. Educators must realize this if they are to provide an adequate program of moral education in the schools. Preparation for moral decision-making involves the intake of values from other people, and rather than being deluded into denying this, educators should recognize it and plan their teaching accordingly. The new models for moral education, despite the glitter of their ideal of autonomy, have left us without the substance we need. When this is recognized it appears that the best new model for moral education is none other than an old model. Why not resurrect the old model and see if it isn't still capable of working well?

NOTES

[1] Henry Veatch has written numerous journal articles about the foundation of ethical theory, as well as two books, *Rational Man: A Modern Interpretation of Aristotelian Ethics* (Bloomington, Indiana: Indiana University Press, 1962) and *For an Ontology of Morals: A Critique of Contemporary Ethical Theory* (Evanston, Illinois: Northwestern University Press, 1971).

[2] Louis E. Raths, Merrill Harmin, and Sidney B. Simon, *Values and Teaching* (Columbus, Ohio: Charles E. Merrill, 1966), ch. 3. This book is the primer of the values clarification model for moral education.

[3] Ibid.

[4] Ibid, ch. 4.

[5] Ibid, ch. 8.

[6] Lawrence Kohlberg, "The Cognitive-Developmental Approach to Moral Education," *Phi Delta Kappan*, LVI (June, 1975), pp. 671–672.

[7] A summary of Kohlberg's stage theory may be found in the above mentioned article which provides a highly readable synopsis of his views on the theory and practice of moral education. As the stage theory is the focal point of Kohlberg's work, he has incorporated a summary of it into most of his writings. For an excellent secondary source on the stage theory see Ronald Duska and Mariellen Whelan, *Moral Development: A Guide to Piaget and Kohlberg* (New York: Paulist Press, 1975). For an extended treatment of Kohlberg's philosophical views see his papers, "From Is to Ought: How to Commit the Naturalistic Fallacy and Get Away With It in the Study of Moral Development," in *Cognitive Development and Epistemology*, Theodore Mischel, ed. (New York: Academic Press, 1971) and "Stages of Moral Development as a Basis for Moral Education," in *Moral Education: Interdisciplinary Approaches*, C. M. Beck, B. S. Crittenden, and E. V. Sullivan, eds. (Toronto: University of Toronto Press, 1971).

[8] Kohlberg sometimes utilizes further technical terminology to describe stage 6: consistency, reversibility, prescriptivity. What these terms seem to represent to him has been incorporated into what I have labelled here as universalizability.

[9] Lawrence Kohlberg and Donald Elfenbein, "The Development of Moral Judgments Concerning Capital Punishment," *American Journal of Orthopsychiatry* (July, 1975).

[10] I know of no better explanation of the value of the humanities as a vehicle for moral education than Henry Veatch's article, "The What and the Why of the Humanities," *Proceedings of the American Catholic Philosophical Association* (1973).

THE PROPER CONTEXT OF MORAL EDUCATION

Jesse A. Mann
Georgetown University

An impressive result of the philosophical reflection of Henry Veatch has been his substantial writing in normative ethics. In particular, he has always championed the ethics of Aristotle. Accordingly, one of his major claims has been that ethics is, above all, a practical science in the Aristotelian sense, and that clearly it ought to have an effect on the actions of man. At the very least, the moral philosopher, according to Henry, has to communicate to rational men consistent and valid reflections on the nature of the good life and on those qualities and virtues that constitute and sustain it. That is, his job is not complete unless he specifies in some way what the content of the good moral life ought to be. Since ethics involves content or proper subject matter about action here and now performed, a formalism which eschews content, such as Kantianism, cannot in Veatch's view carry the load that morals must. Just as the surgeon must not only sharpen the scalpel but also know how to use it, so too the moral philosopher must not only know how to sharpen his awareness of what goes on when we think morally but must also be able to bring that moral thinking to bear on the actual living of life itself.[1]

In this paper I would like to consider some of the implications of this practical "Hoosier" concern with ordinary life and common sense for a theory of moral education. Two recent published reports make clear that moral education is a major concern in this country today.[2] In particular, I wish to make the claim that a good theory of moral education must explicitly consider both formal elements such as reasoning and primary moral principles, and material elements such as the contents of a great tradition embodied in literature. These two elements, the formal and the material, are indeed crucial and they are addressed throughout this volume in papers like those of Casement and McDonnell.

My special concern in this paper will be with what I wish to call the "context" of moral education, that mix of family, friends, school, religious institutions and the workplace which constitute the framework in which a formally adequate moral philosophy with content can be communicated. A crucial problem for moral educators today is that, in addition to the form and matter of moral education, there are other essential factors. Out of my reading the work of Veatch, MacIntyre[3], and others, I would like to discuss what I take to be at least five essential elements operative in any theory of moral education.

One, the form of moral education, must in some way be a rational form. That is, as Henry Veatch insists, reasoning about our moral actions is the very shape of moral education itself.

Two, this form cannot be empty. Our reasoning must be informed by the considerable results of reasoning already done. Thus the content of the reflections of Aristotle, Plato, Aquinas and others must be added to the formal elements involved in the reasoning process. Not only must we reason about wisdom derived from a living tradition but we must somehow be able to reflect adequately on the problems raised by present experience.

Three, the individual student who is examining this form and content is doing so always in some context or environment. This moral context or moral environment is of the utmost importance in the whole question of moral education today. Given our present problems with the traditional family, the school, in some cases, is the only moral institution a student faces.

Four, some theory of freedom has to be implicit in any theory of moral education. Thus Aquinas claims that reason is the very root of freedom and most moral educators agree with this view in one form or another. There are, of course, difficulties for writers like B. F. Skinner who on the one hand is widely read by moral educators but who, on the other, hardly seems to give any real meaning to the notion of individual freedom.

Five, any meaningful theory of moral education has to outline the virtues involved in the moral life. As MacIntyre has shown, for about fifteen hundred years our culture based itself largely on the four cardinal virtues of Plato and Aristotle, namely, prudence, justice, temperance and fortitude, and, for an additional thousand years, our culture added to those fundamental four virtues of the Greeks the three Christian theological virtues of faith, hope and charity.

These then are some of the principles that I would wish to call upon in seeking to make recommendations for a needed new look at the problems involved in moral education in our schools both public and private.

With regard to the whole question of the appropriate content of moral education I am in agreement with the main conclusions reached by William Casement in this same volume. As I see it, Casement is correct in his assessment of the values clarification theories of Simon and others. Casement notes properly that these theories are inconsistent on two grounds. Firstly, their claim to be non-indoctrinative is not sound because they in fact indoctrinate students with the theory that all options in a given moral dilemma are equally worthy of consideration; and, secondly, their claim to being merely formal cannot be sustained because they make the material claim that all moral options are equally to be examined.

The value clarification proponents attempt to engage the student in the act of assessing choices without ever committing him to the defense or rejection of any of the choices he actually makes. Thus, in the work of Simon[4] there is a hidden indoctrination of the student. Explicitly we are told that the teacher is not going to impose values on the student; in fact, the teacher defends the notion that all values are equally important and that the wise thing to do is stand apart from all values and act as if they were all the same. As Casement has pointed out, this is not only implicit indoctrination, but it is philosophical folly.

A second possible solution to the problem of moral education, also commented on in this volume by Casement, is to follow Professor Kohlberg's approach. Kohlberg is far less open to charges of indoctrination inasmuch as in some of his writing he supplements his formal adherence to Kantianism with an implicit claim that he wishes to impart the Platonic notion of Justice.[5] Until quite recently, Kohlberg has not been very friendly to the notion of the virtues as explained by Veatch, and, most currently, MacIntyre. However, it is the strong conviction of this writer that Kohlberg should be very sharply distinguished from the values-clarification movement, such as that of Simon. Kohlberg's recent work with Fowler and Power on a state of morality characterized by religion shows his interest in both justice and religion. This emphasis on such important content seems to me to establish pretty firmly that Kohlberg is interested in the content of moral education. Moral choice is an exercise of character more than a knowledge game for Kohlberg and is further involved in the acts of a community seeking justice.

The question we are left with then is, "Can we ever totally eliminate content from moral education and at the same time be consistent?" The answer seems to be that we cannot unless we can establish a purely Kantian formalism which at the same time that it constitutes moral education is also such that it offers no content. However, my principle concern in this paper is really not with the matter of content but rather with the whole question of the moral environment. It is to this question that I will address the remainder of this paper.

At the outset, one should distinguish the physical environment from the moral environment. It is interesting that Aristotle has claimed that the physical environment can be such that happiness is impossible. Thus, for happiness we must have not only the moral goods of virtue and friendship but we also need such items from the physical environment as health and "external goods" which include housing, food, clothing. Clearly, the extremes of hunger, physical isolation, excessively crowded conditions, prolonged exposure to cold, upheavals such as floods and volcanic eruptions create great havoc in the moral as well as in the physical life of man, the moral institutions of human beings being closely related to the external conditions. The truly moral environment, nevertheless, is quite different from the physical environment.

Perhaps the best way to approach the moral environment concept is to stress the two essential concepts of tradition and community. In this matter of the moral environment it would be my claim that these two are clearly the most central aspects of the whole question of the moral environment. Clearly, no one can divest himself of the influence of community or tradition on his life. One does not choose one's racial or ethnic identity, the date of one's birth, the place among one's other siblings in the family. One has no choice in the whole matter of the major moral education to be given by the mother and later by the father in the earliest years of life. The question of who forms the moral community into which one is born and the further question of just what traditions this moral community follows is crucial to the development of the new child. Thus the task of moral education is to see to it that moral traditions are themselves subjects of proper reflection and assessment. This is of course done routinely in one's life.

For this reason one of the major preoccupations of psychology has been the whole matter of socialization. Psychological studies of socialization, however, especially in this pluralistic society, seek to describe the least common denominator kind of development that all children get. Children are not the unique persons they are simply because of what they have in common with other children. What must also be taken into account is the rich and precious diversity of heritage enjoyed by each individual child. This is too valuable to be left undone or to be left to the initiatives of a school board.

Clearly and immediately, then, we must ask what institutions carry on this kind of practical communication of the moral environment in which the child acts. Obviously there are at least four basic ones in any society: the family, the school, the church, and friends. There are others, of course, such as the courts and the legislatures, the work places such as the great corporations and the guilds of artisans such as the labor unions and the art schools and the technological institutes, scientific societies and so forth. All of these latter are important but I think not as important as the family, the church, the school and one's own network of "friends". I would like to consider each of these in turn.

We must consider how sad it is that the four essential agents of a moral environment one is often not practiced, namely religion, and in our culture two others are in deep trouble, namely the school and the family. That leaves only one as really viable for some youngsters, namely friendship. Yet as Aristotle has advised us, friendship itself requires other virtues.

As I have said, the major institutions which form the moral environment seem to me to be four: the family, the school, the church, and one's network of friends, especially one's authentic friends, although one should include also one's useful and amusing friends. Before discussing each of these in more detail, I wish to add the notion that in our time—or at least in the last four hundred years, "science" has been a kind of institution which gave considerable shape to the moral life of individuals. In general, however, science has been something of a disappointment to those who thought they saw in it an omnipotent character. Thus some—especially in the liberal movements of the eighteenth and nineteenth century—may have thought that science was going to be the new religion of mankind. Accordingly, a dedication to science would be enough to form a moral environment sufficient for mankind. A number of philosophers who have themselves been scientists, one of whom notably is William James, have belied that promise. If we are to believe James—and his arguments seem very cogent— life always present problems to the individual which neither science nor reason can answer. One might also argue that much of the dedication of the existentialists, particularly Marcel and Sartre, to the irrational has been a function of their deep rejection of the notion that "science" is enough—in the sense that, having science, one needs no further religion or system of morality. One must also mention here the major thrust of the vital new movement in Phenomenology. Writers such as Husserl and Heidegger have argued strenuously that the very categories which are central to science such as quantity, space, time, number, relation, are trivial when applied to man. Man is to be appreciated in terms of respect, love, guilt, responsibility, remorse, and other categories which are simply too mysterious and complicated to be adequately and meaningfully subsumed by any known quantitative assessment in science.

The primary institution which is crucial to the context of moral education is the family, however. Perhaps the greatest crisis in moral education comes from the weak position of the family. The number of families which are disrupted by divorce continues to grow and the number of families which are described as "one-parent families" continues to grow. Children are thus in many cases deprived of what used to be the normal pattern of two parents resident in the same house and involved in the moral education of those children. The difficulties being suffered by the nuclear family of parents and children are further complicated by the fact that the extended family is also not as strong as formerly. One factor in its weakening consists of the sheer mobility of modern society. Because the family itself is not strong enough— especially when isolated from a believing community and a vital tradition— to fend off the permissiveness of modern culture in terms of easy abortion and sexual promiscuity, the family is further weakened by additional burdens of care. The reason for this inability of families to cope with moral education is clearly stated by Aristotle in the *Politics*. Families are not themselves perfect institutions. They require the larger society. Not only is this need of the larger society clear in matters of material things, it is also true in terms of moral realities. Families need churches or similar believing communities with vital traditions quite as much as they need supermarkets.

The claim that the family cannot provide enough context for a moral education by itself leads us to the next element to be described as a part of the essential context in which moral education goes on. I call this element the church and by it I mean any church in one of the great religious institutions with which mankind has been blessed, Christianity, Buddhism, Islam are primary examples. I am willing to include also some remnants of these great traditions which are clung to and practiced by individuals who no longer go into the churches. Thus it is clear to me that many are moved by Puritanism and the work ethic who do not consider themselves religious. They work hard, seek to be thrifty, frugal; they are honest and wish to acknowledge God in their lives. They are not formally religious in the sense that they go to church, but they are quite religious in the sense that the meaning of their lives is provided by a doctrine worked out and clarified by the living institutions to whose buildings they no longer go. I am less inclined to view as religious in anywhere near the same sense other movements of a mass kind which, it seems to me, are mainly Dionysiac in character and either transitory or trivial in effect.

It is clear that beyond the family a second essential element in the context of moral education is religion. In my opinion it is religion primarily in the sense of organized religion but I acknowledge that other lesser institutions such as "heritages" can do the same thing though less forcefully and—I think—less adequately.

I wish to argue that the next most important among the elements essential in a moral context is friendship. Here we are faced with a special set of difficulties. Virtue is essential to friendship in the authentic sense. Yet children at the beginning of their moral development do not find enough models of moral virtues from peers who are equally undeveloped humanly as they are. The fact is, of course, that teachers in Aristotle's sense can be, and are, true friends of their students just as parents are. Aristotle has argued effectively that the good man needs friends not because of any dependence on them but because they give him an opportunity to be magnanimous, to be generous in spirit and to be ready to help others substantially and in friendly ways. Just as the man of virtue needs friends, so too the beginning child needs to develop in such a way that he can get beyond his primary narcissism and be able to live in mutuality with his peers. Above all, the school, the family and the church ought to provide the growing child and the maturing young person with a large number of persons in which such mutuality is possible. One of the frequent complaints of students, even of young couples, in a sense of loneliness, a sense that beyond their individual lives there are no persons to whom they are able to go spontaneously and to whom they are ready to give generously of their time and their energy. Erik Erikson has noted that a primary crisis in growing up beyond adolescence is the ability of young couples to treat each other as spoiled children. The result is stagnation and not the generativity needed to form a network of friends.

The last of these four essential institutions for a moral context is the school. It is most dependent on what happens in the other three, the family, the church or its equivalent, and the network of friends. More has been expected of the school than is reasonable. One cannot, for instance, hope that the school can function to provide an effective moral education when there is no support from a family, a church, a network of caring and nurturing friends, including under ideal circumstances both parents, uncles, aunts, cousins, and significant neighbors. It is highly unreasonable, for instance, to expect that an inner city school is going to be able to create a pattern of effective achievement without help from families, churches, friends and significant community persons—including the industries in the area. One thing, however, the school can do is to become an effective instrument for goals set by the wider community. A tragic expectation is that the school is the proper institution to establish the wisdom needed in the lives of the morally developing young. On the contrary, the good school is an effective reflection of the wisdom and tradition already present in a hopefully wise community.

In conclusion, then, I have made the claim that although the form and the context of moral education is quite important for the student of moral theory to consider, there are other areas of investigation of great importance which must be stressed. One of these areas is that of the context in which moral decisions take place. This context includes at least four major institutions of society. These are the family, the church, the school, and a network of friends. Furthermore implicit in these institutions are two of the major needs of all human beings in their moral life: a rich and wise tradition and a large and loving community.

Notes

[1] These themes are especially clear in Henry Veatch's *Rational Man* and *The ontology of Morals.*

[2] I am referring to the recent report (Spring 1983) on education by the Secretary of Education, United States Commission on Excellence in Education (*A Nation at Risk: The Importance of Educational Reform.* Washington, D.C.: U.S. Government Printing Office, 1983), and to the recent five-year study by Dean Goodlad of U.C.L.A., *A Place Called School.* New York, McGraw Hill, 1983.

[3] Veatch has written many articles and given many papers on the philosophy of education, and has completed a book-length manuscript on this topic which is ready for the publisher. In referring to Alasdair MacIntyre, I have principally in mind his recent work, *After Virtue.*

[4]. See Louis Raths, Merrill Harmin, and Sidney B. Simon, *Values in Teaching* (Columbus, Ohio: Charles E. Merrill, 1966). See also Sidney B. Simon, Leland W. Howe, and Howard Kirschenbaum, *Values Clarification: A Handbook of Practical Strategies for Teachers and Students* (New York: Hart Publishing Co., 1972).

[5]. Especially in "Education for Justice: A Modern Statement of the Platonic View," in Nancy F. Sizer and Theodore R. Sizer, eds. *Moral Education: Five Lectures* (Cambridge, Mass.: Harvard University Press, 1970) and also F. Clark Power and Lawrence Kohlberg, "Religion, Morality, and Ego Development," in J. Fowler and A. Vergote, eds., *Toward Moral and Religious Maturity* (Morristown, N.J.: Silver Burdett, 1980).

OUR NON-ETHICAL EDUCATIONAL ETHOS

Theodore A. Young
Grand Valley State College

Ethics *and* Education? Odd. Henry Veatch presumably would agree with Plato that education *is* moral education. And yet in our educational ethos (at least in public education) ethics courses are but one (elective) ingredient *in* education. I suppose this is because our notion of education emphasizes vocational training and science. And even we in the humanities are crypto-scientists: scholars specializing. Among the specialists are the moral philosophers. It cannot be surprising that their expertise lies not in what Aristotle called practical reason, but instead in theorizing about ethics, or in meta-ethics.

To assist an understanding of our educational ethos I propose to look to the past. In my study of George Berkeley I was surprised to find him at heart a classical philosopher. In moral, political, and educational matters his teachers were such as Plato and Aristotle. He lamented the decline of their influence, and blamed it on the spread of the "corpuscularian and mechanical philosophy." Scientific study

> might usefully enough have employed some share of the leisure and curiosity of inquisitive persons. But when it entered the seminaries of learning as a necessary accomplishment, and most important part of education, by engrossing men's thoughts, and fixing their minds so much on corporeal objects and the laws of motion, it hath, however undesignedly, . . . not a little indisposed them for spiritual, moral, and intellectual matters. Certainly, had the philosophy of Socrates . . . prevailed in this age among those who think themselves too wise to receive the dictates of the Gospel, we should not have seen interest take so general and fast hold on the minds of men, nor public spirit reputed to be . . . a generous folly, among those who are reckoned to be the most knowing as well as the most getting part of mankind.[1]

We all know that in metaphysics Berkeley directed his attacks against materialists. Their counterparts in morals, politics and education are free-thinkers. Because free-thinking always presents itself as the champion of enlightened scientific reason against what it takes to be ungrounded or superstitious belief, it was given great impetus by the rise of modern science. The more serious eighteenth century free-thinkers looked to science as the model, and to scientific method as the proper use of reason. The more frivolous believed that any one of us is, as rational, free to interpret and criticize any religious, moral, political, or artistic doctrine in accordance with his own lights, with reverence to no authority whatever. Perhaps it would not be unfair to say that the former were forerunners of today's social scientists; the latter forerunners of today's "experts" in the arts and the humanities. Berkeley opposed both types; and in reviewing his attacks on free-thinking I will not attempt to sharply differentiate the two. Moreover, in today's educational blend of the sciences and the humanities, a compromise between them has been reached; while classical education, opposed to both, has almost ceased to exist.

In morals, Berkeley argued neither utilitarianism nor deontologism, but instead the classical view that achieving a good or happy life requires development of the peculiar human virtues of wisdom, courage, and the like. Thus, when countering the free-thinkers of his time, for whom the moral ideals are liberty and truth, Berkeley succeeds in showing that liberty and truth are better understood as means to our moral well-being. Much vicious activity, for example sexual intemperance, has been defended in the name of liberty. Against this Berkeley writes, "Freedom is either a blessing or a curse as men use it,"[2] and again, "Liberty is the greatest human blessing that a *virtuous* man can possess."[3] Likewise, in the name of truth, how many bright young college teachers delight in undermining the simple faith of unsophisticated undergraduates, without having anything to put in its place, except of course what they take to be truth? Berkeley's point is that promoting truth as a moral end in itself may encourage iconoclasm in us, so that we become skeptics if not cynics.

In politics, Berkeley held the classical position that man is by nature a political animal. In his essay, "Passive Obedience," he argues that loyalty to the supreme political power is as binding upon us as any of the ten commandments. Not because, as Hobbes had theorized, human life in the natural state (a life of complete political — or should we say apolitical — liberty) is solitary, poor, nasty, brutish, and short; but instead because, as Plato had pointed out long before, men need one another and cannot satisfy their physical and spiritual needs save by living together in political community. Berkeley's classical commitment to political stability was also made evident when, in 1715, there was suspicion of Tory support of an imminent Jacobite rebellion, he published "Advice to the Tories who have taken the Oaths." The oaths had been taken in 1701, following the Act of Settlement that gave the crown to the Hanovers upon the death of Queen Anne. The oaths swore allegiance to King George I and abjured any pretence of James III to the throne. Berkeley reminded the Tories that no matter how cloudy this political circumstance might be, there are religious and moral scruples perfectly clear to any Christian and right thinking person: honesty, loyalty, truth. It cannot be known what effect Berkeley's advice had; but in fact, the rebellion that occurred later that year collapsed at least in part because of lack of support from the Tories.

Perhaps it is in education that Berkeley's classical thought is most clearly seen. We might wonder why the issue is not religious vs. scientific education. For after all, the free-thinkers took pride in setting themselves free from religion — all its superstitions, prejudices, oppressions. And Berkeley after all was defending religion. True, Berkeley was an orthodox Christian; but his defense of religion was a philosophical defense, and it was an argument against free-thinking, not against science.

Surely there is such a thing as scientific education. In Berkeley's time and ours there can be no doubt about that. But just as surely, it is not a moral education; that is, whatever it is education is, it is not in instructing us what the good life is and how to achieve it. Hence, the dispute about values is not a scientific one or a religious one, but a philosophical one.

In case that is not altogether clear, let us take another look at it, by noticing Berkeley's introduction in *Alciphron,* his apology for Christianity of the term, "minute philosophy." He borrows the label from Cicero, and prefers it because he does not want to be regarded as being opposed to thinking freely. That ancient Roman philosopher called the free-thinkers of his day " . . . minute philosophers, which name admirably suits them, they being a sort of sect which diminish all the most valuable things, the thoughts, views, and hopes of men; all the knowledge, notions, and theories of the mind they reduce to sense; human nature they contract and degrade to the narrow low standard of animal life, and assign us only a small pittance of time instead of immortality."[4] Alciphron, the free-thinker, agrees to use of the term, but puts his own interpretation on it: "It is my opinion this appellation might be derived from their considering things minutely, and not swallowing them in the gross, as other men are used to do. Besides, we all know the best eyes are necessary to discern the minutest objects: it seems, therefore, that minute philosophers might have been so called from their distinguished perspicacity."[5] Now, there is no denying that great numbers of scientifically inclined and trained thinkers, when they come to wonder about man and the universe, do "degrade and contract human nature to the narrow low standard of animal life." But that is not a part of the teaching of any science. Nor does any science teach that the only way to achieve knowledge is through "considering things minutely." Still, our consideration of the truth of these opposed philosophies must await another day. For now, the question is what the *moral* teaching of each of them is.

Berkeley appeals to the free-thinking literature of his day for the morally significant notions of minute philosophy. One such notion is that man is not different from the beast; another that a man is a machine, and that therefore thought, or reasoning, is nothing but part of the machinery. From these notions comes another, that man is not responsible for his actions and that therefore conscience is a whim and morality a prejudice. Another argues that vice is useful; yet another that loyalty is nothing and that public spirit is an idle enthusiasm. The masterpiece of free-thinking, though, is proof that God does not exist.

The corresponding notions of classical philosophy could not be more different: man is neither a beast, nor a machine, but instead is a rational animal, a little lower than the angels, with a spark of the divine in him; man is responsible for his behavior; virtue is necessary to happiness, vice destructive of it; loyalty is a virtue necessary, as is public spirit, for the welfare of the *polis,* without which man has little chance of living a good life; and finally, there is proof that God, the Divine, Supernature, exists.

According to the classical philosophers, such as Plato, Aristotle, Maimonides, St. Thomas Aquinas, and now Berkeley, education is a long, arduous process, requiring years and years of methodical, disciplined study, best pursued, part of the time anyway, in an academy, withdrawn from the distractions of mundane living. In *Alciphron* Lysicles caricatures the capped and gowned pedants of the eighteenth century poring over dead authors who wrote in dead languages, cut off from the real world; and recommends the new philosophers, ". . . the best bred men of the age, men who know the world, men of pleasure, men of fashion, and fine gentlemen,"[6] who have no method but free and easy conversation. Alciphron, in his turn, caricatures the stuffy bookworms who meditate on ". . . obsolete notions, that are now quite exploded and out of use."[7]

The teachers and students of this new way of education are not found in the academies and universities but instead ". . . in a drawing-room, a coffee-house, a chocolate-house, at the tavern, or groom-porter's. In these and the like fashionable places of resort, it is the custom for polite persons to speak freely on all subjects, religious, moral, or political; so that a young gentleman who frequents them is in the way of hearing many instructive lectures, seasoned with wit and raillery, and uttered with spirit. Three or four sentences from a man of quality, spoke with a good air, make more impression and convey more knowledge than a dozen dissertations in a dry academical way."[8]

Anyone aware of the educational scene in contemporary America will recognize that these are pages rich for commentary. One sympathetic to Berkeley is likely to lament that he foresaw too well. ". . . our chief strength and flower of the flock," speaks Alciphron, "are those promising young men who have the advantage of a modern education. These are the growing hopes of our sect, by whose credit and influence in a few years we expect to see those great things accomplished that we have in view."[9] One noteworthy accomplishment of the minute philosophers in our time is moving from the coffee-houses and taverns right into the academies and universities. Not only have they moved in, but also they have taken over; classical education has all but disappeared from the American educational scene.

Instead of a long, arduous course of methodical, disciplined, academic, and classical study, with its ultimate aim of moral and political insight and leadership, we now have either scientific training and/or "speaking freely" on all controversial subjects, like religion, morals, politics. To be sure, scientific training is exact, methodic, disciplined, and often requiring long hard years of tedious study. However, its aim is the production of specialized experts, and thereby the advancement of scientific knowledge, but not the moral education of leaders of a *polis.* Its aim, in short, is to discover the facts. Values? That is somebody else's department. But whose? Enter the free-thinkers.

From grade school through college students are taught, not to ignore values, but rather to create their own systems of values. In the realm of facts, modern science has produced, by way of highly specialized expertise, relatively few but well respected authorities. But in the realm of values, there is no comparable science, no course of study, no method, no curriculum that will yield expertise. All that can be or is offered, it seems, is free and easy conversation; in short, one virtually endless bull session that the really serious and bright student quickly wearies of.

But, hold. What about the social and behavioral sciences? Have we not there in these young sciences already made great discoveries and advances, in psychology, sociology, anthropology, politics, maybe even history? And is not the future of these sciences even brighter? Have we not here perhaps some bridge between cold, hard, objective scientific fact and warm, soft, subjective value? Berkeley even presaged, albeit sarcastically, behavioral science, which by implication is to replace the meditations of the stodgy pedants of the old way. ". . . we have among us some contemplative spirits of a coarser education, who, from observing the behaviour and proceedings of apprentices, watermen, porters, and the assemblies of rabble in the streets, have arrived at a profound knowledge of human nature, and made great discoveries about the principles, springs, and motives of moral actions. These have demolished the received systems, and done a world of good in the city."[10] We cannot help wondering what Lysicles, the maker of this speech, would think of our cities after two hundred years of such behavioral studies.

Such a wondering is doubtless unfair, both because our modern cities are not the creatures of behavioral science and because of the great care and regard for scientific method that characterizes the social sciences. Nonetheless, it is clear why Berkeley included *social* science in his criticism of minute philosophy. For it is inevitable that to the extent that behavioral studies emulate and imitate the "hard" sciences, they eschew any and all consideration of what ought to be, in order to concentrate on fact. Indeed, they proclaim themselves to be value-free. Hence, to suppose that such studies have anything to do with moral education would be to confuse minute philosophy with classical philosophy.

The point might be clearer, put another way. Berkeley sees that education, willy-nilly, has a moral end. That is, values, "prejudices," beliefs, about what is good and true and beautiful *will* be put into the minds of young people. The only question is, under the aegis of which philosophy, classical or minute? Science is dumb on the question. Indeed, the very uses to which science is put depends upon *its* being under aegis of one or the other of these competing philosophies.

But, someone might wonder, in this critique of contemporary education no mention has been made of professional and academic philosophers. Every college and university, it seems, has its department of philosophy. And if teaching of values does not belong in the science departments, and the "humanities" are mainly free and easy conversation, then does it not naturally fall to philosophers, following in the wake of Berkeley and the like, to teach morality and politics?

It would seem so; and indeed some professional and academic philosophers do still try to teach or inculcate what the good life is, and how to go about reaching it by development of moral and political virtue. But on the academic scene two established trends work against that endeavor. On the one hand, outside philosophy departments "scientific" study of morals and politics thrives. The scientific study of politics is done in a department with the name, usually, of "political science"; in such departments, classical political philosophy is virtually non-existent. And while there is no one department labeled "moral science," still there is no widespread hesitancy on the part of anthropologists, sociologists, psychologists, as well as political scientists and some historians, to pretend expertise in moral values, and even to teach moral "enlightenment" to provincial students, even though, on their own principles only facts, and not values, are accessible to their professed scientific studies.

On the other hand, within professional and academic philosophy the established twentieth century trend, at least in English-speaking countries, is to what is called analytic philosophy. Followers of this trend have in effect surrendered to science, leaving it to experts in various fields to discover the truth in those areas. Philosophy then becomes what these practitioners call a second order discipline; instead of studying (some part of) reality, it studies the logic and language of the varied human inquiries into reality. "Philosophy" then is clearly a misnomer, for as so practiced it is no longer a love or pursuit of wisdom. But wisdom will be pursued. And into the vacuum left by the abandonment, by professional philosophers, of philosophy in the classical sense, there has stepped minute philosophy. Analytic philosophy is but one among other departments or disciplines. Who then guides the education? Surely we do not want and should not have mere handmaidens to the sciences doing it. No; and instead we have either frivolous or serious minute philosophers.

The potentially disastrous effect that Berkeley foresaw may be indicated by a reading of the following, the immodesty and vulgarity of which I apologize for in advance.

Ever since the invention of the printing press, books have been published telling men and women how bad they are, giving advice on how to be a better person, and generally offering an alternative system or "way" which promises salvation or at least more friends and more influence over people. *The Bible,* of course, is the most obvious example of such a book. It fills us with lofty aspirations for personal salvation by loving more, stealing less, and avoiding the mere thought of fornicating with our neighbor's spouse.

More recently, however, beginning perhaps with Normal Vincent

Peale's *How to Win Friends and Influence People [sic]*, there has been an avalanche of such books. Most of the recent books have come from one or more of the psychological fads that have been sweeping our country like hula hoops during the past ten years.

The article presents a list of such fads and goes on to describe the cyclic nature of these fads. The author laments that although none of these systems has worked, we continue to be suckers for them; and instead of achieving perfection or even improvement of personality, we add to our feelings of guilt and frustration. The author's proposed solution:

Somehow we must put an end to all this nonsense and come to appreciate our slob-selves for what we are. Because, like it or not, the chances are excellent that we will be basically the same slobs next year that we are today. So, . . .what is needed is an attempt to develop a psychological system of slobism. Not a system offering personal salvation, or even a few handy guides to living; not a system of moral platitudes or rules to follow; but a system which simply describes and honors the human animal, that offers a modest amount of pride and self-respect to the individual as who he or she is, rather than what they can become, that heretically suggests that *because of* our weaknesses, our foibles, our self-destructive, non-creative, stupid behavior we are still reasonably worthwhile people. In short, let us dump that salvation guilt and spend next Sunday afternoon in front of the boob-tube drinking beer, eating cold pizza and stale popcorn, watching Cartoon Carnival.[11]

A fine example of frivolous free-thinking! In 1713 Berkeley wrote an essay in praise of public schools and universities. He regards them "not only as nurseries of men for the service of the church and the state, but also as places designed to teach mankind the most refined luxury, to raise the mind to its due perfection, and give it a taste for those entertainments which afford the highest transport, without the grossness or remorse that attend vulgar enjoyments."[12] Nonetheless, he is not unaware of what happens to some men when they "come to riper years." "The grateful employment of admiring and raising themselves to an imitation of the polite stile, beautiful images, and noble sentiments of ancient authors, is abandoned for law-Latin, the lucubrations of our paltry newsmongers, and that swarm of vile pamphlets which corrupt our taste, and infest the publick. The ideas of virtue which the characters of heroes had imprinted on their minds insensibly wear out, and they come to be influenced by the nearer examples of a degenerate age."[13]

Vile pamphlets, then, existed in Berkeley's day; and presumably emanated from the coffee-houses or the taverns. The one quoted above comes from within the academy! That it should be authored, as in fact it was, by a dean of a college, is surprising and disturbing enough; but that after publication in the college newspaper of such a treatise he remained so, is enough to make all of us aware of how established minute philosophy is, and make those of us who care about the youth of the country almost despair. Berkeley predicted that "it is more than probable that, in case our Free-thinkers could once achieve their glorious design of sinking the credit of the Christian religion, . . .we who want that spirit and curiosity which distinguished the ancient Grecians would by degrees relapse into the same state of barbarism which overspread the northern nations before they were enlightened by Christianity."[14] But cheer up! Maybe we are only lapsing into "slobism."

Berkeley's dramatically climactic contrast of the aims and consequences of the two philosophies is eloquent.

> The profound thinkers of this way have taken a direct contrary course to all the great philosophers of former ages, who made it their endeavour to raise and refine human-kind, and remove it as far as possible from the brute; to moderate and subdue men's appetites; to remind them of the dignity of their nature; to awaken and improve their superior faculties, and direct them to the noblest objects; to possess men's minds with a high sense of the Divinity, of the Supreme Good, and the immortality of the soul. They took great pains to strengthen the obligations to virtue; and upon all those subjects have wrought out noble theories, and treated with singular force of reason. But it seems our minute philosophers act the reverse of all other wise and thinking men; it being their end and aim to erase the principles of all that is great and good from the mind of man, to unhinge all order of civil life, to undermine the foundations of morality, and, instead of improving and ennobling our natures, to bring us down to the maxims and way of thinking of the most uneducated and barbarous nations, and even to degrade human-kind to a level with the brute beasts. And all the while they would pass upon the world for men of deep knowledge. But, in effect, what is all this negative knowledge better than downright savage ignorance? That there is no Providence, no spirit, no future state, no moral duty: truly a fine system for an honest man to own, or an ingenious man to value himself upon![15]

Anyone who has been to the public schools of our day cannot fail to recognize that it is the notions of minute philosophy that have come to prevail. This is not to say that all modern educators think alike, or have the same system of values. Not only are there among them some who are still classically oriented, but also among the minute kind there is a variety. Moreover, a serious free-thinker might well, at this point, object that Berkeley's *saying,* however eloquently, that all free-thinking is destructive of morals and politics, does not *prove* it. The objection would be well-taken; and Berkeley indeed does attempt to show that each sort of free-thinking is so destructive.

But our showing how Berkeley does it must await another occasion. Let me conclude this jeremiad with the climactic statement in Berkeley's *Alciphron*.

> In good earnest, I imagine that thinking is a great desideratum of the present age; and that the real cause of whatever is amiss may justly be reckoned the general neglect of education in those who need it most - the people of fashion. What can be expected where those who have the most influence have the least sense, and those who are sure to be followed set the worst example? where youth so uneducated are yet so forward? where modesty is esteemed pusillanimity, and a deference to years, knowledge, religion, laws, want of sense and spirit? Such untimely growth of genius would not have been valued or encouraged by the wise men of antiquity, whose sentiments on this point are so ill suited to the genius of our times that it is to be feared modern ears could not bear them. But, however ridiculous such maxims might seem to our . . . youth, who are so capable and so forward to try experiments, and mend the constitution of their country, I believe it will be admitted by men of sense that, if the governing part of mankind would in these days, for experiment's sake, consider themselves in that old Homerical light as pastors of the people, whose duty it was to improve their flock, they would soon find that this is to be done by an education very different from the modern, and other-guess maxims than those of the minute philosophy. If our youth were really inured to thought and reflexion, and an acquaintance with the excellent writers of antiquity, we should see that licentious humour, vulgarly called free-thinking, banished from the presence of gentlemen, together with ignorance and ill taste; which as they are inseparable from vice, so men follow vice for the sake of pleasure, and fly from virtue through an abhorrence of pain. Their minds, therefore, betimes should be formed and accustomed to receive pleasure and pain from proper objects, or, which is the same thing, to have their inclinations and aversions rightly placed. . . This, according to Plato and Aristotle, was the . . . right education. And those who, in their own minds, their health, or their fortunes, feel the cursed effects of a wrong one, would do well to consider they cannot better make amends for what was amiss in themselves than by preventing the same in their posterity.[16]

Notes

[1] *Siris, Works,* Vol. 5 (London, 1953), pp. 150–1.

[2] *Alciphron, Works,* Vol. 3 (London, 1950), p. 217.

[3] "An Essay Towards Preventing the Ruin of Great Britain," *Works,* Vol. 6 (London, 1953), p. 70. Emphasis added.

[4] *Alciphron,* op. cit., pp. 46–7.

[5]*Ibid.*, p. 47.

[6]*Loc. cit.*

[7]*Ibid*, p. 48.

[8]*Loc. cit.*

[9]*Loc. cit.*

[10]*Ibid.*, p. 50.

[11]Quoted by permission of the author, whose name, along with that of the college newspaper in which this article was published, are being suppressed, out of consideration for the college of which the author was dean.

[12]*Essays in the Guardian, Works,* Vol. 7 (London, 1955), pp. 203–4.

[13]*Ibid.*, p. 203.

[14]*Ibid.*, p. 205.

[15]*Alciphron, op. cit.*, p. 54.

[16]*Ibid.*, pp. 328–9.

THE CASE FOR ESTHETICS AND ETHICAL VALUES

Philip Herzbrun
Georgetown University

In our value-vexed world what certifies the arts a place in humane education as we profess it? And among the arts why should literature, by which I mean *belles lettres,* be accorded pride of place in our humanities curricula?

To dispose of the second question summarily: we have a language in common. We think, however erroneously, that the language of *belles lettres* is the language of discourse; hence it is accessible. Education is conducted verbally, so words are the accustomed medium of communication. But in the following pages all the arts, with their several languages, idioms and vocabularies, are susceptible to my argument.

Ethicists, who derive much of their *materia* from plays, poems and novels—especially from the themes they embody—yet have severe reservations about endorsing the esthetic as an end in itself. Most view esthetic enterprise narrowly as it evolved in terms of decadent "aestheticism" and its derisive labels, such as "The Mauve Decade," "Art-for-Art's Sake," and "The Yellow Nineties." This thinking associates the arts at worst with sheer hedonism or, in any event, with their irrelevance to the realm of humane value. At best the arts are seen as effete, empty sterile exercises, inviting concern only within the purview of jejune technical Formalism. Perhaps the key to this distrust lies in the muddle over everything regarding the esthetic, from its definition to its effects (or, more voguishly, *affects).*

The first sticking-point is the relation of the concept to beauty. Etymologically, as the *OED* tells us, the term "esthetic" pertained to "things perceptible to the senses, things material" (as opposed to things thinkable or immaterial"). The Greek verb stem denoted "to feel, apprehend by the senses." Plato meant by the term "sheerly sensate, phenomenal, or phantasmal kind of experience." True, antiquity first flirted with the notion of poetry as one vehicle conveying *to kalon,* the fine or beautiful. But it was the pseudo-Neoplatonic Renaissance that emphasized the arts generally as "fine," "ideal" and "beautiful." By the mid-eighteenth century Alexander von Baumgarten had reared *Aesthetics* (1750) to the status of a "criticism of taste" considered as a science or philosophy. Despite Kant's protest against this wilful misuse of "the science which treats of the conditions of sensuous perception," Baumgarten's extension of *aesthetik* suited the pre-Romantic atmosphere of an age excitedly delineating the Sublime, the Picturesque and the Beautiful in terms that generated much heat, but only diffuse and fitful light. For two hundred years raging controversy has not eased the quandary over "beauty"—its essence, its province and its appeal. In *The Foundations of Aesthetics,* for instance, Richards, Ogden and Wood determined at least sixteen wildly varying meanings of the term *beauty.*[1]

The issue of beauty as an esthetic criterion is now so befogged that it should no longer be argued or begged, but dropped. If after two and a half millenia it is no longer tenable to revert to the etymological origins of *esthetic* as a term signifying literal sensation, why not use it *figuratively,* as pertaining to that realm "sensed" through the agency of the imagination? Then it can be reserved for contention with human imaginative creativity exclusively, in *belles lettres,* the fine arts (including painting, sculpture, music, dance), and architecture. Thus our response to nature—and its beauties—becomes a matter apart, to be dismissed from critical discourse in the interest of clearing the air. What a boon to criticism! *Esthetic,* so delimited, would be the figurative antonym of *anesthetic,* which we still understand in its literal, physical sense.

This speculation raises a second crux for the ethicist in his confrontation with the arts. Can what we "feel," rather than "think," be instructive? If so, how? Does what we feel about an artwork amount to more than self-indulgent, ephemeral impressions? What orders our experience so that it becomes value-laden, hence formative, and not an adjunct to, but the essence of humane education.

When Max Eastman regards poetry as a "pure effort to heighten con-sciousness,"[2] he is reverting, perhaps unconsciously, to a view that pervaded antiquity. Then it was instrumental in achieving that unity of civilization, culture, tradition, literature and education that Werner W. Jaeger celebrated in his monumental study *Paideia.*[3] The function of the *paideia* was to promote virtue "by shaping or moulding character," *plattein,* as Plato puts it. Art was considered the instrument enabling man to complete or *fulfill* nature. Aristotle thought the "useful arts," ranging from handicrafts through medicine, essentially were extensions of nature that ministered to human practical needs. He saw the purpose of "fine" arts as the enlargement, nourishment, and development of human awareness and insight, hence, to Walter Jackson Bate, the fulfillment of man's humanity by the completion of his unique capacity for "converting awareness into emotion—into *felt [my emphasis] persuasions and active response."*[4] *(Note that "felt" is used in the sense I intend.)*

Their belief that "art has a limitless power of converting the human soul"[5] informs the most noble Greek imputation to art: that it is "psychagogic." *Psychagogia* has been variously translated as "leading hearts," "soul expan-sion," "soul persuasion." (What a debasement in today's attribution of "mind expansion" to drugs like peyotl and LSD!) All these phrases attest to the immense power the Greeks invested in art, specifically by Aristotle in *poesis* or, as we would say, *belles lettres,* as moulder of human character.

The Latin *educere,* pertaining etymologically to "the leading forth" of the soul toward the fulfillment of human potentiality, is the counterpart of the Greek *psychagogia*. And *educere* is related to *educare*, expressive of "rearing, upbringing." The end sought was *areté, or virtue, the ideal of Greek aristocratic education*. The Latin *virtus* derives from *vir*, man, and suggests the ideal condition of manliness. For Aristotle *(Politics)*,

> virtue consists in *rejoicing* and *loving* and *hating* aright; and there is clearly nothing which we are so much concerned *to acquire* and *to cultivate* as the power of *forming* right judgments, and of *taking* delight in good dispositions and noble actions.

The active verbals I have underscored emphasize process, by which virtue is wrought through desiring and moving toward the good by reacting to and, indeed, *feeling* the truth, hence the valuable. The state is not static, nor is the subject passive. And nothing here has to do with "learning," as the term is commonly understood. It also says nothing regarding instruction, the instilling of facts, precepts or opinions. Indeed it involves the assimilation of truth gained in experience, not by the agency of the rational intellect, through which we *comprehend*, but by the faculty of the sympathetic imagination, through which we *apprehend* and thus appropriate to psychagogic purpose. As Bate says,

> By gradually enlarging and unconsciously shaping man as a desiring, reacting, and living organism, and by calling forth his ability to convert insight or awareness into feeling, art is capable of developing his capacity to react vitally and sympathetically to the truth.[6]

This is the position held by Matthew Arnold, especially telling during the time when "Aestheticism" was gaining force. He too deplored as naive the extraction of didactic implication from poetry—we are reminded that the Victorians wanted from poetry a pot of message—and stressed its moral function, in that we derive from it a sense of *"how to live,"* the most pressing of humane considerations.

All this argues for the uses of the intrinsically esthetic in art. It is certainly not the argument of the Aesthetes' "art-for-art's sake," but rather art-for-truth's-sake, the ostensible goal of the academic ethicist. The professor of Ethics 101, however, is as dubious about the pedagogical value of this figurative sensorium as he would—rightly—be about the literally sensuous (or sensual. Like a marauding homilist, he ransacks literature for *exempla* illustrative of good and evil—or whatnot. His concern is with the knowable, not the experiential; with what can be "learned from," not vibrantly "sensed in" a work. Yeats says that man can embody truth, but that he cannot know it. Thus with literature, that a compelling work is the embodiment of its truth; its particulars, no matter how alluring, we can only know *about*, then forget. It is not discreditable to use literary examples for instructive purposes, but these purposes are ulterior to psychagogic ends. As Robert Frost says: "Of course we can translate poems. All we lose is the poetry." And it is the poetry, with all its manifold, unpredictable powers, that perplexes our ethicist.

This poetry—and access to it—is the substance conveying the ethical quantum of humane education. It must be trusted, not feared. The instrument for accessibility to *poesis* projected by the creative imagination is *Spieltrieb,* best translated as "the play impulse," a term attributable both to the artist and his audience. The concept and the term derive from the previously castigated Baumgarten. Transformed in several ways by Friedrich von Schiller and Coleridge, it has come to twentieth century critical thought in all its extensive implication through Johan Huizinga's study *Homo Ludens.*[7]

Human enterprise has often been conceived in terms of *Spieltrieb:* "playing the horses," "playing the stockmarket," "The Games People Play," "role models," "Life is a stage," etc. Play in Huizinga's sense is not synonymous with games, either diversionary, as in sport, or committed, as in art. It is vital—indeed, quintessential—human activity. The seriousness of play is implicit in Freud's observation that "play is a child's work." this is not to deny that we do "play" games. Even art in its game formality is evident in Frost's remark when asked why he refused to write free verse, that it was "like playing tennis with the net down."

Spieltrieb, however, has meant for those who use it something of greater significance, for both performer and receptor. In *Aesthetical Letters* Schiller conceives the "play theory of art," in which the "instinct for play" is essential to complement the "formal instinct of the reason" and the "sensuous instinct." *Spieltrieb* to Schiller means "the highest degree of self-spontaneity (autonomy) and of freedom with the fullest plenitude of existence." He contends that man is "completely a man only when he plays," that is, when the formal and sensuous instinct in counterpoise are freely experienced in our engagement with an artwork. The object of the "play instinct," hence, is form-shaping-life, for which Schiller's term is "living form."

To go no further into the theoretical ramifications of the play impulse, let us assert its primacy in inducing the intrinsic value of art into humane education. This view does not traffic with educational curricula *per se.* Art history, art appreciation, *germanische Philologie, explication de texte,* literary theory, and the like are beside the point if the arts are to yield transcendent esthetic value to their students. Note that critical esthetics is itself of no avail. When Barnett Newman says that art criticism is for the painter like ornithology is for the birds, he is speaking, however extravagantly, for both artist and audience.

There is no salvation to be found in pedagogical technique or methodology, and the informational component of the art under study serves only to satisfy the reason. The point of my argument is that the artwork is more under exposure than study. T. S. Eliot says that the poet, like a burglar entering a house with a piece of meat to preoccupy the dog, gives the mind enough substance to chew on so that it is pacified while the insidious poetry does its work.

In a recent provocative article Bate contends that the arts are an essential form of knowing. I take it that Bate must intend "knowing" to be a process provocative to the active, participating imagination. He invokes as normative "a trust in the moral and educative effect on human character of knowledge, as the act of knowing penetrates to the confused emotion and the slippery *imagination* [my emphasis] of the human psyche."[8] With somewhat different stress this is but a redaction of Schiller's components in a nutshell.

Veritas vos liberabit compels our assent, but only from the arts if *veritas* has been sensed fully and freely. The arts do not bear ethical freight as message. (Nabokov says that the postman delivers messages.) Rather they—literature particularly—in Arnoldian terms, embody the "best that has been thought and said in the world." I insist that absorption in this "best" is activity of fullest ethical significance. If truly liberal education, worthy of its designation, is to be imbued with humane value, it must embrace the esthetic, the poetic in art without equivocation, with no pandering to the "truth" of philosophical discourse, but with liberating enthusiasm.

Notes

[1] I. A. Richards, C. K. Ogden and James Wood, *The Foundations of Aesthetics*, 2nd ed. (New York: Lear Publishers, 1948) pp. 20–21.

[2] *The Literary Mind; Its Place in an Age of Science* (New York, London: Scribner's, 1931), p. 170. The context is the chapter entitled "What Poetry Is," pp. 161–94.

[3] Werner Wilhelm Jaeger, *Paideia: the Ideals of Greek Culture,* 3 vols., trans Gilbert Highet (Oxford: Blackwell, 1939).

[4] *Criticism: the Major Texts* (New York: Harcourt, Brace, 1952), p. 6.

[5] Jaeger, I, 36.

[6] *Criticism,* p. 7.

[7] *Homo Ludens: a Study of the Play-Element in Culture,* trans. (New York: Roy Publishers, 1950). See especially "Nature and Significance of Play as a Cultural Phenomenon," pp. 1–27.

[8] "The Crisis in English Studies," *Harvard Magazine,* Sept.-Oct. 1982, p. 47.

THE WRITINGS OF HENRY BABCOCK VEATCH IN CHRONOLOGICAL ORDER*

Books:

Intentional Logic: A Logic Based on Philosophical Realism, New Haven, Conn.: 1952.

Realism and Nominalism Revisited, Milwaukee, Wisc.: 1954.

Logic as a Human Instrument. With Parker, Frank. New York, N.Y.: 1959.

Rational Man: A Modern Interpretation of Aristotelian Ethics, Bloomington, Ind.: 1962. Translated by Garcia del la Mora, J.M., as *Etica del ser racional*. Barcelona: 1967.

Two Logics: The Conflict between Classical and Neo-Analytic Philosophy, Evanston, Ill.: 1968.

For An Ontology Of Morals: A Critique of Contemporary Ethical Theory. Evanston, Ill.: 1968.

Aristotle: A Contemporary Appreciation, Bloomington, Ind.: 1974.

---

*I would like to thank Rocco Porreco for suggesting I update a bibliography of Veatch's writings that I had compiled in 1968. I would like to thank Professor Porreco's student Barry Smith and my own student Maureen Connors for their help in updating the earlier bibliography. A caveat is in order. The list of writings is meant to give as complete a listing of Henry's work as is possible, but it cannot claim to be definitive. It was compiled mainly from cataloguing old reprints and searching philosophical bibliographies, mainly the Philosopher's Index. If there were works in non-philosophical journals or works with no offprints they would not be listed. Nevertheless, the list does give an indication of Henry's philosophical output and thus seems a worthwhile inclusion in this festschrift. If anyone can enlighten me on works of Henry's not listed I would be appreciative. I have added to the bibliography a list of reviews of some of Henry's books which should be of interest to scholars.

Ronald Duska
Rosemont College.

ARTICLES IN ANTHOLOGIES

"For a Realistic Logic." In *The Return to Reason*, pp. 177-198. Edited by John Wild. Chicago: 1953.

"Intentional Logic." In *Philosophy in the Mid-Century*, pp. 9-11. Edited by Raymond Klibansky, Firenze: 1958.

"Proposition and Knowledge." Reprinted from *Intentional Logic*, pp. 154-169. In *Philosophy of Knowledge*, pp. 154-169. Edited by R. House and J. Mullally, pp. 185-199. New York: 1960.

"Minds: What and Where in the World Are They?" In *Theories of the Mind*, pp. 314-329. Edited by Jordan M. Scher. New York: 1962.

"For a Renewal of an Old Departure in Ethics." In *Faith and Philosophy*, pp. 141-157. Edited by Alvin Plantinga. Grand Rapids: 1964.

"Aristotelianism." In *A History of Philosophical Systems*, pp. 106-116. Edited by Vergilius Ferm. New York: 1965.

"A Case for Trans-Empirical and Supernaturalistic Knowledge Claims." In *Mind, Matter and Method*, pp. 314-329. Edited by Feyerabend and Maxwell. Minneapolis: 1966.

"Intentionality." In *The New Catholic Encyclopedia*, vol. 7, pp. 564-566. Washington, D.C.: 1967.

"A Contemporary Interpretation of Aristotle." In *The Future of Ethics and Moral Theology*, pp. 114-137. Chicago: 1968.

"Intentional Logic." In *Contemporary Philosophy: A Survey*, pp. 41-43. Edited by Raymond Klibansky, Firenze: 1968.

"A Variation on the Theme of the Hollow Universe." In *Melanges a la memoire de Charles de Koninck*, pp. 417-432. Quebec: 1968.

"Philosophy and Ethics." With M. S. Gram. In *The Great Ideas Today*, pp. 228-270. Encyclopaedia Britannica Inc.: 1970.

"The Philosophy of Logical Atomism: A Realism Manque." In *Essays on Bertrand Russell*, pp. 102-117. Edited by E. D. Klemke, Champaign-Urbana, Ill.: 1970.

"To Gustav Bergmann: A Humble Petition and Advice." In *Festschrift for Gustav Bergmann*, pp. 65-85. Edited by M. S. Gram and E. D. Klemke. Iowa City: 1974.

"Telos and Teleology in Aristotelian Ethics." In *Studies in Aristotle*, pp. 279-295. Edited by Dominic J. O'Meara, Washington, D. C.: 1981.

Variations, Good, and Bad on the Theme of Right Reason in Ethics." The *Monist* 66 (1983): 49-70. In *The Questions Behind the Answers: A Sampler of Philosophy.* Edited by Donald R. Gregory. Washington, D.C.: University Press of America, 1983.

Translations

Dufrenne, Mikel. *Language and Philosophy.* Translated by Henry B. Veatch, Bloomington, Ind.: 1963.

Published Contributions to Discussions

Comments on "Questions de Pedagogie ou de Recherche Scientifique," with M. Dufrenne, W. Frankena, *et al. Babel* 8 (1962): 125-163.

Interrogator of John Wild. *Philosophical Interrogations.* Edited by Sydney and Beatrice Rome. New York: 1964.

Articles in Periodicals and Proceedings

"Some Suggestions on the Respective Spheres of Science and Philosophy." *The Thomist* 3 (1941): 177-116.

"Concerning the Distinction between Descriptive and Normative Sciences." *Philosophy and Phenomenological Research* 6, (1945): 284-306.

"A Note on the Metaphysical Grounds for Freedom, with Special Reference to Professor Lovejoy's Thesis in *The Great Chain of Being." Philosophy and Phenomenological Research* 7 (1947): 622-625.

"A Rejoinder to Professor Lovejoy." *Philosophy and Phenomenological Research* 7 (1947) 622-625.

"Concerning the Ontological Status of Logical Forms." *The Review of Metaphysics* 2 (1948): 40-64.

"Aristotelian and Mathematical Logic." *The Thomist* 13 (1950): 50-96.

"In Defense of the Syllogism." *The Modern Schoolman* 26 (1950): 184-202.

"Formalism and/or Intentionality in Logic." *Philosophy and Phenomenological Research* 11 (1951): 348-365.

"Discussion: Reply to Professor Copi." *Philosophy and Phenomenological Research* 11 (1951): 373-375.

"Basic Confusions in Current Notions of Propositional Calculi." *The Thomist* 14 (1951): 238-258.

"The Significance of Current Criticisms of the Syllogism." *The Thomist* 15 (1952): 624-641.

"Metaphysics and the Paradoxes." With Theodore Young. *The Review of Metaphysics* 6 (1952): 199-218.

"Reaffirmation of Intentionality: A Rejoinder to Monsignor Doyle." *The New Scholasticism* 28 (1954): 253-271.

"Colloquium on Judgment." With D. Walhour, B. Blanshard, I. C. Lieb, and D. B. Terrell. *The Review of Metaphysics* 9 (1956): 650-651.

"Putting the Square Back into Opposition." With Joan B. Ogden. *The New Scholasticism* 30 (1956): 409-440.

"Logical Truth and Logic." A symposium with Hughes Leblanc and C. D. Rollins. *The Journal of Philosophy* 53 (1956): 671-679.

"Tillich's Distinction Between Metaphysics and Theology." *The Review of Metaphysics* 10 (1957): 529-533.

"Some Recent Developments in Logic: Their Implications for Ontology and Intentionality." *Proceedings of the American Catholic Philosophical Association* (1958): 98-107.

"Why Not Intentionality?" *International Congress of Philosophy*, 1958.

"A Caveat Against Professor Fehl." *Anglican Theological Review* 41 (1959): 270-275.

"On Being Old-Fashioned in Philosophy." A review of C. A. Campbell's *On Selfhood and Godhood*. *The Review of Metaphysics* 13 (1960): 439-446.

"On Trying To Say and To Know What's What." *Philosophy and Phenomenological Research* 24 (1963): 83-96.

"Is There a New-Found Time in the New-Found Philosophy?" *Anglican Theological Review* 45 (1963): 331-344.

"Matrix, Matter and Method in Metaphysics." *The Review of Metaphysics* 17 (1964): 372-395.

"The Truths of Metaphysics." *The Review of Metaphysics* 17 (1964): 372-395.

"St. Thomas and the Question 'How are Synthetic Judgments A Priori Possible?' " *The Modern Schoolman* 42 (1965): 239-263.

"On the Metaphysical Status of Natural Law." A symposium on *Justice* with Wilford O. Cross, John S. Marshall, Lewis Hammond, and Justus George Lawler. *Anglican Theological Review* (1965): 170-180.

"Two Cultures—Two Kinds of Knowledge." A symposium with William Earle and Scott Greer. *Tri-Quarterly* (Winter, 1965): 74-79.

"Non-Cogniticism in Ethics: A Modest Proposal for its Diagnosis and Cure." *Ethics* 76 (1966): 102-116.

"A Modest Word in Defense of Aristotle's Logic." *The Monist* 52 (1968): 210-228.

"Good Reasons in Ethics: A Source of Gratuitous Logical Embarrassment." *Proceedings of the International Congress*, 1968.

"The Defense of Natural Law in the Context of Contemporary Analytic Philosophy." *The American Journal of Jurisprudence* 14 (1969): 54-68.

"Language and Ethics: 'What's Hecuba to him, or he to Hecuba?' " *Proceedings of the American Philosophical Association* (1970–71): 45-62.

"Good Reasons and Prescriptivism in Ethics: A Metaethical Incompatibility." *Ethics* 80 (1970): 102-111.

"A Contemporary 'Modus Vivendi' for St. Thomas." *Proceedings of the American Catholic Philosophical Association* 45 (1971): 11-15.

"Two Logics, or One, or None?" *The New Scholasticism* 47 (1973): 350-360.

"Religion, Morality and Natural Law." *Listening* 8 (1973): 95-115.

"The What and Why of the Humanities." *Proceedings of the American Catholic Philosophical Association* 47 (1973): 21-26.

"Kant and Aquinas: A Confrontation on the Contemporary Meta-Ethical Field of Honor." *The New Scholasticism* 48 (1974): 73-99.

"Essentialism and the Problem of Individuation." *Proceedings of the American Catholic Philosophical Association* 48 (1974): 64-73.

"The Rational Justification of Moral Principles: Can There Be Such a Thing?" *The Review of Metaphysics* 29 (1975): 217-238.

"Paying Heed to Gerwirth's Principle of Categorical Consistency." *Ethics* 86 (1976): 278-287.

"A Neglected Avenue in Contemporary Religious Apologetics." *Religious Studies* 13 (1977): 29-48.

"On the Use and Abuse of the Principle of Universalizability." *Proceedings of the American Catholic Philosophical Association* 51 (1977): 162-170.

"Is Quine A Metaphysician?" *The Review of Metaphysics* 31 (1978): 406-430.

"Natural Law: Dead or Alive?" *Literature of Liberty* 1 (1978): 7-31.

"Contemporary Theology: Is It to Be With or Without Benefit of Metaphysics?" *Listening* 13 (1978): 11-19.

"Are There Non-Moral Goods?" *The New Scholasticism* 52 (1978): 471-499.

"Plato, Popper and the Open Society: Reflections on Who Might Have the Last Laugh." *Journal of Libertarian Studies* 3 (1979): 159-172.

"Is Kant the Gray Eminence of Contemporary Ethical Theory?" *Ethics* 90 (1980): 218-238.

Reviews

God and Philosophy, By Etienne Gilson. In *Philosophy and Phenomenological Research* 1 (1941): 505-510.

Proceedings of the American Catholic Philosophical Association 13 (1943). In *Philosophy and Phenomenological Research* 4 (1945): 605-608.

Physics and Philosophy, by James A. McWilliams and *The Nature and Unity of Metaphysics*, by George M. Buckley. In *Philosophy and Phenomenological Research* 8 (1948): 734-735.

Modern Science and Its Philosophy, by Phillip Frank. In *The New Scholasticism* 24 (1950): 223-225.

The Bond of Being, by James Anderson. In *Philosophy and Phenomenological Research* 12 (1951): 152-154.

Philosophical Analysis: A Collection of Essays, edited by Max Black. In *The Thomist* 15 (1952): 169-173.

The Doctrine of Being in the Aristotelian Metaphysics, by Joseph Owens. In *The Modern Schoolman* 30 (1953): 146-151.

Medieval Logic: An Outline of Its Development from 1250 to c. 1400, by Philotheus Boehner. In *Philosophy and Phenomenological Research* 13 (1953): 578-579.

Thomism and Aristotelianism: A Study of the Commentary by Thomas Aquinas on the Nichomachean Ethics, by H. V. Jaffa. In *Speculum* 28 (1953): 176-178.

Conventional Logic and Modern Logic: A Prelude to Transition, by J. T. Clark. In *Speculum* 29 (1954): 266-268.

Translations from the Philosophical Writings of Gottlob Frege, edited by Peter Geach and Max Black. In *The Thomist* 17 (1954): 104-111.

Freedom, Loyalty and Dissent, by Henry Steele Commager. In *Indiana Magazine of History* 50 (1954): 295-298.

The Development of Academic Freedom in the United States, by Richard Hofstadter and Walter P. Metzger, and *Academic Freedom in our Time,* by Robert MacIver. In *Indiana Magazine of History* 52 (1956): 420-423.

Bergsonian Philosophy and Thomism, by Jacques Maritain. In *Speculum* 31 (1956): 532-534.

Acquinas, by F. C. Copleston. In *Speculum* 32 (1957): 152-154.

Contemporary Philosophy: Studies of Logical Positivism and Existentialism, by F. C. Copleston. In *The New Scholasticism* 31 (1957): 422-425.

An Etienne Gilson Tribute: Presented by His North American Students, edited by Charles J. O'Neil. In *The New Scholasticism* 35 (1961): 231-233.

Medieval Philosophy, by Armand A. Maurer. In *The New Scholasticism* 37 (1963): 523-525.

St. Thomas and Cajetan: Commentary on Aristotle's 'On Interpretation,' translated by Jean T. Oesterle. In *The Journal of the History of Philosophy* 3 (1965): 121-125.

A Metaphysics of Authentic Existentialism, by Leo Sweeney. In *Philosophy and Phenomenological Research* 37 (1966): 140-141.

Acquinas' Search for Wisdom, by Vernon Bourke. In *Speculum* 41 (1966): 521-522.

The Conditions of Philosophy: Its Checkered Past, Its Present Disorders and Its Future Promise, by Mortimer Adler. In *The Modern Schoolman* 43 (1966): 407-409.

Aspects of Scientific Explanation and Other Essays in the Philosophy of Science, by Carl Hempel. In *Philosophy of Science* 37 (1970): 312-314.

Aristotle's Theory of the Syllogism: A Logico-Philosophical Study of Book A of the Prior Analytics, by Gunther Patzig. In *Studies in History and Philosophy of Science* 2 (1972): 369-378.

Interpreting Modern Philosophy, by James Collins. In *International Philosophical Quarterly* 13 (1973): 446-449.

Savoir et Pouvoir: Philosophie Thomiste et Politique Clericale en XIXᵉ Siécle, by Pierre Thibault. In *Philosophy of Religion* 6 (1975): 256-257.

Causal Powers: A Theory of Natural Necessity, by R. Harré and E. H. Madden. In *The New Scholasticism* 50 (1976): 537-541.

Substance, Body and Soul: Aristotelian Investigations, by E. Hartman. In *The Review of Metaphysics* 32 (1978): 138-140.

Reason and Morality, by Alan Gewirth. In *Ethics* 89 (1979): 401-414.

Heidegger: The Critique of Logic, by Thomas A. Fay. In *International Philosophical Quarterly* 19 (1979) 115-117.

Dimensions of Morality: Paradigms, Principles and Ideals, by A. S. Cua. In *The Review of Metaphysics* 32 (1979): 742-745.

Social Order and the Limits of Law, by Iredell Jenkins. In *The American Journal of Jurisprudence* 26 (1981).

Reviews of Veatch's Books

Intentional Logic, by John A. Oesterle. In *The Thomist* 16 (1953): 413-425.

Rational Man, by David A. O'Connell. In *The Thomist* 29 (1965): 337-338.

Two Logics: The Conflict between Classical and Neo-Analytic Philosophy, by W. C. Wilcox. In *Philosophical Forum* 10 (1971): 384-385.

————, by Adelhard Scheffczyk. In *Archiv für Geschichte der Philosophie* 54 (1972): 294-297.

For An Ontology of Morals: A Critique of Contemporary Ethical Theory, by Kenneth Pahel. In *Ethics* 82 (1972): 349-353.

————, by Janko Zagor. In *The Thomist* 36 (1972): 343-345.

————, by Rukavina Thomas. In *The New Scholasticism* 46 (1972): 384-401.

————, by Harry Ruja. In *Philosophy and Phenomenological Research* 33 (1972): 127-128.

————, by Lee C. Rice. In *The Modern Schoolman* 50 (1972): 123-124.

_____, by Joel Kupperman. In *The Philosophical Review* 82 (1973): 244-246.

_____, by Michael Robins. In *The International Philosophical Quarterly* 13 (1973): 135-139.

_____, by Michael Robins. In *The Review of Metaphysics* 26 (1973): 770.

_____, by A. C. Ewing. In *Mind* 83 (1974): 308-310.

Aristotle: A Contemporary Appreciation, by Ronald H. Epp. In *Teaching Philosophy* 1 (1975): 86-87.

_____, by John F. Peterson. In *The Thomist* 39 (1975): 142-145.

_____, by John L. Treloar. In *The Modern Schoolman* 53 (1976): 311-313.

_____, by Robert Bolton. In *The Philosophical Review* 85 (1976): 251-253.